DATE DUE

DEC 2 1 1990			
[illegible] 0 4 2002			

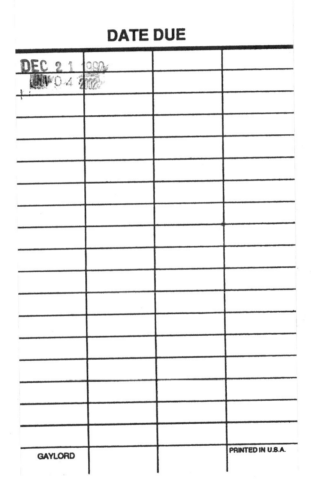

Fundamentals of Indian Philosophy

Fundamentals of Indian Philosophy

R. Puligandla

ABINGDON PRESS
Nashville
New York

FUNDAMENTALS OF INDIAN PHILOSOPHY

Library of Congress Cataloging in Publication Data

Puligandla, R 1930- Fundamentals of Indian philosophy.
Bibliography: p. 1. Philosophy, Indic—History. I. Title.
B131.P84 181'.4'09 74-30009

ISBN 0-687-13704-7

ISBN 0-687-13705-5 pbk.

Acknowledgment is made to the following publishers for permission to reprint copyright material:

George Allen & Unwin and Humanities Press for material from *Central Philosophy of Buddhism* by T. R. V. Murti.

The Association Press, Calcutta, for material from *Hymns from the Rigveda* by A. A. Macdonell.

The Clarendon Press for material from *The Vedanta Sutras of Badarayana, with the Commentary of Ramanuga,* translated by George Thibaut. Reprinted by permission of The Clarendon Press, Oxford.

Harper & Row and Bruno Cassirer for material from *Buddhist Texts Through the Ages,* edited by Edward Conze and others.

The Hokuseido Press, Tokyo, for material from *Nāgārjuna, A Translation of his Mūlamadhyamakakārikā with an Introductory Essay,* by Kenneth K. Inada.

Oxford University Press, Delhi, for material from *The Thirteen Principal Upanishads* by R. E. Hume.

Prentice-Hall for material from *Presuppositions of India's Philosophies* by Karl H. Potter.

The Vedanta Society of Southern California for material from *The Upanishads,* translated by Swami Prabhavananda and Frederick Manchester and published by Vedanta Press.

MANUFACTURED BY THE PARTHENON PRESS AT NASHVILLE, TENNESSEE, UNITED STATES OF AMERICA

To

My Parents

Venkata Raman and Venkata Ratnam

Preface

It is no exaggeration to say that in American colleges and universities the past decade has been one of unprecedented interest in the history, philosophies, and religions of Asia. During this period, many colleges and universities have either established departments of Asian studies or strengthened and enlarged the already existing ones. Departments of philosophy and religion have introduced courses pertaining to India, China, and Japan in which more and more students enroll. Among the various courses, those dealing with India are usually in great demand and accordingly draw a large number of students. Although there are many excellent books on Indian philosophy, such as S. Radhakrishnan's *Indian Philosophy*, Hiriyanna's *Outlines* and *Essentials*, Chandradhar Sharma's *Critical Survey*, and Chatterjee and Datta's *Introduction*, there are practically none suitable for a quarter or semester introductory course. The few anthologies that are available cannot profitably be used in a beginning course. The present book is intended to fill such a need. Its contents, organization, and method of treatment have grown out of my experience in teaching a course in Introduction to Eastern Thought for the past seven years at the University of Toledo.

This book does not presuppose any background in philosophy, although those with such a background will be able to readily identify the problems in Indian philosophy and compare them with their counterparts in Western philosophy. The main aim of this book is not only to introduce the student to the problems, methods, goals, and temper of Indian philosophy, but also to arouse in him or her sufficient interest in the subject to undertake further study of Indian philosophy and culture. If the present book succeeds in this modest objective, I will have been justified in writing it.

R. Puligandla
The University of Toledo

Acknowledgments

The number of scholars, colleagues, and students to whom I owe a great debt in writing this book is so large that it is not possible to mention all of them individually. Like any other author of a book of this nature, I am indebted to such distinguished scholars as S. N. Dasgupta, S. Radhakrishnan, Junjiro Takakusu, T. R. V. Murti, Edward Conze, and H. V. Guenther, whose works invariably form the background. Among younger scholars on whose writings I have freely drawn, I should mention Dale Riepe, Eliot Deutsch, Kenneth Inada, and Karl Potter.

I am especially grateful to Kay Wenzel for her meticulous and elegant typing of the manuscript and other secretarial assistance. Her cheerful patience with the scholarly idiosyncrasies of authors is truly amazing.

I also wish to thank Kaisa Puhakka, my former student, for her perusal of the manuscript and for her help in preparing the Glossary and Bibliography.

I am grateful to the authorities of the University of Toledo for granting me sabbatical leave during the winter quarter of 1973–74, thereby making it possible for me to complete the writing of this book and meet the deadline with the publishers.

Finally, I would like to thank Professor Eliot Deutsch, editor, *Philosophy East and West,* and Dr. Nalinaksha Dutta, chairman, editorial board, *The Maha Bodhi,* for their permission to reproduce in this book parts of my articles which appeared in their journals.

Contents

Chapter I

General Introduction

It is a widespread belief in the West, among philosophers and nonphilosophers alike, that philosophy as systematic inquiry into the nature of things is a uniquely Western activity, conspicuously absent in non-Western cultures and civilizations. Lest this assertion be deemed specious and unfounded, we shall document it. Two well-known contemporary American philosophers write:

> *Few of the ancient peoples advanced far beyond the mythological stage, and perhaps none of them can be said to have developed a genuine philosophy except the Greeks.* It is for this reason that we begin our account with them. They not only laid the foundations upon which all subsequent systems of Western thought have been reared, but formulated nearly all the problems and suggested nearly all the answers with which European civilization occupied itself for two thousand years. Their philosophy is one of the best examples that any people has furnished of the evolution of human thinking from simple mythological beginnings to complex and comprehensive systems. *The spirit of independence and the love of truth which animated their thinkers have never been surpassed and rarely equaled.*[1]

And even while they grant that every people may have had a philosophy of its own, Western philosophers quickly assert that only philosophy as conceived and practiced in their own tradition is the true and genuine philosophy, those of others being no more than poetry, faith, and ethics at best and mythology at worst. Thus, according to Thilly and Wood,

> a universal history of philosophy would include the philosophies of all peoples. Not all peoples, however, have produced *real* systems of thought, and the speculations of only a few can be said to have had a history. *Many do not rise beyond the mythological stage. Even the theories of Oriental peoples, the Hindus, Egyptians, and Chinese, consist, in the main, of mythological and ethical doctrines, and are not complete systems of thought: they are pervaded with poetry and faith.* We shall, therefore, limit ourselves to a study of the Western countries, and begin with the philosophy of the ancient Greeks, on whose culture our own civilization, in large part, rests.[2]

Small wonder, then, that every book on the history of Western philosophy, with perhaps the single exception of Bertrand Russell's, is entitled "History of Philosophy," without qualification, thereby implying that there is no philosophy other than Western philosophy. How does one account for this pervasive attitude among Western philosophers? I venture to say that such an attitude is due on the one hand to massive ignorance of alien intellectual traditions, and on the other to inveterate parochialism. Another reason why Western philosophers so cavalierly dismiss non-Western philosophies as mythico-religious thought is that, since in their own tradition there was a sharp opposition between religion and philosophy and the latter had to free itself through a long and arduous struggle from the authority of the former, they uncritically assume that any civilization in which there never existed such an opposition cannot be said to have a philosophy. Underlying such misguided thinking is the unwarranted view that the terms "philosophy," "religion," and "religious consciousness" must mean the same to non-Western peoples as they do to Westerners. But the fact that in such cultures as the Indian and Chinese religion and philosophy have always been inseparable does not mean that their modes of thought are less rational and worthy of our attention than Western philosophies. Yet another source of the negative attitude toward non-Western philosophies is Western philosophers' belief that any thought worthy of the title of philosophy must necessarily deal with science as understood and practiced in the West during the last three hundred years; since the Indian systems of thought do not deal with problems arising out of modern Western science, we are told that they are not philosophies at all, but mythology and religion. To sum up, by the fiat of definition Western philosophers rule out non-Western thought from the domain of philosophy and relegate it to myth, religion, and poetry.

In sharp contrast to the above attitude, we wish to point out that the philosophy of any people is not to be identified with any particular mode of thought—metaphysical, scientific, ethical, sociopolitical, artistic, mythological, or religious. Nor does it make sense to judge whether or not the thought of a given people is philosophic by preconceived criteria, especially those of one's own tradition. The philosophy of any people is the cream of its culture and the integrated expression of its styles of thinking, feeling, and living. The philosophy of each people is thus a product of its environment and its specific modes of cognitive, intellectual, aesthetic, moral, and religious experience. As such, to judge the philosophies of others by standards and criteria of one's own culture is an act of blind self-glorification wholly unconducive to understanding other peoples. To understand a people and its culture is to understand how it sees the world, itself, and other peoples; and unless and until members of each culture approach the philosophies of others with an open mind and study them seriously, there will be neither the understanding of other peoples nor the enlightenment and enrichment of one's own philosophy and culture that can only result from such understanding.

Although comparative philosophy is still a young discipline, enough work has been done in this field to break the barriers to philosophical communication between East and West. Nevertheless, owing to intellectual chauvinism and delusions of cultural supremacy, philosophers of each tradition continue to contemptuously dismiss the philosophies of other traditions. The result is that blissful ignorance, benevolent indifference, unmitigated intolerance, worn-out clichés, pious platitudes, and self-serving shibboleths still rule the day.

It is interesting to note that, in spite of their vast cultural differences, the basic philosophical problems raised, as well as the majority of solutions proposed, by the Indian and European traditions are astoundingly similar.[3] Every problem that occupied the attention of European philosophers also engaged Indian philosophers: monism and pluralism, change and permanence, appearance and reality, materialism, atomism, idealism, realism, pragmatism, the nature of self and consciousness, perception, language and reality, theories of meaning and names, the problem of universals and particulars, nominalism, conceptualism, criteria of valid knowledge, laws of logic, theories of inference, freedom and determinism, the individual and society, the good life—these are but a few issues common to both Indian and European philosophies. Who can fail to discern the philosophical astuteness of Nāgārjuna, Āryadeva, Vasubandhu, Candrakīrti, Dignāga, Dharmakīrti, Dharmottara, Annambhaṭṭa, Kumārila Bhaṭṭa, Prabhākara, Gaṇgesa, Śaṁkara and Rāmānuja? Only someone wholly ignorant of these thinkers and their works could write that "even the theories of . . . the Hindus . . . consist, in the main, of mythological and ethical doctrines."

The Sanskrit terms for philosophy are *darśana* and *tattva,* which mean "vision of truth and reality" and "nature of reality," respectively. Like philosophers of other traditions, Indian thinkers were concerned with the fundamental questions of existence: What is the nature of reality? What is the real nature of man? How has the world come to be? Is it created or eternal? If it is created, what is the creator's relation to man? What is knowledge as distinct from mere belief and opinion? What are the criteria of reliable knowledge? What is truth? What is error? How do we know? What are the ultimate constituents of the world? Is man free, or is his behavior determined by circumstances external to him? If he is not free at the present, can he attain freedom? Are there any paths to freedom? What is the good life? How to attain it? Before we proceed further, it should be pointed out that, although the Indian answers to these questions are in some respects strikingly similar to the Western ones, there is an important difference between the Indian and Western methods of philosophical inquiry.[4] Thus, whereas Western philosophers treat metaphysics, epistemology, psychology, ethics, etc., separately, Indian philosophers do not; rather, they discuss each problem from all these points of view. The *modus operandi* of the Indian philosopher consists of three stages. The first is known as *pūrvapakṣa* (prior view), in which the philosopher presents his opponent's position along with the latter's arguments in defense of it; in the second, known as *khaṇḍana* (refutation), the philosopher refutes his opponent's position by systematic criticism and argumentation; and in the last, namely, *uttarapakṣa* (the subsequent view), he presents his own position along with proofs and arguments in defense of it. The last stage is also called *siddhānta* (conclusion).

In a very real sense, Indian philosophies are pragmatic because of their strong practical bent. That is to say, according to Indian thinkers the aim of philosophy is not just the satisfaction of intellectual curiosity or the pursuit of theoretical truths; the more important aim is that philosophy should make a difference to the style and quality of life.[5] If a philosophy, no matter how sophisticated and intellectually satisfying it may be, has no bearing on our life, it is deemed an empty and irrelevant sophistry. The character and life of a philosophical idealist must differ from that of a philosophical realist in some significant sense; similarly, the disposition and life-style of a man who accepts a philosophy according to which God exists should differ from that of one whose philosophy rejects the notion of God. The point, then, is that for the Indians philosophical wisdom does not consist in intellectual inquiry for its own sake; rather, one should go beyond to assimilating the intellectually discerned and established truths into one's own personality and leading a life of freedom and enlightenment. The philosopher in the Indian society is thus not just a man of intellectual virtues, but one who is a living example of knowledge, peace, freedom, and wisdom. For this reason, philosophers are revered and admired in the Indian culture. A philosopher is not respected merely for his subtle dialectical powers and vast theoretical knowledge; he is respected and looked up to as an inspiration because of the wisdom his life reflects.[6] No man, however great his learning and scholarship, will be considered a philosopher in the Indian culture unless he is also free from egoism, greed, and pettiness and has the positive virtues of a noble disposition, a tranquil mind, and a universal outlook. In brief, the life-style of a philosopher must in some important ways be different from that of the masses. We are not hereby implying that every Indian philosopher fits this conception; rather, we are merely calling attention to the Indian conception of the philosopher in general. We might remark that a similar image of the philosopher is to be found in the traditions of China and Japan. Thus, the Buddhist philosopher should do no violence to any living being in thought, word, or deed. Accordingly, while he may present his own viewpoint and defend it by argument, the Buddhist philosopher refrains from coercing his opponents or mocking them or their views. The reason for this is that Buddhist philosophy (and Indian philosophy in general), unlike Western philosophy, does not recognize the law of contradiction and the law of excluded middle as absolutely valid and unchallengeable. Consequently, during a discourse, the Buddhist philosopher may sometimes not reply in clear-cut affirmations and negations. This may be totally disconcerting to the Western thinker. Thus, Arthur Koestler,

> a typical intellectual of the twentieth century, at one time of his life seemed to be more of a machine gun than a human being.[11] In consequence he was completely baffled by the *ethos* of the Easterners he met, so strikingly different from the ruthless rough and tumble of European disputants. Both in India and Japan he noted an aversion to clear-cut affirmations. "Nothing could be more shocking to a Japanese than

> the injunction 'Let your communication be Yea, yea, Nay, nay.' He would regard it as inconceivably rude."[12] Deprived of any food for his logomachia, Mr. Koestler was most disappointed to meet again and again with the refusal to fight when attacked. And though he thus had plenty of opportunity to study ahimsa (non-violence) at first hand, it taught him nothing except contempt for the "logical confusion"[13] of its practitioners.[7]

Commenting in the same vein on the West's "peculiar elevation of the laws of thought to an absolute status," Professor E. A. Burtt, a noted scholar in the field of comparative philosophy and religion, writes:

> Occidental philosophy makes what progress it does through the medium of hostile argumentation. . . . This makes for spicy debates and hilarious argumentation; when two redoubtable pugilists engage in such intellectual sparring the rest of us crowd the sidelines in the philosophic journals and watch the fray with excited absorption. . . . But it is a terribly slow, wasteful, and cantankerous way of getting ahead in philosophy. Satisfying though it is to our belligerent instincts, sober consideration must recognize that it puts us under serious handicap in comparison with thinkers who can grow toward the larger truth without battering each other through these obstructive conflicts.[8]

We have quoted at length in order to substantiate our point that from the Indian standpoint a philosopher's vision of reality should have a serious bearing upon his life and conduct. If it does not, it can in no way serve him or others as a guide for realizing the four basic ends of human life (*puruṣārthas*)[9] recognized by the Indian tradition: *dharma, artha, kāma,* and *mokṣa.*

Dharma has several meanings in Sanskrit and defies any attempt to render it exactly into English. Nevertheless, we can convey its basic sense by noting that it derives from the root *dhṛ* meaning "to sustain," "to maintain," "to support." Thus duties, obligations, justice—in general rules of conduct and guides for action—come under *dharma* since they are essential to the protection and perpetuation of the individual and society. That is, *dharma* is the duties and obligations of the individual toward himself and the society as well as those of the society toward the individual. Thus it is *dharma* which makes it possible for men to live and function harmoniously in their society by fulfilling themselves and at the same time contributing to the well-being of the society at large. Different individuals have different duties and obligations, depending on their aptitudes, abilities, and stations in life at any given time. It is obvious, however, that all individuals have certain duties and obligations in common.

Like *dharma, artha* has many meanings in Sanskrit. Its root meaning is "that which one seeks." Broadly speaking, *artha* may be translated as one's means of supporting one's life. It is clear that *artha* covers job, wealth, and all other material means necessary for the maintenance of life. This does not mean that *artha* excludes the spiritual life of man. Quite the contrary, material well-being is a necessary condition for spiritual life. It is absurd to talk about the spiritual life of a man in the grip of grinding poverty and emaciating sickness. Thus all means of livelihood are *artha.* However, man should not earn his living and acquire wealth in violation of *dharma*—for instance, by deceiving, stealing, killing.

But wealth is only a means and not an end in itself. The purpose of wealth is *kāma*—pleasure and enjoyment in general, such as food, drink, sex, home, friendship. Pleasure and enjoyment are not to be thought of as unworthy and sinful; on the contrary, they are one of the main aims of life. It is important, however, that *artha* and *kāma* be in harmony with each other and with *dharma.*

The fourth aim of life is *mokṣa.* The term *mokṣa* derives from the root *muk,* meaning "to free," "to emancipate," "to release." In short, *mokṣa* is complete freedom. But, one might ask, freedom and release from what? The answer to this question is the quintessence of Indian wisdom. Let us first point out that the very fact that Indian philosophies regard *mokṣa* as the ultimate goal of life points to the extraordinary significance they attach to the essentially spiritual nature of man. According to all Indian schools of philosophy, man's state of suffering and unfreedom is not due to any original sin on his part but to original ignorance (*avidyā*) of his true being and nature. Thus the *Upaniṣads* teach that man in his true being is Ātman (Brahman, ultimate reality), which is infinite, eternal, and immortal. But in his ignorance, man identifies himself with finite and perishable things, such as his body, mind, ego, and thereby develops attachments to them and suffers sorrow and misery when he loses them, as he inevitably does. It is only by attaining the knowledge that in his true being he is indeed ultimate reality that man can conquer ignorance and bondage and become free. In other words, freedom consists in self-realization—the realization that man is the infinite, eternal, immortal Pure Being. It is important to note that "immortality" is not to be understood as endless existence in some distant and unknown corner of the cosmos, but as man's discovery that he is identical with the all-encompassing eternal reality. On such realization, birth and death are seen to be no more than products of ignorance, pertaining only to the world of phenomena and having no ultimate reality. Equally important is the fact that all schools of Indian philosophy teach that *mokṣa* is not a state to be looked forward to after death. Quite the contrary, it is to be attained here and now while one is still in one's bodily existence. It is for this reason that all Indian philosophies and religions hold that the body is not something to be disparaged as the source of sin and depravity, but rather is the vehicle for attaining *mokṣa*—for it makes no sense to talk about knowledge, liberating or otherwise, without a body. It should be obvious now why every school of Indian philosophy recognizes Yoga in some form or other as the physical-mental discipline necessary for the attainment of *mokṣa*. The same point may be expressed by saying that biological and social fulfillment is a necessary but not a sufficient condition for the attainment of *mokṣa*.

Each Indian philosophical system is classified as orthodox or unorthodox according as it accepts or rejects the authority of the Vedas, the oldest and most sacred scriptures of the Hindus. A word of caution for the Western reader is necessary here. The fact that a system is orthodox does not necessarily mean that it is theistic; as such, a system can be both orthodox and atheistic. The reason for this is that theism and atheism are both compatible with the teachings of the Vedas. The following are generally regarded as orthodox systems: Sāṁkhya, Yoga, Nyāya, Vaiśeṣika, Mīmāṁsā, and Vedānta. The unorthodox systems are Cārvākism (materialism), Jainism, and Buddhism. One may, however, consider Sāṁkhya, Yoga, Nyāya, and Vaiśeṣika to be neither orthodox nor unorthodox, since they originated independently of the Vedas—that is, without accepting or rejecting them. It may also be noted that in their original forms Sāṁkhya and Yoga are atheistic, whereas Nyāya and Vaiśeṣika are theistic; however, the former are theistic in their later developments. We may remind the reader that all these are generally classified as orthodox schools.

From another point of view, some scholars combine the orthodox schools in pairs: Yoga-Sāṁkhya, Nyāya-Vaiśeṣika, and Mīmāṁsā-Vedānta. The basis for this coupling is that the first element of each of the three pairs pertains to practice, and the second to theory. Thus, Yoga is essentially a practical discipline of physical and mental training for the realization of the truths taught by the theoretical system of Sāṁkhya; similarly Nyāya is primarily methodology, whereas Vaiśeṣika is the metaphysical system upheld by Nyāya. Similar considerations hold with respect to Mīmāṁsā and Vedānta.

The following characteristics are common to all systems of Indian philosophy, with the single exception of materialism: (1) All the schools insist that no account of reality which fails to do justice to reason and experience can be accepted. By "reason" is meant here the canons of formal reasoning as well as those of inductive inquiry. Similarly, "experience" is to be understood in its broadest sense, which includes everyday commonsensical experience, scientific experience, and extraordinary states of consciousness. (2) All the systems maintain that every acceptable philosophy should aid man in realizing the *puruṣārthas* (the chief ends of human life). Briefly, all philosophies of India are philosophies of life. Any philosophy worthy of its title should not be a mere intellectual exercise but should have practical application in enabling man to live an enlightened life. A philosophy which makes no difference to the quality and style of our life is no philosophy, but an empty intellectual construction which may quench the thirst of the curious but is otherwise irrelevant. To put it differently, philosophy should have soteriological power—the power to transform man's life from one of ignorance, darkness, and bondage to one of knowledge, wisdom, and freedom. (3) All the systems of philosophy acknowledge man's essential spirituality, regard freedom as his highest and ultimate goal, and demand that philosophy show him the way to attain freedom. (4) All the schools teach that man's state of ignorance and suffering is not due to original sin but to original ignorance. (5) Accordingly freedom and liberation can only be won by conquering ignorance through knowledge. (6) All the systems hold that there is no limit to the perfectibility of man—he is infinitely perfectible. The reason for this view is that man contains within himself the secret of all existence, for, as the Upaniṣads teach, man's inmost Self (Ātman) is Brahman, and, as Buddhism teaches, every man is Buddha, only he should know that to be the case. (7) All the schools argue that complete freedom (*mokṣa, nirvāṇa*) is to be attained here and now in the bodily existence. (8) All the systems accept Yoga in some form or other as the spiritual discipline *par excellence* for the attainment of freedom. (9) All the philosophies acknowledge through the doctrine of *karma* and rebirth an impersonal universal moral order, with the explicit understanding that this doctrine pertains not to ultimate reality but only to the empirical world. (10) All the schools emphatically reject as absurd any suggestion that man is nothing but a material entity. (11) All the systems hold that ultimate reality cannot be grasped through the senses and intellect, but can only be experienced in direct, nonperceptual, nonconceptual, intuitive, mystical insight. (12) All the schools are initially pessimistic, in that they begin their philosophizing by drawing attention to the fact of man's present state as one of ignorance, suffering, misery, and bondage. (13) Nevertheless, all the schools are ultimately optimistic, in that they unqualifiedly affirm that it is within the power of man to attain knowledge, wisdom, peace, freedom. In short, Indian schools of philosophy categorically reject nihilism as well as philosophies of the Absurd, Angst, and Nothingness, and unequivocally proclaim the ultimate triumph of the human spirit.

Chapter II

Cārvākism: Materialism

Introduction

Among the various non-Vedic schools of philosophy, materialism is quite old. Chronologically, its origins may roughly be located in the post-Upaniṣadic period before the Buddha. Tradition has it that a sage named Cārvāka founded Indian materialism, but in some quarters it is believed that Cārvāka was a prominent disciple of Bṛhaspati, the actual founder of the school. In any case, it is interesting to note that the term *Cārvāka* has its etymology in *carv* which means to chew or eat. Accordingly, *Cārvāka* has acquired the status of a common noun, used derogatorily to refer to anyone who is thought to be a materialist or a preacher and practitioner of the doctrine of "eat, drink, and be merry." Indian materialism is also known as *Lokāyata-mata,* "the view of common folk."

As there are no extant original writings of the Cārvāka school (with perhaps the exception of a much later work, Jayarāśi Bhaṭṭa's *Tattvopaplavasiṁha*), our knowledge of the doctrines of Indian materialism is based exclusively on the works of other schools,[1] which seem to be more interested in discrediting and lampooning materialism than in presenting an objective account of its tenets. Small wonder, then, that materialism could never occupy a dominant place in the Indian philosophic scene.

Epistemology

Like every other school of philosophy, materialism is concerned with inquiring into the sources, nature, validity, and limits of man's knowledge of reality. According to the materialist, *pratyakṣa* (sense perception, hereafter referred to simply as "perception") is the only source and criterion (*pramāṇa*) of knowledge;[2] that is, all claims to knowledge must stand or fall according as they are based on perception. In order to defend this fundamental epistemological doctrine of the exclusive reliability of perception, the materialist attempts to refute[3] two other sources and criteria of knowledge, namely, inference and testimony, which are accepted by almost all other schools of Indian philosophy as valid and reliable.

Inference is the process by which we claim one proposition to be true or false on the basis of other propositions. There are two patterns of inference which in modern terminology may be referred to as "deductive" and "inductive" inference. From an epistemological point of view, the Cārvāka rejects not only the distinction between deductive and inductive inference but also inference itself as an invalid and unreliable source of knowledge.[4] An example of the deductive pattern of inference is the following syllogism:

> All men are mortal.
> All Greeks are men.
> Therefore, all Greeks are mortal.

The materialist points out that we cannot accept the truth of the proposition "All Greeks are mortal" unless we already know that the propositions "All men are mortal" and "All Greeks are men" are true. At this point, let us illustrate the inductive pattern of inference. Particular men X, Y, Z, etc., are mortal. Therefore, all men are mortal. The general problem of inductive inference may now be stated as that of providing justification for asserting a universal proposition on the basis of particular propositions. It can be seen now why, as far as the problem of knowledge of the world is concerned, the Cārvāka regards the deductive and inductive patterns of inference as inextricably bound up with each other. Let us clarify this point with respect to our example of deductive inference. The Cārvāka asks: How do we know, for example, that "All men are mortal" is true? We cannot, he says, know this proposition to be true, since all we are entitled to assert by our experience is that all men we have encountered thus far are mortal, but not that all men, in the past, present, and future, are mortal. The point of this criticism is that there is no basis for our thinking and claiming that the future will be like the past. Consequently, the inferred proposition "All Greeks are mortal" cannot be reliable knowledge. It is only by a leap in the dark, that is, by assuming that the future will be like the past, that one can assert that all men are mortal. But since there is nothing in our experience that can justify such a leap, this proposition, and every proposition inferred on the basis of it, cannot constitute valid and reliable knowledge. Thus deductive inference is shaky and untrustworthy as a source and criterion of knowledge.

The second objection of the materialist against deductive inference is closely related to the first. It is that deductive inference is a *petitio principii*—arguing in a circle and begging the question. Thus to assert that all men are mortal is at the same time to assert that all Greeks are mortal, since Greeks are classified as men. Hence the inferred proposition, "All Greeks are mortal," gives us no knowledge or information not already contained in the original proposition on the basis of which the inference is made.

One might object to the criticisms of the materialist by saying that "All men are mortal" is assertible because of the invariable connection we have perceived between being man and being mortal. To take another example, one might say that "Where there is smoke, there is fire" can be asserted universally because of the invariable connection we perceive between smoke and fire. But the materialist would retort that all talk about the so-called invariable connections is futile and misguided in establishing the universality of the claims made.[5] For, he asserts, arguments from invariable connections go beyond what is actually perceived and perceivable. It is one thing to say that all instances in which smoke has been perceived are also instances in which fire has been perceived, and quite another to claim on the basis of such observed instances that all instances of smoke, past, present, and future, are also instances of fire. We have no grounds in our experience for going from statements of limited, perceived instances to unlimited, unrestricted, universal generalizations. Universal truths cannot be asserted, because they have no foundation in our perceptual experience, which is the only trustworthy and valid source and criterion of knowledge. It follows then that according to the materialist there can be no such thing as knowledge of universal truths.

We may ask, however, whether the materialist can successfully avoid drawing inferences at all. Without going into any detailed and complex considerations, we answer this question negatively. The Cārvāka cannot do without inference. Take the simple situation of the materialist teaching his doctrines. In order to teach, he has to employ language and to assume that his listeners understand what he is saying. It is important to note that when the Cārvāka says something, he actually utters a sequence of noises, which are directly perceived by his hearers. Unless the hearers interpret these noises as symbols for certain concepts and ideas, they will not be able to understand what the materialist is saying. But how do they go about interpreting and understanding the noises made by the materialist? Obviously, the hearers *infer* from the noises the meaning and content of the Cārvāka's utterances. In particular, they have to rely on their memory for the meanings of the words. But if the materialist forbids them to use their memory, on the grounds that memory can only point up to something that is not now being perceived, not only do his hearers find it impossible to understand the materialist, but, more importantly, the materialist's own aim of teaching them becomes self-stultifying. It is also worth noting that, although the Cārvāka denies inference at the theoretical level, he himself cannot help employing it in his everyday commerce with the world of men and objects around him. He thus appears as a curious spectacle to others. The point here is that the materialist's philosophic view of inference as an invalid source of knowledge is incompatible with his own actual practice in living. Finally, one might ask whether the materialist's central claim that perception is the only reliable source of knowledge is based on perception alone. It is easy to see that this claim is not itself given in perception, but is the result of a theoretical construction which goes beyond perception. It would seem that the materialist has arrived at his general claim that perception is the only reliable source of knowledge in the following manner: He first observes that certain perceptions, X, Y, Z, etc., are reliable and then goes on to assert that perception in general is reliable. But such a generalization shows at best that perception is *a* reliable source of knowledge, not that it is the *only* source, which is what is to be vindicated if the materialist is to successfully defend his claim of the exclusive reliability of perception. It is clear, then, that the materialist is guilty on two counts. First, while claiming to reject inference, he surreptitiously makes use of it in asserting the generalization that perception is reliable; and second, he commits the error of asserting that only perception is reliable, on the basis of the generalization that perception is reliable. We may note in passing that the materialist's criticism of deductive inference is very similar to that of the utilitarian philosopher John Stuart Mill.[6]

We now come to the Cārvāka critique of testimony. A great deal of our knowledge is based on the testimony of others whom we regard as competent and reliable persons. We accept it as true that there is a continent called "Australia" on the testimony of others, although we ourselves may never have been to Australia. Similarly, one accepts it as true that there are certain organisms called "microbes" on the testimony of the microbiologist, although one has never seen them oneself. Thus it would seem that testimony is an indispensable and widely employed source of reliable knowledge. But the materialist rejects testimony on the following grounds: Accepting something as true on the basis of testimony presupposes that we regard the person or persons giving the testimony as reliable, honest, and trustworthy. But, the materialist asks, on what grounds are we justified in so presupposing? The answer, according to the Cārvāka, can only be an inference of the following kind. Mr. X proved reliable in his testimony concerning matters P, Q, and R. Therefore, Mr. X is to be regarded as reliable concerning matter S. In short, Mr. X's testimony is in general reliable. But such an inference is invalid, the materialist continues, for we have cases where authorities hitherto regarded as reliable turned out to be unreliable and untrustworthy. No authority's testimony can be regarded as universally reliable on the basis of his proven reliability in the past, no matter how great. Notice that the materialist's rejection of testimony as a valid source of knowledge is but a special case of his rejection of inference in general.[7] Thus, according to Cārvāka, both inference and testimony are to be rejected as invalid and unreliable sources and standards of knowledge. Perception is the only valid source and criterion of knowledge.

Metaphysics

The metaphysics of the materialist is a direct consequence of his epistemological doctrine that perception is the sole source of reliable knowledge. He holds that gods, souls, heaven, hell, and immortality have no basis in our experience (perception) and hence are to be rejected as nonexistent and fictitious. They are concocted by the priestly class in order to protect its vested interests of money, status, and power by presiding over and performing rituals and ceremonies on behalf of the gullible masses at the latter's expense.[8]

According to the Cārvāka, matter is the only reality. The world is constituted of matter in the form of the four elements, air, fire, water, and earth.[9] All objects, both inanimate and animate, are the result of different combinations of these elements. Consistent with his doctrine of the exclusive status of perception as the source of valid knowledge, the Cārvāka rejects ether (space, *ākāśa* in Sanskrit), which is regarded as an element by other Indian schools. The reason for such a rejection is that ether cannot be perceived but only inferred. Our senses are also the result of various combinations of the four elements. Everything that can enter into our experience is to be accounted for without appealing to unperceivable and mysterious entities and qualities. Just as the intoxicating quality of wine arises out of fermented yeast, and saltiness out of a certain combination of sodium and chlorine, so also consciousness arises out of the four elements combining to produce a certain aggregate.[10] What others call "the soul" is no more and no less than the conscious body. Thus consciousness or mind is an epiphenomenon, a by-product of matter. To appeal to God or some supernatural being in order to explain consciousness is nothing but argument from ignorance. It is clear, then, that according to the Cārvāka qualities not possessed by any of the elements individually may arise in the aggregates constituted of them: for example, although neither hydrogen nor oxygen is wet, water, produced by a certain combination of them, is wet. Thus the Cārvāka teaches the doctrine of emergent evolution concerning qualities, including consciousness.

God, like the soul, is a fiction, a nonexistent entity, forever beyond the realm of our perceptual possibilities. Whereas many philosophers argue that God is the creator of the universe, the Cārvāka rejects the notion of God by saying that God, by the admission of his own advocates, is not a perceivable reality. To the question how the universe could have come into being without a creator, the materialist answers that it is logically consistent to hold that the universe has neither a beginning nor an end. Matter has always existed and will always exist. The elements themselves, by their intrinsic natures, act as the efficient cause bringing about the different objects constituting the world. Thus matter is both the material and efficient cause of the universe. Nor is there any reason for us to believe that the universe is a product of design or is the work of a designing agent, such as the so-called God. If someone maintains that God is both the material cause and the designer of the universe, says the materialist, we can significantly ask him to tell us what brought God into being in the first place and what caused him to design the universe. The Cārvāka points out that these questions can only be answered at the cost of infinite regress and question-begging. The materialist therefore concludes that God as the explanatory principle of the existence and character of the world is simply unilluminating and useless.

Ethics

Concerning ethics and the conduct of life, the materialist teaches the doctrine of hedonism, according to which the pursuit of pleasure and the enjoyment of worldly goods are the only proper and sensible ends of life.[11] Since according to him death is the annihilation of life,[12] men should pursue and secure for themselves the maximum pleasure and enjoyment compatible with their lot in life. It is sheer folly and the height of unwisdom for man to relinquish the pleasures this life has to offer in the hope of finding some state of greater and permanent enjoyment elsewhere after death. For death is the ultimate end, there being no other world than this.[13] Accordingly, the Cārvāka teaches that asceticism, self-immolation, and self-mortification are the epitome of stupidity and delusion. Religion, God, soul, the afterlife, heaven, and hell are the fabrications of priests for assuring themselves a comfortable livelihood. Of the four ends of human life *(puruṣārthas)*, namely, *artha, kāma, dharma,* and *mokṣa,* the materialist recognizes and commends the first two and rejects the last two as illusory and hence as unworthy of man's attention. Accordingly, men are exhorted to acquire wealth—not, however, as an end in itself, but only as a means to pleasure and enjoyment, They may employ any means whatever, straight as well as crooked, to attain wealth and through it pleasure and enjoyment. Nevertheless, the Cārvāka warns us that we should not seek a pleasure or enjoyment if it brings in its wake pain and misery. An action is good if it produces more pleasure than pain, and bad if it results in more pain than pleasure. The wise man is he who, under the circumstances of life in which he finds himself, successfully seeks and secures maximum pleasure while avoiding pain altogether or experiencing it only minimally.[14] It is clear from the foregoing that the ethics of the Cārvāka are hedonistic ethics.

It should, however, be pointed out in fairness to the materialist school that not all followers of it were crude and egoistic hedonists. To be sure, a good number of materialists did draw a distinction between crude and egoistic hedonism and refined and altruistic hedonism. These thinkers not only felt the need to distinguish qualitatively between pleasures but also recognized the need for society, law, and order[15] and therewith the need for sharing one's pleasure and enjoyment with one's fellowmen. It would be gross injustice and malicious distortion to describe the Cārvāka as a blind, fierce, and insensitive pursuer of pleasure for himself without concern for his fellowmen. In conclusion, it is worth noting that the Cārvāka of ancient India and the Epicurean of ancient Greece bear a striking resemblance to each other in many respects. Both were philosophical materialists whose hedonism was tempered with self-discipline, discriminating intelligence, refined taste, and genuine capacity for friendship.

Chapter III

Jainism

Introduction

Jainism is both a philosophy and a religion. It is an ancient, non-Vedic, unorthodox system of thought and practice, though it is highly likely that it arose as both a reaction to and a reform of the Brahmanism of the Vedas. The popular belief that Vardhamāna was the founder of Jainism seems to be false, for, according to the tradition of Jainism, Vardhamāna was the twenty-fourth in a long line of *Tīrthaṁkaras* (perfect souls, seers, guides of mankind, and trail-blazers). Vardhamāna, then, was a Tīrthaṁkara who, living in times of priestly corruption, moral bankruptcy, and spiritual decay, keenly felt the need to help mankind and resuscitated an ancient faith.

Born about 540 B.C. at Kundagrāma in Modern Bihar, Vardhamāna was of princely lineage. Like most other princes, he married early and led the life of a householder until he was nearly thirty years old. Then, having set himself the task of finding a way out of the misery, suffering, illness, and death which so unmistakably characterize sentient existence, Vardhamāna renounced the worldly life and practiced meditation and other disciplines, living the simple and austere life of a mendicant. After thirteen years of arduous quest, Vardhamāna proclaimed to the world his discovery of the path to freedom from all forms of bondage and illness. This discovery made him the *Jina* (the conqueror) and *Mahāvīra* (the great spiritual hero). After becoming the Jina, Vardhamāna spent the rest of his life teaching the way so that every man could become the conqueror. He is said to have died in 468 B.C.

Metaphysics

In that it draws a sharp distinction betwen animate substances (*jīvas* = souls) and inanimate substances (*ajīvas* = non-souls), Jainism is thoroughgoing dualism. It is also pluralistic *(anekāntavāda)* in that it recognizes the existence of an infinite number of animate and inanimate substances, each possessing an infinite number of characteristics of its own.[1] Further, since it teaches that the infinite number of substances exist independently of our perceptions or awareness of them, Jainism may also be described as epistemological and metaphysical realism.

The Jaina theory of substances is very much like that of Aristotle. A substance *(dravya)* is that which possesses characters. The various characters are divided into the essential and the accidental, also called "qualities *(guṇas)*" and "modes *(paryāyas)*," respectively.[2] An essential character is one by possession of which a substance is what it is; and an accidental character is one which a substance might possess at one time and not at another. The essential characters of a substance are eternal and unchanging; consequently, substances are also eternal and unchanging. Thus it is the essential characters which underlie the permanence of the world. On the other hand, the changing character of the world is due to the accidental characters of substances. In this manner, then, the Jainas recognize and accommodate change and permanence as both genuine and real features of all existence.[3] Let us illustrate all this. Consider the soul. It is a substance in that it has the essential character of consciousness. Pain and pleasure, for example, are its accidental characters. The soul is thus both permanent and changing. Jainism rejects the concept of an absolutely unchanging substance, such as the Brahman of the Upaniṣads, as well as that of absolute change devoid of anything abiding, such as the pure flux of Buddhism.[4]

On the basis of extension, Jainism divides substances into two classes: those that are extended in space and those that are not. Under the former come souls *(jīvas),* matter *(pudgala),* space *(ākāśa), dharma,* and *adharma;* under the latter there is only one, namely, time (kāla). That is, time is the only unextended substance.[5]

The *jīva* is an eternal substance whose essential character is consciousness.[6] The *jīva* animates the physical body in which it dwells at the time. But, importantly, whereas in the Upaniṣads the *jīva,* in the sense of Ātman, is considered unchanging—that is, atomic or omipresent—Jainism teaches that the *jīva* is capable of change in magnitude. Thus, the magnitude of the *jīva* varies according as it inhabits a smaller or a larger body.[7] Without doing violence to the Jaina teachings, we may say that for Jainism "consciousness," "sentience," and "knowledge" are equivalent concepts. Consequently, we can rightly say that knowing is the essential character of the *jīva.* The *jīva*'s knowledge, as long as it is ensconced in a material body, is imperfect and incomplete, owing to the limitations imposed upon the *jīva* by the material body. Were it not for such limitations, the *jīva*'s knowledge would be perfect and complete—in short, the *jīva* would be omniscient. It is worth noting, however, that according to Jainism, there can be no disembodied consciousness; consciousness is always associated with some body. Curiously enough, our sense organs, which are regarded by many as necessary for knowledge, are considered by the Jainas to be obstacles to knowledge. The reason for this is to be found in the Jaina conception of knowledge. The soul, in its original state, unencumbered in the nexus of matter, is omniscient. As such, the sense organs, which are material entities serving as means for only partial and imperfect knowledge, are really impediments depriving the soul of its primordial omniscience. Accordingly, the aim and goal of the *jīva* is to overcome the limitations and obstacles emanating from its entanglement with matter, and thereby to regain its original state of knowledge, pure, perfect, and all-encompassing.[8] In that state, there is nothing hidden from the soul, and it commands the knowledge of existence in all its varied aspects as well as of past, present, and future. It should be clear that the soul attains such a state of perfection, not through ordinary modes of knowledge such as perception and thought, but through a direct, immediate, intuitive, nonperceptual, nonconceptual grasp of reality.

Like all other schools of Indian philosophy, with the single exception of the Cārvākas, Jainism upholds the universal law of *karma,* according to which every event, be it thought, word, or action, produces its effects, which in turn serve as causes bringing about other events, and so on.[9] It is this chain of causes and effects that is referred to as "karmic bondage" or simply *karma.* Naturally enough, Jainism subscribes to rebirth and transmigration. It follows, then, that the state of the *jīva* at any given time is due to the nature of the *karma* it has accumulated over aeons of time. We should, however, point out that Jainism holds that man is not powerless over *karma;* quite the contrary, by effort, discipline, and knowledge man can not only courageously acknowledge past *karma* but also prevent the accumulation of new *karma.* He who has thus completely freed himself from all *karma* is indeed the liberated soul.

It should be emphasized that although Jainism recognizes souls, unlike Hinduism it rejects the notion of an ultimate single, universal soul. Such a rejection is also the rejection of the notion of a Supreme Being, traditionally known as God, the creator and sustainer of the universe. In the absence of God, the law of *karma* is fully autonomous in its operation. That is, it is not God that dispenses rewards and punishments to individual souls in accordance with their *karma,* but the impersonal law of *karma* itself. The particular form which a *jīva* assumes and the kind of body it inhabits are determined entirely by the *jīva's karma* in its past existence; likewise, the future mode of existence of a *jīva* is determined by its *karma* in the present existence. At this point, it is worth pointing out the peculiarly Jaina conception of *karma*. How does *karma* manifest itself? Is it material or immaterial? In sharp contrast to the Hindu conception of *karma,* according to which *karma* is immaterial, Jainism teaches that *karma* is constituted of fine and subtle particles of matter.[10] Although this view of *karma* may at first seem fantastic and incredible, it does make sense in the light of the Jaina doctrine that it is matter which limits the knowledge and perfection of the soul. If *karma* is bondage and limitation due to the soul's involvement with matter, it is only natural, within the framework of Jaina metaphysics, to identify *karma* with subtle particles of matter. It is also worth noting that such a material view of *karma,* though incompatible with the atomic conception of the soul, is in harmony with the Jaina conception of the soul as a composite entity. For if the soul is atomic and hence indivisible, it is impossible for the subtle particles of *karma* to penetrate it. On the other hand, the composite soul, being by definition made up of parts, is susceptible to the ingression of the fine particles of matter constituting *karma.* In conformity with their doctrines of the materiality of *karma* and the composite nature of the soul, the Jainas maintain that souls in their mundane existence are of different grades, depending on the number of sense organs they possess. A soul with just one sense organ—for example, a plant, which has that of touch—is of the lowest grade, whereas the soul of man is of the highest grade possessing all six sense organs, the mind included.[11] It is obvious that inanimate matter, such as a stone, possesses no sense organs at all and hence has no soul.

In contradistinction to *jīvas,* matter is atomic in its ultimate constitution.[12] What we perceive is gross, composite matter, not the constituent atoms, which are imperceptible. Such properties as touch, color, taste, and smell belong only to gross matter but not to the ultimate atoms, which are without qualities and indistinguishable from each other. Observed differences in the qualities of objects are due to differences in the number and configuration of their constituent atoms. Our senses, mind, and breath are also composed of atoms.[13] Unlike other schools, Jainism does not regard sound as a quality, but as a mere modification of gross (but not atomic) matter.[14] The elements earth, water, fire, and air are products of different combinations of the qualityless and indistinguishable atoms. As such, one element can be transformed into another through changes effected in the atomic structure. We might mention in passing that the Jainas hold that even atoms have their own souls, although these souls are to be distinguished from the *jīvas* possessing sense organs and consciousness. For Jainism, then, the whole universe is throbbing with souls,[15] a view similar to the ancient Greek hylozoism.[16]

We shall now consider the remaining four *ajīvas,* namely, space, *dharma, adharma,* and time. Space is infinite, eternal, and imperceptible. Its existence is inferred as the condition of extension. Space is not, however, to be equated with extension, but is that which makes it possible for extended objects to exist. To put it differently, space is the power of accommodating extended substances, such as souls, matter, *dharma,* and *adharma.* It is important to note here that the Jainas, unlike other philosophers, consider extension an intrinsic or essential character of substances.[17] They point out that it does not make sense to define "space" as extension. On the contrary, the Jainas maintain, space is the condition which makes it possible for extended substances to exist and appear.[18] It is to be emphasized that the Jaina conception of space avoids the circularity involved in defining "objects" as those which occupy space, and "space" as that which is occupied by objects. As a point of contrast, it may be noted that the Jaina conception of space, while incompatible with that of Descartes, closely resembles that of Locke. According to the Jainas, space is divisible into two parts: that which contains the world (world-space) and that which is empty beyond the world.

The terms *dharma* and *adharma,* in the context of *ajīvas,* are not to be understood in their usual senses of moral merit and demerit. According to Jainism, *dharma* and *adharma* are extended substances which are eternal, formless, passive, and imperceptible.[19] The former is the condition for the possibility of motion, while the latter is the condition for the possibility of rest. *Dharma* and *adharma* both pervade the whole of the world-space. Their existence is inferred from the facts of motion and rest. Being passive, they can neither initiate nor arrest motion. *Dharma* is merely the condition favorable for motion, and *adharma* for rest; that is, they are necessary but not sufficient conditions for motion and rest respectively. To illustrate this point: water cannot initiate the motion of a fish, but only makes its motion possible; on the other hand, earth cannot arrest the motion of bodies, but only supports those which rest upon it.

We come now to the last of the *ajīvas,* namely, time. It is important to note first that time differs from *jīvas* as well as from the other *ajīvas* in that it is a substance not extended in space. Like space it is infinite, eternal, and imperceptible. Its existence is inferred from the facts of continuity, modification, activity, newness (nowness), and oldness (thenness);[20] that is to say, time is the condition for the possibility of all these. Time is unitary and indivisible and all things are in it.[21] Further, according to Jainism, time is of two kinds, empirical *(vyavahārika)* time and real *(paramārthika)* time. The latter is primordial, infinite, indivisible, and underlies the possibility of continuity and duration. Empirical time is divisible into units, such as seconds and minutes, and is produced by imposing upon the formless indivisible real time conventions, distinctions, and limits.[22] Whereas real time alone makes possible duration, empirical time makes possible all changes. This last point, it may be remarked, is in harmony with Henri Bergson's distinction between the measurable time science deals with and the duration of lived experience.[23]

Epistemology

Jainism divides all knowledge into two classes, the mediate *(parokṣa)* and the immediate *(aparokṣa).* Mediate knowledge is any knowledge which the soul comes to have by the mediation of sense organs, including the mind—in short, any knowledge whose acquisition involves something other than the soul itself. By contrast, immediate knowledge is that which the soul obtains without the intervention of the sense organs. It is clear, then, that the Jaina classification of knowledge is based on the manner of acquiring knowledge rather than on the objects of knowledge. Knowledge by direct perception, internal or external, which is regarded by many schools as immediate knowledge, Jainism regards as mediate, since the senses and mind (things other than the soul itself) play a role in it. Sometimes Jainism speaks of such direct perceptual knowledge as relatively immediate, as distinct from absolutely immediate knowledge, which the soul has in virtue of that consciousness which it attains by freeing itself from all the karmic obstacles. Such consciousness is, like the sun, self-luminous and illuminates all objects, internal and external, without the mediation of the senses and the mind. We may call the absolutely immediate knowledge "suprasensual, non-conceptual, non-perceptual, intuitive knowledge (*kevala-jñāna*)." [24] From the foregoing, it should be clear that knowledge is not something external to be grasped and possessed by the soul, but is a state of the soul itself. We might mention in passing that Jainism, like many other Indian schools, accepts in respect of mediate knowledge the three criteria (standards, *pramāṇas*), namely, perception, inference, and testimony.[25]

Jainism believes that there are an infinite number of independently existing atoms, objects, and souls. All of these have innumerable characters and aspects, and consequently they stand in innumerable relations to each other.[26] Only an omniscient being, such as the liberated soul, can know all objects in all their aspects. No soul entrapped in the karmic network of mundane existence is capable of such all-encompassing and perfect knowledge. As ordinary, unliberated *jīvas* we can only have partial, imperfect knowledge of any object. Our knowledge of any object, as long as we are in the unliberated state, is always from a certain point of view and of a certain aspect of the object. A judgment is the proposition through which we express our knowledge of objects. But since our ordinary knowledge can only be partial, the judgments we pass can only be partial too. A partial judgment is known as *naya*.[27] Any judgment we make can only be from a certain standpoint and about a certain aspect of the innumerable aspects of an object. The Jainas point out that it is only by forgetting the essential incompleteness of ordinary knowledge that philosophers lay absolute, dogmatic, unconditional, and exclusive claims of truth for their own necessarily partial and incomplete judgments and theories of the world. Small, wonder, then, that dogmatism and ignorance invariably lead to vehement but futile arguments and disputes concerning the nature of reality. Philosophers who claim absolute and unconditional truth for their own knowledge, owing to their unawareness of its essential incompleteness, are like the proverbial blind men, each of whom sternly claimed that his own description of the elephant was true. The Jaina view that all our ordinary knowledge is necessarily partial, being always relative to some particular point of view and about particular aspects of objects, is known as *syādvāda*,[28] the doctrine of relativity of knowledge and judgments (*syād* = relative to some standpoint, *vāda* = doctrine, theory, view). Thus, the judgment "This object is blue" would, according to the Jainas, be correctly expressed as "Relative to a certain standpoint and to a certain aspect, this object is blue," meaning that looked at from a certain place at a certain time, at a certain angle, in a certain light, etc., the object is blue. The qualifications indicating the point of view and aspects may refer to place, time, quality, quantity, etc., as well as to the act of perception itself. The *syādvāda* theory logically leads Jainism to the recognition of many alternatives between judgments of mutually exclusive simple affirmation and negation. Accordingly, the Jainas classify judgments into seven kinds, hence the *saptabhaṅgīnaya*, the schema of sevenfold judgment.[29] For our purposes, we need not go into a detailed discussion of this schema. Suffice it to present here the seven forms of judgment. Thus let S stand for subject, P for character, and R for the phrase "relatively." Then the seven forms of judgment are as follows:

1. R, S is P.
2. R, S is not P.
3. R, S is P, and S is not P.
4. R, S is indescribable.
5. R, S is P, and S is indescribable.
6. S is not P, and S is indescribable.
7. R, S is P and S is not P, and S is indescribable.

We have two main criticisms of the Jaina doctrine of relativity of judgment and the sevenfold schema. The Jainas, while rightly drawing our attention to the relativity of all judgments and knowledge, fail to understand that all talk of relativity makes sense only in the light of some absolute, real or imagined. But Jainism never seems to leave the plane of the relative toward that of the absolute. We shall see in a later chapter that though, like Jainism, the Mādhyamika school of Buddhism emphasizes the relativity of all knowledge, unlike the Jainas it calls attention to the absolute by drawing the distinction between the empirical, mundane, lower, relative truth and the supramundane, higher, absolute truth. Further, the sevenfold schema is merely a mechanical assembly of the various possible judgments but not a synthesis of them. As such, the Jainas are mistaken in thinking that the conjunction of all partial truths is equivalent to the whole truth. In other words, the Jaina theory of judgment is merely a theory of identity added to difference but not one of identity-in-difference, which is what is needed to account for the identity-in-difference manifested in reality. To be sure, the Jaina concept of *kevala-jñāna* of the liberated soul does seem to be indistinguishable from that of absolute knowledge. But by absolutizing the relativity of knowledge, Jainism contradicts its own notion of *kevala-jñāna*. The only way out of this contradiction is for the Jainas to admit the Mādhyamika distinction between the lower, relative truth and the higher, absolute truth. But, needless to say, such an admission would compel Jainism to give up ultimate and unconditional claims, not only for realism and pluralism, but for relativism itself.

God and Liberation

As a religion, Jainism, unlike Buddhism, is confined to India and never commanded any following outside the subcontinent. This observation is not, however, to be construed as a reflection on the merit and worth of Jainism. It merely expresses a fact.

Jainism believes that the universe is infinite and eternal. It is atheistic in its unqualified rejection of any God or Supreme Being as the creator and sustainer of the universe. The Jainas advance a number of arguments against the existence of God.[30] We shall present two main arguments, one dealing with the concept of God as creator, and the other with that of his perfections.

The Jainas first point out that the claim that God exists is not based on perception but on inference, and then go on to show that the inference is doubtful and unwarranted. Consider the following Nyāya argument for the existence of God. Just as every product—for example, a jar—is the work of an agent, so also the world must have an agent or creator. Such an agent is indeed God. The Jainas object that this argument assumes that the world is a product, and that in order for the argument to be acceptable, its proponent should establish that the world is a product. According to the Jainas, this cannot be done. For what does it mean to say that something is a product? One might say, as the Naiyāyika (follower of the Nyāya school) does, that anything is a product if it is composed of parts. But the Jainas point out that, although the Naiyāyika holds that space has parts, he does not regard it as a product; quite the contrary, he claims it to be an eternal substance not produced by anything else. The Jainas therefore contend that the world cannot be shown to be a product merely on the ground that it has parts. As such, they maintain, the assertion that the world is the work of a creator is unwarranted. The Jainas further point out that the concept of product implies that the agent does some work on the material in order to produce the object. But if God is bodiless, as the theist claims, it is hard to see how he can work on matter to produce the world. The Jainas thus conclude that the argument for the existence of God through the concept of creation fails.

Theists maintain that God is omnipotent, unitary, eternal, and perfect. The Jainas say that the grounds for attributing these qualities to God are as doubtful as those for asserting his existence. If God is omnipotent, he should be the cause of all things. But we see everyday objects not produced by God, such as houses and jars. Again, God is held to be unitary on the ground that if there were many gods, each with his own plans, purposes, and activities, the world would not be a harmonious world, as it in fact is. To this the Jainas object by saying that there is no absurdity in thinking that a plurality of gods working together harmoniously could produce the world, just as masons, and even lower animals like bees and ants, collectively produce castles, hives, and anthills. There is therefore no reason, the Jainas argue, to hold that God is unitary. Finally, God is said to be eternally perfect. The Jainas object to this claim by saying that the phrase "eternally perfect" is an absurd locution; for perfection is merely the removal of imperfections, and consequently to attribute perfection to a being who was never imperfect is nonsensical.

But it would be a gross misunderstanding to interpret atheism here as lack of or opposition to religious quest. It is one of the unique features of the Indian mind, hardly comprehensible to the Westerner, that there can be no incompatibility or opposition between atheism and sublime spirituality and profound religious experience. That is, belief in God is neither a necessary nor a sufficient condition for a deeply religious life. Jainism confirms this Indian trait by having produced a long line of great spiritual masters.

Jainism's rejection of God does not entail rejection of such activities as prayer and worship on the part of devout

Jainas. The Jainas worship and offer prayers to the Tīrthaṁkaras, the liberated souls, in order to receive guidance and inspiration in their own quest for liberation.[31] It deserves to be emphasized that the motive behind such prayers and worship is neither to seek mercy and forgiveness nor to indulge in self-deprecation and confession of guilt, as is so often the case with the followers of theistic religions. Given the Jaina doctrines of thoroughgoing atheism and the autonomous character of the law of *karma*, each man has to attain freedom and perfection by his own efforts and cannot expect to be saved by others, not even by the Tīrthaṁkaras. That is, each man must work out his own salvation. Meditation on the perfections of the free souls only serves to remind one of one's own potential for perfection, thereby inspiring one to tread the path. Reliance on one's own efforts to the exclusion of grace, divine or human, in one's struggle for perfection and freedom renders Jainism a religion fit only for the courageous, not for the weak and the timid.

Ethics

The ethics of Jainism are austere, simple, and straightforward. The practice of nonviolence in thought, word, and action is the cardinal virtue. The Jainas should, under no circumstances, inflict pain and suffering on any sentient being, but should always act with kindness, charity, gentleness, and compassion toward all living beings. Truthfulness, utter lack of greed, and purity of heart are to be cultivated by every follower of the Jina.[32] These moral virtues, meditation on the profound truths taught by the Jina, and faith in oneself lead men to liberation, a state characterized by the four perfections: infinite knowledge, infinite faith, infinite power, and infinite bliss. Like all other Indian religions, Jainism emphasizes the inseparability of moral perfection and perfection of knowledge. Perfect knowledge cannot be had without perfect conduct, and vice versa.

There are two principal sects of Jainism, the *Śvetāmbaras*

and the *Digambaras,* the sect of the saints of the white robes and that of the naked saints, respectively. We need not concern ourselves with the minor doctrinal differences between the two sects. Suffice it to point out that the Digambaras maintain that souls who have attained perfection, such as saints and ascetics, should cast off everything, including their robes, and go about naked. They also believe that women cannot attain liberation unless reborn at a future time as men. The Śvetāmbaras reject these views. In light of these differences, it would not be misleading to describe the Śvetāmbaras as religious liberals and the Digambaras as religious conservatives.

Chapter IV

Buddhism

A. THE BUDDHA'S TEACHINGS

Introduction

Gautama Siddhārtha was born in 563 B.C., of royal descent, into the Śākya clan, in Kapilavastu, a hilly principality at the foot of the Himalayas, in the north of India. He was brought up in the comfort, luxury, and pomp of his father's palace. At the age of sixteen, he was married to a princess named Yasodharā, and some time later a son, named Rāhula, was born to them. It was about this time that Gautama, who thus far had been carefully shielded from all the pains and miseries of life, happened to witness sickness, old age, and death. The sight of suffering and death made a profound impression on him, and he became keenly aware of the utter vanity and ignorance of his princely life in the light of the essential suffering and futility of all life. Shortly thereafter, Gautama came across a wandering ascetic who had completely renounced the world and led a life free from all cares and passions. Gautama then felt that such an ascetic way of life offered an escape from pain and suffering. Having resolved to renounce the world in order to discover a solution to human suffering, Gautama left his family and princely life and became an ascetic. He wandered far and wide seeking teachers and practicing severe disciplines, including the mortification of the body. Six years passed in this manner before Gautama realized that the ascetic practices had failed him in his quest for freedom from suffering, and rejected harsh ascetism as a means to liberating knowledge and wisdom. Undaunted by his failure, Gautama embarked once again on his search for the cause and cessation of suffering, this time relying wholly on his own resources. The path he chose was self-discipline and self-analysis through concentration and meditation, avoiding equally the extreme of asceticism and self-mortification on the one hand and that of unrestrained pursuit of pleasure and enjoyment on the other. At last, while absorbed in concentration under the Bo tree, Gautama grasped in extraordinary clarity the cause and cessation of suffering. He thus became the Buddha, the Enlightened One. From then until his death in 483 B.C., at the ripe old age of eighty, Gautama traveled untiringly, teaching his message to men and women, irrespective of their race, caste, color, and station in life. In course of time, the Buddha's message gave rise to Buddhism as a religion and philosophy which spread far and wide, to Ceylon, Burma, and Thailand in the south and to Tibet, China, Japan, Korea, and Mongolia in the north.

The Pali Canon

Buddhist literature is vast and rich. It is customarily divided into two parts: *Hīnayāna* and *Mahāyāna*. The former is written in Pali and the latter in Sanskrit. The heart of Hīnayāna literature is known as the Pali Canon, also called the *Tipiṭaka* meaning the *Three Baskets*. Like all other great teachers of ancient times, the Buddha taught orally, usually in the form of a sermon or a dialogue. The Pali Canon was composed long after his death and is generally regarded as the authentic teachings of the Buddha as reported by his intimate disciples. The first basket is the *Vinaya-Piṭaka*, which deals with rules of conduct and discipline of the Order, the *Samgha;* the second is the *Sutta-Piṭaka* (also known as the *Nikāyas*), a collection of the sayings, sermons, and dialogues of the Buddha; and the third basket, the *Abhidhamma-Piṭaka,* is a discussion of philosophical matters. The noncanonical part of Hīnayāna literature includes such works as *Milinda-Pañha, Visuddhimagga, Dīpavamsa, Mahāvamsa,* and innumerable commentaries on the *Tipiṭaka.*

The Mahāyāna literature is even vaster and more prolific. During the long period of development and dissemination of Buddhism beyond the borders of India, many of the Mahāyāna works were translated from Sanskrit into Tibetan and Chinese. Unfortunately, during this process a number of Sanskrit originals left India and were lost, and a good part of modern Buddhist scholarship is concerned with retranslating certain Tibetan and Chinese treatises into Sanskrit.

Important Hīnayāna as well as Mahāyāna works are listed in the Bibliography.

Approach to the Problem of Suffering

Although the Buddha was a man of penetrating intellect, as can be gathered from his analysis of the problem of suffering, the overall emphasis of his teaching is on the practical matters of morality and conduct leading to the conquest of suffering, rather than on abstruse philosophical inquiries. In other words, the Buddha was primarily an ethical teacher and not a metaphysician. For him, the most urgent task is to lead man out of suffering and illness. Appropriately enough, the Buddha is often described as "the great physician." If a man is struck by a poisoned arrow and is writhing in pain, the first thing for us to do is to alleviate his pain by pulling the arrow out of his body, not to insist on eliciting information as to the origin and nature of the arrow, the man who shot the arrow, or the man struck by the arrow before we can pull the arrow out and nurse the injury.[1] Similarly, if the poisoned arrow of suffering is embedded in humanity, it would be the height of unwisdom for men to preoccupy themselves with such metaphysical questions as: Is the world eternal? Is it finite or infinite? Is there a God? Is the soul different from the body? Inquiry into these questions, says the Buddha, is not in the least conducive to solving the immediate and pressing problem of suffering.[2] Consequently, anyone who indulges in metaphysical inquiry is either blind to the fact of suffering or wasting his time by hoping to cure men of suffering by making them swallow metaphysical medicines. In view of this attitude toward the problem of suffering and its cure, the Buddha is sometimes described as an antimetaphysical pragmatist. We shall now present the Buddha's analysis of the problem of suffering and his solution to it.

The Four Noble Truths[3]

Life is suffering (*duḥkha*). If we examine the phenomenon of life, says the Buddha, one thing that no discerning person can fail to notice is the all-pervading fact of suffering. Want, desire, greed, jealousy, anxiety, animosity, egoism, as well as sickness, old age, and death are too apparent for us not to notice them. Frustration and disappointment at not gaining things we desire and pain at the thought of losing those we have are also suffering. Some might object to the Buddha's observation that life is suffering by saying that life consists of pains as well as pleasures and the Buddha is therefore guilty of emphasizing the darker side of life to the exclusion of the brighter. The answer to this objection is that what seems to be pleasure at the moment eventually ceases to be pleasure by leading to boredom and dissatisfaction, which clearly are pain and suffering. It is only because of a shortsighted view of things that men fail to realize that every pleasure contains within itself the seeds of pain. Moreover, at the peak of all suffering is death itself, ready to lay its icy hands on us anytime and turn our dreams and hopes into dust and ashes. The thought of death is sufficient to produce terror and anxiety not only in oneself but in all those who are physically and psychologically dependent on one. How, then, asks the Buddha, can one be blind to the fact of universal suffering? The term *duḥkha* is often rendered as suffering in the sense of physical and psychological pain. But more correctly *duḥkha* is to be understood in its fundamental meaning, namely, impermanence *(anitya)*.[4] Impermanence is the basic characteristic of all existence, animate and inanimate. If we look around, we find all things changing. There seems to be nothing permanent within man or without. According to the Buddha, it is this impermanence that is the foundation of all suffering. Thus if men do not lose what they have and obtain everything they desire and do not disintegrate and die, then there will be no suffering. But analysis of existence shows that everything is constantly changing. Consequently, an unchanging and permanent world can only be a figment of the imagination and the product of wishful thinking. Impermanence is the basic trait of reality as we experience it with our senses and mind. And wherever there is impermanence there is bound to be suffering. Thus the First Noble Truth is that existence is *duḥkha* (impermanence), out of which arises all suffering.

The Second Noble Truth is that suffering is not due to chance and caprice but is brought about by certain conditions which constitute the warp and woof of existence itself. If suffering is uncaused, then there can be no way of eliminating it. It is important to note that every phenomenon, including our sensations, feelings, desires, impulses, sickness, old age, and death, is produced by causes which are themselves phenomena. In short, the whole of existence, as we experience it, is a vast causal nexus. This fact is expressed by the formula "This arising, that arises; this ceasing to be, that ceases to be"; or, equivalently, "This phenomenon is dependent upon that phenomenon." We may also express this by saying that nothing exists unconditionally and absolutely; everything is dependent upon something other than itself. The doctrine that everything is caused by (or arises in dependence upon) other things is known as the "Doctrine of Dependent Origination

(*Pratītyasamutpāda*)." [5] It is the foundation not only of the teachings of the Buddha but also of the various philosophical schools of Buddhism, as we shall see later. For now it is sufficient to point out that in the light of the Doctrine of Dependent Origination, the Second Noble Truth may be stated thus: Suffering (*duḥkha*), like all else, depends upon certain conditions—or, briefly, suffering has a cause. The various conditions which produce suffering are expressed by the Buddha in the form of a chain of causes and effects made up of twelve links. Hence "the twelvefold chain of causation" [6] is another name for the Doctrine of Dependent Origination. The links are as follows: We first observe that if a man is not born, then he cannot experience suffering. But a man cannot be born unless there is the will to be born. The will to be born is due to man's clinging to objects, physical and mental. But on what does clinging depend? Clinging depends upon man's craving or thirst for objects. But why is there craving? Craving arises out of our sense experience; that is, if we did not have sense experience, then there would be no objects for us to crave. But, one asks, how is sense experience possible? Sense experience arises out of the contact of senses with objects; were it not for the sense-object contacts, there would be no sense experience. How do sense-object contacts arise? The contacts are due to the six sense organs of cognition, including the mind. These organs in turn are dependent upon the embryonic psychophysical organism. But the embryonic organism itself depends upon some initial consciousness. What makes the initial consciousness possible? The initial consciousness arises out of impressions (karmic forces) from past existence. Finally, the karmic forces are themselves due to ignorance; that is, where there can be no ignorance, there can be no karmic forces and impressions. For clarity and quick reference, we list the twelve links as follows:

1. Ignorance (*avidyā*)
2. Karmic impressions (*saṁskāra*)
3. Initial embryonic consciousness (*vijñāna*)
4. Embryonic psychophysical organism (*nāma-rūpa*)

5. Six sense organs, mind included (*ṣaḍāyatana*)
6. Sense-object contact (*sparśa*)
7. Sense experience (*vedāna*)
8. Thirst for sense objects (*tṛṣṇā*)
9. Clinging (*upādāna*)
10. Will to be born (*bhava*)
11. Birth or rebirth (*jāti*)
12. Suffering, sickness, old age, and death (*jarā-maraṇa*)

We may note that the first two factors pertain to past life, factors 3 through 10 to present life, and the last two to future life. It is also to be noted that the twelvefold chain is not a linear but a circular chain,[7] because the twelfth factor is joined to the first. More importantly, some of the links are only necessary but not sufficient for the ones that follow them. Thus old age and death are only necessary but not sufficient for ignorance; similarly, sense experience is only necessary but not a sufficient condition for thirst and desire. If the chain were one of necessary *and* sufficient conditions, it would be impossible to break it. Then old age and death would necessarily bring about ignorance; and since men do become old and die they would forever be caught up in ignorance and go through the rounds of birth and death without ever being able to break the chain and get out of the circle of causation. Further, the chain has no beginning in time; that is, it did not begin at some moment in time. This is another way of saying that ignorance is beginningless. However, by following the Buddha, each man can break the chain and attain liberation by eliminating ignorance, the root cause of suffering. We may remark here that in the Indian tradition in general and Buddhism in particular, unlike the Western tradition, the primordial burden of man is not original sin but original ignorance. Ignorance is suffering and bondage, which can only be overcome by knowledge and wisdom.

The twelvefold chain of causation, the foundation of all the other teachings of the Buddha, is variously referred to as the *Dharma-Cakra* (the Wheel of Becoming), *Saṁsāra-Cakra* (the Wheel of Existence), *Janma-maraṇa-Cakra* (the Wheel of Birth and Death), *Bhava-Cakra* (the Wheel of Rebirth), *Dvādaśa-nidāna* (the Twelve Sources), and *Pratītyasamutpāda* (Dependent Origination).

Having understood the causes of suffering, the next thing to do is to eliminate it. This brings us to the Third Noble Truth, which may be stated thus: Since suffering is caused, it can be eliminated by eliminating its causes. The cessation of suffering can be brought about by the removal of the conditions on which suffering depends. It is the dependence of suffering on certain conditions that makes it possible for us to overcome suffering and become free from all fetters of existence. What is it, then, that has to be removed in order for pain, misery, sorrow, and suffering to cease? It is clear from the twelvefold chain that ignorance is the fundamental condition of suffering. Accordingly, it is ignorance that has to be combated in order to gain freedom from suffering. But how is ignorance to be conquered? Man can, according to the Buddha, rid himself of ignorance by clearly comprehending the truth of the nature of existence and acquiring perfect insight and wisdom leading to non-attachment, tranquility, freedom, and bliss—in short, by attaining Nirvāṇa. But one would like to know whether there is a path to Nirvāṇa. The answer to this question is the Fourth Noble Truth: there is indeed a path, the one discovered and traversed by the Buddha himself. It is the Eightfold Path (*aṣṭaṅgika-mārga*),[8] the perfect blending of knowledge and conduct. The eight steps of the path are as follows:

1. Right views (*sammādiṭṭhi*)
2. Right resolve (*sammāsaṅkappa*)
3. Right speech (*sammāvācā*)
4. Right conduct (*sammākammanta*)
5. Right livelihood (*sammā-ājiva*)
6. Right effort (*sammāvāyāma*)
7. Right mindfulness (*sammāsati*)
8. Right concentration (*sammāsamādhi*)

Of these, right speech, right action, and right livelihood pertain to conduct; right effort, right mindfulness, and right concentration, to discipline; and the remaining two, right views and right resolution, to knowledge and wisdom. Perfect knowledge is insight into the nature of existence and the factors that produce craving and suffering; perfect discipline, coupled with perfect knowledge, enables one to master the cravings; and perfect conduct, guided by perfect knowledge and discipline, leads to a life free from all forms of suffering and bondage. Such a life is the life of wisdom, a life no longer laboring under the burden of ignorance. The attainment of such perfection of wisdom is indeed the attainment of Nirvāṇa. He who has attained Nirvāṇa is the *Arhat,*[9] the Venerable One.

Nirvāṇa

At this point we need to say a few words about Nirvāṇa which has been a subject of great controversy among Buddhists and non-Buddhists alike.[10] The term Nirvāṇa literally means "blown out." [11] This meaning is the source of the negative interpretation of Nirvāṇa as annihilation and cessation of existence. Thus it is maintained by some that by teaching the way to Nirvāṇa the Buddha has pointed the way for men to extinguish themselves. While readily acknowledging the complexity of the concept of Nirvāṇa, we should point out that such an annihilationist interpretation of Nirvāṇa is simply absurd. For the Buddha, who himself attained Nirvāṇa, surely did not blow himself out of existence; nor could his teachings be understood as an exhortation for men to extinguish themselves; nor is it correct to equate Nirvāṇa with death. According to the Buddha himself, Nirvāṇa is to be attained here and now while one is still alive, not a paradise to be looked forward to after death. What, then, is Nirvāṇa? We answer that Nirvāṇa is the state in which one is completely free from all forms of bondage and attachment, having overcome and removed the cause of suffering. It is also the state of perfect insight into the nature of existence. He who has attained Nirvāṇa has once and for all freed himself from all the fetters that bind man to existence. He has perfect knowledge, perfect peace, and perfect wisdom.[12] It is true that when the Buddha was asked whether one who attains Nirvāṇa exists or ceases to exist after death, he simply refused to answer the question and instead maintained complete silence. The Buddha's silence is to be interpreted as indicating the inappropriateness of the question itself: the question is inappropriate in that not only the asking of the question but any attempt to answer it can only lead one into the quagmire of idle metaphysical speculations and futile philosophical disputes. Further, and more importantly, the Buddha's silence is due to his awareness that Nirvāṇa is a state that transcends every mundane experience and hence cannot be talked about; for all talk is possible only within the perceptual-conceptual realm wholly governed by the Doctrine of Dependent Origination, whereas Nirvāṇa is beyond the senses, language, and thought.[13]

It would be well to dispel here another popular but false conception of Nirvāṇa. The view is often expressed that one who attains Nirvāṇa cuts himself off from the world of toil, tears, and turmoil and spends his life in a state of total inactivity and indifference to the world around him.[14] How false this view is can be seen simply by remembering the kind of life the Buddha himself led for forty-five years, from his enlightenment to the day of his death. Far from living a passive life withdrawn and secluded from the world of ordinary men with all their cares and passions, the Buddha was always in the midst of people from all walks of life, discoursing with them, counseling them, giving aid and comfort to them, and teaching them the way to freedom and perfection. In view of this fact, it is absurd to describe Nirvāṇa as a state of inactivity, stupor, and indifference. The man who attains Nirvāṇa is a man of knowledge, discipline, and nonattachment. As a man of perfect wisdom, he desires nothing for himself but always works for the well-being and liberation of his fellowmen. This way of life is in full conformity with the spirit of the Buddha's teaching that wisdom consists in treading the middle way, avoiding the extreme of asceticism, inactivity, and indifference on the one hand and that of frantic activity and mindless pursuit of pleasure on the other. The Nirvāṇic man, then, is the true follower of the Buddha, in that he neither always sits absorbed in meditation nor wholly withdraws from activity. He is the living testimony that the middle way is indeed the way to enlightenment.

B. PHILOSOPHICAL FOUNDATIONS OF THE BUDDHA'S TEACHINGS

Introduction

The Buddha was primarily an ethical teacher and not a metaphysician or philosopher. He saw his urgent task as that of showing man the way out of suffering and not one of constructing a philosophical theory about man and the world. The Buddha's teachings therefore lay great emphasis on the practical matters of discipline and conduct leading to liberation through nonattachment and freedom from all passions. According to the Buddha ignorance is the root cause of suffering, and it is only by removing ignorance that suffering can be removed. But ignorance is to be combated by knowledge—insight into the nature of existence. What is the nature of ignorance that has to be overcome? What constitutes the knowledge that dispels ignorance? In order to answer these questions, we should turn our attention to the philosophical implications of the Buddha's teachings; that is, we should uncover the intellectual insights on which the Buddha's teachings are based. These insights are what are referred to as "Right Views," the first step of the Eightfold Path.

Process Ontology, Dependent Origination, and Impermanence

It is customary to divide philosophies into the substance and process varieties—philosophies of Being and Becoming, respectively. The term "ontology" means the study of the most general and pervasive traits and modes of existence.[15] Those ontologies which hold that underlying the seeming change, variety, and multiplicity of existence there are unchanging and permanent entities (the so-called substances) are known as "substance ontologies." On the other hand, those according to which there exists nothing permanent and unchanging, within or without man, are known as "process ontologies," also referred to as "modal ontologies." In the West, the philosophies of Parmenides, Aristotle, Descartes, Leibniz, Spinoza, Locke, and Kant are but a few examples of substance ontology, whereas those of Heraclitus, Henri Bergson, and Alfred North Whitehead are instances of process ontology. On the Indian philosophical scene, Jainism, Sāṁkhya, and Vedānta are representatives of substance ontology, while the teachings of the Buddha are based on process ontology.[16] We may thus say that the Buddha is a process philosopher. We shall now present the grounds for describing the Buddha's philosophy as process philosophy (or philosophy of Becoming).

One of the central teachings of the Buddha is the doctrine of universal change and impermanence. Everything in the world is changing and impermanent. There is nothing that endures and abides eternally. Birth, growth, and decay are the all-pervading features of existence. Things come into being and pass away. The seed germinates, the sprout grows into the plant, the plant becomes the tree, the tree bears fruit and flower and withers away. The child is born, grows into the adult, suffers sickness and old age, and dies. Mountains arise and crumble away, continents are formed and dissolved, stars appear and disappear, and the face of the earth as well as that of the heavens itself changes. Thus it appears that no matter when and where we look we find all around us continuous change and impermanence holding sway. Wherever there is birth, there is death; wherever there is growth, there is decay; wherever there is meeting, there is parting; wherever there is a beginning, there is an end; wherever there is arising, there is passing away. In the light of such inescapable observations, the Buddha taught that change and impermanence are the basic traits of all existence.[17] If impermanence is the fundamental characteristic of existence, one might ask, Why do men believe that there exist permanent entities called substances? Our answer to this question is that the notion of permanence arises in part out of language and thought. Consider, for example, my writing desk. I proudly and sentimentally describe it as the *same* desk my father, grandfather, and great-grandfather used. But in what sense is it the same desk? Has it not in the course of four generations undergone any change at all? Look at it and you will see for yourself. Surely it looks worn, the varnish had faded away, the wood has become weak, and the surface is warped. Why then do I refer to it as the *same* desk? There must be something of it that has remained the same since my great-grandfather made it a hundred years ago. But there is nothing about the desk that we can point to that has not undergone some change or other. The reason why we are led into thinking that it is the *same* desk is to be found in the fact that we use the same term "desk" to describe it at different times. That is, by overlooking the fact that it is words that we hold constant in time in order to facilitate communication, we think that since the same word is used at different times the object to which the word refers has also remained constant and unchanged in time. It is of the utmost importance to note that words (and symbols in general), which make possible thought and communication by virtue of the constancy of their meanings, also lead us into the illusion that what they refer to is unchanging and permanent. Language, then, is the source of our mistaken belief that there exist permanent and unchanging objects.

It is worth noting that the doctrine of universal change and impermanence follows from the fundamental teaching, namely, the Doctrine of Dependent Origination,[18] according to which nothing exists unconditionally and absolutely—this arising, that arises and this ceasing to be, that ceases to be.[19] If anything exists absolutely and unconditionally, then it is incapable of entering into interaction with anything else, for to enter into interaction is to undergo change. Thus the view that anything exists permanently contradicts the Doctrine of Dependent Origination. The conclusion, then, is that the thesis of universal change and impermanence logically follows from the Doctrine of Dependent Origination, the foundation of the Buddha's teachings.

It should be emphasized that the Buddha recommends the Doctrine of Dependent Origination as the Middle Way which avoids the two dogmatic extremes of eternalism and annihilationism.[20] Eternalism is dogmatic since according to it reality consists of permanent and unchanging entities, the so-called substances, although none of these can be objects of our experience, actual or possible. Annihilationism is the equally dogmatic teaching that, contrary to our experience, reality is made up of entities that simply perish away without leaving any trace. The Doctrine of Dependent Origination is truly the Middle Way, the way of becoming, in that it teaches not only that the objects of our experience exist—not, however, absolutely and unconditionally, but dependently and conditionally—but also that owing to its conditional existence every object, instead of simply perishing away, produces some effect or other. It may be remarked in passing that in the light of the Doctrine of Dependent Origination the common expression "the world is changing" is misleading, in that it suggests that there exists some permanent entity called "the world" undergoing change; instead, the correct expression is "The world *is* change," "change" being understood in the sense of conditional existence.

The Doctrine of Karma[21]

The Doctrine of Dependent Origination, expressed as the twelvefold chain of causation, contains as links karmic impressions from past existence and rebirth. These two links signify the proposition that the present existence of a man is dependent upon his past existence; that is, his present existence is the effect of his thoughts, words, and actions in his past existence. Similarly his future existence is dependent upon his present existence. This is precisely the law of *karma:* every event, be it thought, word, or action, produces its effects, which in turn become causes for other effects, and so on, thus generating the karmic chain. It is easy to see, then, that the law of *karma* is but a special case of the Doctrine of Dependent Origination which governs all existence.[22] One form of the Doctrine of Dependent Origination is: "If this is that comes to be; from the arising of this that arises; if this is not that does not come to be; from the stopping of this that is stopped." [23] We can now state the law of *karma* explicitly as an instance of this doctrine: Depending on the past, there is the present and depending on the present, there will be the future. In other words, our present and future are neither capricious nor unconditional, but are conditioned by our past and present, respectively.

The Doctrine of Non-self (Anattā)

Another consequence of the Doctrine of Dependent Origination is the doctrine of non-self (*anattā*). It is an age-old belief in almost all cultures that there exists in man an eternal and permanent entity variously known as the "soul," the "self," or the "spirit"—in short, there exists in man a substance called the "soul." Philosophers as well as primitive peoples subscribe to this belief. Among the world's great religions, Judaism, Christianity, Islam, Jainism, and Hinduism teach that the soul of man is an immortal substance. Such great philosophers as Socrates, Plato, Descartes, and Kant acknowledge the soul as an eternal substance.[24] These philosophers hold that the soul is the essence of man. Thus, although man's body changes and perishes, his soul is changeless and immortal, abiding and immutable. It is the soul which animates the body. The soul is to be equated neither with any part of the body nor with the body as a whole. The soul is known in Jainism as the *jīva* and in Hinduism as the *Ātman*.[25] In sharp con-
that there is no permanent and enduring entity in man.[26]
trast to these philosophies and religions, the Buddha teaches
According to the Doctrine of Dependent Origination, everything exists dependently and conditionally; and we have seen that the fact of universal change and imperma-

nence logically follows from the Doctrine of Dependent Origination. As such, there can be nothing which is permanent and unchanging. Much like David Hume,[27] the Buddha asks every man to enter into his deepest recesses and examine whether he could ever become aware of an unchanging entity called the "soul": All one could become aware of when one thinks of one's self or soul is a sensation, an impression, a perception, an image, a feeling, an impulse, etc., but never a thing or substance called the "soul." Accordingly, the Buddha analyzes man into five groups (*skandhas*): (1) form (matter), (2) feeling (pleasant, unpleasant, neutral), (3) perceptions (sight, smell, etc.), (4) impulses (hate, greed, etc.), and (5) consciousness.[28] Anything a man thinks he is or has must fall into one or other of these five heaps. The self or soul is simply an abbreviation for the aggregate of these *skandhas* and not some entity over and above the aggregate. Thus there is no distinct substance known as the "self" or "soul." To think otherwise is to labor under a fond but dangerous illusion. Notice also that every one of the *skandhas* is subject to the Doctrine of Dependent Origination. And if man is no more and no less than the collection of the *skandhas,* there can be no substances in him, material or spiritual. Here it is important to dispel a common misunderstanding concerning the doctrine of *anattā*. It is often said that through his doctrine of *anattā* the Buddha denies man a self or soul. This view is mistaken, for the Buddha does not deny the existence of self or soul understood as the collection of the *skandhas;* what he does deny is the belief that there exists behind and beyond the *skandhas* a self or soul as a permanent and unchanging entity. To put it differently, the Buddha readily acknowledges a changing self, but rejects an unchanging substantial self as an illusion traceable partly to our linguistic habits and partly to such psychological factors as craving,[29] grasping, insecurity, and, most importantly, fear of vanishing away with death. We shall have more to say later about this last point.

How, then, one might ask, does the Buddha explain not only our feeling of continuity and unity of experience but also *karma* and rebirth? If the Buddha denies a permanent soul, what is it that is reborn according to the law of *karma?* How can we even say that it is the child which has grown into the adult? Moreover, if there is no identical, unchanging self, how can we hold a man responsible for his actions and apportion praise and blame and reward and punishment? After all, if, as the Buddha teaches, there is no enduring soul, the man who performed an action and the man who is being judged and rewarded or punished cannot be the same. Surely, the objector continues, the Buddha's *anattā* doctrine makes a mockery of morality and responsibility.

Let us admit immediately that these questions are natural and pertinent reactions to the doctrine of *anattā*. But can they be satisfactorily answered by the Buddha without doing violence to his doctrine of non-self? [30] We submit that they can be answered. The Buddha accounts for the felt continuity and unity of our experience by drawing attention to an analogy. Consider, for example, a chain made up of several links. The chain is continuous and unbroken, although there is no single strand which runs from one end of the chain to the other. What provides for the continuity of the chain is the connection between successive links. Similarly, the unity and continuity of our experience is due to the causal connections of our successive experiences. Or, to take another example, consider a candle. The candle gives continuous light as a single flame. But is there something persisting in the flame from one moment to another? Further, we can light one candle by the flame of the other. Does this mean that the continuity between the first and the second flame is due to some persistent entity? The answer to both these questions is a definite "no." When a candle burns, its flame at any moment is dependent upon certain conditions which are different from those governing the flame at another moment. The observed continuity of the flame is due to the unbroken succession of the casual connections between the flame at one moment and that at the immediately succeeding moment. And when we light one flame by another, no enduring entity is being transferred from one to the other. Though the two flames are different, they are continuous owing to the causal connection between them. But if someone were to maintain that the continuity is due to some permanent entity, he should tell us whether the entity is located in the first flame, or the second flame, or in both at the same time. It is easy to see now the insurmountable difficulties which the advocate of permanent entities faces. The upshot of these analogies is that we can cogently account for our feeling of continuity and unity of experience without having to postulate some mysterious permanent entity called the "soul" or "self." The feeling of continuity and unity of experience is due to the fact that the various states constituting our experience form an unbroken succession of causes and effects in accordance with the Doctrine of Dependent Origination. In a similar maner, karmic impressions of our past existence constitute a casual chain of which our present life is the effect. It is important, then, to bear in mind that rebirth in the context of the Buddha's teachings is not to be understood as transmigration—the migration of the same soul from one body into another—but as the causation of our present life by the past and future life by the present. Much like William James[31] twenty-five hundred years later, the Buddha discredits the notion of a permanent soul and teaches that consciousness is neither abiding nor an entity, but is merely an unbroken stream, each moment of the stream arising in dependence on the conditions in the immediately preceding one. Thus it is the unbroken stream of consciousness and not an enduring soul that provides the continuity between our past and present lives on the one hand and our present and future lives on the other. Finally, in connection with the Buddha's teachings, it is best to avoid the term "reincarnation" altogether on account of its misleading connotation of an enduring entity, and to use instead the term "rebirth." It becomes clear now that moral responsibility presents no problem to the doctrine of *anattā*. A man is held responsible for his actions, not because he possesses a permanent soul, but because his existence is an unbroken stream in which the past, present, and future are bound together by causal chains. In other words, it is by virtue of the continuity of his existence and not because he possesses a permanent soul that a man is responsible for his actions.

The implications of the doctrine of *anattā* to ethics and morality are both striking and far-reaching. It is belaboring the obvious to point out that while man's material progress is truly astounding, ethically he has made little or no progress. He is no better than his hoary ancestors of the cave and the jungle. Why is it that morally man is a dismal spectacle? Today, as thousands of years ago, he makes war with a zest and enthusiasm unmatched elsewhere in the animal kingdom; he is greedy, cruel, wicked, and bloodthirsty, takes pleasure and delight in killing both beasts and his fellowmen, and enjoys inflicting untold suffering and destruction. The reason, it seems to me, is to be sought in the incompatibility between his ethics and ontology. Almost all philosophies and religions teach on the one hand that man has a permanent soul or self (which has to be saved) and exhort him on the other to practice compassion, charity, and, above all, selflessness. But as long as man believes that he has an eternal self or soul, he finds it not only difficult but even unnatural to be unselfish, for, after all, he has been taught that it is in the very nature of things that he has a self. No wonder the conflict between the ontological view of what we are and the ethical teachings on how we ought to be leads to a life of doubt, tension, guilt, and anxiety. The Buddha is unique among the teachers of the world in that he not only clearly saw the bearing of ontology on ethics but also taught an ontology that is most conducive to the moral development of man. Thus the Buddha's ethics flow from his doctrine of *anattā*, which in turn is ontologically firmly grounded in the Doctrine of Dependent Origination. The remarkable insight of the Buddha is that moral perfection cannot be attained without knowledge (right views) concerning existence. We can see now why right views constitute the first step of the Eightfold Path. We can also understand why the Buddha untiringly exhorted men to give up the pernicious illusion of a permanent self. The destruction of this illusion is the first step toward enlightenment, conquest of suffering, and perfection itself.

We close this section by noting that the freedom of thought and intellectual independence allowed—nay, encouraged—by the Buddha are unique in the history of religions. The Buddha insisted that no one accept his teaching merely out of reverence for him, but that each man subject the teaching to rigorous reflection and analysis and accept it only after all doubts and perplexities are overcome.[32]

C. BUDDHIST SCHOOLS OF PHILOSOPHY

The Hīnayāna-Mahāyāna Division

Shortly after the death of the Buddha, the First Buddhist Council was held at Rāja-gṛha in order to formulate the Discipline of the Order (the Vinaya Canon). Nearly a hundred years later, as a result of a stormy controversy over certain matters of discipline (*vinaya*), the followers of the Buddha found themselves divided into two camps, the *Sthaviravādins* (upholders of the Doctrine of the Elders) and the *Mahāsāṁghikas* (the Great Assembly-ites). The Second Buddhist Council was held at Vaiśālī to deal with the controversial points. At the behest of Emperor Asoka, the Great, the Third Buddhist Council was held at Pāṭaliputra (about 249 B.C.). About a thousand monks attended the conference, the chief purpose of which was to clarify and compose a systematic body of the doctrine according to the Elders (*Sthaviras*). In all likelihood, what has come to be known as the Pali Canon was the work of this council. In course of time, owing to doctrinal and disciplinary differences, further divisions arose among both the Sthaviravādins and the Mahāsāṁghikas, leading to the formation of about twenty different schools. Among these, the most important is known as the Sarvāstivāda, so called for its doctrine of the reality of all things, mental and nonmental. The Fourth Buddhist Council was summoned (first or second century A.D.) by King Kanishka. The task of the council was to systematize the fundamental doctrines of the Sarvāstivāda. The Sarvāstivāda later gave rise to the *Sautrāntika* school, so called because of its exclusive emphasis on the authority of the *Sutta-Piṭaka*. The history of the origins and development of the various schools from this point on is too complex for us to trace here in any detail.[33] Suffice it to mention that eventually Buddhist schools fell into two broad divisions, the *Hīnayāna* (the Lesser Vehicle) and the *Mahāyāna* (the Greater Vehicle). The Hīnayāna is also known as the *Theravāda* school, whose adherents regarded themselves as the true followers of the Elders (*Theras* in Pali). Sometimes the Theravāda is also referred to as the Southern school owing to its dominance in Ceylon, Burma, and Thailand. The Mahāyāna, also referred to as the Northern school, holds sway in Tibet, China, Japan, Korea, and Mongolia. Besides many minor schools, there are at least thirty major schools under Hīnayāna and Mahāyāna.

We shall now present some of the major differences between the two vehicles. Hīnayāna has often been critized by Mahāyāna for its narrow conception of the Arhat as one who seeks Nirvāṇa for himself without any concern for his fellowmen.[34] Such a single-minded concern of the Arhat for his own salvation, no matter how sublime and elevated it may be, is regarded by Mahāyāna as selfish, ignoble, and unworthy, falling short of the ideal of the liberated man as one of both enlightenment and unbounded compassion (*mahākaruṇa*) for all sentient beings. Thus Mahāyāna replaces the concept of the Arhat by that of the *Bodhisattva*.[35] The Bodhisattva, moved by sympathy, love, and compassion, refuses to enter into Nirvāṇa until he has helped all living beings to attain liberation.[36] Accordingly, on attaining enlightenment, the Bodhisattva, instead of withdrawing himself from the world of pain and suffering and leading the secluded and inactive life of the recluse, lives and works among the multitudes and helps them to attain their salvation. In his infinite compassion, the Bodhisattva gladly exchanges the fruits of his own good deeds to relieve men of their suffering and suffers the consequences of their actions himself. Having overcome all passions and attachments, the Bodhisattva acts always out of compassion for suffering men and never out of selfishness, egoism, greed, and personal gain. His actions therefore do not breed *karma.* Thus the Bodhisattva may be compared to the beautiful lotus which, although it grows out of dirt and mire, rises above it and is unblemished and undefiled.[37] In short, the Bodhisattva lives *in* the world but is not *of* the world.[38]

A second difference between Hīnayāna and Mahāyāna concerns the divinity of the Buddha. Hināyāna is thoroughly atheistic and hence refuses to look upon the Buddha as God.[39] Mahāyāna, on the other hand, clearly sees that the masses of men are too weak and frail to face life fraught with suffering and misery without turning to some transcendental source of solace, help, love, and mercy. Accordingly, Mahāyāna, while not denying the primacy and efficacy of one's own efforts in attaining Nirvāṇa, assures the masses that the Transcendental Buddha knows and helps every suffering being. In this manner, Mahāyāna offers faith and hope to the weak and timid. As such, prayer and worship play a great role in popular Mahāyāna.[40] It should be borne in mind, however, that the Transcendental Buddha,[41] the *Mahāyāna* equivalent of God, is not to be identified with the historical Buddha, who is only an incarnation of the former.

A third point of divergence between Hīnayāna and Mahāyāna pertains to the potential buddhahood of all living beings, also called "Buddha-nature," "suchness," and "thusness."[42] Whereas according to Hīnayāna Buddha nature is something to be attained by each man at a certain time during his round of births and deaths, Mahāyāna teaches that Buddha nature is always present in every sentient being and that one should only realize that this is so. Consequently, Mahāyāna considers every living being a potential Buddha. Thus Mahāyāna teaches that *Saṁsāra* (mundane existence) and Nirvāṇa are not two different ontological realms but one and the same reality[43] seen from different points of view. When ignorance, the source of bondage and suffering, is overcome, this same world will be experienced as Nirvāṇa in its primordial splendor. One then realizes that one has always been in Nirvāṇa, only one was not aware of it owing to the veil of ignorance.[44]

This brings us to the fourth point of disagreement between the two vehicles. The ontology of Theravāda is plurastic realism. It is realism because it holds that the ultimate constituents of reality, *dharmas,*[45] are the same as the ones which constitute the world of our empirical experience. That is, Theravāda rejects any distinction between the world as appearance and the world *as it is in itself.* It follows from this that according to Theravāda we directly perceive ultimate reality. Theravāda is pluralistic because it teaches that the ultimate constituents (*dharmas*) are distinct and irreducible. Mahāyāna rejects pluralism and realism as untenable and dogmatic. According to Mahāyāna, the number and quality of the *dharmas,* the so-called ultimate constituents, are inextricably tied down to the perceptual-conceptual schema one employs to describe reality; further, there is not one but many different schemas according to which we may describe reality. The point is that since each description of the nature and constitution of the world depends upon a certain schema, no description can be claimed to be absolute and ultimate. Each description is relative to some point of view. Further, the descriptions are applicable only to the world as phenomena—to the world as grasped through our senses and intellect—and not to ultimate reality, which is beyond all perceptions and conceptions. Ultimate reality is Emptiness (*Śūnyatā*), in the sense that it is nondual, nameless, formless, unborn, uncreated, and ineffable. It can only be apprehended in nonsensual, nonintellectual, direct intuition (*prajña*).[46] Thus the *dharmas* of Theravāda are valid in the phenomenal realm only. They are neither absolute nor ultimately real.[47]

We have pointed out in connection with the concept of the Bodhisattva that in certain forms of Mahāyāna the historical Buddha is regarded as an incarnation of ultimate reality; the historical Buddha is the phenomenal manifestation of the transcendental reality. Gautama is only one among many incarnations of the ultimate reality. There were Buddhas before Gautama, and there will be after him. Seen in this way, the transcendental reality of Mayāyāna is strikingly similar to the Nirguṇa-Brahman (Brahman as beyond names and forms) of Advaita Vedānta, while the various Buddhas are the Mahāyāna counterparts of the Saguṇa-Brahman (Brahman thought of as describable) (Īśvara) of Advaita Vedānta.[48] The world as it appears to us is known in Mahāyāna as the *Dharmakāya*[49] (*dharma*-body) of the Buddha as transcendental reality. Buddha as the incarnation of the transcendental reality is regarded as God who responds to the prayers of the devotee with help, love, and mercy. Buddha in this respect is known as Amitābha Buddha, the Buddha of Infinite Light.[50]

Having set forth the salient differences between Hīnayāna and Mahāyāna, we shall now consider in some detail the doctrines of four important Buddhist schools of philosophy: the Sautrāntika and Vaibhāṣika schools under Hīnayāna, and the Yogācāra and Mādhyamika schools under Mahāyāna.

The Vaibhasika School

The *Abhidhamma* treatises[51] of Theravāda constitute the foundation of philosophical realism. There are innumerable commentaries on the *Abhidhamma.* The Vaibhāṣika derives its name from the fact of its exclusive emphasis on a particular commentary, the *Abhidhammamahāvaibhāṣā.*[52]

The Vaibhāṣika is thoroughgoing process philosophy. It is also pluralism, realism, and nominalism.[53] In the true spirit of the Doctrine of Dependent Origination, the Vaibhāṣika holds that reality is pure flux and change, there being no permanent entities, the so-called substances, either within man or without.[54] For the Vaibhāṣika existence is constituted of pulses, also referred to as "point-instants," which constantly arise and pass away. Hence the Vaibhāṣika ontology is sometimes described as "the doctrine of momentariness" (*kṣaṇika-vāda*). The chief argument of the Vaibhāṣika against substance ontology is as follows: A substance, by definition, is an entity that remains identical in time; that is, it is permanent. And if anything is permanent, says the Vaibhāṣika, it cannot be causally efficacious, for to be causally efficacious is to be able to enter into interaction with other entities and undergo change in time. But we observe incessant change all around us. Therefore reality cannot be of the nature of substance. The ontological dictum of the Vaibhāṣika is thus: "To exist is to be causally efficacious and *vice versa*."[55] It follows from this dictum that if something is not causally efficacious, then it does not and cannot exist. Substances, in that they are thought of as permanent and unchanging, are causally inefficacious and hence are nonexistent.

According to the Vaibhāṣika, the world is in reality as it appears to us. The ultimate constituents (*dharmas*) of reality are the same as those which make up the world of our empirical experience. In other words, the Vaibhāṣika rejects any distinction between the world as it appears to us and as it is in itself.[56] The *dharmas*, ultimate constituents of existence, are absolute, and independent of our consciousness. For this reason the Vaibhāṣika is realism. The Vaibhāṣika is pluralism in that it further asserts that the *dharmas* are distinct and irreducible. Reality, then, according to the Vaibhāṣika, is flux made up of point-instants constituted of *dharmas*, each point-instant succeeding the other in an unbroken chain. The continuity of existence is accounted for by the Vaibhāṣika through the causal connections between successive point-instants. A given point-instant is the effect of its immediately preceding one and the cause of its immediately succeeding one. This explication of the continuity of existence, it should be noted, presupposes that the past, present, and future are all equally real.[57] If it were not so, the Vaibhāṣika argues, it would be impossible to explain how the present, which is real, can arise out of an unreal past and give rise to an equally unreal future.

The problem of universals arises in connection with general terms such as "red," "cow," and "triangle." These terms are understood as denoting the properties redness, cowness, and triangularity, possessed by different red objects, cows, and triangles. Some philosophers, known as "essentialists," advance the thesis that these properties are the essences by virtue of which different objects are what they are. The essentialists further hold that these properties are entities having reality of their own independently of the particular objects which exemplify them. For this reason, the essentialists are also called "realists." The essences so conceived are called "universals," which are unchanging, nonspatial, and nontemporal. In Western philosophy, Plato is the most celebrated upholder of the independent reality of universals. In contrast, those philosophers who deny the universals an independent ontological status are traditionally known as "nominalists." [58] According to nominalists, universals are merely concepts which we form by abstracting from actual objects their common properties. The nominalists therefore consider universals merely conceptual-linguistic entities having no ontological status apart from the particulars exemplifying them. The Vaibhāṣika argument for nominalism is as follows: If universals are entities, as claimed by the essentialist, how is one to explain the existence of a given universal in objects widely separated in space and time? Further, the Vaibhāṣika asks, what happens to a universal when an object in which it exists changes or is destroyed? When a tree burns to ashes in a jungle fire, what exactly happens to the universal "treeness"? Does it also change into "ashness"? Or is it still present in the ashes in some mysterious manner, since it is eternal and indestructible? More importantly, how does one come to know the existence of a universal in a given object? According to the Vaibhāṣika, we come to know the universal and the particular in which it exists through one and the same perception. Those who maintain the independent reality of universals should, the Vaibhāṣika demands, show that there are two perceptions, one which reveals the particular and the other which reveals the universal. But even the most ardent defender of the separate ontological status of universals admits that perception is always of particulars and that we do not know what it is to perceive universals without at the same time perceiving the particulars in which they exist. Thus the Vaibhāṣika concludes that all talk of the real and independent existence of universals inhabiting a spaceless and timeless realm is both misguided and unwarranted by our actual experience. The Vaibhāṣika therefore maintains that universals are merely conceptual-linguistic abstractions, and for that very reason we are able to apply them to different objects, not because they constitute a separate reality. For the Vaibhāṣika, reality is particular through and through and is devoid of any universal, unchanging entities. It is important to emphasize that the Vaibhāṣika's rejection of the reality of the universals logically follows from his rejection of substances. For to regard the universals as substances (and substances, we have seen, cannot enter into interaction and undergo change) is to contradict the dictum "To exist is to be causally efficient and vice versa," and therefore universals, thought of as substances, simply cannot exist.

The Vaibhāṣika is realist in that it maintains that the external world exists independently of our perceptions and that the ultimate constituents of the world, *dharmas,* are revealed to us by our perceptions. That is, we perceive external objects as well as their ultimate constituents directly. One might ask how the Vaibhāṣika supports its claim that we directly perceive external objects. The Vaibhāṣika answer is as follows: First, we have no other source of knowledge of the external world than our perceptions. How else, the Vaibhāṣika asks, can we account for what our perceptions reveal than by admitting the independent existence of external objects? The existence of external objects cannot be explained by inference alone, contrary to the Sautrāntika belief. Unless we sometime or other directly perceive external objects, inference will be of little avail in establishing the existence of external objects. Consider the case of someone inferring the existence of fire from his perception of smoke. The Vaibhāṣika points out that unless sometime in the past the person has perceived fire and smoke together, he will not now be able to infer the existence of fire from his perception of smoke. Thus if external objects are never perceived, they cannot be inferred, either. The Vaibhāṣika therefore concludes that direct perception of some external objects is a necessary condition for inferring the existence of others.[59] The existence of external objects cannot be inferred from our mental forms or pictures of them. The Sautrāntika is mistaken in thinking that our perceptions are representations (copies) of external objects, because for one who is not acquainted with external objects perceptions do not appear as copies or representations but rather as objects existing originally and independently. Thus it would be absurd to say that although we never perceive external objects, we can infer their existence from our perceptions. This same point can be put in the form of a paradox: If the thesis that we never perceive external objects but our perceptions are copies of them is true, then the thesis is necessarily false; for how can we say that our perceptions are copies of external objects if we never perceive the latter? Thus the very truth of the thesis constitutes its refutation. We should therefore admit, says the Vaibhāṣika, that we do perceive external objects directly. We may note here in passing that the Vaibhāṣika is realist with respect to both the nonmental and the mental. That is, the Vaibhāṣika admits the reality not only of the external world but also of consciousness.

The Sautrāntika School

The name of the Sautrāntika school[60] derives from the fact that it attaches exclusive importance to the authority of the *Sūtra-Piṭaka* (*Sutta-Piṭaka* in Pali) of the Pali Canon.

Like the Vaibhāṣika, the Sautrāntika subscribes to the reality of both the mental and the nonmental. Nevertheless, there is an important difference between the realism of the Vaibhāṣika and that of the Sautrāntika. While the Vaibhāṣika maintains that we perceive external objects directly, the Sautrāntika holds that external objects are not perceived by us directly, but are inferred from our perceptions, which are representations or copies of external objects.[61] For this reason, the Saùtrāntika epistemology is called "representationism" or "copy-theory of knowledge," which closely resembles that of John Locke.[62] It should be emphasized, however, that the Sautrāntika representationism does not entail the denial of the independent existence of external objects. On the contrary, the Sautrāntika defends the independent existence of external objects by the following argument: Suppose that the thesis of the independent existence of external objects is false. How then, asks the Sautrāntika, are we to distinguish between illusionary and nonillusionary experiences? If a thirsty man traveling in a desert experiences the optical illusion of seeing water at a distance and rushes to the place only to find that there is no water, how is he to explain his experience of seeing water? If the traveler had never perceived water, he could not in the first place even entertain the belief that what he perceived from a distance looked *like* water. The Sautrāntika thus concludes that belief in the independent existence of external objects is warranted by the fact of our experience of perceptual illusions. To be sure, the Sautrāntika grants that we never directly perceive external objects, but only infer them from our perceptions. The Sautrāntika also rejects as absurd the Yogācāra thesis that external objects are not real but are merely our own mental forms—consciousness appearing to itself as external objects. The Sautrāntika points out that if, as the Yogācāra claims,[63] all we ever perceive are our own mental forms, then the Yogācāra is not entitled to say that consciousness appears to itself as *external* objects, for where no genuine contrast between "internal" and "external" is admitted, the use of the term "external" can only be vacuous. The Sautrāntika also rejects as untenable the Yogācāra claim of the unreality of external objects based on the following argument: Since consciousness and its object are simultaneous, they are also identical; and since there can be no experience of objects apart from consciousness, only consciousness is real, and not its object. The Sautrāntika's objection to this argument is that it does not follow from the simultaneity of consciousness and its object that the two are identical; further, it is arbitrary to say that of two things which are simultaneous one is real and the other unreal. What is more, the Sautrāntika continues, not even the most convinced and enthusiastic follower of the Yogācāra would, while having the perception of, for example, a stone, say, "I am the stone," instead of "I see a stone." This in itself shows that the Yogācāra cannot help distinguishing between the perceiving subject and the object of perception.

A second important difference between the Sautrāntika and the Vaibhāṣika stems from the fact that, unlike the latter, the former distinguishes between the world as it appears to us (phenomena) and as it is in itself (noumena). In the light of this distinction, the Sautrāntika rejects the Vaibhāṣika contention that the ultimate constituents, *dharmas,* of existence are the same as the ones which make up the world of our empirical experience. Thus the Sautrāntika denies the *dharmas* absolute, ultimate, and independent ontological status.

A more serious point of disagreement between the Sautrāntika and the Vaibhāṣika concerns the nature of the relation between successive point-instants (pulses) of existence. For the Vaibhāṣika past, present, and future are all equally real. The Vaibhāṣika's reason for this position is that the present, which is admittedly real, cannot be the effect of an unreal past and the cause of an equally unreal future. Consequently, the Vaibhāṣika argues, the past and future must somehow be contained in the present. But this in turn is possible only if the point-instants have duration. The Vaibhāṣika's point here is that a point-instant which has no duration at all cannot be causally efficacious in bringing about its succeeding point-instant; cause and effect cannot be simultaneous. In this manner, then, the Vaibhāṣika comes to regard point-instants as having duration, no matter how small. The Sautrāntika rejects this view on the ground that to attribute duration to point-instants is to regard them as permanent entities, contrary to the Docrine of Dependent Origination. It is important to note that the Sautrāntika's rejection of the view that point-instants have duration logically leads him to the rejection of the thesis that the relation between successive point-instants is causal relation. According to the Sautrāntika, the relation between point-instants is one of replacement in accordance with the principle of conditioned origination; that is, each point-instant is replaced by its succeeding one, the latter being merely dependent upon, but not caused by, the former.[64] It is clear, then, that for the Sautrāntika the arising and the passing away of a point-instant are not two processes, but one and the same process. This is another way of saying that "existence" and "nonexistence" are two different labels for the single reality of becoming.[65] This point may be dramatically and vividly illustrated by pointing out that the process of dying is the same as the process of birth and growth.

Concerning the status of universals, the Sautrāntika, like the Vaibhāṣika, advocates nominalism.

The Yogācāra School

There are two different accounts of the origin of the name of the Yogācāra school.[66] According to one account, the Yogācāra is so called because the followers of the school emphasized critical inquiry (*yoga*) along with exemplary conduct (*ācāra*); according to the other, the adherents of the school practiced yoga for the realization of the truth that reality is of the nature of consciousness.

The distinguishing doctrine of the Yogācāra is that consciousness (mind) alone is ultimately real.[67] Consequently, external objects are regarded by the Yogācāra as unreal. The Yogācāra accepts the Doctrine of Dependent Origination and therewith pure process ontology, in that it holds that consciousness is not a substance but an everchanging stream. All objects, internal and external, are ideas of the mind. According to the Yogācāra, it is impossible to demonstrate the independent existence of external objects. The main argument for this view is that since consciousness and its object are simultaneous, they are identical. To put it differently, no object can ever be experienced apart from consciousness; therefore, consciousness and its object are one and the same. We have already presented the Vaibhāṣika and Sautrāntika criticisms of this argument.

The Yogācāra also offers other arguments against belief in the independent existence of external objects.[68] These arguments may be construed as the Yogācāra critique of the Sautrāntika and Vaibhāṣika. Assume, for example, that there exists an external object. This object must be either indivisible, partless, and atomic, or divisible and composite. If it is the former, it cannot be perceived, since atoms are too minute to be perceived. On the other hand, if it is composite, we can never perceive all the parts and the sides of the object simultaneously. Thus in either case the assumption of the existence of external objects is fraught with insurmountable difficulties.[69] The Yogācāra now points out that his own thesis of the identity of consciousness and its object is not open to the above objections and difficulties, for one cannot sensibly ask whether consciousness is atomic or composite.

Another argument of the Yogācāra against the thesis of the independent existence of external objects is based on the ontology of momentariness. The Yogācāra points out that, since objects are not substances but durationless point-instants, it is difficult to see how a momentary object can be the cause of consciousness; for if it is the cause of consciousness, there must be a time lapse between the arising of the object and our consciousness of it. But such a time lapse is impossible on two counts: (1) the object as point-instant is durationless, and hence it cannot be causally efficacious; and (2) the object and the consciousness of it are experienced by us simultaneously. Therefore, the Yogācāra concludes, the external object cannot be the cause of consciousness; quite the contrary, being simultaneous with consciousness, it can be no more and no less than consciousness itself.[70] The Yogācāra further points out that it is equally absurd to argue that we become conscious of an object after the object has vanished away and ceased to exist, because in that case it would be impossible to account for our immediate (present) consciousness of the object. On the other hand, says the Yogācāra, if consciousness and its object are one and the same, there can be no difficulty in explaining the fact of our immediate perception and knowledge of objects.

Because of its central doctrine that ultimate reality is of the nature of consciousness (*vijñāna*) the Yogācāra school is also called *Vijñāna-vāda*. We have seen that for the Yogācāra external objects are nothing but ideas in the mind (states of consciousness). This is the same as saying that for the Yogācāra the external world is not only epistemologically but also ontologically dependent upon the perceiving mind or consciousness. It may be noted that the Yogācāra position is remarkably similar to the subjective idealism of George Berkeley.[71]

The chief objection against the Yogācāra is as follows: If external objects are identical with consciousness (mind), how is it that we cannot perceive whatever we want to perceive? How is it that we seem to be powerless over the appearance, change, and disappearance of the objects of our perception? In order to answer this objection, the Yogācāra appeals to the law of *karma*.[72] The mind (consciousness), according to the Yogācāra, is a stream of ideas and states containing within themselves the karmic impressions from our past existence. As such, what one perceives at a given time depends upon certain karmic impressions; in other words, the karmic impressions from the past, latent in the stream of consciousness, rise to the surface under appropriate circumstances. An analogy may shed some light on this point. Just as of the countless things that make up our memory we remember and recall only certain things at certain times and places, so also of the myriads of impressions that lie deep in consciousness only some rise to the surface under certain circumstances and appear as objects, internal and external. It is from this point of view that the Yogācāra calls consciousness *Ālaya-vijñāna*[73] (the repository or storehouse of all past impressions). It should be emphasized, however, that for the

Yogācāra consciousness is not an unchanging substance but an unbroken stream of states and impressions.[74] As long as one is in bondage and ignorance, impressions, thoughts, ideas, desires, etc., arise in accordance with the law of *karma*. The practice of yoga, coupled with exemplary conduct, enables man to put an end to the arising of mental states which, by breeding attachment to the illusion of the external world, perpetuate the round of births and deaths.[75] One who thus overcomes attachment and illusion realizes the sole reality of consciousness. According to the Yogācāra, the attainment of consciousness, pure and serene, is indeed the attainment of Nirvāṇa.

The Mādhyamika School

Introduction

The literal meaning of the term *Mādhyamika* is "the farer of the Middle Way." The Mādhyamika avoids all extremes, such as eternalism and annihilationism, self and non-self, matter and spirit, body and soul, substance and process, unity and plurality, affirmation and denial, identity and difference—in general all dogmatic and exclusive dualisms—and treads the Middle Way in the true spirit of the teachings of the Buddha.

Nāgārjuna (second century A.D.) is generally regarded as the founder of the Mādhyamika school. Although some of the unique insights of the school are already to be found in the celebrated *Mahāyāna-Śraddhotpāda-Śāstra* (*The Awakening of Faith in the Mahāyāna*) of Aśvaghoṣa, the author of *Buddhacarita,* it is to Nāgārjuna's penetrating intellect and extraordinary dialectical skill that the school owes its power and glory. Nāgārjuna's famous *Mūlamadhyamakakārikā*[76] is the fountainhead of the method, teaching, and spirit of the Mādhyamika school. Besides Nāgārjuna, Āryadeva, Candrakīrti, Kumārajīva, and Śāntideva are among the most illustrious figures of the school.

The Mādhyamika Conception of Philosophy

Philosophies, both in India and elsewhere, can be divided into two classes: the *Ātman* schools (eternalism) and the

Anātman schools (annihilationism). The term *Ātman* here is to be understood not just in its ordinary meaning of soul but in its generic meaning of unchanging, permanent, eternal entity. The Ātman schools, then, are those whose fundamental doctrine is that ultimate reality is of the nature of unchanging and eternal substance. On the other hand, the Anātman schools are those according to which ultimate reality is devoid of any unchanging and eternal entities, but is pure flux. In a very real sense the perennial conflicts between philosophical schools are grounded in the fundamental clash between the Ātman and Anātman views of reality. Thus, in Greek antiquity, the opposition between Parmenides and Heraclitus[77] is none other than the Ātman-versus-Anātman conflict. Similarly, in India,[78] the controversy between the orthodox schools and certain Buddhist schools stems from the fundamental divergence between the Ātman ontology of the former and the Anātman ontology of the latter. It is worth noting that Ātman philosophies, in that they regard ultimate reality as unchanging and eternal, may also be described as "philosophies of identity"; on the other hand, Anātman philosophies, since they reject the Ātman doctrine and advocate instead the view that reality is pure change with no abiding entities, may also be characterized as "philosophies of difference." For these reasons, the Ātman and Anātman views are sometimes referred to as "the doctrine of the One" and "the doctrine of the Many," respectively; or, equivalently, as "monism" and "pluralism."

One of the most original insights of Nāgārjuna concerns the origin and nature of philosophies and philosophical conflicts. According to Nāgārjuna, philosophical doctrines originate in man's unquenchable thirst for the real, the ultimate, the unconditioned, and the absolute.[79] Confronting the world as something other than himself, man embarks on the search for the knowledge of the world as non-self (the other). But knowledge is always a relation between the knower and the known in that it brings the two together. Knowledge is the means by which man seeks to unite the self and the other. In this manner, the thirst for knowledge is at bottom the quest for being. To put it differently, in his very attempt to know the world man appropriates the world to himself. But, Nāgārjuna asks, what exactly is knowledge? How is it produced? Nāgārjuna's answers to these questions constitute another of the great and revolutionary insights of the Mādhyamika school. Knowledge, insofar as it is expressible at all, is propositional, and propositions in turn are constituted of concepts and percepts, which the Mādhyamika refers to as names and forms.[80] Accordingly, the reality which philosophers create in their knowledge is the reality of names and forms and not reality as it is in itself. But in their thirst for the real, philosophers forget this and mistake the reality they construct out of names and forms for reality itself. Thus they are like thirsty travelers in a desert who, not knowing the difference between reality and illusion, are tempted by the mirage and rush in vain from place to place hoping to quench their thirst. But just as mirages cannot quench our thirst, so also imaginative constructions of reality cannot quench man's thirst for the real. Man thus becomes a wanderer in the jungle of his own imaginative constructions (*vikalpa*) of the real. The failure to distinguish between reality in itself and reality of names and forms is ignorance, which breeds suffering (*duḥkha*). Each school, in its thirst for the real and quest for being, claims absolute truth and validity for its own doctrines of the real and condemns those of other schools as false and misguided. Thus, philosophies become dogmatic, and dogmatism produces blindness, intolerance, opposition, and conflict.

The question now arises whether one can ever hope to capture reality through names and forms. The Mādhyamika answer to this question is a definite "no." How does the Mādhyamika support this negative answer? The key is to be found in the Mādhyamika analysis of the nature of thought and knowledge. According to the Mādhyamika, thought originates in and thrives on the polar nature of concepts. Every concept is polar in that it acquires meaning in contrast with other concepts. This is the case not just with such explicitly polar concepts as "short" and "long," "convex" and "concave," "light" and "dark," but with respect to all concepts. Consider, for example the concept "table." The meaning of this concept is dependent upon that of the concept "non-table." Were it not so, we could not explain to someone what a table is; all we could say is "A table is a table," which is tautologous and unilluminating as a means to knowledge of table. When we say, "A table is . . . ," the statement is necessarily to be completed with concepts other than "table" if our explication of "table" is to be informative and knowledge-producing. In brief, where there is no concept of non-table there can be no concept of table either. The point, then, is that knowledge and intelligibility are made possible by the polar character of concepts—the polar nature of thinking itself. Language, thought, and knowledge would become crippled and vanish away were it not for the dependence of one concept on another. The important question now is: Is there a unique way in which concepts can be brought together in order to produce knowledge? The Mādhyamika answer to this question is in the negative: there is no unique way of relating concepts to each other. The concepts a thinker generates, the ways in which he joins them, and, consequently, the particular body of knowledge and truths he claims, are dependent upon many considerations, the most important of which are the presuppositions of the given thinker. It should be clear, therefore, that it is impossible to demonstrate within a given system (or theory) of reality the presuppositions of that system itself. Any purported demonstration is bound to be circular for the reason that the demonstration has to employ the very concepts and categories determined in the first place by the presuppositions themselves. We may introduce here the notion of the transcendental deduction of a conceptual system, a notion first introduced by Immanuel Kant.[81] To provide a transcendental deduction for a conceptual system is to demonstrate not only that people employ that conceptual system for an objective description of reality, but also that it is the *only* one suitable for objectively dealing with reality. The latter part of this demonstration is known as "uniqueness demonstration." But it is impossible to offer a noncircular demonstration for the uniqueness of any system, because by the very claim of uniqueness the given system is the only one which can describe reality objectively. This in effect means that uniqueness demonstrations beg the very question at issue and so become circular. Thus transcendental deductions are necessarily circular and worthless.[82] This is precisely the Mādhyamika observation that every claim to describe the real is bound to be dogmatic and every attempt to demonstrate the truth of the claim circular.

The main points of the Mādhyamika school covered thus far can now be summarized. Concepts as well as conceptual systems are relative to each other. No concepts or conceptual systems can stand by themselves and generate truths. The truths generated by one system are necessarily dependent upon those generated by others. Consequently, no system can lay claim to absolute truth and validity. The truths of each system can only be relative and partial. All theories of reality are conceptual constructions (*vikalpa*), each construction emphasizing some particular aspect and point of view. But the advocate of each system, forgetting that his own system necessarily depends upon others, including his opponents', claims absolute truth and unconditional validity for it and rejects other systems as false and misguided. The cause of such forgetfulness is man's quest for the real, the absolute, the ultimate, and the unconditioned. Philosophers and other system-builders thus cling to their own views and constructions of reality. Such clinging is due to ignorance—the failure to distinguish between a *view of reality*[83] and *reality itself.* This ignorance is the source of *duḥkha.* Another way of saying the same thing is, the disparity between a view of reality and reality manifests itself as despair, anxiety, and ill-being in general. Keenly aware of the emphasis the Buddha placed on non-clinging in overcoming suffering and bondage, Nāgārjuna tries to free men by calling attention to the relativity of all thought-constructions, thereby eliminating the very basis for all clinging.

According to the Mādhyamika, true philosophy, in the sense of liberating wisdom, is the dialectical consciousness of the limitations of our constructions of reality out of *nāma* and *rūpa*—it is reason discovering its own shortcomings and powerlessness to give us insight into reality as it is.[84] Freedom, according to Nāgārjuna, is freedom from being enamored of conceptual constructions of reality, and the recognition of the relativity of all views of reality. *Prajñā-pāramitā,* the highest wisdom, is on the one hand the keen awareness of the limitations and relativity of all thought-constructions of reality, and direct, nonperceptual, nonconceptual, intuitive insight into reality on the other.[85] *Prajñā* is thus at once perfect freedom and perfect peace.

The Method of the Dialectic

Consistent with its fundamental teaching of the relativity of all views, the Mādhyamika entertains no views, doctrines, theories, and principles of his own to propound and defend.[86] Accordingly, the technique of the Mādhyamika dialectic is *reductio ad absurdum* (*prasaṅga*) through and through.[87] This means that the Mādhyamika takes a thesis or view exactly as stated by its proponent and, by employing only the principles, rules, and propositions accepted by the advocate of the view himself, proceeds to demonstrate that the thesis at hand is self-contradictory. And since the supporter of the thesis himself regards freedom from contradiction as a necessary condition for its truth, he has now to withdraw his claim to the truth of his thesis. It is clear from this that the proponent of the thesis could himself have discovered the self-contradictory nature of his thesis, were it not for the fact that in his own thirst for the real he was held captive by his own construction of reality and fell victim to illusion and dogmatism. It is extremely important to note that for the Mādhyamika the demonstration of the falsity of a given view, say T, does not entail the truth of its antithesis not-T.[88] In this respect, the Mādhyamika method of *prasaṅga* differs from the *reductio ad absurdum* as employed by other philosophers. Thus, Zeno of Elea, having shown that the Heraclitean thesis that reality is of the nature of pure change is self-contradictory, claimed the truth of the Parmenidean antithesis that reality is One, unchanging, and eternal. The Mādhyamika points out that Zeno is not entitled to this claim, because we can demonstrate the Parmenides' thesis too is self-contradictory. It is precisely for this reason that the Mādhyamika does not attach himself to any thesis about the real, the absolute, the ultimate, and the unconditioned.

We shall now illustrate the Mādhyamika dialectic with respect to the concept of origination (causation). Concerning causation, Indian philosophical schools fall into two groups: the *satkāryavāda* and the *asatkāryavāda*. According to the former, the material effect is identical with (or preexists in) the material cause; according to the latter, the material effect is different from (or does not preexist in) the material cause. Sāṁkhya and Advaita Vedānta are *satkāryavāda,* whereas Nyāya, Vaiśeṣika, and certain Buddhist schools, such as Sautrāntika and Vaibhāṣika, are *asatkāryavāda.*

The Mādhyamika recognizes four possible alternatives concerning any concept.[89] With respect to "causation," they are: (1) a thing arises out of itself; (2) a thing arises out of a not-self; (3) a thing arises out of both itself and a not-self; and (4) a thing arises neither out of itself nor out of a not-self.[90] The first and second of these alternatives are respectively the *satkāryavāda* and the *asatkāryavāda.* Let us first present the Mādhyamika refutation of these.

The Mādhyamika points out that if, as the *satkāryavāda* claims, effect and cause are identical in the sense that the former preexists in the latter, then there can be no difference between the two, and it does not make sense to talk about causality; for causality is a relation between two things, and for it to be a genuine relation there must be a difference between the cause and its effect. But, the Mādhyamika continues, by identifying the cause and its effect the *satkāryavāda* renders the whole concept of causality meaningless.[91] The Mādhyamika then goes on to point out that it would not do either to argue that cause and effect are identical in some respects and different in others. For if the cause and effect are identical in just those respects which are relevant to causation, then the fact that cause and effect are different in other respects is irrelevant, and causation is still unexplained. On the other hand, if cause and effect are different in just those respects that are relevant to causation, then surely the thesis that cause and effect are identical is manifestly false. Thus in either case the claim that cause and effect are identical is absurd. All this can be expressed by saying that if cause and effect are identical, then everything that can be affirmed or denied of the one should be capable of being affirmed or denied of the other. If the tree is the effect of the seed and cause and effect are identical, although it makes sense to say that the tree is thirty feet tall it is simply false to say that the seed is thirty feet tall. Therefore, the Mādhyamika concludes, the thesis of the identity of cause and effect is self-contradictory and absurd.

Turning now to the thesis of the *asatkāryavāda,* namely, that cause and effect are absolutely different, the Mādhyamika argues as follows: If cause and effect are totally different from each other, what precisely is the relation between the alleged cause and its effect? It is absurd to answer that the relation is causal relation, for that is to beg the question and not to answer it. Any sensible answer to the question should tell us what it means to say that of two different things one is the cause and the other the effect. Unless the reason for calling one the cause and the other the effect is given, all talk about something being the cause of something else is just babble and word magic. The Mādhyamika points out that anyone who talks like that must be deluded in thinking that something becomes a cause because he has given it the name "cause," or an effect because he has given it the name "effect." If this were so, we could turn one thing into another merely by calling it by a different name.

Further, if the effect is wholly unrelated to the cause, then not only should nothing be able to produce anything but also anything could be produced from anything[92]—for example, milk from stone, and oil from sand. But no one has so produced. The Mādhyamika's point here is that the view that cause and effect are absolutely different is as sterile and absurd as its antithesis that they are absolutely identical. To put the point more generally, the *satkārya-vāda* as well as its opponent, the *asatkāryavāda,* forgets that a relation has two functions: it unites and separates two things. Where there is no separation, there can be no uniting, and vice versa.[93] It is only by being unaware of this dual role of relation that men can lay dogmatic claims to one aspect of relation to the exclusion of the other. Such claims, as has been shown, can only lead to absurdities and contradictions.

The third alternative is refuted merely by noting that the refutation of the first and that of the second together constitute the refutation of the third. That is, if the thesis that a thing arises out of itself is absurd and the thesis that it arises out of a not-self is also absurd, then surely it is absurd to say that a thing arises out of both itself and a not-itself.[94] The fourth alternative needs no refutation, for it is itself the abandonment of causality; this is the view that there is no relation of any kind between cause and effect and hence things happen randomly. This does not mean that Nāgārjuna upholds this view. Quite the contrary, he is drawing attention to the fact that the view that things happen randomly is a claim about reality. More importantly, anyone who holds such a view has no right to employ the terms "cause" and "effect." The point here is that if things happen randomly, then "cause" and "effect" are empty and meaningless. As such, to hold the randomness thesis on the one hand and employ the concepts of cause and effect on the other is to contradict oneself. Nāgārjuna thus concludes his criticism of causation by saying that "at nowhere and at no time can entities ever exist by originating out of themselves, from others, from both (self-other), or from the lack of causes (i.e., and only)." [95]

The moral of this dialectical criticism of origination

(causation) is that causes and effects understood in an absolute sense can only lead to contradictions. "Cause" and "effect" refer to entities that exist relatively and dependently; but if taken as referring to entities existing independently and unconditionally—self-existents—these concepts engender absurdities. Another way of saying the same thing is, "cause" and "effect" are mutually dependent concepts having different referents in different conceptual frameworks and conventions.[96]

Nāgārjuna analyzes the notion of substance and attribute in a similar manner. Some advance the thesis that only attributes are real and not substance, while others claim the counterthesis, namely, only substance is real and not attributes. But, says Nāgārjuna, without attributes substance cannot be known, and without substance attributes cannot exist. Where do attributes exist? Do they exist within or without substance? Substance and attributes are neither the same nor different. Here too the dogmatic advocate commits the error of claiming reality exclusively for one or the other of two mutually dependent existents. Where there are no substances there can be no attributes, and vice versa. It must be emphasized, however, that in saying that substance and attributes are mutually dependent existents the Mādhyamika is not saying that substance and attributes both exist absolutely and ultimately. What he means by "mutually dependent existents" is that the reality of each is conditioned by that of the other. Neither of them exists absolutely, but both exist dependently and relatively.[97] The Mādhyamika accordingly warns us against falling victim to the illusion that simply because we have the concepts "substance" and "attribute" there are in reality some independent entities called "substances" and "attributes." Nāgārjuna subjects to similar analysis[98] such other concepts as "existence" and "nonexistence," "self" and "non-self," "unity" and "plurality," "subject" and "object," "rest" and "motion," and concludes that none of these concepts refers to any independent, absolute entities in reality. Taken as mutually dependent concepts, they signify relative existents; but if taken as referring to absolute, ultimate, and independent existents, these concepts lead to contradictions and absurdities.

Śūnyatā (Emptiness, Void) [99]

By denying causation is not Nāgārjuna denying the existence of the world? Is he not embracing and endorsing nihilism? Does not the destructive dialectic controvert the Buddha's teaching that wisdom consists in avoiding the dangerous extremes of eternalism and nihilism and treading the Middle Way? Let it be immediately said that the Mādhyamika school is not nihilism; quite the contrary, it is truly the Middle Way. Nāgārjuna teaches that it is absurd to talk of reality being true or false. Reality simply is.[100] What does it mean to deny reality? Denial of causation can entail the denial of reality only on the supposition that reality is constituted of causes and effects; and unless and until this supposition is shown to be true, Nāgārjuna cannot be charged with denying reality. What Nāgārjuna demonstrates by his dialectical critique of the concept of causation is precisely the untenability of the assumption that reality is constituted of causes and effects. Thus the import of the Mādhyamika critique is not the denial of reality, but only the denial that the concepts of cause and effect have any absolute referents in reality, for any claim that they do is self-contradictory. It is this point that is expressed by Nāgārjuna when he says that concepts are empty and void (*śūnya*).[101] It is worth emphasizing that emptiness of concepts does not entail the emptiness of reality.[102] It is true, however, that sometimes Nāgārjuna does refer to reality as Emptiness (Śūnyatā). What he means by this is not that reality is nonexistent or illusory, but only that it is devoid of any entities which we think our concepts refer to as existing in an absolute, independent, and unconditioned manner.[103] Thus the Mādhyamika is not a nihilist. Only he who mistakenly identifies concepts and conceptual constructions with reality can go from the emptiness of the former to that of the latter, thus becoming a nihilist. We have seen that according to the Mādhyamika it is the *thirst for the real and the absolute that drives men to mistake their own constructions of reality for reality itself.*[104]

Nāgārjuna points out[105] that despite their claims to be the true followers of the Buddha the various Buddhist schools have failed to comprehend in its full depth and significance the central teaching of the Buddha, namely, the Doctrine of Dependent Origination. No wonder they fell prey to ignorance, illusion, and dogmatism. Thus the Sautrāntika and Vaibhāṣika claimed absolute, independent, and unconditioned reality for the *dharmas* of their own systems. On the other hand, the Yogācāra made exclusive claims to the reality of consciousness (*vijñāna*). All these schools, in their thirst for the real and unconditioned, have forgotten the heart of the Buddha's teaching that nothing exists unconditionally and absolutely and that everything exists in dependence upon other things. To say that nothing exists absolutely, independently, and unconditionally is to say that there are no self-existent entities or natures—all *dharmas* (existents) are devoid of own-being and own-nature (*svabhāva-śūnya: sva* = own, *bhāva* = being or nature, *śūnya* = empty, void)—and bear in mind that everything exists relatively, conditionally, and dependently. Thus the relativity and Śūnyatā (Emptiness) of the Mādhyamika are none other than the Doctrine of Dependent Origination,[106] for teaching which Nāgārjuna salutes the Master.[107]

The Lower and Higher Truths

According to Nāgārjuna, the Buddha taught two truths, one pertaining to the phenomenal world, the world as grasped through names and forms, and the other to reality as it is in itself, beyond all names and forms. The world of names and forms is governed through and through by the Doctrine of Dependent Origination. Therefore, every truth generated by any conceptual system is relative to and dependent upon other truths and systems. In the realm of phenomena, there can be no absolute truth or truth of the absolutely real. All phenomenal truths are relative, conditioned, and valid within particular domains of our perceptual-conceptual experience. For this reason, Nāgārjuna calls phenomenal truths "conventional," "relative," "mundane," and "lower truths" (*saṁvṛti-satya*).[108] On the other hand, there is the absolute, supramundane, unconditional, higher truth, beyond percepts and concepts, ineffable and defying all descriptions. Nāgārjuna calls the higher truth *paramārtha-satya*.[109] It is grasped in *prajñā*—direct, intuitive insight[110] into reality as it is in itself. The Buddha maintained silence with respect to such nonempirical questions as whether the world is eternal or noneternal, finite or infinite, whether the soul is the same as or different from the body, whether or not one who attains Nirvāṇa (also referred to as the *Tathāgata,* the "thus-gone") exists after death, and what Nirvāṇa itself is. Such silence is due to the Buddha's awareness that these questions transcend reason and sense-experience and that consequently any attempt to answer them through names and forms can only serve to detract men, by producing confusion, ignorance, and dogmatism, from the immediate task of overcoming suffering. Such questions and the puzzlement they generate simply vanish away in the light of *prajñā,* transcendental wisdom.

Dogmatic opponents of Nāgārjuna, both ancient and modern, have condemned his dialectic as destructive and charged him with exhorting men to reject common sense, science, and philosophy as false and useless. Such a charge is based on a serious misunderstanding. Nāgārjuna does not deny the usefulness and validity of common sense, science, and philosophy in the phenomenal realm, the realm of relative truths. Quite the contrary, he fully acknowledges their importance and efficacy in dealing with the world as phenomena. He emphatically declares that without logic and reason man cannot know anything, but with them there is nothing that he cannot know.[111] It is clear, then, that what Nāgārjuna rejects is not the limited, phenomenal validity and pragmatic worth of logic and reason but their pretensions to reveal the real. He therefore exhorts men to guard themselves against these pretensions and illusions, lest they should forever remain in the grip of ignorance and suffering.

Before concluding, we shall say a few words about Nāgārjuna's most cryptic and bewildering utterance: that there is no difference whatever between mundane existence (*Saṁsāra*) and Nirvāṇa.[112] The point of this utterance is that mundane existence and Nirvāṇa, are not two numerically distinct ontological realms, but are one and the same reality seen from different standpoints, the lower and the higher; that is, the movement from Saṁsāra to Nirvāṇa is epistemological and not ontological. When we rid ourselves of illusion, ignorance, dogmatism, and, above all, attachment to thought-constructions, Saṁsāra, the very world of our ordinary experience, becomes transformed into Nirvāṇa. The distinction between Saṁsāra and Nirvāṇa, like all other distinctions, can only be relative. *Prajñā* is both the power to experience the world so transformed and the wisdom such experience brings about. Thus we may say that *prajñā* has a soteriological effect on man. It transforms him into a radically different kind of man, a man without greed, egoism, ignorance, and fear of any kind. That is, *prajñā,* the insight into the real, brings in its wake perfect freedom and perfect peace.

Consistent with his teaching of *prajñā* as the highest wisdom as well as freedom from all attachments and illusions, Nāgārjuna teaches that one should not be attached even to the Sūnyatā (emptiness), relativity, Nirvāṇa, or the Buddha himself.[113] Clinging to anything as the unconditioned reality, including the relativity of all views, breeds illusion and suffering. It is in this spirit that Nāgārjuna exhorts men to free themselves even from the Buddha, from the Noble Truths, and from Nirvāṇa itself. Nirvāṇa cannot be existence, for if it is, like all other existents it will be subject to birth and death. It cannot be nonexistence either, for, if it is nonexistence, it will necessarily be dependent upon existence. Nirvāṇa too, therefore, is only an illusion and not reality.[114] It should be emphasized, however, that when Nāgārjuna says that Nirvāṇa is not a reality he is to be understood as saying that Nirvāṇa, thought of as an independent reality referred to by the concept Nirvāṇa, is unreal. Thus Nāgārjuna does not deny the reality of Nirvāṇa, but warns men against clinging to the concept of Nirvāṇa.[115]

In conclusion, we note that the profound and sublime teachings of Śākyamuni Buddha receive their clearest expression in Nāgārjuna's dialectic. Thus the Mādhyamika is the flower of Buddhist wisdom. In course of time, the Mādhyamika school became the source of inspiration for the great wisdom of Tibetan as well as Zen Buddhism. Only the Zen master, in the light of the *prajñā* Nāgārjuna speaks of, could have commanded a student to cleanse his mouth for uttering the name of the Buddha, because of its purported sanctity.

D. BUDDHIST PSYCHOLOGY AND ETHICS [116]

The Concept of Identity

We saw earlier that Buddhist ontology is process ontology through and through. This means that the world is continuous change, there being no permanent and enduring objects, the so-called substances, either inside or outside man. We shall now show that the Buddhist denial of substances stems from the Buddhist analysis of the concept of identity.

The term "identity" has two meanings, one trivial and the other nontrivial. Thus the proposition "For any X whatever, X is identical with itself at any given time" is true, no matter what ontology one subscribes to; for this reason, we shall call this sense of identity trivial. But the proposition "For any X whatever, X is identical with itself at all times" asserts identity in the nontrivial sense. And whereas the first sense of identity is independent of any particular ontology, the second sense presupposes substance ontology; for to say that "X is identical with itself at all times" is to say that "X remains unchanged through time," and, given the definition of "substance" as "that which remains unchanged through time," it follows that X is a substance. But, the Buddhist asks, how does one know that something remains unchanged through time? Notice that this question is the same as that which asks: How does one know substances exist? This is an epistemological question in that it demands an answer in terms of methods of knowledge. Let us illustrate the kind of difficulties one encounters in answering it. Suppose I want to know the length of my desk. I can know it by measuring, and for measuring I need a measuring rod or tape. Having measured, I say that the desk is, say, four feet long. Suppose that at a later time I want to know whether the length of the desk has changed. I use the measuring rod I employed earlier and come up with a measurement of, say, 3.9 feet. But if the measuring rod itself is changing through time, I cannot use it to find out whether my desk has undergone change in length. Thus, in order to know whether or not something has changed, we need to have a standard of comparison (or measurement) which itself must remain unchanged in time. But, the Buddhist inquires, where do you find such unchanging standards? Nowhere, is his simple and emphatic answer. And if there are no unchanging things to serve as standards, continues the Buddhist, surely the claim that substances (unchanging entities) exist is empty and idle babble. Nevertheless, we may ask the Buddhist, if there are no unchanging entities to serve as standards by which to determine whether or not something changes, how does he know that *everything* changes. That is, in the absence of any standard, how does the Buddhist detect change? The Buddhist answer is as follows: Given anything in the world, you may choose anything else as your standard to determine whether the first thing is changing. But then the object serving as the standard can itself be compared with some other object as the new standard, which in turn can be compared with a still new standard, and so on ad infinitum. It follows that what is considered unchanging and hence chosen as a standard in one context is not unchanging with respect to another standard. That is, there are no absolutely unchanging entities, since anything you choose as standard can be shown to be changing with respect to something or other. The Buddhist warns against the fallacy of inferring from these considerations that there must be some ultimate standard, such as God or the so-called fixed stars of Newtonian cosmology. What is to be correctly inferred, says the Buddhist, is that there are no ultimate standards, for everything and anything you choose as standard and unchanging can be shown to be changing. Absolute rest, absolute motion, and absolutely unchanging entities are thus all figments of the imagination. However, the Buddhist readily grants that with respect to some *arbitrary* standard one may talk about something as unchanging, but he cautions that this does not mean that there is something absolutely unchanging, which is presupposed by "identity" in the nontrivial sense. Thus he concludes that since everything is changing nothing is identical with itself at all times and hence there are no substances. This is precisely what is meant by the Doctrine of Dependent Origination, according to which there are no self-existent entities in the world. A substance, in that it is thought to be unchanging, is thought of as a self-existent entity. Change, according to the Buddhist, is the interaction of one thing with another. Thus anything unchanging is not entering into interaction with anything else, hence the term "self-existent." But anything that exists is changing. Therefore anything unchanging is nonexistent. It is in this manner that the phrase "self-existing entity" is self-contradictory. Hence the Buddhist ontological dictum, "To exist is to be changing and vice versa." Further, "change" and "causal efficacy," are synonymous, for a change which is neither a cause nor an effect is indetectable and therefore fictitious, like a substance. Hence the second dictum, "To exist is to be causally efficacious." More importantly, existence and nonexistence are not different. They are one and the same, because everything arises and vanishes simultaneously. This must be so; otherwise, one would be compelled to say that something comes into existence, endures for a while, and then starts to become nonexistent—a line of thought which contradicts the denial of any enduring entities. Thus "existence" and "nonexistence" are two different names for one and the same process. From the foregoing, it also follows that there is only motion but no thing moving. The so-called moving thing is an abstraction and hence unreal:

> The Buddhist, therefore, regards all attempts to explain the world or the individuals by means of one or more "eternal substances" (such as God, soul, original matter, atoms, etc.) as just as useless as if one tried to tie the reflection of the moon to the water with the hair of a tortoise. There are no permanent entities of any sort; and all that exists is conditioned and will again pass away. Philosophically analysed, the whole universe and everything in it reveals itself as a strictly ordered sequence of dynamic processes, as a play of the forces of dharma. The theory that each individual event is functionally dependent is now further refined in that only a multiplicity of factors can bring about a new one, a single one being insufficient to do so. Thus there is no arising from one single original cause from which something develops, but only a new coming into existence by mutual co-ordination of a multitude of conditions. And so the Cosmic law manifests itself ultimately as a continuous and irrefrangible "condition (alism)." There are no isolated factors, and all things are connected with each other. Personality too, is an ever-changing stream of dharmas which arise from multiple conditions, are active for a short time, and again cease, to make room for others.[117]

Psychological Significance of the Concept of Identity

If analysis of experience leads to the conclusion that substances are nonexistent, why do men persist in believing the contrary? We shall answer this by considering the psychological significance of the implications of the Buddhist analysis of identity.

The first point to notice is that the concept of security is the psychological counterpart of the ontological concept of identity and arises out of it. In a very real sense both the Buddhist and the ordinary unenlightened man are trying to resolve the puzzle generated by an initial existential disquietude as to the whither and whence of man and the world. But the resolutions they arrive at are governed by their respective ontologies, and we shall see that they are as different as anyone could imagine. Let us examine the ways in which the Buddhist analyzes the phenomenon of insecurity that bedevils man, and the solution he proposes. Finding himself in a world in which nothing seems to be permanent, and exposed to suffering, sickness, and death, man is terrified and restless and seeks to conquer these dismal and sorry aspects of his existence. The first step man takes toward overcoming the overwhelming impermanence of existence is to somehow convince himself that his life and works are not in vain and that something of him endures. The feeling that he will, like all else, pass away is awesome and frightening, hence the need to find a standard that ensures something permanent in himself. Such a standard is the God of religions, and the permanent entity in man which is generated and sustained by it is the so-called self, soul, ego, etc. But in reality, says the Buddhist, the standard is a gratuitous fiction produced and maintained by man's attempt to overcome his sense of fear and insecurity. Thus, according to Chögyam Trungpa,

> where there is an external person, a higher Being, or the concept of something which is separate from oneself contrary to the Doctrine of Dependent Origination of Things, then we tend to think that because there is something outside there must be something here as well. The external phenomenon sometimes becomes such an over-whelming thing and seems to have all sorts of seductive and aggressive qualities, so we erect a kind of defence mechanism against it, failing to see that that is itself a continuity of the external thing. We try to segregate ourselves from the external, and this creates a kind of gigantic bubble in us which consists of nothing but air and water or, in this case, *fear and reflection of the external thing.* So this huge bubble prevents any fresh air from coming in, and that is "I"—the Ego. So in that sense there is the existence of Ego, but it is in fact illusory. Having established that *one generally wants to create some external idol or refuge,* subconsciously one knows that this "I" is only a bubble and it could burst at any moment, so one tries to protect it as much as one can—either consciously or subconsciously. In fact we have achieved such skill at protecting this Ego that we have managed to preserve it for hundreds of years.[118]

These observations of Lama Trungpa are worth some elaboration because they bring into focus the vicious circle involved in man's attempt to seek permanent entities in a world which is pure change. Man is first driven by insecurity and fear of passing away to look for something permanent in himself. But in order to arrive at something permanent in himself, he is forced to postulate the existence of something outside of himself as permanent and standard. But, paradoxically enough, man's fear and insecurity are not allayed by the postulation of such an entity. On the contrary, they take on a new dimension; for insofar as he derives and sustains his own permanence from that of the postulated external entity (God), man has constantly to live in a state of obedience to that entity, lest any transgression of its laws, whatever he imagines them to be, should bring upon him eternal damnation (now that he thinks he has an eternal self), which is worse than passing away. On the other hand, since he has convinced himself that there is something permanent in him, call it the "self," "soul," "ego," or whatever, man cannot help engaging in ego-aggrandizement and satisfying the cravings of the ego, thereby treading the path of greed, jealousy, and selfishness, all of which, while reinforcing the ego, nevertheless produce tension, unease, guilt, and conflict. The vicious circle should be clear by now. One fiction, the permanent ego, is maintained by another fiction, the postulated external permanent object. But one may wonder why man needs to engage in ego-aggrandizing activities in spite of having convinced himself that he has a permanent ego. The answer is that such activities are not an appendage to the ego; on the contrary, they *constitute* the ego. Ceasing to engage in these activities is to be in the egoless state; that is, the ego cannot be maintained unless the activities which constitute it are performed. Thus performing these activities is both a necessary and a sufficient condition for the very possibility of maintaining the ego. Notice, for example, that even in acts of charity there is the feeling that someone, the "I," is being charitable. This point is poignantly expressed by Trungpa when he contrasts the Bodhisattva with the ego-bound man:

> The Bodhisattva does not even think in terms of his own psychological benefit; he does not think, "I would like to see him

> not suffering." "I" does not come into it at all. He speaks and thinks and acts spontaneously, not thinking even in terms of helping, or fulfilling a particular purpose. He does not act on "religious" or "charitable" grounds at all. So in this case compassion does not refer to kindness alone, but to fundamental compassion, selfless compassion. He is not really aware of *himself,* so compassion has greater scope to expand and develop, because here there is no radiator but only radiation.[119]

We have said that the need to find something permanent in himself is rooted in man's fear of vanishing away. This need is fulfilled by the postulation of an external permanent entity. But once it is postulated, man has to live in constant fear of it. Thus in either case, he lives in fear—one kind of fear before he got himself an ego, and another after acquiring it. Such a man, according to the Buddhist, is a victim of illusions which are the foundation of the alienation of man from himself and from his fellowmen. As an illustration of this point,[120] consider the medieval Western man, whose sole preoccupation was with doing God's will and saving his soul. A certain man was brought before the Inquisition, tried for heresy, and condemned to be burned at the stake. As he was slowly burning, some men were deeply touched by his pain and suffering and were sobbing and shedding tears. But they looked at the sky and quickly wiped away their tears, assuming solemn and self-righteous expressions. What is the point of the story? These men, in their total loyalty and obedience to the external permanent entity (God), could not afford feelings of pity, sympathy, and humanity toward a man in immense pain and suffering, because to feel sympathy and compassion toward him (a heretic) would have been to betray their obedience to God and thereby lose their souls. In other words, man's sense of obedience to a fiction is so powerful that he is ashamed and afraid of feeling compassion for his fellowman, for fear of losing his own soul, another fiction. These men were alienated from themselves because their reality was predicated not upon themselves but upon some imagined permanent entity; they were also alienated from their fellowman because they were incapable of kindness and compassion toward him—he was not even human. Notice that alienation from one's fellowman follows from alienation from oneself.

It is easy to show that all this follows from the Buddhist analysis of identity. According to the Buddhist analysis, "identity" in the nontrivial sense is a concept exemplified by nothing that exists, because to exist is to change continuously. Therefore, anything which is claimed to be both an existent and identical in time is nonexistent. In short, the phrase "an existent identical in time" is self-contradictory. But the fear of passing away compels man to find in himself something that is unchanging. This he manages to fabricate by postulating an external, standard, permanent entity. In traditional religious terminology, such a standard is God, and the permanent in man is the ego, the self, or the soul. Since man derives his own permanence from the postulated permanent entity, his loyalty and obedience to it are single-minded and superior to those to any other entities. Moreover, once he persuades himself that he has a permanent self, man cannot help performing selfish and egoistic activities; for such activities are what constitute the ego. Man's loyalty and obedience to the source of his own permanence and the actions which constitute and reinforce the ego result in the alienation of man from himself and from his fellowman: alienation from himself, because his own reality is not based on himself but on something other than himself; alienation from his fellowman, because of egoism and a sense of utter subservience to something nonhuman. Now that he believes he has an ego, man has to save it from the wrath and anger of God on the one hand and from attacks by his fellowman on the other. Thus, according to the Buddhist analysis, the first mistake of man is the attempt to find something permanent in a world which is pure change. Such an attempt can only lead to illusion, which in turn produces fear, resulting in alienation and ill-being.

But one might object to the above analysis by saying that it applies only to men who believe in an external, permanent standard God and not to others and hence fails as a general account of the psychological insecurity of man. The

Buddhist points out that such an objection is mistaken. To be sure, in the above discussion the postulated permanent entity is taken as God. But it need not be a God, although this has been the most prevalent and powerful way in which man has attempted to resolve his insecurity by seeking an external, enduring standard. It is true that modern men—or those who call themselves rational and scientific—do not seek, at least overtly, to overcome their insecurity through the God of traditional religions. But this does not mean that they are not looking for enduring entities through which to generate and maintain their own identity as selves, souls, egos, etc. These men postulate their own standards of permanence by which to identify and sustain themselves, such as state, nation, progress, science, love, friendship, work. All these are substitutes for God as a permanent entity. Let us illustrate how these function as permanent entities and standards. Three decades ago, the world saw millions of men go mad and berserk and offer everything they had to serve their state, race, and flag. Like that of the medieval man, the loyalty of such men is to an intangible, invisible entity by relating to which they seek to establish their own identity. Without such a relationship, these men will be lost, for then they cannot know who they are. Even Marx, who prided himself on being a scientific philosopher of man and the world, fell for the illusion of permanence, the millennium marked by the emergence of the classless society.[121] He was never clear as to what will keep history moving once the classless society is realized and hence, on his own account of history, all possibility of dialectical conflict generating history will have vanished with the vanishing of the classes. The paradox here is that even such a thoroughgoing process philosopher as Marx should have ended up with something permanent and unchanging. And men are exhorted to devote themselves to that distant but supposedly certain abstraction and to strive to hasten the day of its appearance. The Buddhist point is not that different men choose different standards of identification, but that every man is driven to choose a standard at all, and that as long as men seek standards of permanence and identification the problem of insecurity remains unsolved and manifests itself as both inner and outer conflicts—guilt, tension, sheer boredom, aggression, war, and general ill-being.

Consider the obsession with work, play, or anything whatever. Man starts out saying that he is doing something because he enjoys it. But after a while he cannot help doing it. The activities become compulsive and so enable him to identify who he is. In the absence of such activities he is terrified by the question who he is. He says that he is bored. This point is succinctly expressed by Professor Jacobson:

> Man suspects the loose footing of all his endeavours [remember Trungpa's words that one is dimly aware that the "I" is a bubble that could burst at any moment], and he expresses this suspicion by exaggerating every venture. He believes with more zest than the mere facts allow. He solves his problems with more energy than their gravity requires. He overdoes everything. He gives himself to his work and play with a tenacity that ends by enslaving him. He imagines that he is merely expressing himself productively, when actually his creation wins by taking him captive. . . . *Everything he does has this forced quality*. He cannot afford not to know, he cannot afford not to discover; he is driven. Being this kind of creature, he uses most of his ingenuity to keep himself from perceiving that this is the way he is. . . . Culture is the human animal's clever and wholly inventive way of acquiring for himself an identity.[122]

The import of these remarks is that

> man builds his towers of Self because he cannot face the possibility that there is no permanent ego. He cannot face the truth that his self-concept is meaningful either in a purely conventional sense, or as a mere postulate in a theoretical system having no ultimate status at all.[123]

> "Non-ego," "Not-self (*anattā*)," i.e. the fact that neither within these bodily and mental phenomena of existence, nor outside of them, can be found anything that in the ultimate sense could be regarded as self-reliant real Ego entity, personality, or any other abiding substance.[124]

Becoming painfully aware from time to time of the essential emptiness of his existence, man is driven to fabricate a self. But "the Buddhist contention is that we will never be at ease before we have overcome this basic anxiety, and that we can do that only by relying on nothing at all." [125]

In terms of the concept of identity, all this can be expressed by saying that if man does not think and act in an obsessive manner he has no means of identifying himself. Identity is the relation or set of relations in which man stands to something, be it a person, object, thought, or activity. If this something is not there he will be lost, and so he has to create it in some form or other. He will be lost in the typically psychological sense of becoming anxious, restless, bored, and frighteningly lonely. And what is it to be lonely? To be lonely is to suffer from not having anything to relate to; and since one's own identity depends upon one's standing in relation to something (as a matter of fact, it is just such a relation or set of relations that constitutes the so-called oneself), loneliness is a feeling of loss and lack of identity and hence is terrible and unbearable. In a very real sense, then, man's life is a continuous search for something or other to relate to in order to overcome the emptiness and the feeling that he is really a mere passing phenomenon. But it should be noted that not any kind of relation and any kind of object or person will do the job of providing a sense of identity and security. John Doe may meet a person on a bus, chat with him, and part from him at Devilsville without any feeling of restlessness or loss of identity. But there are bound to be certain persons and objects in John Doe's life that he cannot think of losing, for fear of losing himself. It is true that John Doe is not always aware that such persons and objects are necessary for his own security and identity. He is a master at rationalization and talks in edifying and moving tones about the joy and pleasure of lasting friendships, viable marriages, priceless possessions, and absorbing activities. But rationalization offers as little protection and security as a mask of thin air offers a pugilist. Thus when John Doe's beloved wife dies, he weeps like a child. His neighbors say how much he loved his wife. But has John Doe ever learned that all things pass away? If he has, why is he weeping? The truth is that his love for his wife is a convenient rationalization for his love of himself, and he is really weeping for himself, weeping over the identity crisis brought about by the loss of one of the objects whose relations to John Doe are his identity. Having lost such an object, John Doe is terrified at having to face the question "How can I go it alone from now on?" It should be noted that after a time John Doe finds something else—a person, object, or activity—to relate to and regains his sense of identity; this is precisely what is meant by the common saying that time is the greatest healer. It is also true that sometimes a man attempts to regain his identity by living in his memories and fantasies. In any case, the Buddhist point is that the unenlightened man cannot help seeking permanent entities, be they persons, objects, activities, by relating to which he produces and maintains the illusion of his own identity. But such a search, according to the Buddhist, is from the beginning doomed to failure and can only result in sorrow, frustration, and anxiety. Let us give one last example. A man has a very close friend whom he regards as precious because he thinks the friend is kind, loyal, loving, and trustworthy. He does not want to lose the friend. But one day he discovers that his friend has betrayed him. He is shocked and enraged. Why? Because one of his sources of identity is gone. More importantly, what grounds did he have in the first place for thinking that his relations with his friend were unchanging and permanent? None at all, except the image of the friend he himself built. But he is unaware that he is an ingenious image-builder and that only images and thought-constructions can be permanent, and not existents. The Buddhist point here is that man is an image-building animal because it is precisely by such activity that he produces and maintains the illusion of his own identity. Even more important, from the Buddhist point of view, is the fact that in spite of several disillusionments, man does not stop image-construction and therewith the quest for the permanent and unchanging in him. Such, according to the Buddhist, is the height of man's ignorance and unwisdom.

We may now sum up our discussion of the psychological implications of the Buddhist analysis of identity. In order to overcome insecurity and the fear of passing away, man searches after something permanent (identical in time) in himself. He cannot find such an entity in himself except through his relations to some entity other than himself thought to be permanent and unchanging. But every entity he regards as permanent and hence capable of generating and maintaining his own identity and permanence turns out to be otherwise—impermanent and changing. Since this is the case, man constantly suffers disillusionments and identity crises. Identity crisis may take place in two ways: (*a*) by losing the identity-producing object and (*b*) by being bored with it. To be bored with something means that that something is no longer responding to one's ego-needs. In either case, man moves on to find something else to which he may relate in order to establish his own identity. But, according to the Buddhist, nothing in the world is permanent, for existence and change are one and the same. Therefore, if man grasps this truth he does not look for permanent entities either within himself or without. Once man clearly sees that there is nothing to cling to and that there is no need to cling to anything at all, he becomes free. For the Buddhist, then, wisdom and enlightenment consist in the realization that there is nothing permanent in the world and hence that all search after enduring entities, in particular an enduring self or ego, is foolish and can only lead to illusion, sorrow, and suffering. But such a realization is not to be mistaken for the mere parroting of these views. What is needed is an existential realization of their truth, which can only come about by an excruciating analysis of every aspect of one's experience. The various exercises and techniques of meditation[126] are all methods for attaining such a realization of this fundamental ontological truth. The knowledge that there is nothing to cling to and no need to cling to anything at all conquers the psychological insecurity that plagues man and triggers the futile quest.

Since there is no ego and nothing permanent, there is no

boundary separating man from all else. From this basic ontological premise follows the Buddhist ethic. The central point of this is that if there is no permanent ego, there is nothing to be saved and protected; and since all craving, greed, and selfishness arises from the illusion of the enduring ego, a clear insight into the fictitious character of the ego leads to freedom from selfishness and all that goes with it. Such an insight is what makes the Bodhisattva the supremely compassionate being, without an iota of the "I." One may point out here that all the great religions have more or less the same fundamental ethical precepts. But each religion explains, justifies, and grounds its ethics in a different ontology. For example, Judaism, Christianity, and Islam exhort man to be kind, compassionate, and unselfish because the God (s) of these religions commanded it so. It is interesting, however, that all three religions recognize an enduring soul or self, which can only be saved by obeying God's will. But the paradox is that while their ethics demand that man be unselfish, their ontologies assure him that he has a permanent self which has to be saved. These religions fail to see that once man is granted a permanent self, he finds it hard to be unselfish. Thus their ontology of a permanent self clashes with their ethical demand that man be unselfish, which results in inner and outer conflicts. It is appropriate to point out here that Whitehead, the process-philosopher *par excellence* in the West, clearly saw the incompatibility between ethics and substance ontology. Thus Professor Hartshorne, one of the most distinguished interpreters of Whitehead, writes:

> Egoism rests on a superstitious absolutizing of non-identity with other persons. The concrete units of reality are not you and I, but you now, or you then, or I now, or I then. If "I now" care about me later on, it can also care about you later on, and much the same act of imaginative sympathy is involved. Calculating self interest is one arbitrarily limited strand of concern for life beyond the present self. Whitehead humorously summed up the ethical objection to substance theories by remarking, "I sometimes think that all modern immorality is produced by Aristotle's theory of substance." A Buddhist would understand this.[127]

Moreover, a code of ethics whose sole justification consists in its being regarded as a command of a God, while readily acceptable to those who believe in a God who is creator, commander, and judge of man, presents immense difficulties to those who find it hard, if not impossible, to believe in a God. The result is an ethical code which hangs in the air without any acceptable ontological support. In sharp contrast, Buddhism neither recognizes a God nor accepts any arguments for unselfish conduct in terms of commands, punishments, etc. The Buddhist wants to ground his ethics in his ontology, according to which there is nothing permanent in the world, either inside or outside of man. Thus, on gaining the insight that the ego is a pure fabrication and illusion, man becomes free, spontaneous, and compassionate. His compassion is not conditioned by the self and the non-self. It should be emphasized, however, that the Buddhist is not under the illusion that merely by studying Buddhist ontology as an intellectual exercise one becomes a supremely ethical man. The Buddhist is keenly aware of the danger that words and systems of thought may become substitutes for the practice of analysis and the acquisition of insight that verify the truth of his teachings and lead to liberating wisdom. The illusion of the permanent ego is so overwhelming that prolonged and extraordinary efforts are required to overcome it. Nevertheless, the intellectual awareness that a permanent self is a fiction which man constructs in order to overcome fear and insecurity is the first step toward the realization of freedom and wisdom.

To conclude, the Buddhist ontological premise that the world is process through and through is not an isolated philosophical proposition. On the contrary, it is fundamental to the whole Buddhist analysis and understanding of man and world. The Buddhist philosophy of life, freedom, and wisdom follows as systematic implications of this ontological premise. For example, Buddhist psychology and ethics are not disconnected reflections on these matters but are logical consequences of the proposition that there are no substances in the world. The concept of identity in the nontrivial sense, which underlies the concept of substance, is incompatible with the concept of process. Therefore, the concept of self, soul, or ego as a permanent entity is empty and does not refer to any existent. Having shown this, the Buddhist inquires why man constantly searches for a permanent entity within him and how he attempts to obtain this by postulating a standard of permanence, be it a God, state, race, art, science, play, or work. All these are ways in which man desperately tries to cover up the terrifying and paralyzing emptiness of his existence. The Buddhist analysis shows that all such attempts are doomed to failure because of their incompatibility with the world as process; and even if man temporarily succeeds in putting himself in the comfortable coma of fiction and illusion, he eventually suffers disillusionments one after another. And as long as he is in ignorance, he continues his quest for identity and permanence. He does not learn from disillusionments. Psychology and ethics built on false ontologies, according to the Buddhist, will only result in fear, anxiety, guilt, and other forms of unease and conflict, as well as man's alienation from himself and from his fellowman. According to the Buddhist, the existentialists are mistaken in their cry that man has come *into* this world; quite the contrary, man has come *out of* the world—that is, he is part of the world process. Hence he is not a stranger in the world. All alienation is rooted in man's feeling that he is somehow thrown into the world from some other place. It may be well to recall here that from the Buddhist point of view there is nothing called the "world" undergoing change; the world *is* change. If to exist is to be causally efficient, then permanent entities are causally inefficient; that is, they are simply not existents. Freedom consists in the existential realization that there is nothing to latch on to and no need to latch on to anything at all, not in the mere verbalizing of this truth. Once the so-called permanent ego is seen as no more than an illusion to be overcome and as nonexistent, the way is open for man to become free, spontaneous, unselfish, and compassionate. With the expulsion of the illusion of the enduring ego, all boundaries between man and man and between man and nature crumble, and his compassion becomes boundless and unconditioned. A study of the history of philosophy as well as civilization discloses that man's ethical failure can only be matched by his ignorance. The reason for such a dismal picture is that ethics has been left without an ontological support, or rests upon dogmatic theologies and revealed religions which, by their very nature, cannot withstand rational scrutiny. According to the Buddhist analysis, only by grounding ethics in a true ontology can man triumph as an ethical being. In such a grounding, knowledge, wisdom, freedom, and conduct are inseparable. A separation of these into compartments and isolated units results in schizophrenia, a not uncommon disease afflicting even those who proudly look upon themselves as rational, scientific, and wise. When they leave their libraries and laboratories men who claim to live by the cool light of reason turn to all kinds of superstitions and fictions in order to preserve their precious egos. The churchman who loudly preaches that his God who is the Father of all men commands them to live like brothers is not ashamed of offering prayers to the very same God for victory for his nation, tribe, or race, and for death and decimation to his brothers. The Buddhist analysis shows that such absurdities are not accidental and comical, but are the inevitable and tragic consequences of a view of man and world emanating from an ontology which has not a whit of truth in it. Is it surprising, then, that mistaken ontologies can only produce mutilated men?

Chapter V

Sāṁkhya

Introduction

Sāṁkhya is among the oldest of Indian philosophies.[1] Having its roots in the Vedas, it has influenced all other Indian schools, orthodox and unorthodox alike. Thus the basic tenets of Sāṁkhya can be seen in Jainism as well as in Yoga, Nyāya, Vaiśeṣika, and Vedānta. A great sage by the name of Kapila was the founder of the Sāṁkhya school. Tradition has it that Kapila formulated the Sāṁkhya system in a work entitled *Sāṁkhya-sūtra* (*The Principles of Sāṁkhya*), followed by a detailed treatise, *Sāṁkhya-pravacana-sūtra.* In course of time, a great number of expositions, commentaries, and interpretations of Sāṁkhya appeared. Of these, the earliest available and the most important is *Sāṁkhya-kārikā* by Īśvarakṛṣṇa (fifth century A.D.). Other significant works of Sāṁkhya include Gauḍapāda's *Sāṁkhya-kārikā-bhāṣya,* Vācaspati Misra's *Sāṁkhya-tattva-kaumudī,* and Vijñānabhikṣu's *Sāṁkhya-pravacana-bhāṣya.*

There are two different accounts of the origin of the name of the school. According to the one, Sāṁkhya derives its name from the word *sāṁkhya,* which means number, in that the school concerns itself with providing the right knowledge and understanding of reality by specifying the number and nature of the ultimate constituents of the universe. According to the other account, the term *sāṁkhya* means perfect knowledge, and since the philosophy is regarded by its followers as the system of perfect knowledge they gave it the name Sāṁkhya.

Metaphysics

Sāṁkhya is dualistic realism. It is dualistic because of its doctrine of two ultimate realities: *Prakṛti,* matter, and *Puruṣa,* self (spirit). Sāṁkhya is realism in that it holds that both matter and spirit are equally real. With regard to the self, Sāṁkhya is pluralistic because of its teaching that Puruṣa is not one but many. The Sāṁkhya distinction between Puruṣa and Prakṛti is fundamentally that between the subject and the object. The subject can never be the object, and the object can never be the subject. The self (Puruṣa) and the non-self (Prakṛti) are radically different from each other. The dualistic metaphysics of Sāṁkhya is thus founded on the undeniably bipolar character of our everyday experience as made up of the experiencer and the experienced. We shall now turn to a detailed presentation of the Sāṁkhya account of Prakṛti and Puruṣa.

We experience the world as constituted of a manifold of objects. The Sāṁkhya asks: What is the cause of these objects? How did they come about? He answers by saying that Prakṛti is the ultimate (first) cause of all objects,[2] including our body, senses, mind, and intellect. We observe that every object is caused by (or arises out of) other objects. Thus, curd is produced from milk, and cloth from thread. But, according to the Sāṁkhya, milk and thread are only proximate not ultimate causes of curd and cloth. He wants to know how milk and thread themselves come to be. More generally, the question is: What is the ultimate stuff of which the various objects of the world are made?

The Sāṁkhya points out that it would not do to say, as, for example, Jainism and Nyāya-Vaiśeṣika do, that objects are produced by the combination of material atoms thought of as ultimate constituents of the physical world;

for although we can explain gross objects as arising out of material atoms, we cannot explain how material atoms can produce such subtle objects as mind and intellect. When we inspect the world around us, we find that the cause is always subtler and finer than its effect. Thus, the seed is finer than the tree, and the egg subtler than the chicken. Consequently, material atoms cannot themselves be the cause of such subtle and fine objects as mind. Therefore, the Sāṁkhya argues, there must be some finest and subtlest stuff or principle underlying all physical existence. Prakṛti is such a principle; it is the first and ultimate cause of all objects, gross and subtle. It is both the material and the efficient cause of the physical world. Being the ultimate cause, Prakṛti itself is uncaused, eternal, and all-pervading; and being the subtlest and finest, Prakṛti cannot be perceived, but can only be inferred [3] from its effects. The Sāṁkhya inference of the existence of Prakṛti is as follows: Every object of our experience is dependent upon and caused by other objects. Nothing arises out of nothing. In this manner, the whole physical world is a series of causes and effects. But, the Sāṁkhya continues, the series of causes and effects can only account for the arising of one object from another and cannot explain the fact of there being any objects at all. The existence of the physical world, then, must either remain an unfathomable mystery or be traced to a primordial cause. The first alternative is certainly unsatisfactory, since mystery cannot be a substitute for knowledge and the understanding of reality. Only the second alternative is in accord with reason and experience. Thus the Sāṁkhya infers Prakṛti as the primal cause of all physical existence.[4]

Prakṛti is the non-self and is devoid of consciousness[5] and hence can only manifest itself as the various objects of experience of the Puruṣa, the self. According to the Sāṁkhya, Prakṛti is constituted of three *guṇas,* namely, *sattva, rajas,* and *tamas.*[6] The term *guṇa* ordinarily means quality or nature. But in the context of Prakṛti, *guṇa* is to be understood in the sense of constituent (component). *Sattva* is the component whose essence is purity, fineness, subtlety, lightness, brightness, and pleasure. It is *sattva* which is most closely associated with ego, consciousness, mind, and intelligence. It should be emphasized, however, that *sattva* is only a necessary but not a sufficient condition for consciousness, for consciousness is exclusively the Puruṣa. *Rajas* represents the principle of activity and motion. In material objects *rajas* is responsible for motion and action of objects. In man *rajas* is the cause of activity, restlessness, and pain. *Tamas* is the constituent which manifests itself in material objects as heaviness as well as opposition and resistance to motion and activity. In man it is the cause of ignorance, coarseness, stupidity, laziness, lack of sensitivity, and indifference.

It is important to note that the three *guṇas* constitute Prakṛti as a dynamic complex and not a static entity; Prakṛti is thus not a mechanical aggregate of the three constituents, but an organic unity in which the three *guṇas* are in a state of dynamic equilibrium.[7] That is, the *guṇas* not only oppose but are also dependent upon each other.[8] On account of the homogeneous, nonmechanical, organic unity of Prakṛti, the *guṇas* cannot be separated. This is another way of saying that Prakṛti cannot be decomposed into the individual *guṇas*, for otherwise the *guṇas* and not Prakṛti would be the ultimate causes of all physical existence.

Before considering the emergence of the heterogeneous world of variety and multiplicity from the imperceivable homogeneous Prakṛti, it will be appropriate to present the Sāṁkhya theory of causation. The Sāṁkhya holds that the material effect is identical with (or preexists in) its material cause.[9] In short, the Sāṁkhya upholds the *satkārya-vāda*.[10] In accordance with *satkāryavāda*, the Sāṁkhya maintains that since Prakṛti is the ultimate cause of all physical existence, the three *guṇas* which constitute Prakṛti also constitute every object of the physical world. Every object therefore produces in us pleasure, pain, or indifference.

Prior to its evolution and differentiation into the world of objects, Prakṛti exists in a state of dynamic equilibrium due to the perfect balance between the three *guṇas*. It is worth emphasizing that even before evolution Prakṛti is in a state of constant change and transformation—the *guṇas* constantly balancing each other. Thus Prakṛti is never in a static state. Change and activity are its very essence.[11] Consequently, every object in the world, being an effect of Prakṛti, is also in a state of constant change. Thus, my writing desk which is perceived as unchanging and static is really a dynamic entity in perpetual change. It is interesting to note that the Sāṁkhya view of objects as dynamic entities is in accord with the finding of modern physics that all objects are complexes of molecules, atoms, electrons, etc., in a state of incessant motion and transformation.[12] According to Sāṁkhya, evolution of Prakṛti into the multiplicity of objects is followed by dissolution, a process in which the world of objects is transformed back into the undifferentiated primordial Prakṛti. Dissolution will again be followed by evolution. In this manner cosmic cycles arise. It is of the utmost importance to note that there are two different interpretations of *satkāryavāda;* these are *pariṇāmavāda* and *vivartavāda*. According to the former, the transformation of Prakṛti into the manifold of objects is a real transformation. According to the latter the transformation is not real but only apparent. The Sāṁkhya defends *pariṇāmavāda,* whereas Advaita Vedānta upholds *vivartavāda*.[13]

Sāṁkhya teaches that the evolution of Prakṛti is due to the imbalance and disequilibrium brought about by the dominance or preponderance of one or the other of the three *guṇas*. The evolution of Prakṛti results in twenty-three different kinds of objects.[14] The first of these is intellect (*mahat, buddhi,* the great one), arising out of the preponderance of *sattva*.[15] *Mahat* is the basis of all our intellectual modes. It is thus the faculty by which we discriminate, deliberate, judge, and make decisions. It is by *mahat* that we distinguish between the subject and object, self and non-self, experiencer and experienced.[16] The second, namely, ego (*ahaṁkāra*), arises out of *mahat*. *Ahaṁkāra* is the source of the sense of "I" and "mine." It is what causes us to appropriate objects, set goals for ourselves, and initiate actions to realize them. From *ahaṁkāra* emanate two sets of objects. The first consists of the five sense organs, the five motor organs, and mind (*manas*); the second is comprised of the five elements which, according to the Sāṁkhya, may exist in two forms, subtle and gross.[17] It is obvious that the members of the first group pertain to our conscious life and consequently arise out of the sattvic component of *ahaṁkāra*. On the other hand, the objects of the second group, of which the objective world is constituted, emanate from the *tamas* component of *ahaṁkāra*. The *rajas* aspect of *ahaṁkāra* does not produce any objects of its own but supplies the energy for the other two *guṇas* to produce their respective objects.

We have said that the elements exist in subtle and gross forms. Accordingly, there are five subtle elements (*tanmātras*) and five gross elements, namely, space (*ākāśa*), water, air, fire, and earth. The gross elements arise as a result of combinations of the subtle elements. The five *tanmātras* are: elemental sound, elemental touch, elemental color, elemental taste, and elemental smell. From elemental sound is produced the gross element space with the property of sound; the gross element air is produced by the combination of elemental sound and elemental touch and has both the qualities of sound and touch; the gross element fire is produced by the combination of elemental sound, elemental touch, and elemental color and has all three attributes of sound, touch, and color; the gross element water arises out of the combination of the first four *tanmātras* and has the corresponding four qualities; and earth, the fifth gross element, is produced by the combination of all five *tanmātras* and has all five qualities. All gross objects are produced by different combinations of the five gross elements. It is worth noting that only the gross elements and objects formed out of their combinations are perceivable, and not the *tanmātras*. It is also important to note that Sāṁkhya distinguishes between two kinds of disintegration. That in which a gross object is reduced to its constituent gross elements and that in which it is reduced to the *tanmātras*. The former takes place during the evolutionary phase of Prakṛti, whereas the latter takes place only during the dissolution of the physical world into the primordial Prakṛti. To put the matter differently, once Prakṛti has evolved, all reversible transformations are at the gross level. It is only at dissolution that reversible transformations at the subtle level take place; not only do all gross objects disintegrate into gross elements, but, furthermore, the gross elements disintegrate into the subtle elements, which in their turn disintegrate, resulting in the undifferentiated, homogeneous Prakṛti in dynamic equilibrium.

The complex formed of *mahat, ahaṁkāra,* and *manas* is known as the internal organ (*antaḥ-karaṇa*), the basis of sensation, perception, and conception—in short, of all of our mental life. It should be kept in mind, however, that the internal organ and its components are all physical entities, and hence none of them is to be confused with the Puruṣa (self). The internal organ is thus only necessary but not sufficient for the possibility of the self's experience of the world. From a physiological point of view, the internal organ, together with the sensory and motor organs, may be looked upon as the brain and the nervous system.

We come now to the Sāṁkhya account of the Puruṣa.[18] Sāṁkhya is dualistic[19] in that it recognizes two ultimate realities: Prakṛti, the physical world, and Puruṣa, the self. The physical world is the manifestation of Prakṛti, which is subtle and devoid of any consciousness. On the other hand, Puruṣa is the self within, which is pure consciousness and sentience. Sāṁkhya rejects any suggestion of reducing the Puruṣa to Prakṛti or the Prakṛti to Puruṣa as misguided and unwarranted by the nature of our experience; for, the Sāṁkhya argues, experience is always constituted of two poles, the experiencer and the experienced, the awareness and the object of awareness. Consequently, the distinction between Puruṣa and Prakṛti is absolute and indissoluble.[20] Puruṣa is radically different from the body, the senses, the *manas,* the ego, and even the intellect, all of which are physical. The self is not to be thought of as an object whose attribute is consciousness. Quite the contrary, the self *is* pure consciousness itself. The self cannot be an object, because if it were it would in principle be possible to experience it as one among many objects. It is the pure subject and hence can never be the object. It is what reveals objects to us.[21] Being totally different from the ever-changing and active Prakṛti, the self is unchanging, wholly passive, and can have neither will nor knowledge. As such, the self is pure enjoyer (*bhoktṛ*) and not an agent (*kartṛ*). However, like Prakṛti, the self is eternal, uncreated, and all-pervading. According to some Sāṁkhya philosophers, the self is neither the enjoyer nor the enjoyed and is thus beyond pleasure and pain, bliss and sorrow. It is the passive witness (*sākṣin*). This view of the self as being beyond even bliss is in sharp contrast with the Advaita Vedāntin view of self as blissful consciousness. The question now arises how and why people think that it is the self which experiences pain, sorrow, pleasure, and happiness. The Sāṁkhya answers by saying that in its ignorance the self identifies itself with the objects of its experience, thereby falling into the illusion that it is the experiencer of pleasure, pain, joy, and sorrow.

Like Prakṛti, Puruṣa cannot be perceived. Consequently, the existence of the latter, like that of the former, is inferred.[22] First and foremost, one's own existence is the most indubitable of all one's experiences. It is so indubitable and incontrovertible an experience that one cannot deny it without self-contradiction. It would be absurd to be able to doubt one's own existence, for the very act of doubting presupposes the doubter. Thus, the Sāṁkhya concludes, the existence of the self is self-evident and beyond doubt. It may be noted that this Sāṁkhya argument for the existence of the self is remarkably similar to the Cartesian dictum "I think, therefore I am." There is, however, a difference between the two: whereas for Descartes thinking is the attribute of the self, for the Sāṁkhya the self is not something which has attributes, but is pure consciousness itself. According to the Sāṁkhya, thinking belongs to the internal organ but not to the self. It would seem, then, that what Descartes calls the self or "I" is not the self of Sāṁkhya but the ego (*ahaṁkāra*). The second argument of the Sāṁkhya for the existence of self is based on linguistic considerations. When someone says, "I am fat," he is not saying that his self is fat but that his body is. In this manner our feeling of the distinction between the self and the body is reflected in our language. The third argument is expressly teleological. The Sāṁkhya says that the evolution of Prakṛti into the various objects, subtle and gross, would be pointless if it did not serve any purpose. Each object of the physical world serves as a means to the realization of some end or other. Therefore, the Sāṁkhya argues, there must exist conscious subjects or selves for serving whose ends Prakṛti evolves into the physical world.[23] In short, the evolution of Prakṛti is for the sake of Puruṣa. The Sāṁkhya further supports this observation by saying that the very fact that the first products of evolution, namely, *mahat, ahaṁkāra,* and *manas,* are aids to conscious life requires us to infer that there must be conscious subjects whose ends govern the order of evolution of Prakṛti. *Per contra,* if no conscious subjects exist, one cannot understand why Prakṛti should evolve at all, and also why the first products should be necessary for conscious life. The fourth argument for the existence of self consists in drawing our attention to the fact that men, notwithstanding their ignorance and capacity for evil, feel the urge for self-perfection, and saying that such a spiritual urge and impulse would be inexplicable if there did not exist a subject seeking perfection.[24] Therefore, the Sāṁkhya argues, there must exist a conscious subject striving toward perfection. In view of these considerations, it would be quite correct to say that Sāṁkhya employs the notions of both first cause and final cause in its metaphysics. Prakṛti is the first cause of the physical world, and the evolution of Prakṛti is governed by the final cause, namely, the end or goal of Puruṣa. What is the end and goal of Puruṣa? According to Sāṁkhya, the end and goal of Puruṣa is liberation from the imperfections and limitations of man that arise out of his involvement with Prakṛti. We may note that

Sāṁkhya finds itself in the curious position of claiming on the one hand that the imperfections of the self are due to its entanglement with Prakṛti, and on the other that the evolution of Prakṛti is the means by which the self liberates itself from the imperfections. It would, however, be unfair to the Sāṁkhya if we left this observation unexplained. What this apparently paradoxical and inconsistent position of the Sāṁkhya means is that the self in its ignorance falls victim to the illusion that its involvement with Prakṛti is real; and that salvation consists in its realization that such an involvement and the attendant imperfections are unreal and spring from its false identification with Prakṛti. Thus liberation of the self consists in the knowledge of its eternal and absolute independence from Prakṛti.

According to the Sāṁkhya, there is not one but many Puruṣas, selves. For this reason, Sāṁkhya is spiritual pluralism. Sāṁkhya defends the plurality of selves from the fact of the existence of men as distinct and unique individuals.[25] The distinctness and uniqueness of men from each other is in turn supported by the undeniable fact of mental and moral differences between them. In short, no two men are mentally and morally identical. Therefore, the Sāṁkhya concludes, there must be distinct selves. We may note that the Sāṁkhya argument for the plurality of selves is open to the following objections: If selves are not perceivable but are transcendent subjects, how is the Sāṁkhya entitled to claim the plurality of selves from the fact of the plurality of empirical individuals? In sharp contrast, Advaita Vedānta teaches that only empirical egos are many, but there is one and only one Self, the Ātman.[26] Another serious objection against the Sāṁkhya theory of the self concerns its pervasiveness. If selves are many, what does it mean to say that each of them is all-pervading? If "all-pervading" is taken to mean being simultaneously present everywhere, then it is hard to see how a self which at a certain time is associated with a certain body can also be associated at the same with other bodies. In other words, the Sāṁkhya claim that the self is all-pervading is incompatible with its claim of the plurality of selves. It is possible, however, that the Sāṁkhya may be saying that only in its liberated state is the self all-pervading. The most telling criticism of the Sāṁkhya metaphysics concerns the relation between Prakṛti and Puruṣa.[27] According to the Sāṁkhya, Prakṛti is unconscious and prior to evolution it is in a state of dynamic equilibrium in which the three *guṇas* exist in perfect balance. Further, Prakṛti cannot itself initiate evolution but requires contact with Puruṣa. Only by coming into relation with Puruṣa can Prakṛti begin to evolve. The question now is: If, as the Sāṁkhya teaches, Prakṛti and Puruṣa are absolutely different, how can they interact? If Puruṣa is wholly inactive and unchanging, how can it initiate the evolution of Prakṛti? The Sāṁkhya answer to this objection is unsatisfactory; for all that the Sāṁkhya has to say in reply to this objection is that Prakṛti and Puruṣa are like a lame man and a blind man who can harmoniously cooperate to find their way out of a jungle.[28] But unfortunately this is not an argument but merely an analogy. In the absence of any other reply to this objection, the relation between Prakṛti and Puruṣa the Sāṁkhya speaks of remains a total mystery. We may note in passing that it is the singular achievement of the Mādhyamika to draw attention to precisely this kind of difficulty that philosophical systems generate for themselves by absolutizing concepts. Thus in the case of Sāṁkhya Prakṛti and Puruṣa are absolutized and made wholly independent. No wonder, the Mādhyamika would continue, the Sāṁkhya is unable to explain how two entities which are thought of as absolutely independent and self-existent can interact. The Mādhyamika point here is that in the first place the Sāṁkhya has no basis for thinking that Prakṛti and Puruṣa are absolutely independent and wholly unrelated existents. And anyone who violates the Doctrine of Dependent Origination is bound to pay the heavy price of falling into inconsistency, absurdity, and unintelligibility itself. However, the Mādhyamika readily grants that the Sāṁkhya can claim that Prakṛti and Puruṣa are relative, dependent, and conditioned existents.

Epistemology[29]

The Sāṁkhya, like almost all other Indian schools, recognizes the three independent sources and criteria (*pramāṇas*) of valid knowledge: perception, inference, and testimony. According to the Sāṁkhya, the self comes to have knowledge through the vehicles of the sense organs, *manas,* and *mahat.* Sensations and impressions arise as a result of contacts between the sense organs and objects. The *manas* analyzes the sensations and impressions into various forms and passes them on to the *mahat.* The *mahat* thus becomes transformed into the form of the particular object. But being a physical entity, the *mahat* lacks consciousness and so cannot itself generate knowledge. Because of its predominantly sattvic nature, however, the *mahat* reflects the consciousness of the self, the Puruṣa. In this manner, the unconscious yet eminently sattvic *mahat* becomes conscious of the form into which it has been modified. Thus arises perception as a cognitive act. An analogy may illustrate this point further. A mirror in a dark room, although situated in front of an object, cannot reveal the object to us, but needs the light of a lamp for reflecting and revealing the object. Similarly, the *mahat,* an unconscious, physical entity, needs the light of consciousness of the Puruṣa in order to produce cognition and therewith knowledge. It is clear, then, that without the Puruṣa as pure consciousness there can be no knowledge.

Sāṁkhya distinguishes between two kinds of perception, which may be described as pure sensation and perception. In pure sensation one is aware of the presence of something, although there is no knowledge of what that something is. That is, in pure sensation there is neither categorization nor analysis nor synthesis of the sensa. Pure sensation is thus wholly devoid of any conceptual components. To put it differently, in sensation there can only be cognition but no *re*cognition, for recognition means to identify that which is being sensed as such and such; such identification necessarily involves categorization, analysis, synthesis, and interpretation of that which in sensation is given as merely present. Thus, a baby's experience of the world is, to use William James' phrase, a blooming and buzzing confusion. The baby has no concepts by which to label the various sense-data and thereby to generate the notion of identity and with it objects and individuals. On the other hand, with the acquisition of language one learns to label one's sensations and identify them as this or that object—for example, this is a red flower and that is an elephant. In Sāṁkhya literature, sensation and perception are also referred to as indeterminate and determinate perceptions,[30] respectively.

We shall now persent an outline of the Sāṁkhya theory of inference. Inference is needed only when we do not know everything about the world. It is the process by which we assert, on the basis of what we perceive or know, something that we have not yet perceived or known.[31] The connection between what is perceived and what is asserted is one of invariable relation. Thus, having observed that smoke and fire invariably and unfailingly occur together, one infers from the perception of smoke the existence of fire. It should be emphasized, however, that the relation between what is perceived and what is inferred must be universal and grounded in experience; that is, mere coincidental (or isolated instances of conjoint) occurrence of phenomena cannot serve as the basis of inference from the perception of one to the existence of the other.

Broadly speaking, Sāṁkhya divides all inferences into two classes, *vīta* (affirmative) and *avīta* (negative). The first consists of inferences based on universal affirmative propositions, and the second of those based on universal negative propositions. The first class is further divided into two groups, one group consisting of inferences based on universal affirmative propositions that are grounded in empirical experience, and the other of inferences based on universal propositions not so grounded. Let us illustrate each of these three kinds of inference.[32] The smoke-fire example given above belongs to the first group of the first class. The following is an example of inferences of the second group of the first class. Consider the question, How do we know that we have sense organs? According to the

Sāṁkhya, it would be absurd to say that we know we have sense organs because we perceive them, for the sense organs are those by which we perceive all objects but not the sense organs themselves: the eye cannot see itself. Nevertheless, says the Sāṁkhya, we can infer the existence of the sense organs by the following argument: Every action requires for its performance some instrument or device. Perceiving is an action. Therefore, since we do perceive, we must possess instruments or means of perception, namely, the sense organs. According to the Sāṁkhya this inference is justified, not because we have *observed* our sense organs to be invariably related to perceptual acts, but because of our general conception of action as something that requires an instrument. (One might question the Sāṁkhya conception of perception as action, but we shall not pursue this objection here.) We shall now illustrate inference based on universal negative propositions. It consists in progressive elimination of all but one of the possible alternatives. Thus one infers that something is a substance by showing that it is neither a quality nor a relation nor an activity nor anything else. We may mention that the Sāṁkhya accepts the five-membered syllogism of the Nyāya as the most adequate pattern of inference. This pattern we shall discuss in detail in the chapter on Nyāya.

The Sāṁkhya recognizes testimony as appropriate where neither perception nor inference can serve as means to knowledge.[33] Testimony is of two kinds, namely, *laukika* and *vaidika:* that which in principle is open to confirmation by perception and inference, and that which is not so open, respectively. The former kind pertains to knowledge of objects constituting the world of ordinary experience, whereas the latter pertains to knowledge of supersensuous, transcendental reality. Thus when the geographer makes the claim that there is a continent called "Australia," we accept it as true because we ourselves can in principle certify it on the basis of perception and inference. Similarly, when the microbiologist asserts that there exist certain minute organisms, aided with the appropriate theory and instruments we ourselves can in principle determine the truth or falsity of this assertion. On the other hand, in matters beyond perception and inference, the Sāṁkhya accepts the testimony of the Vedas. The reason for this is that the Sāṁkhya regards the Vedic seers as men who, by freeing themselves from all the imperfections of mundane existence, have gained insight into ultimate reality. Their utterances are expressions of their direct intuitive knowledge of ultimate reality; consequently, the Vedas constitute the most authoritative and infallible[34] source of knowledge of the transcendental reality. It should be kept in mind, however, that the Sāṁkhya does not regard the Vedas as eternal, since they are founded in the transcendental experiences of men who lived and died at certain times and places. Thus the Vedas are infallible, not because they are eternal, but because they are the intuitive insights of perfect men. Nevertheless, the Sāṁkhya considers Vedic knowledge timeless in the sense that it is not the exclusive possession of this or that group of men living in a certain place at a certain time, but instead is grounded in the universal, unchanging spiritual experience of all men in all times and places.

We conclude our discussion of the Sāṁkhya metaphysics and epistemology by noting a few more salient points. The Sāṁkhya metaphysics is dualistic realism, since according to it there are two ultimate principles, Prakṛti and Puruṣa, which are equally real. Consequently, the Sāṁkhya rejects monism, whether materialistic or idealistic. The reason for this is that materialistic monism commits the error of affirming the reality of Prakṛti (matter) and denying the reality of Puruṣa (spirit); on the other hand, idealistic monism is guilty of the reverse error of affirming the reality of Puruṣa and denying the reality of Prakṛti. The Sāṁkhya points out that neither of these monisms can do justice to the incontrovertible fact of our experience as constituted of the two poles, the subject and the object. For the Sāṁkhya, knowledge arises out of the coming together of Prakṛti and Puruṣa. Prakṛti and Puruṣa complement each other, the former providing the objects of knowledge, and the latter the principle of consciousness. Neither Prakṛti nor Puruṣa is in itself capable of producing knowledge. The Sāṁkhya epistemology is also realist in that it holds that external objects actually possess the properties and relations that we apprehend in our perceptions of them. Nevertheless, the Sāṁkhya maintains that the knowing subject is not a passive spectator of the world but plays an active role in the production of knowledge. This is not to say that our knowledge is purely subjective and lacks any objective basis. What the Sāṁkhya means by the "active role of the knowing subject" is that, of the innumerable aspects, properties, and relations of the objects constituting the world, the subject selects and concentrates on some and ignores the others. This results in a perspectival theory of knowledge, according to which different persons perceive reality differently because of the differences in their perspectives. What is more, the same person experiences the world differently at different times. How a certain person experiences the world at a certain time depends upon a number of factors, the most important of which include the dispositions of the person as deriving from the *karma* of his past existence. The point of all these observations is that the Sāṁkhya considers reality much richer and more complex than can be grasped from any single perspective. The Sāṁkhya reminds us, however, that this does not mean that perspectives are merely subjective and hence do not reveal the real. Quite the contrary, each perspective reveals to us a certain aspect of the world. In defense of this claim the Sāṁkhya points out that different perspectives overlap, and that this cannot be the case unless there is in reality an objective basis for the perspectives.[35] True, the Sāṁkhya admits, more often than not perspectives disagree; but he quickly points out a truth that we are prone to overlook: there can be no disagreement unless there is some agreement. The agreement is due to the fact that the sense organs, *manas, ahaṁkāra,* and *buddhi,* of different persons have evolved from the single Prakṛti. The disagreement is to be accounted for in terms of the differences in the degree and nature of the ignorance that afflicts different men.

God [36]

The Sāṁkhya system, as formulated by its founder Kapila, is avowedly atheistic. Kapila teaches not only that the existence of God cannot be proved but also that God does not exist.[37] The following are the Sāṁkhya arguments against the existence of God. They are not so much proofs for the nonexistence of God as refutations of arguments for the existence of God.

The main target of the Sāṁkhya critique is the view that God is the first cause of the world. The Sāṁkhya points out that if, as the defenders of God's existence claim, God is eternal, permanent, and unchanging, he cannot be the cause of the world; for to be a cause is to interact and consequently to undergo change in time. Thus it would be self-contradictory to hold that God is both eternal and unchanging and also the cause of the world. Therefore God does not and cannot exist. This conclusion also follows from the *satkāryavāda* view of causation which the Sāṁkhya upholds. Prakṛti is ever active and changing. If God is the cause of Prakṛti, then by the *satkāryavāda* God too must be active and changing. But this contradicts the assertion that God is unchanging. Hence God does not exist. According to the Sāṁkhya, Prakṛti is the first cause of the physical world and needs no God for its existence, evolution, or dissolution.[38]

The opponents of the Sāṁkhya contend that Prakṛti, being physical and unconscious, cannot evolve unless guided by an intelligent being; such a being, they claim, is God. The Sāṁkhya rejects this argument by saying that it is essentially the same as the earlier argument; for guiding something is an action, and to act is to undergo change. Thus if God is the guiding agent of Prakṛti, he cannot be eternal and unchanging. God, therefore, does not exist.

The Sāṁkhya also rejects the argument for the existence of God based on his goodness. It is an incontestable fact, argues the Sāṁkhya, that there is an enormous amount of suffering and misery in the world. But if God is an all-good being, it is absurd that he should cause (or guide the evolution of Prakṛti into) such a world as we know. Hence God cannot be both an all-good being and the cause or guiding intelligence of the world.

Finally, one may want to argue against the Sāṁkhya that God is the creator of Prakṛti as well as Puruṣa. The Sāṁkhya counters this argument by saying that if anything is creatable then it is also destructible. But both Prakṛti and Puruṣa are eternal and indestructible. As such, they cannot be the creations of anything, including God.

The Sāṁkhya points out that the argument for the existence of God in terms of his purpose also leads to absurdity. If God is perfect, as the defenders of his existence claim, he lacks nothing and hence cannot have any desire or purpose; for only imperfect beings can entertain desires and purposes. Thus to say that God is perfect and has a purpose in creating the world is contradictory. Consequently, God does not exist.[39]

We should point out that not all Sāṁkhya philosophers endorse Kapila's atheism. Certain later interpretations of the Sāṁkhya system are clearly theistic.[40] For example, in his *Sāṁkhya-pravacana-bhāṣya,* Vijñānabhikṣu argues that without God we cannt explain the evolution of Prakṛti. We shall discuss other theistic interpretations of Sāṁkhya in the chapter on Yoga.

Bondage and Salvation[41]

We have seen that, according to the Sāṁkhya, the self is eternal, uncaused, and all-pervading. It is wholly passive and has neither will nor knowledge. The self is pure consciousness. But in its ignorance the self identifies itself with the *manas, ahaṁkāra,* and *mahat,* which are products of Prakṛti (the non-self). It is through such false identification that the self falls victim to illusion and comes to feel that it is the experiencer of pain and suffering. In this manner, the self develops attachment to the objects of the world. Such an attachment constitutes its state of bondage and unfreedom. And as long as the self is ignorant of its true being, its attachment to the non-self, and consequently its state of bondage, will continue in accordance with the law of *karma*. The self thus becomes entangled in the cycle of births and deaths. It is clear that the Sāṁkhya school, like all other Indian schools, regards ignorance as the root cause of bondage and suffering. Accordingly, salvation consists in the self's breaking the chains of ignorance and illusion, thereby realizing its true being as Puruṣa, eternal, immortal, free, and utterly independent of Prakṛti. That is, liberating knowledge is the knowledge that the self is neither the ego nor the mind nor the intellect nor any other product or aspect of Prakṛti; it is beyond space and time and pleasure and pain. Such knowledge is called *vivekajñāna* (discriminatory knowledge),[42] for it is the knowledge of the self's absolute distinction from Prakṛti.[43] In contrast, ignorance is known as *aviveka,* the failure to discriminate between the self and the non-self. The Sāṁkhya warns us against thinking that liberation and freedom of the self are the result of its development from a less perfect to a more perfect state. The reason for this is that the self in its true being as Puruṣa is eternally beyond joy and sorrow and hence beyond perfection and imperfection. It is correct, then, to say that for the Sāṁkhya salvation does not consist in the attainment of moral or intellectual perfection but in the knowledge of the total and eternal independence of the self from the non-self.[44] This is not to say that moral and mental perfection is irrelevant to the attainment of liberation. Quite the contrary, for while in bondage to Prakṛti the self can only discover its state of bondage through the operation of the intellect. In this manner, intellectual perfection is necessary for the self to know that its present state of unfreedom is due to its ignorance. It is also important to note that as long as the self attaches itself to the objects (and the pleasures and pains they bring) of Prakṛti, it cannot become aware of its bondage. Thus calming the senses and mastering desires and passions is necessary for the self to discern its true nature. In this manner, moral perfection becomes relevant to the attainment of freedom and salvation.

Since, according to the Sāṁkhya, the self is eternally free and independent of Prakṛti, salvation is not something to be attained or looked forward to after the death of the physical body. In other words, salvation is not a spatio-temporal, causally determined event. If it were, it would be absurd for the Sāṁkhya to say that the self in its true being is eternal and free. Quite the contrary, says the Sāṁkhya, salvation is to be attained here and now, while one is still living. It does not even make sense to talk about one's *realizing* anything when one does not exist in a physical body. He who realizes the absolute and eternal independence of the self from Prakṛti is known as *jīvanmukta*—one who is free while still alive. The *jīvanmukta,* although he still has a physical body, is free from all passion and attachment because of his realization of the true nature of his self. He has broken the *karmic* chain which binds him to Prakṛti and has therefore emancipated himself from the round of births and deaths. The death of the *jīvanmukta* is consequently his final and total liberation from all manifestations, gross and subtle, of the Prakṛti.[45] Such a state of absolute freedom and final isolation of the self from Prakṛti is known as *kaivalya* (or *videhamukti,* freedom without body).

The question now arises: Is there a method, a discipline, a technique by which man can cut through the veil of ignorance, the source of suffering and bondage, and realize his true nature as the eternally free Puruṣa? The Sāṁkhya teaches that there is indeed such a discipline and it is the Yoga, the topic of our next chapter.

Chapter VI

Yoga

Introduction

Yoga[1] is a uniquely Indian discipline of theory and practice for the realization of the ultimate truth concerning man and the world. Contrary to the belief, common even in scholarly circles, that Yoga sprang from the Vedic culture of the Āryans, its roots are to be found in the Dravidian culture of pre-Āryan India. The archaeological excavations of Harappa and Mohenjo-daro clearly reveal the non-Āryan origin of Yoga.[2] The great achievement of the Vedic Āryans, then, did not lie in founding Yoga but in incorporating it into the Vedic wisdom and perfecting it.

Yoga is an integral part of all Indian philosophies, orthodox and unorthodox alike, which concern themselves with the attainment of the highest wisdom and spiritual realization of man. Thus Jainism, Buddhism, and Hinduism (whether in the form of Sāṁkhya, Nyāya, Vaiśeṣika, or Vedānta) recognize and recommend the practice of Yoga in one form or another. We do not know when exactly Yoga became a school of philosophy, but we do know that Patañjali's *Yoga-sūtras* is the first and most systematic and authoritative presentation of Yoga in both its theoretical and practical aspects. Other important works of the Yoga school include Vyāsa's *Yoga-bhāṣya* (commentary on *Yoga-sūtras*), Vācaspati Misra's *Tattva-vaiśāradī* (commentary on *Yoga-bhāṣya*), Bohjarāja's *Yoga-sūtra-vṛtti,* and Vijñānabhikṣu's *Yoga-sāra-saṁgraha.* Besides these, there are innumerable expositions and interpretations of Yoga, both ancient and modern.

Metaphysics and Epistemology

As a system of philosophy, Yoga is traditionally regarded as being closely associated with Sāṁkhya. The reason for this is twofold. On the one hand, Sāṁkhya explicitly acknowledges Yoga as the practical means to the realization of the various truths taught by Sāṁkhya as a theory of reality; on the other hand, the Yoga school regards the Sāṁkhya as providing the theoretical basis and interpretation of Yoga as a practice and technique for attaining liberation (*kaivalya*). That is, the Yoga school accepts Sāṁkhya metaphysics and epistemology as the most appropriate and adequate rational framework for the discipline of Yoga. In this way, the two schools complement each other. Nevertheless, there are certain important differences between them. Though both Sāṁkhya and Yoga hold that there is not one but many Puruṣas, Yoga, unlike Sāṁkhya, also teaches that there is God (Īśvara), the Supreme Puruṣa or Self.[3] No other self, even in the wholly liberated state of *kaivalya,* can be identical with or equal to the Supreme Puruṣa, because the latter, unlike the former, has never been and cannot be in bondage to Prakṛti. Further, according to the Yoga, the Supreme Puruṣa is also a person, eternally free from the pain and misery of physical existence, which can only plague the other Puruṣas. The Supreme Puruṣa, however, is not the whole of reality, for besides him there exist Prakṛti and other Puruṣas. In other words, because of the very existence of Prakṛti and other Puruṣas, the Supreme Puruṣa, notwithstanding his highest power and perfection, cannot be the sole reality. The Yoga school offers, among others, two arguments for the existence of the Supreme Puruṣa. Since Prakṛti is purely physical and hence lacks consciousness, its unmistakably goal-directed evolution cannot have been due to Prakṛti itself.

There must therefore be some being of the highest wisdom, power, and perfection as the guiding intelligence behind the evolution of Prakṛti. Further, since Prakṛti does not and cannot begin to evolve except by contact with Puruṣa, Yoga argues that the Supreme Puruṣa is needed to bring the other Puruṣas, who are imperfect, into contact with Prakṛti to start its evolution. By his very persence, the Supreme Puruṣa prompts and influences the other Puruṣas to interact with Prakṛti, thereby triggering its evolution. It should be emphasized, however, that the Yoga does not regard the Supreme Puruṣa as the creator of either the Prakṛti or the other Puruṣas. The other argument for the existence of the Supreme Puruṣa is based on the concept of gradations of perfection. The Yoga points out that there can be no talk of gradations except in the light of a lower and a higher limit. Prakṛti, altogether lacking perfection, is the lower limit; and since Puruṣas are of varying degrees of perfection, there must be a being as the upper limit of perfection. Obviously, only a Puruṣa and not Prakṛti can be such a being. That most perfect being is indeed God, the Supreme Puruṣa. We may note that this Yoga argument for the existence of the Supreme Puruṣa is strikingly similar to one of Thomas Aquinas' Five Ways.[4]

Patañjali himself does not recognize any theoretical necessity for the existence of God. His reason for introducing God as an integral part of the system of Yoga is purely practical—to inspire men by providing them with a model of the highest perfection of knowledge and power.[5] Meditation upon God as the Supreme Puruṣa not only makes man keenly aware of his own imperfections but also inspires him to free himself from them. Further, God as the Supreme Person, capable of perfect love and mercy, can help man in his struggle against ignorance and bondage. By a complete surrender of oneself to the Supreme Puruṣa, one overcomes the greatest obstacle to liberation, namely, egoism and all its attendant suffering and evil. Nevertheless, Patañjali teaches that not all forms of Yoga require devotion to God, and consequently Yoga can serve even the atheist as a means to freedom and liberation.[6]

Structure of the Yoga-sūtras

Patañjali's *Yoga-sūtras* consists of four parts (*pādas*). The first part, known as *samādhipāda,* is a general introduction to the nature, goal, and methods of Yoga in its various forms. It also describes the various modifications of the internal organ, *citta,* as well as the different Yogic techniques leading to the cessation of the modifications. The second part, called the *sādhanapāda,* is concerned with an analysis of suffering, its causes, and its elimination. Under the causes of suffering are discussed not only mental states but also actions, their fruits, attachment to the fruits, therewith *karma* and bondage. The third part, entitled *vibhūtipāda,* deals with Yoga psychology, including paranormal phenomena and the acquisition of supernormal powers. The fourth and final part, the *kaivalyapāda,* deals with liberation (*kaivalya*), the reality of the self as the transcendent Puruṣa, and various realms of being.

The aim of Yoga, according to Patañjali, is to obtain that knowledge which frees man from the shackles of Prakṛti. It is the knowledge that the self in its true being is immortal, all-pervading, and absolutely independent of Prakṛti. Such knowledge at once destroys the ignorance and illusion that bind the self to Prakṛti, and reveals the real being of the self as Puruṣa (pure consciousness) in its eternal splendor. The liberating knowledge cannot be had unless man subdues his senses, desires, and passions, and acquires perfect calm and tranquillity. In other words, complete control and mastery of the internal organ (the complex of *buddhi, ahaṁkāra,* and *manas*), which Patañjali refers to as *citta,* is the most important part of Yogic practice.[7] Yoga, as expounded by Patañjali, is known as the *aṣṭāṅga-yoga,*[8] the eight-limbed Yoga, on account of the eight constituent steps and stages.

Yogic Meditation

The aspirant for Yogic knowledge must prepare himself for embarking on Yogic concentration and meditation.

This preparation consists in the practice of certain physical and mental exercises and several observances such as cleanliness, contentment, truthfulness, nonviolence, nonpossessiveness, nonacquisitiveness. These exercises and observances are known as the first five *aṅgas* of Yoga: *yama, niyama, āsana, praṇāyāma,* and *pratyāhāra.* The first two eliminate distractions arising from uncontrolled desires and emotions. *Āsana* and *praṇāyāma* eliminate disturbances arising from the physical body. The function of *pratyāhāra* is to detach the sense organs from the mind, thus cutting the mind off from the external world and the sense impressions produced on it by the external world. The subject's mind is now completely isolated from the world and is therefore ready to practice concentration and meditation without any distractions, bodily or mental. Freed from all kinds of hindrances, be they beliefs, desires, emotions, theories, or feelings, the mind is now in a position to direct full attention to any object whatever and grasp it in its primordiality. But before the subject can arrive at the originary or primordial intuition, he has to pass through three stages of concentration, namely, *dhāraṇā, dhyana,* and *samādhi,* the last three *aṅgas* of Patañjali's Yoga. Attainment of *samādhi* is the first goal of Yogic meditation, but, contrary to popular belief, it is not the ultimate goal. It is merely the stage which opens the door to *kaivalya,* variously known as *mokṣa,* "final liberation," and "total freedom from bondage." We come now to a consideration of the three stages of meditation.

Dhāraṇā. "Concentration is the confining of the mind within a limited mental area (object of concentration)." [9] In ordinary thinking, the mind constantly shifts from one object to another. What the subject aims at in the *dhāraṇā* stage is to keep the mind continuously engaged in the consideration of one object and to bring it quickly back to the object whenever it shifts to some other object. Thus in this stage the mind is fixed and is yet variable in that it shifts away from the chosen object of concentration, and the success of the subject is measured according to the frequency with which his mind shifts. The smaller the number of shifts and interruptions, the more successful the *dhāraṇā*.

Dhyāna. "Uninterrupted flow (of the mind) toward the object (chosen for meditation) is contemplation." [10] Thus the subject passes from the *dhāraṇā* to the *dhyāna* stage by being able to keep the mind steadily on one and only one object. Here it will be helpful to introduce and explain the meaning of *pratyaya*. The term refers to the total content of the mind at any given time. This does not mean the total information of a mind at any given time. It merely refers to the content which is the object of meditation. In order to understand this better, it is enough to note that in ordinary thinking the mind is constantly shifting from one *pratyaya* to another, and in *dhāraṇā* the frequency of *pratyaya* change is made very small. In the *dhyāna* this *frequency* is reduced to zero; that is, the mind has now one and only one object as its total content. Even so, it is important to note that the mind is variable, the shifting taking place within the limits of the *pratyaya*. This is no defect or disadvantage, but is in fact how it should be, for the purpose of *dhyāna* is to study the chosen object in its various aspects. The point here can be illustrated by analogy with the use of a microscope. When one focuses the microscope on an object, one is directing attention to one object, which is the *pratyaya*. But one also scans the various parts of the object; one's attention is shifting but only within the limits of the *pratyaya*. Thus the Yogic aspirant reaches the *dhyāna* stage when he is able to hold his mind on one *pratyaya*. The success of the student is judged by the frequency of *pratyaya*-change and hence the frequency of his efforts to bring the mind back into the chosen *pratyaya*. The lower these frequencies, the more successful is *dhyāna*.

Samādhi. "The same (contemplation) when there is consciousness only of the object of meditation and not of itself (the mind) is *samādhi*." [11] This is an extremely important *sūtra* and needs detailed explanation. First one would like to ask: If the subject has been able to keep his mind on the object, where is the need to go beyond *dhyāna* to the *samādhi* stage? What is to be gained by this additional step? It is true that as the student progresses from *dhāraṇā* to *dhyāna* his concentration increases and hence he knows the object much more clearly and intimately than in ordinary thinking. In the *dhāraṇā* and *dhyāna* stages all distractions are removed and the mind is occupied with one single object. Nevertheless, there is yet one distraction which prevents the subject from seeing the essence of the object, and that distraction is the subject's awareness of himself. This awareness stands between him and the object, no matter how slightly, and prevents the object from being grasped in its primordiality. This distraction is to be eliminated by going from the *dhyāna* to the *samādhi* stage, in which all self-awareness of the mind disappears and the object shines in its primordiality. This point becomes clearer if we consider briefly Patañjali's view of the manifested world. According to Patañjali, everything in manifestation has two forms: *rūpa* and *svarūpa*. *Rūpa* is the superficial and inessential form, and *svarūpa* is the essential form. Thus, during *dhyāna,* the *rūpa* of the mind is its *pratyaya* (the object of meditation), and it is through this that the mind finds expression. The *svarūpa* is the residual consciousness of the mind's own action and role in the process of *dhyāna* and is essentially the subjective nature of the mind. As one goes from *dhāraṇā* to *dhyāna,* the mind's residual consciousness of itself becomes weaker and weaker, and the concentration of the object stronger and stronger. Thus in the *dhyāna* state, the *svarūpa* of the mind is still there, albeit in a weak manner. When one goes to the *samādhi,* the *svarūpa* (residual awareness of the mind of itself) completely disappears, giving place to the object; that is, there now takes place the fusion of the mind with its object—the fusion of the subject and the object. There are no longer two things here; there is only one, pure consciousness, which is not an object. At this point the structure of consciousness and that of the object coincide.

"In the case of one whose modifications of the mind have been almost annihilated, fusion or entire absorption in one another of the cognizer, cognition, and cognized is brought about as in the case of a transparent jewel (resting on a coloured surface)." [12] It is obvious that the clear jewel in this *sūtra* is the mind which undergoes no modifications—not even those due to self-awareness, for self-awareness itself is eliminated in the *samādhi* state—and the colored surface is the object of meditation. The object is grasped in its primordial reality without any modifications imposed upon it by the mind. The pure, real, internal knowledge regarding the object is isolated from the mixed, external object, and the Yogi can then know the real object by making the mind one with it. Such, then, is the nature of *samādhi* and knowledge obtained through it. The three stages, *dhāraṇa, dhyāna* and *samādhi,* taken together constitute what Patañjali calls the *saṁyama.*[13] According to Patañjali, in the *samādhi* state the subject is freed from the brain-bound intellect and acquires intuition, known as *buddhi* or *prajñā.* It is through this intuition that the Yogi grasps the subtler and profounder aspects of objects in the manifested universe.

Saṁyama can be performed on any object whatever, and knowledge of it at different levels can be obtained. Thus Patañjali classifies knowledge as *śabda, artha,* and *jñāna. Śabda* is knowledge based on words alone. *Artha* is the knowledge which the Yogi seeks, the true knowledge of any object whatever as grasped by intuition in the *samādhi* state. *Jñāna* is knowledge based on perception and reasoning, under which come all empirical sciences. Patañjali also distinguishes between the *savitarka* and *nirvitarka samādhi* stages. In the former, the separation of knowledge into the above three kinds takes place; in the latter, which is the culmination of the *saṁyama,* the pure, real, internal knowledge regarding the object is obtained, and the Yogi then knows the real object through making the mind one with it.

Yogic Knowledge

The knowledge obtained through Yogic meditation is not to be confused with ordinary kinds of knowledge, for instance, common sense and scientific knowledge. The latter are always based on presuppositions which cannot be validated within the disciplines themselves. Thus Patañjali says that "the knowledge based on inference or testimony is different from direct knowledge obtained in the higher states of consciousness because it (the former) is confined to a particular object or aspect." [14] For Patañjali there are three sources of right knowledge in the realm of intellect: direct cognition, inference, and testimony. Direct cognition through sense organs plays a very limited role and cannot itself provide knowledge unless corrected, checked, and supplemented by inference and testimony. But the knowledge obtained through *prajñā* (intuition) is based on neither testimony nor inference but on direct cognition. This cognition is different from direct cognition through sense organs and is free from the error and illusion which bedevil the latter. The Yogi's knowledge is thus through and through intuitive and nonconceptual. One may say that this kind of knowledge is nonrational. It should be noted that "nonrational" is not the same as "irrational," for the latter means opposition to reason and intellect, whereas the former means something that is outside the province of reason and intellect. This simply means that the intuitive knowledge of the Yogi is radically different from conceptual, mediated, intellectual knowledge. It does not mean that Yogic knowledge is necessarily opposed to intellect and reason, but simply that it transcends reason and intellect.

One may ask here whether knowledge so obtained can be used as a basis for intellectual knowledge, such as that of the sciences. The Yogic answer to this question is "yes" at one level and "no" at another. In the *savitarka* stage of *samādhi* the separation of knowledge into three kinds, *śabda, artha,* and *jñāna,* takes place, and by going to the stage of *nirvitarka* (nondiscriminatory) *samādhi* the Yogi obtains the pure knowledge of the object. Thus if one stops at the *savitarka* stage, surely one can obtain the *jñāna* component, knowledge based on perception and reasoning, and use it as a basis for constructing conceptual knowledge. But the knowledge attained at the *nirvitarka* stage cannot be so used. This does not mean that it cannot be used at all by the Yogi. On the contrary, the Yogi makes full use of such knowledge by directly reaching the corresponding plane of consciousness. He does not employ any instruments, perceptions, or concepts for acquiring and using such knowledge. Thus Patañjali says, "Thence, instantaneous cognition without the use of any vehicle and complete mastery over *Pradhāna* (manifested universe)." [15] Consequently, it seems correct to say that the Yogi's knowledge is of the noumena (things-in-themselves).

The Yogi, very much like Kant, maintains that intellectual, perceptual, conceptual knowledge is of phenomena only. But with that he parts company with Kant, for according to Kant it is not given to man to have knowledge of the noumena.[16] The Yogi emphatically rejects this position and claims that man can know the noumena through Yoga. (The difference between Kant and the Yogi can in part be explained in terms of the difference between their respective cultural traits. Thus the finitude of man, his limited perfectibility, and his dependence on the grace of God are among the central tenets of Christianity, an integral part of Kant's heritage. For the Yogi, on the other hand, man is infinitely perfectible and is God himself. Therefore there is nothing that he cannot know. These notions are indeed part of the cultural heritage of the Yogi.)

Kaivalya (Liberation)

The Yogi, by sinking deeper and deeper into his own consciousness, realizes the state of pure subjectivity, which is not an object. He also realizes that the ordinary feeling of his involvement with Prakṛti is the product of illusion and ignorance (*avidyā*). Thus in the *nirbījasamādhi,* the *samādhi* in which there is no seed or object at all, the seeker himself becomes the object. This is the final goal of all Yoga, the attainment of the highest consciousness, the realization of transcendental subjectivity, the self discovering its own nature as the immortal Puruṣa. He who thus knows his true being as eternal Puruṣa (the transcendent subject), as absolutely distinct from Prakṛti, attains *kaivalya,* the state of absolute freedom from bondage and ignorance.

Concluding Remarks

In conclusion, we may note the following important points of general similarities and differences between the various Indian schools. According to Sāṁkhya and Yoga, the goal of Yoga is the self's realization of its true nature as the immortal and all-pervading Puruṣa, utterly separate from Prakṛti. For Advaita Vedānta,[17] the goal of Yoga is the realization of the fundamental unity and identity of the individual self with the absolute self, Brahman. For the Nyāya-Vaiśeṣika,[18] the end of Yoga is the elimination of all pleasure and pain and joy and sorrow and therewith the attainment of a state of total repose, devoid of even consciousness. Advaita Vedānta, Sāṁkhya, and Yoga disagree with the Nyāya-Vaiśeṣika on this point. Thus, according to Advaita Vedānta, the liberated state of the self is one of pure bliss; for Sāṁkhya and Yoga, it is one of pure consciousness. Another important difference in the context of Yoga concerns God. Sāṁkhya rejects God as both creator and designer of the universe. Yoga admits God as the most perfect Puruṣa, instrumental in bringing about the evolution of the purely physical, unconscious Prakṛti. For Yoga, God is also the Supreme Person who, in his perfect knowledge and power, aids men in attaining salvation. For the Nyāya-Vaiśeṣika, God is not only the creator but also the designer of the universe. Advaita Vedānta recognizes God but maintains that he is not the ultimate reality. Only Nirguṇa-Brahman, the undifferentiated pure being, is the ultimate reality. According to Advaita Vedānta, God is thus Brahman thought of by imperfect men as having qualities and capable of bestowing love, grace, and mercy on men. Advaita Vedānta does not recognize any creator of the universe. The universe is Brahman, eternal, unborn, and uncreated.

In spite of all these theoretical differences, all Indian schools, with the single exception of the Cārvāka, recognize and recommend the practice of Yoga for attaining *mokṣa*. This fact in itself is ringing testimony to Yoga as the spiritual discipline *par excellence.*

Chapter VII

Vaiśeṣika

Introduction

It is generally believed that Vaiśeṣika originated as an unorthodox (non-Vedic) system but eventually turned orthodox by accepting the authority of the Vedas in certain matters. Vaiśeṣika is younger than Sāṁkhya and at least as old as Jainism and Buddhism. A sage named Kaṇāda was the founder of the Vaiśeṣika system. Naturally enough, Kaṇāda's *Vaiśeṣika-sūtra* (*The Principles of Vaiśeṣika*) was the first systematic work of this school. In course of time, there appeared a number of expository and commentarial works, the most important of which include Praśastapāda's *Padārtha-dharma-saṅgraha,* Udayana's *Kiraṇāvalī,* and Śrīdhara's *Nyāyakandalī.*

The school derives its name from its great emphasis on the category of particularity (*vaiśeṣa*). Vaiśeṣika is also known as "the atomistic school" because of its elaborate atomic theory. The ordinary meaning of the term *vaiśeṣa* is distinguishing quality or feature. But in the context of the Vaiśeṣika vaiśeṣa means particularity, of which atoms are only one exemplification. In other words, the Vaiśeṣika school recognizes various kinds of particulars besides atoms. Thus it would be best to understand Vaiśeṣika as the school whose central tenet is that existence is constituted through and through of particulars, some of which are atomic, and others nonatomic.

The Vaiśeṣika system is essentially an ontology, in that its main concern is not with logical and epistemological matters but with the enumeration and delineation of the ultimate constituents of the universe. For this reason, it may also be regarded as a system of descriptive metaphysics. It may be mentioned in passing that Nyāya school takes over the Vaiśeṣika ontology and defends it with sophisticated logical and epistemological analyses.

Metaphysics and the Categories

Vaiśeṣika metaphysics is pluralistic realism. It is pluralistic on account of its central claim that variety, diversity, and plurality are the warp and woof of reality; in other words, ultimate reality is constituted of irreducible particulars. Vaiśeṣika is realism because of its teaching that reality as particulars exists independently of our perceptions. Thus Vaiśeṣika rejects monism, whether materialistic or idealistic. It is to be noted, however, that Vaiśeṣika is not materialistic pluralism, for its pluralism includes not only material but also nonmaterial entities, for example, souls (selves). Further, Vaiśeṣika metaphysics is substance metaphysics as contrasted with the process (flux) metaphysics of Buddhism.

The Vaiśeṣika term for category is *padārtha,* whose literal meaning is "the meaning of a word" as well as "the thing or object referred to or signified by a word." Thus *padārtha* stands for all objects which can be thought, named, experienced, or inferred. In the context of Vaiśeṣika metaphysics, *padārtha* is the category under which all knowable things are to be comprehended. Vaiśeṣika recognizes seven *padārthas*—categories of objects making up the world.[1] They are as follows: (1) substance (*dravya*), (2) quality (*guṇa*), (3) action (*karma*), (4) generality (*sāmānya*), (5) particularity (*vaiśeṣa*), (6) inherence (*samavāya*), and (7) nonexistence (*abhāva*). It may be mentioned that the founder of the system did not regard nonexistence as a separate category and accordingly listed only the first six categories. Nevertheless, since he did discuss nonexistence as a possible object of knowledge, later writers considered nonexistence to be an independent category and consequently added it to the original list of six.

1. *Substance (Dravya)*.[2] Substance is that in which qualities and actions exist. It is thus the substratum of qualities and actions. According to the Vaiśeṣika, although substances can exist independently of qualities and actions, these cannot exist independently of substances. Being the substratum, substance is also the material cause of things. Substances are of two kinds: material and nonmaterial. Further, substances may be composite, transient, and finite, or simple, ultimate, eternal, and infinitesimal or infinite. Composite substances are made up of ultimate substances;[3] the former can be produced and destroyed, whereas the latter can neither be produced nor be destroyed—in short, they are eternal. It is clear, then, that according to the Vaiśeṣika anything which is composite and hence has parts and is divisible cannot be eternal; only the simple, indivisible, and noncomposite is eternal.

The Vaiśeṣika recognizes five material substances: (1) earth, (2) water, (3) fire, (4) air, and (5) ether (*ākāśa*).[4] Each of these substances has a *unique* quality by possessing which it is what it is. Thus, smell is the peculiar quality of earth, taste that of water, color that of fire, touch that of air, and sound that of *ākāśa*. It is worth emphasizing that to say that every material substance of a certain kind possesses a unique quality is not the same as saying that it does not possess other qualities but simply that it is distinguishable from material substances of other kinds by its unique quality. Thus, what distinguishes earth from the other four substances is not taste, touch, color, or sound, but smell, which only it has. Further, according to the Vaiśeṣika, since we sense the various qualities each by a specific sense organ, each sense organ is constituted of the respective substance.

The substances earth, water, fire, and air exist in two

forms: (1) composite and transient and (2) simple and eternal.[5] As eternal substances, they exist in the form of indivisible atoms (*paramāṇus*), which are not finite but infinitesimal. Atoms are uncreatable and indestructible. All gross objects, such as trees, mountains, cups, and saucers, exist as composite substances. They can be produced and destroyed. But the atoms of which they are constituted can be neither produced nor destroyed. According to the Vaiśeṣika, atomic substances are not perceivable but can only be inferred. Thus when an object, say a rock, is broken into fragments, which in turn are further broken into smaller fragments, and so on, we should arrive at entities which are not further divisible; such ultimate, indivisible entities are atoms. But one might ask: Why cannot the process of division of an object go on indefinitely? The Vaiśeṣika answers by saying that if the process of division can continue indefinitely, then two objects of vastly different magnitudes—for example, a stone and a mountain—must both contain the same number of atoms. But this cannot be the case, for then we would not be able to explain the undeniable fact that one of the objects is smaller than the other. Therefore, the Vaiśeṣika continues, in order that we may account for the observed differences in magnitude, we should require that the process of division and subdivision terminate at some point, namely, that at which we reach entities not further divisible.[6] The Vaiśeṣika further maintains that since each of the four material substances, earth, water, fire, and air, has a characteristic quality, there must be four different kinds of atoms as ultimate material substances. In other words, all atoms of a given kind have the same characteristic quality. Thus, all atoms of water are alike and are different from all atoms of earth. The reason why the Vaiśeṣika says that atoms themselves have qualities is that otherwise we would not be able to explain the observed qualitative differences between objects—for example, between water and earth. The Vaiśeṣika offers the following account of the process of formation of objects from the atoms. Atoms are infinitesimal,[7] supersensible, and originally lack motion. God imparts motion to the otherwise inactive atoms. Two atoms combine to form the dyad, which is also infinitesimal and imperceivable. Three dyads combine to form the triad, which is the smallest perceivable object of finite magnitude. The Vaiśeṣika example of the triad is the mote in the sunbeam. All objects of the material world, including our bodies, are produced by different combinations of triads. In the dyad, the relation between its constitutive atoms is called *saṁyoga* ("conjunction") and the relation between the dyad as a whole and its atoms is called *samavāya* ("inherence").[8] Similar considerations hold with respect to the triad. The triad, which is the whole, stands in the relation of *samavāya* to the three dyads constituting it, whereas the three dyads are related to each other through *saṁyoga*. The Vaiśeṣika point here is that, whereas parts are merely conjoined to each other, the whole inheres in the parts. We shall have more to say later about the Vaiśeṣika concepts of conjunction and inherence.

At this point, we may draw attention to some important differences between Vaiśeṣika atomism and the Greek atomism of Leucippus and Democritus. According to the Vaiśeṣika, atoms differ not only in quantity but also in quality. Thus, water atoms differ both qualitatively and quantitatively from fire atoms. This is another way of saying that for the Vaiśeṣika atoms have secondary qualities, such as taste, smell, color, and touch. In contrast, according to Greek atomism atoms are devoid of secondary qualities, and hence are all alike and can only be distinguished quantitatively and numerically; consequently, observed differences in the qualities of objects are due to differences in the number and configuration of their constituent atoms.[9] A second difference between Vaiśeṣika and Greek atomism is that whereas according to the former atoms originally lack motion, according to the latter atoms are active and exist in a state of incessant motion. This leads us to another significant difference. Since according to the Vaiśeṣika atoms are originally inactive and lack motion, the Vaiśeṣika requires an agent who set atoms in motion; such an agent is the Vaiśeṣika God. On the other hand, Greek atomism, by making motion inherent to atoms,[10] seeks to explain the evolution of the world in purely mechanical terms. A fourth difference between Vaiśeṣika atomism and Greek atomism is that according to the former souls are radically different from atoms, whereas according to the latter souls are as much the products of atoms as are material objects.[11] Finally, whereas the Vaiśeṣika, through its recognition of God as the efficient cause of the world, sees a moral order in the universe, the Greek atomists seek to explain all aspects of the world, including the moral and spiritual, through the mechanical interplay of the all-sufficient atoms. It should be clear by now that the Vaiśeṣika God is like Aristotle's prime mover.[12]

The fifth material substance, namely, *ākāśa* (ether), not to be confused with space, is the substratum of the quality of sound. Like atoms, *ākāśa* is indivisible, eternal and imperceivable; but, unlike them, it is infinite and all-pervading. *Ākāśa* is inferred from the sensed quality of sound.[13]

We come now to the Vaiśeṣika theory of the nonmaterial substances. There are four nonmaterial substances: (1) space (*dik*), (2) time (*kāla*), (3) soul (*ātman*), and (4) mind (*manas*). Space is one, imperceivable, indivisible, infinite, all-pervading, and eternal.[14] The existence of space is inferred from our cognitions of direction and location, such as east, west, left, right, here, there, near, and far.[15] Time, like space, is one, imperceivable, indivisible, infinite, all-pervading, and eternal. It is inferred from our cognition of temporal modes, such as now and then, past, present, and future, and new and old. Time is thus the substratum of our temporal cognitions.[16] It should be emphasized, however, that the divisions and the distinctions we make in space as well as time are purely conventional and hence do not reflect any real divisions in the indivisible, unitary, all-pervading substances of space and time.[17]

The soul (self, *ātman*), like time and space, is an individual, all-pervading, and eternal substance.[18] It is the substratum of the quality of consciousness.[19] It should be kept in mind that, according to the Vaiśeṣika, consciousness is not an essential quality of the soul, but is merely an accidental quality, which the soul acquires through its association with the body. In other words, when the soul dissociates itself from the body, it no longer has consciousness. The Vaiśeṣika distinguishes between two kinds of souls, the individual soul and the Supreme Soul. Individual souls are many,[20] whereas there is only one Supreme Soul, namely, God (Īśvara). We become aware of ourselves as individual souls through internal perception. Thus when someone says, "I am sad," [21] he is saying that it is his self not his body that is sad.

The mind (*manas*) is also an indivisible, imperceivable, eternal substance; it is the substratum of our internal sense (*antarindriya*).[22] Unlike *ākāśa,* space, time, and soul, mind is atomic;[23] but unlike the material atoms mind cannot give rise to composite entities. Being atomic, mind cannot be perceived but can only be inferred.[24] It is through the operation of the mind that the self comes into contact with objects. The existence of mind is inferred as follows: Just as we need our sense organs, such as the eyes and ears, for perceiving external objects, so also we need an internal sense organ for the perception of internal objects such as the soul, cognition, feeling, and willing. It is of the utmost importance to note that, according to the Vaiśeṣika, mind is necessary even for the perception of external objects; for unless the mind turns its attention to the object with which the external senses are already in contact, there can be no cognition. To put it differently, although our sense organs, such as the eyes and ears, are in contact with an external object, we can only become aware of some particular aspect of the object one at a time—for example, color or smell—owing to the selective attention of the mind on that aspect. The Vaiśeṣika argues that the selective character of perception lends evidence to the existence of mind.[25]

Finally, the Vaiśeṣika recognizes nine ultimate substances in all, of which five are material and four nonmaterial. The five material substances are earth, water, fire, air, and *ākāśa;* of these, only the first four are atomic and infinitesimal, while the fifth is nonatomic, all pervading and hence infinite. All five are imperceivable, indivisible, and eternal. All composite and hence divisible and impermanent substances are perceivable and are made up of the atoms of the four substances, namely, earth, water, fire, and air. The nonmaterial substances are space, time, soul, and mind. All of these are indivisible, all-pervading, and eternal. However, of these only the first three are all-pervading, whereas the last is atomic; but unlike the atomic material substances, mind does not give rise to composite substances. Further, all the nonmaterial substances except the soul are inferred. The soul is directly known through one's awareness of oneself.

2. *Quality* (*Guṇa*). Quality is that which can only exist in a substance as its substratum; that is, qualities cannot exist independently of substances. A quality cannot belong to another quality or action, but only to a substance.[26] Qualities can be either material or mental and are not necessarily eternal.[27] Qualities are completely passive and do not produce any composite object. The Vaiśeṣika recognizes twenty-four qualities, both material and mental:[28] (1) color, (2) taste, (3) smell, (4) touch, (5) sound, (6) number, (7) magnitude, (8) distinctness, (9) conjunction (*saṁyoga*), (10) disjunction, (11) nearness, (12) remoteness, (13) cognition, (14) pleasure, (15) pain, (16) desire, (17) aversion, (18) effort, (19) heaviness, (20) fluidity, (21) viscidity, (22) tendency, (23) moral merit, and (24) moral demerit. One might ask how the Vaiśeṣika arrived at the figure twenty-four for the number of qualities. All one can say in reply is that the exact number is unimportant, and that the number would be greater if one also counted the subdivisions of qualities; for example, one may count under color the various particular colors. It seems reasonable to suppose that the Vaiśeṣika enumeration of qualities is guided by considerations of simplicity and irreducibility. Thus different colors, such as red and blue, can be categorized under color, which itself cannot be reduced to any other quality; similarly, different tastes, such as sweet, sour, and bitter, can be placed under the

category of taste, which itself cannot be reduced to any other quality. We may remind the reader that for the Vaiśeṣika qualities are passive and simple (further unanalyzable) and can only exist in substances.

3. *Action* (*Karma*). Like quality, action can only exist in substance. It always belongs to some substance or other.[29] Whereas quality is static and passive, action is dynamic and transient. In other words, actions and not qualities can be causally efficacious in the production of composite entities. Thus action can separate two entities which exist in disjunction.[30] An action cannot possess another action or quality, for both action and quality can only be supported by substance. The Vaiśeṣika distinguishes five kinds of action:[31] (1) upward movement, (2) downward movement, (3) expansion, (4) contraction, and (5) locomotion. However, not all actions are perceivable. For example, the action of mind, an imperceivable substance, cannot be perceived but can only be inferred through our internal perceptions. In contrast, the actions of all perceivable substances, which are necessarily composite, are perceivable.

4. *Generality* (*Sāmānya*). We are all familiar with the fact that we denote different things of a certain kind by the same term. For example, all horses, irrespective of their differences, are referred to by the term "horse." It is generally believed that the reason why we use the same word to refer to different objects of a certain variety is that all these objects have some property in common. Thus the term "horse" is a general name, since it does not refer to this or that horse, but to horses in general. Words like "horse" are also called "class-names," because they enable us to classify different objects as falling under different concepts. The question now is: What is it that a collection of objects should possess in common in order that they may all be referred to by the same term? The Vaiśeṣika answer to this question is that the various objects under consideration possess a certain common essence. Such a common essence is known as the "universal" (*sāmānya*).[32] But what

is the ontological status of universals? In Indian philosophy, just as in Western philosophy, this question has three different answers: the nominalist, conceptualist, and realist answers.[33]

According to the nominalist, there are no such things as universals (common essences); that is, there is no positive essence that is present in different objects denoted by the same name. What is common, says the nominalist, is merely the name. Thus, Buddhists argue that we refer to a certain group of animals by the term "horse," not because there is present in all these animals a certain common essence, but because they are all unlike all animals which we do not call "horse." In short, the Buddhist maintains that there are no essences but only common names which serve to set apart certain objects from other objects. The Buddhist nominalism is known as *apohavāda*. Nominalism, then, is the doctrine that only particulars and not universals exist.

According to the conceptualist, the universal is not something that exists apart from the particular which exemplifies it. On the contrary, as far as existence is concerned, the universal and the particular are identical. This in turn means that the universal does exist, but not separately from the particulars. The conceptualist warns us against thinking that the universal is merely a name and a figment of our imagination. Quite the contrary, asserts the conceptualist, universals are real existents, but their reality is not independent of or over and above that of the particulars. We may note that Jainism and Advaita Vedānta defend conceptualism.

The Vaiśeṣika upholds thoroughgoing realism with respect to universals. It disagrees with both nominalism and conceptualism and maintains that as essences universals are not only real but independent of the particulars exemplifying them. Thus the Vaiśeṣika teaches that universals and particulars are of equal ontological status. However, the Vaiśeṣika points out that universals are not existents but subsistents. This simply means that universals subsist in substances, qualities, and actions and are nonspatial and nontemporal (eternal).[34] It is worth noting that the

Vaiśeṣika view of universals as nonspatial and nontemporal reals is similar to the Platonic doctrine of the reality of the Ideas. According to the Vaiśeṣika, it is impossible for one universal to subsist in another, for otherwise one and the same thing would have contrary natures. The Vaiśeṣika divides universals into three kinds:[35] (1) Beinghood, which has maximal scope, since all other universals are subsumed under it; (2) Beinghood of a particular kind, which has minimal scope; for example, horseness, under which come all horses; and (3) Thinghood (substancesness, *dravyatva*), the universal whose scope falls between those of the first and the second. This is another way of saying that there are more substances than any particular kind of substance, and that the realm of Being is not exhausted by substance, because Being encompasses, besides substance, quality and action.

5. *Particularity* (*Vaiśeṣa*). As the very name of the school indicates, particularity is the most important and unique of the Vaiśeṣika categories. Particularity, also referred to as "individuality," is best understood as the opposite of generality. According to the Vaiśeṣika, particularity belongs to all substances which are indivisible and eternal.[36] Thus atoms, *ākāśa,* space, time, souls, and minds come under the category of particularity.[37] The Vaiśeṣika doctrine of particularity may at first sound somewhat strange, for one wonders how one can talk about the particularity of indistinguishable entities, for example, the atoms. The Vaiśeṣika reply is that although all atoms of one kind, say water, are qualitatively identical and hence indistinguishable, there must nevertheless be some difference between one atom and another; each atom is different from the others in being a unique individual. Otherwise, continues the Vaiśeṣika, all talk about the plurality of identical atoms is empty and idle. Thus it is particularity that distinguishes a given atom from all the other atoms. It should be emphasized that according to the Vaiśeṣika particularity belongs only to indivisible and eternal entities and not to composite ones like tables and chairs. In other words,

vaiśeṣa is the particularity that can only be predicated of ultimate entities and not of any other entities. Thus we may correctly regard *vaiśeṣa* as the peculiarity by virtue of which something is an ultimate entity. Further, according to the Vaiśeṣika, since there are innumerable particulars (individuals), there must necessarily be innumerable *vaiśeṣas* (particularities). *Vaiśeṣa,* then, is particularity which subsists in individuals.

6. *Inherence* (*Samavāya*). Inherence is also an important and unique Vaiśeṣika category. We shall explain the meaning and significance of this category by drawing attention to the conjoint existence of two objects. Two things which exist separately may be joined to each other in such a way that the act of joining them does not change the nature and mode of existence of the things. Conversely, two entities which exist joined to each other (exist conjointly) may be separated in such a way that the act of separating does not change the nature and mode of their existence. For example, the book on my table can be removed without destroying the nature of the book or that of the table. Also, the book on the floor may be removed and placed on the table without destroying the nature of the book, the table, or the floor. Such a state of conjunction between two objects which can be either brought about or terminated without altering the nature of the objects concerned, the Vaiśeṣika calls *saṁyoga* ("conjunction"). In other words, *saṁyoga* is a contingent, external, mechanical relation between two objects. There is no *inner* necessity to the conjoint existence of two objects.

On the other hand, there is, according to the Vaiśeṣika, another kind of conjoint existence of objects, such that the objects cannot be separated without at the same time destroying one of them. Such conjointness the Vaiśeṣika calls *samavāya* ("inherence").[38] Thus in *samavāya,* unlike *saṁyoga,*[39] one object inheres in the other; consequently, the objects cannot be separated without doing violence to one or other of them. The existence of the whole in parts, of quality and action in substance, of the universal in the particular, of the particularity in an indivisible, eternal individual are all examples of *samavāya*. Thus to say, for example, that the pot inheres in its parts is to say that when we destroy the pot the whole disappears; that is, if we try to separate the parts, the whole will be necessarily destroyed. Similarly, quality inheres in substance and cannot be separated from it. It is clear, then, that according to the Vaiśeṣika, whereas *saṁyoga* is a temporary, contingent, mechanical, and external relation, *samavāya* is an eternal, necessary, and internal relation.[40] Moreover, *samavāya,* unlike *saṁyoga,* is irreversible; for example, it is impossible for substance to inhere in quality or action and for the particular to inhere in the universal. The Vaiśeṣika argument for the eternality of *samavāya* is as follows: Assume *samavāya* is not eternal. This means that two objects which now stand in the relation of *samavāya* some time ago existed separately. But if two things can exist separately, then they can only be brought together through *saṁyoga* and not *samavāya*. Thus to say that two things which once existed in *saṁyoga* now exist in *samavāya* is self-contradictory. Hence the assumption that *samavāya* is not an eternal relation is false; which in turn means that *samavāya* is eternal. It should also be noted that *samavāya* is eternal in the sense that it cannot have a beginning in time. For to say that *samavāya* has a beginning in time is to say that two things which once did not exist in *samavāya* have come into that relation at a certain time. But this implies that *samavāya* can exist between two separable things, which is a contradiction. Hence *samavāya* cannot have a beginning. Nor can *samavāya* have an end. For to say that it has an end is to say that two things which are in *samavāya* can be separated without destroying one of them. But we have seen that, according to the Vaiśeṣika, *samavāya* is a relation which can only be destroyed by destroying one or other of the two entities standing in that relation. One may break the pot, but one would be mistaken in thinking that one had thereby terminated the relation of *samavāya* between the pot and its parts; because once the pot is broken, one *no longer has two entities,* the whole and its parts, but only the parts and hence cannot sensibly talk about any relation between them. Inherence, according to the Vaiśeṣika, is one and not many and is not perceivable but only inferrable.[41]

7. *Nonexistence (Abhāva)*.[42] The Vaiśeṣika holds that nonexistence, like existence, is perceivable. Nonexistence is of four kinds:[43] (1) antecedent nonexistence, (2) subsequent nonexistence, (3) absolute nonexistence, and (4) mutual nonexistence. The Vaiśeṣika regards absolute nonexistence and its logical counterpart, namely, absolute negation, as pseudo-ideas. Just as one cannot perceive pure nothing but always perceives something or other, so also there can be no pure negation but only negation of some affirmation or other. Every negation necessarily implies some affirmation, and perception of the nonexistence of something implies the perception of something else. It is worth noting that the first three kinds of nonexistence can be expressed as "A is not *in* B," and the last as "A is *not* B." Antecedent nonexistence is the absence of something prior to its production: the table does not exist before the carpenter makes it; that is, prior to its making, the nonexistence of the table is *in* the wood. Subsequent nonexistence is the absence of a thing after it is destroyed: the table does not exist after it is consumed by fire; that is, after its destruction, the nonexistence of the table is *in* the ashes. Note that antecedent nonexistence is beginningless but has an end, and subsequent nonexistence has a beginning but has no end. Absolute nonexistence is the absence of one thing *in* another at all times, past, present, and future. Thus, the square is forever absent *in* the circle, the married man is forever absent *in* the bachelor, and color is forever absent *in* space. Mutual nonexistence is the exclusion of one thing by another; it is the absence of any connection between two things because of their difference; thus, being a chair excludes being a flower, and vice versa. To put it differently, the chair is *not* a flower, and the flower is *not* a chair. It is to be noted that although it is a pseudo-idea, absolute nonexistence is beginningless and endless. In short, it is eternal. Similarly, mutual nonexistence is eternal, for two

things which are different from each other exclude each other at all times and under all circumstances.

Epistemology

The Vaiśeṣika epistemology is thin and meager, for the prime concerns of the Vaiśeṣika are ontological. Nevertheless, since ontology can never be wholly divorced from epistemology—that is, the question of what there is cannot be divorced from how we come to know what there is—the Vaiśeṣika does have some, albeit unsystematized, epistemological doctrines. The Vaiśeṣika accepts the two *pramāṇas* (criteria of valid knowledge), namely, perception and inference, and maintains that the other two, comparison and testimony, can be reduced to perception and inference. For this reason, the Vaiśeṣika, unlike the Nyāya, does not regard comparison and testimony as independent *pramāṇas*.

As to the question how knowledge arises, the Vaiśeṣika offers the following answer. Sensations and impressions arise as a result of contact between the sense organs and objects. Sensations and impressions cannot in themselves result in knowledge unless the mind (internal sense organ) turns its active attention to one or other of the incoming sensations and impressions.[44] Thus the selective attention of the mind is necessary for perception as a cognitive act. Without such a role of the mind, one can only be aware of the presence of something but not of that something as this or that kind of object. To be able to identify and recognize objects, one needs to transform pure sensations and impressions into percepts by categorizing the former by means of concepts. It is only when the mind accomplishes such transformation that knowing as a conscious act arises in the soul. It is clear, then, that without the soul, the substratum of consciousness, there can be no knowledge.

The Vaiśeṣika upholds epistemological realism, the doctrine that the perceived qualities and relations of objects are not subjective appearances but belong to the objects independently of our perceptions.[45]

We may note that the Vaiśeṣika maintains the *asatkāryavāda* view of causation, the doctrine that effect is not identical with (does not preexist in) cause.[46] The Vaiśeṣika position concerning the relation between whole and parts best illustrates its *asatkāryavāda*. Thus, whereas the defender of the *satkāryavāda* maintains that the table as effect preexists in the wood, the Vaiśeṣika asserts that the table emerges as a genuinely new object neither identical with nor preexisting in the wood. *Asatkāryavāda* also governs the Vaiśeṣika account of the evolution of objects from atoms. Thus the dyad does not preexist in its constituent atoms but arises as a new entity.

God

Kaṇāda, the founder of the Vaiśeṣika system, has himself little to say about God.[47] There is a remark of his to the effect that the authority of the Vedas is due to their being *tadvacana*.[48] This remark, however, is ambiguous because the term *tadvacana* can be understood as meaning "his word" or "their word." It is highly likely that Kaṇāda meant that the authority and infallibility of the Vedas is due to their being the word of great seers and sages ("their word"). Nevertheless, subsequent Vaiśeṣika writers interpreted Kaṇāda as saying that the Vedas derive their authority and infallibility from being the word of God. This point need not detain us, for almost all the subsequent Vaiśeṣika philosophers defend the existence of God. Even the Nyāya philosophers, who have assimilated the Vaiśeṣika into their own system, are clearly theistic. Thus Udayana, a Nyāya philosopher, offers a series of arguments for the existence of God.[49]

God is the Supreme Soul, perfect, omniscient, and eternal. Guided by the law of *karma* (referred to as *adṛṣṭa*, "the Unseen Power"),[50] God creates, governs, and destroys the world. The Vaiśeṣika holds that the law of *karma*, the Unseen Power, is unintelligent and hence needs the guiding intelligence of God in determining the lots of the various selves. In this manner, the Vaiśeṣika comes to see a moral order in the universe as stemming from God, the most perfect soul and Lord of the universe. It should be borne in mind, however, that God is not creator in the sense that he creates the universe out of nothing. The atoms and other individuals are eternal and hence cannot be the creation of God or any other being. They are co-existent with God. God is called "creator" only in the sense that he is the designer and architect of the universe. Even as designer and architect, his power is not unlimited, owing to the Unseen Power of the law of *karma*. Very much like the Sāṁkhya, the Vaiśeṣika maintains that every creation is followed by destruction, and every destruction by creation, and so on ad infinitum. Having neither a beginning nor an end, the cycle of creation and destruction of the world is an eternally repeating process. Part of the function of God as creator is to impart motion to atoms which originally lack motion. That is, after the destruction of the world the primordial atoms remain in a state of rest and inactivity, and the next creation does not start until God sets the atoms in motion. Whereas in the atomism of Democritus motion is original to atoms, in the Vaiśeṣika atoms originally lack motion and God imparts motion to them, thereby initiating the formation of the elements and other bodies.[51] We may therefore say that for the Vaiśeṣika, whereas atoms and other substances are the material cause of the universe, God, coupled with the Unseen Power of *karma,* is its efficient cause.

Bondage and Liberation

Like all other Indian schools of philosophy, with the exception of the Cārvāka, the Vaiśeṣika regards mundane existence as one of bondage and ignorance[52] concerning the nature of the soul as the cause of bondage; and knowledge as the means to freedom and liberation. In its ignorance, the soul identifies itself with the non-soul, such as the body and mind, and falls prey to desire and passion. Desires and passions drive the soul to actions which in turn breed attachment and bondage in the form of *karma,* thus perpetuating the round of births and deaths. Those actions which are in accord with the *Vedas* breed good *karma,* and those in discord bad *karma;* in any case, the soul has to reap the consequences of every action, good or bad.[53] Thus it is due to its actions that the soul gets firmly entrenched in the karmic mesh. The only way to overcome bondage and suffering is to break the karmic chain through the cessation of all action. Once the soul realizes its true nature as distinct from the body and mind, it can no longer be afflicted by desire and passion and hence will have no urge to act.[54] Thus, according to the Vaiśeṣika, freedom and liberation come with the cessation of all action.[55] The Vaiśeṣika consistently maintains that where there can be no pain there can be no pleasure either. Thus for the Vaiśeṣika liberation is freedom from pain as well as pleasure, sorrow as well as joy. It is to be noted that the Vaiśeṣika conception of salvation as being beyond both pain and pleasure is in contrast with that of the Advaita Vedānta, according to which salvation is a state of pure bliss (*ānanda*). The reason why the Vaiśeṣika rejects the notion of liberation as one of bliss is twofold: knowledge and consciousness are not essential but adventitious qualities of the soul; consequently, if the state of liberation is one in which the soul cannot experience pain, it cannot experience pleasure and bliss either.[56] In short, liberation is the state of utter lack of consciousness, which is necessary for experiencing anything, painful or pleasurable. For the Vaiśeṣika, then, the liberated soul exists as a substance devoid of any attributes, including consciousness. Nevertheless, the Vaiśeṣika teaches that since particularity (*vaiśeṣa*) is an eternal characteristic of the soul, the soul exists as a unique individual even in the liberated state. The most serious objection against this is that, although the Vaiśeṣika asserts on the one hand that the liberated soul lacks all qualities, it asserts on the other that the liberated soul retains its individuality. Particularity, continues the objection, makes sense only with respect to entities which are atomic, and not to an all-pervading entity such as the soul; particularity implies distinguishability of two entities of the same kind. But if two entities are both all-pervading, they cannot be distinguished from each other. Thus the Vaiśeṣika claim of the individuality of liberated souls is unintelligible and unwarranted.

We conclude with a criticism of the Vaiśeṣika conception of God as wholly transcendent to man and the world. It is hard to see how such a God could be the creator, sustainer, and destroyer of the world. Further, the Vaiśeṣika God, lacking power to do anything independently of the law of *karma,* cannot respond to the plight of man by aiding him in his struggle for freedom and liberation. The Vaiśeṣika God satisfies neither the atheist nor the theist; the former rejetcts him as an unnecessary and arbitrary appendage to the all-sufficient law of *karma,* and the latter rejects him as wholly uninspiring and inadequate to the supreme religious quest of union with him.

Chapter VIII

Nyāya

Introduction

Nyāya is an ancient orthodox school of philosophy founded by a sage named Gautama (also spelled Gotama), not to be confused with Gautama the Buddha. The goal of Nyāya, like that of all the other Indian schools, is liberation through knowledge of ultimate reality.[1] There is, however, an important difference between Nyāya and the other systems: whereas they conducted their inquiry into reality without a clear conception and articulation of their methods of inquiry, Nyāya is unique not only for its recognition of the need for and priority of method but also for its explicit and elaborate formulation of the principles of inquiry. Nyāya, then, is chiefly concerned with the canons of correct thinking and valid reasoning as methodological tools for acquiring knowledge of reality. For this reason, Nyāya is often referred to as *tarkaśāstra,* the science of reasoning (or simply, logic). This is not to say that Nyāya is not concerned with metaphysics and ontology; quite the contrary, knowledge of ultimate reality is the aim and end of Nyāya. But it is Nyāya's conviction that this cannot be had without a clear formulation of the canons and criteria of valid knowledge.

The earliest work of the Nyāya school is the *Nyāya-sūtras* (*Principles of Nyāya*) of Gotama (third century B.C.). Subsequent works of the school include Vātsāyana's *Nyāya-*

bhāṣya (a commentary on the *Nyāya-sūtras*); Uddyotakara's *Nyāya-vārttika;* Vācaspati's *Nyāya-vārttika-tātparya-ṭīkā* (commentary on Uddyotakara's work); and Udayana's *Nyāya-vārttika-tatparya-pariśuddhi* and *Kusumāñjali.* At this point, we may note that there are two schools of Nyāya philosophy: the ancient or original (Prācīna-nyāya), and the modern (Navya-nyāya). Ancient Nyāya is Nyāya as formulated by Gotama and clarified and defended by his followers. Modern Nyāya, with its roots still in Gotama's work, differs from it in certain important respects, the differences being the result of arguments, counterarguments, criticisms, and countercriticisms over a long period of time. Gaṅgeśa (A.D. 1200) was the founder of modern Nyāya, and his *Tattvacintāmani* marks the definitive turning point from the ancient to the modern school of Nyāya.[2]

The Nyāya system may be described as logical realism and atomistic pluralism. It is realism on account of its doctrine that the world exists independently of our perceptions and knowledge of it—in sharp contrast to subjective idealism, for example, the Vijñāna-vāda school of Buddhism. The realism is logical because of the Nyāya contention that the independent existence of the world can be defended, not by appeal to naive belief, faith, or intuition, but by logical arguments and critical reflection on the nature of experience. Nyāya is a system of atomism because of its atomic theory of the constitution of matter. Finally, Nyāya is pluralistic because it rejects both materialistic and spiritualistic monism and holds that there is not one but many entities, material and spiritual, as ultimate constituents of the universe. It is worth mentioning here that Nyāya accepts the Vaiśeṣika metaphysics, including the atomic theory, and accordingly incorporates the seven Vaiśeṣika categories in its own list of sixteen categories.

The Sixteen Categories (Padārthas) [3]

The term "category" (*padārtha*) here means philosophical topic. According to the Nyāya, there are in all sixteen categories:

1. *Pramāṇa* is the way in which we come to know anything truly and objectively.

2. *Prameya* is anything that can be known truly and objectively (or simply, the knowable).

3. *Saṁśaya* is doubt or lack of certainty.

4. *Prayojana* is the end, goal, or purpose for which one either pursues or refrains from pursuing a given course of action.

5. D*ṛṣṭānta* is any fact or state of affairs concerning which there is no dispute, and therefore serves as an instance of a general truth, principle, or rule.

6. *Siddhānta* is a theory, view, or doctrine which is upheld by a person or school.

7. *Avayava* is a part, member, or organ of the Nyāya syllogism; an *avayava* may be either a premise or conclusion of a syllogism. We shall say more about this under inference.

8. *Tarka* is the indirect way of demonstrating the truth of a certain claim by showing that its negation leads to absurdities. Such a process of reasoning is called "hypothetical reasoning"; it is the Nyāya counterpart of the *reductio ad absurdum* in Western logic.

9. *Nirṇaya* is true and certain knowledge arrived at by the application of only the legitimate and permissible means and methods of knowledge.

10. *Vāda* is an argument or discussion in which the premises and conclusion as well as the means and criteria of knowledge are explicitly stated.

11. *Jalpa* is a seeming dispute or argument in which one or other of the parties engages with the aim not of arriving at truth but merely of winning the argument.

12. *Vitaṇḍā* is an argument or debate in which each party is merely interested in refuting and discrediting the other's position rather than establishing its own.

13. *Hetvābhāsa* is something that is offered as a valid reason but is in fact not so.

14. *Chala* is any device employed by one of the disputants to dodge a question or objection raised by the other. The device usually consists in distorting the meaning of the opponent's words, quibbling, and playing on pun and ambiguity, although the opponent's meaning has been clear all along.

15. *Jāti* is the employment of false and inappropriate analogies to defend one's own position or refute that of others.

16. *Nigrahasthāna* is the basis on which an argument is lost. Thus, in the course of an argument, one party demands that the other concede defeat by showing that the latter has either grossly misunderstood its own position (or that of the former) or is unaware of the implications of its own thesis (or that of the former).

We may immediately note that the seven categories of the Vaiśeṣika are subsumed by the Nyāya under the single category of *prameya* (the knowable).[4]

Epistemology

According to Nyāya, knowledge is not an essential but only an adventitious property of the self.[5] Knowledge arises as a result of contact between the self and the non-self.[6] Nyāya's fundamental definition of "knowledge" is phenomenological: knowledge is cognition, apprehension, consciousness, or manifestation of objects. It is of the utmost importance to note that for Nyāya knowledge is different from both the knowing subject and the object known. This view of knowledge as distinct from the subject as well as the object follows from Nyāya realism. Nyāya compares knowledge to the light of the lamp which reveals the lamp as well as the objects around it. That is, the light is different from both the lamp and the objects. Nyāya divides knowledge into two broad varieties: presentative and representative (also called "nonpresentative"). Each of these two varieties is further divided into two kinds: valid knowledge and invalid knowledge. Let us clarify all this. Valid knowledge is the true and correct apprehension of an object. In other words, valid knowledge consists in the manifestation of an object as it really is. Needless to mention, this characterization of valid knowledge is a consequence of the correspondence theory of truth which Nyāya upholds. According to the correspondence theory of truth, a proposition is true if and only if the proposition corresponds to (or reflects) the appropriate state of affairs.[7] That is, truth is the correspondence between a proposition and reality. Thus, the proposition "Snow is white" is true if and only if snow is white. Presentative knowledge arises when the object of knowledge is *directly* present to the knowing subject. My perception of my typewriter now is thus an instance of presentative knowledge.

Valid knowledge is called *pramā*. According to Nyāya, there are four sources of valid knowledge: (1) perception, (2) inference, (3) comparison, and (4) testimony.[8] Invalid knowledge is produced by memory, doubt, and hypothetical reasoning. Memory, by definition, is always the present recollection of some past cognition. Consequently, knowledge by memory is not presentative but representative and is accordingly classified by Nyāya as invalid knowledge. Nevertheless, memory can serve as a source of valid knowledge if it can be shown that what is recalled or remembered was experienced in the past as a presentative cognition.[9] Doubt is lack of certainty of cognition. Error is misrepresentation of what is cognized: a man steps on a rope in the dark and thinks that it is a snake. Error, then, is misapprehension, which is of two kinds: (1) thinking that a thing exists when in fact it does not, and (2) thinking that a thing has a certain property when in fact it does not have it. Hypothetical reasoning, although important as a tool of formal reasoning, does not produce any new knowledge. Thus, given the claim that wherever there is smoke there is fire, one asserts by hypothetical reasoning that wherever there is no fire there is no smoke. The reason why Nyāya classifies hypothetical reasoning as a source of invalid knowledge is that it can only confirm what one already knows but cannot produce any new knowledge. Suppose that two persons, X and Y, both say that they perceive smoke on a distant hill. Now suppose further that one of them, X, asserts that therefore there is fire on the hill, and the other, Y, contends that there is no fire. Then, in order to show that Y is mistaken, X employs hypothetical reasoning as follows: In our past experience wherever we have perceived smoke, there we have also perceived fire; therefore, wherever there is no fire there is no smoke. We are now perceiving smoke on the hill. Consequently, it would be absurd to say that there is no fire on the hill. But this does not mean that X is now perceiving fire. For this reason, Nyāya holds that hypothetical reasoning can only confirm one's past inference of fire from smoke but cannot produce any presentative cognition.

Nyāya maintains the correspondence theory of truth, according to which our knowledge of a given object is valid provided the knowledge agrees with (or corresponds to) the real nature of the object. By contrast, invalid knowledge lacks such agreement and correspondence. Further, according to Nyāya, action and behavior based on valid knowledge lead to success and fulfillment, while those based on invalid knowledge lead to failure and disappointment. This might lead one into thinking that the Nyāya theory of truth is also pragmatic. Such, however, is not the case, for Nyāya, unlike modern pragmatism,[10] draws a clear distinction between truth and the test (criterion) of truth. Since Nyāya upholds realism—the view that the existence and characteristics of external objects are independent of the experiencing subject—the correspondence between knowledge and the object of knowledge is in no way dependent upon the knower. Thus, "The rose is red" is true even when no one is perceiving the rose. But how we validate (certify) the claim that the rose is red is a different question. According to Nyāya, one certifies the claim as true or false according as actions based on the claim lead to success or failure. To sum up, Nyāya is realistic with respect to the nature of truth and pragmatic with respect to the test or criterion of truth. In short, truth and how we come to know it are two different issues. For this reason, we may describe the Nyāya theory of knowledge as realistic pragmatism. Concerning causation, Nyāya, like Vaiśeṣika, subscribes to *asatkāryavāda.* We shall now consider the four *pramāṇas,* sources of valid knowledge, recognized by Nyāya.

Perception. Perception, according to Nyāya, is the direct and immediate cognition produced by the interaction between the object and the sense organs.[11] The self, mind (*manas*), sense organs, objects, and contacts between them are necessary for perception. Thus, unless the self is in contact with the *manas* and the *manas* with the sense organs, there can be no sense-object contacts and hence no perception. Like the Vaiśeṣika, Nyāya holds that each of the sense organs derives from the respective element.[12]

Nyāya, like the Vaiśeṣika, distinguishes two stages of perception: the indeterminate (*nirvikalpa*) and the determinate (*savikalpa*).[13] Indeterminate perception is perception involving no conceptual activity, such as naming and relating. In other words, indeterminate perception consists of pure, uncategorized, sensations. For example, when one is looking at an apple, one's indeterminate perception of the apple consists in one's merely being aware of certain visual sensations. Such sensations are the raw material of knowledge. On the other hand, determinate perception, unlike indeterminate perception, arises when one brings the raw sensations under various concepts. That is, while sensations are the material of knowledge, conception is the imposition of form on the sensations. In the above example, knowledge of the apple consists not only in having certain sensations but in categorizing them under such concepts as "color," "shape," "taste," "size." It is by rendering the indeterminate sensations determinate with the aid of concepts that one comes to say that the thing one is sensing is red, round, tart, etc., and that it is an apple and not an orange (see n. 13). For Nyāya, just as for Kant, knowledge is thus constituted of sensation and conception.[14] Sensation without conception is blind, and conception without sensation is empty. This is the same as saying that knowledge has both content and form, the former deriving from sensation and the latter from conception. However, it should be emphasized that, although we can talk about indeterminate and determinate perceptions as two different stages of perception, it would be a mistake to think that we in fact experience each stage separately. Quite the contrary, according to Nyāya, all perception is determinate. The reason for this is that it is impossible to experience sensations without already classifying them, no matter how vaguely. Thus, even if a person does not know what it is that he is sensing, he is certain that it is something different from other things; or, what is the same, anything that is sensed is sensed against some background or other. In this manner, even if the person is unable to say anything *about* what he is sensing, he is necessarily aware that it is this rather than that. Thus he already has to make the figure-background distinction. According to Nyāya, then, the distinction between indeterminate and determinate perception is a distinction only in thought and not in experience. It is interesting to note that this is just what William James was drawing our attention to when he said that for a baby the world is a blooming and buzzing confusion of colors, sounds, etc. It should be clear by now that from a *logical* point of view indeterminate perception is a necessary condition for determinate perception.

Nyāya divides perception into two kinds: ordinary (*laukika*) and extraordinary (*alaukika*).[15] We have ordinary perception whenever our sense organs contact the object in the ordinary way. Thus, my seeing the tree in the yard with the aid of my eyes is ordinary perception. Extraordinary perception arises whenever the contacts between sense organs and objects occur in an unusual manner. We shall say more about this later. Nyāya further divides ordinary perception into two kinds: internal (*mānasa*) and external (*bāhya*). Ordinary perception is internal whenever it is due to contact between the mind (internal sense organ) and its objects. Thus cognition, desiring, feeling, willing, etc., are examples of internal perception. It is obvious that the object of internal perception can only be a psychic state or process. Perception is external whenever it is due to contact between our external sense organ (s) and an object. The five external sense organs of sight, smell, hearing, taste, and touch bring about external perceptions. We have already pointed out that each of the external sense organs is derived from an element distinguishable by the respective sense-quality. Thus, the sense organ of smell is constituted of earth atoms, whose distinctive quality is smell. It may be noted that we have already discussed the Nyāya distinction between determinate and indeterminate perception.

Nyāya recognizes three kinds of extraordinary perception:[16] *sāmānyalakṣaṇa, jñānalakṣaṇa,* and *yogaja. Sāmānyalakṣaṇa* is the perception of universals, the essences by possession of which a number of objects are recognized as being all of a certain kind. Thus when someone says that a given animal is a horse he is classifying that animal under the class "horse." But what enables him to so classify the animal? According to Nyāya, the person could not have classified the animal as a horse unless he had grasped the essential characteristics by virtue of which a given animal is a horse. In other words, in addition to perceiving this or that individual horse, one perceives the universal horse (universal horseness). But, according to Nyāya, one does not and cannot perceive the universal horse in the same way as one perceives a particular horse. The universal horse *inheres* in each particular horse. To take another example, when we say that man is mortal, we are not saying that this or that man is mortal, but that men in general are mortal. How is it possible for us to say this? In ordinary perception we perceive only particular men. It can never be the case that all men, past, present, and future, are perceived by us. Hence ordinary perception cannot enable us to say that all men are mortal. It is only by the extraordinary perception of manhood as the essence of being man we say that all men are mortal.

The second kind of extraordinary perception, *jñānalakṣaṇa,* is perception through complex association. We sometimes hear people say that they not only smell the fragrance of the rose but also *see* the fragrance of the rose; that the ice not only feels cold but *looks* cold, and so on. This way of talking sounds at first bizarre and nonsensical. But on careful analysis one finds that such expressions, far from being absurd and nonsensical, reveal a complicated association of perceptions. Suppose that a person has always in the past experienced a certain flower as having a certain color and a certain fragrance. Owing to such invariable association of color and smell, the person's present visual perception of the flower triggers in his mind the memory of the fragrance of the flower. This results in his saying that he sees not only the color of the flower but also its fragrance. In that the present perception of the fragrance of the flower is not brought about by the sense organ of smell but by the eye, which is ordinarily the organ of sight and not of smell, Nyāya regards perception by complex association as extraordinary perception.

The third kind of extraordinary perception, namely, *yogaja,* is not perception through the instrumentality of sense organs. It is a radically different kind of perception—the intuitive and immediate apprehension of all existence, past, present, and future, and of all objects, the infinitesimal as well as the infinite. According to Nyāya, only those who have attained spiritual perfection are capable of such spontaneous and intuitive perception. It is worth noting that in his *Yoga-sūtras* Patañjali recognizes such extraordinary perception and refers to men capable of it as *siddhas.*[17]

Inference. Nyāya distinguishes between perception and inference[18] as instruments of knowledge; the former gives us immediate knowledge (*aparokṣa*), whereas the latter gives us only mediate knowledge (*parokṣa, anumāna*). Generally speaking, inference may be described as the process of reasoning which enables us to pass from claims of present perceptions or nonperceptions to claims of the existence or nonexistence of things not perceived at the time.[19] That which is perceived is a mark that a certain thing, not perceived now, exists. Let us give an example of inference. There is smoke on that hill, therefore there is fire on that hill, because wherever there is smoke there is fire and wherever there is no fire there is no smoke. Here the speaker perceives only the smoke on the hill, and he infers the presence of fire on the hill on the basis of the perception of smoke. Thus smoke serves as a mark of fire. Further, he says that he is entitled to claim the existence of fire on the basis of his perception of smoke, because in the past wherever he perceived smoke he also perceived fire and he never encountered smoke where there is no fire; in short, there is an invariable relation between smoke and fire. It is this invariable relation, known as "pervasion" (*vyāpti*), that serves as the basis for inferring the existence of fire from the perception of smoke. Let us now state the above inference in the form of a complete argument, which may be called "the Nyāya syllogism":

Hypothesis (*pratijñā*):	(1)	*That hill* is *fire-possessing.*
Reason (*hetu*):	(2)	Because *that hill* is *smoke-possessing.*
Examples (*dṛṣṭānta*):	(3)	(*a*) Like *the torch.*
		(*b*) Unlike *the river.*

This syllogism consists of three members and five terms.[20] The members are the statements numbered 1, 2, and 3, respectively known as "hypothesis" (*pratijñā*), "reason" (*hetu*), and "example (s)" (*dṛṣṭānta*). Hypothesis is that which is being inferred or established; reason is that which is offered as the basis for inferring the hypothesis; and examples are of two kinds, positive and negative, the former providing an example of something which is both smoky and fiery, and the latter an example of something which is neither smoky nor fiery. We shall now indicate and explain the terms. "That hill" is known as *pakṣa;* "fire-possessing" is called *sādhya;* "smoke-possessing" is termed *hetu,* not to be confused with the member *hetu;* "the torch" is called *sapakṣa;* and the term "the river" is known as *vipakṣa.* From this we can state generally that in any Nyāya syllogism terms which occupy the positions occupied in the present example by "that hill," "fire-possessing," "smoke-possessing," "the torch," and "the river" shall be referred to respectively as *pakṣa, sādhya, hetu, sapakṣa,* and *vipakṣa.* An important point to bear in mind in the context of Nyāya inference is that these terms are not to be thought of as referring to individual objects but should be regarded as class terms. Thus "that hill" refers to the class whose only member is that particular hill; "fire-possessing" refers to the class of all fire-possessing objects, etc.

The above Nyāya syllogism can be exhibited as a diagram.[21] Let us denote *pakṣa* by P, *sādhya* by S, *hetu* by H, *sapakṣa* by S_1 and *vipakṣa* by S_2, and symbolize the syllogism as follows:

1. P is S.
2. Because P is H.
3. *a*) *like* S_1.
   b) unlike S_2.

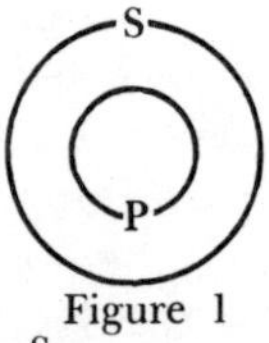

Figure 1

Figure 2

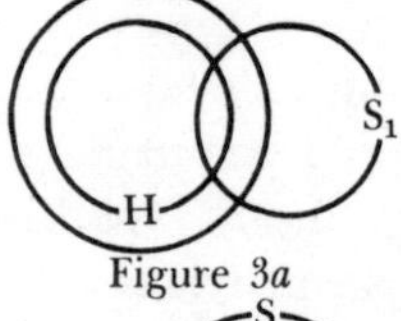

Figure 3*a*

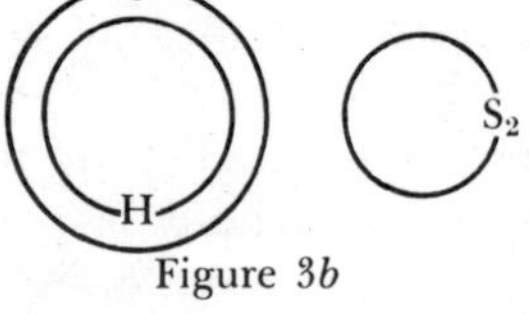

Figure 3*b*

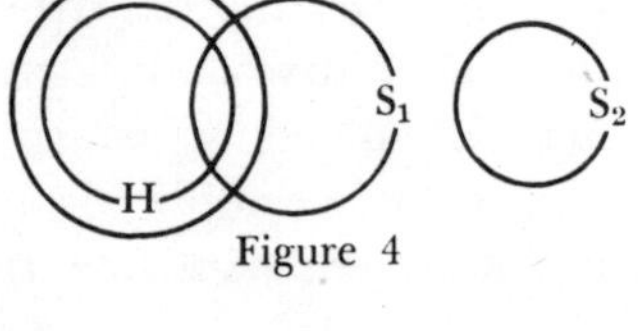

Figure 4

Figure 1 represents the hypothesis that the class whose only member is that hill is included in the class of all fire-possessing things. Figure 2 represents the reason, namely, the class whose only member is that hill is included in the class of all smoke-possessing things. Figure 3*a* represents the fact that the torch is both smoke-possessing and fire-possessing—or, what is the same, that the class of smoke possessing things and that of fire-possessing things overlap. Figure 3*b* represents the fact that the river is neither smoke-possessing nor fire-possessing; that is, the class of things which are neither smoke-possessing nor fire-possessing is excluded from the class of things which are both smoke-possessing and fire-possessing. The fourth and final figure expresses simultaneously all these relationships; that is, it telescopes the entire syllogism.

At this point, we may distinguish between the validity and the soundness of an inference. A valid inference is one in which *if* the basis (premises) of the inference is true *then* that which is inferred (conclusion) is also true.[22] But the inference itself cannot tell us whether its basis is true or false. It is only by inspecting the world that we can determine whether the basis of the inference is true. Thus, in our example above, the basis of the inference consists of the two premises: smoke is being perceived on that hill, and wherever smoke is perceived there exists fire. On the other hand, a sound inference is one which is not only valid but whose premises are determined to be true and hence whose conclusion is true. It should be clear that although every sound inference is also valid the converse is not necessarily the case; that is, an inference may be valid but not sound.

Without distorting the distinctive structure and character of the Nyāya syllogism, we can reconstruct it so that it resembles the familiar categorical syllogism of Aristotelian logic.[23] For this purpose, we shall ignore the member known as "example" (*dṛṣṭānta*). The Nyāya syllogism will then have three members and three terms. Our example above can now be stated as follows:

1. All smoke-possessing things are fire-possessing things.

2. That hill is a smoke-possessing thing.
3. Therefore, that hill is a fire-possessing thing.

It is well known that the categorical syllogism of Aristotelian logic contains three terms and three propositions. The three terms are the major, the minor, and the middle. The proposition containing the major term is the major premise, that containing the minor term is the minor premise, and the third proposition is the conclusion. The major term is the predicate of the conclusion, and the minor term is the subject of the conclusion. The remaining term is the middle term. Further, each of these terms occurs twice. The major term represents the class with the largest extension, the minor term the class with the smallest extension, and the middle term represents the class which serves as the link between the other two classes. Thus, in our example, "fire-possessing things" is the major term, "that hill" is the minor term, and "smoke-possessing things" is the middle term. Proposition 1 is the major premise, proposition 2 is the minor premise, and proposition 3 is the conclusion. Let us now present the Aristotelian version of the Nyāya syllogism in a diagrammatic form. Thus let S stand for smoke-possessing things, F for fire-possessing things, and H for that hill; the syllogism can now be symbolized as—

1. All S are F.
2. H is S.
3. Therefore, H is F.

The corresponding diagram is as follows:

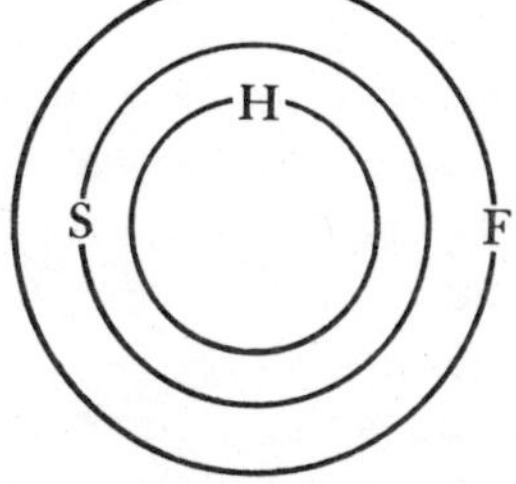

The Nyāya inference is sometimes presented as being constituted of five members. This form is generally regarded as the most complete statement of the Nyāya inference. Here is an illustration:

1. *Pratijñā:* Tom is a rational animal.
2. *Hetu:* Because Tom is a man.
3. *Udāharaṇa:* All men are rational animals, e.g., John, Joseph, Richard, etc.
4. *Upanaya:* Tom is a man.
5. *Nigamana:* Therefore, Tom is a rational animal.

Here *pratijñā* is the assertion to be established by inference; *hetu* is the reason (or ground) for the assertion; *udāharaṇa* is the proposition asserting, together with examples, the universal (invariable) connection, *vyāpti,* between the assertion to be established and its reason; *upanaya* is the subsumption of the present case under the universal proposition; and *nigamana* is the conclusion which logically follows from propositions 2, 3, and 4. Notice that propositions 1 and 5 are one and the same, except that the latter contains "therefore," thereby indicating that it is the result of the inference.

We shall now point out some fundamental differences between Indian and Western logic. By Western logic we mean not only Aristotelian logic but also modern mathematical logic as founded by such thinkers as George Boole, Gottlob Frege, Bertrand Russell, Alfred North Whitehead.[24] Similarly, by Indian logic we mean not only logic as formulated by the Nyāya school but also logic as conceived and practiced by the various other Indian schools.[25] First and foremost, Western logic is an exclusively deductive and formal discipline. This means that logic in the West is concerned with discovering and formulating the canons of valid inference, without any regard to the content of the propositions constituting the inference. In other words, Western logic is the investigation of the relations obtaining between various symbolic sentences merely on the basis of their formal structure. Consider, for example, the following inference pattern: All P are Q and all Q are R, therefore all P are R. Every argument that can be obtained by substituting particular terms for P, Q, and R is a valid argument because its form, irrespective of its content, is that of the above valid inference pattern. As an illustration, let us substitute Californians for P, Americans for Q, and Canadians for R. We then obtain the following valid categorical syllogism: All Californians are Americans, and all Americans are Canadians; therefore all Californians are Canadians. It is to be noted that, because of the particular choice of the terms we have substituted for P, Q, and R, the conclusion of the categorical syllogism is in fact false. Nevertheless, the syllogism is valid because it is a substitution instance of a valid inference pattern. To say that the syllogism is valid is merely to say that *if* it is true that all Californians are Americans and all Americans are Canadians, *then* it is true that all Californians are Canadians. Western logic does not consider it its business to inquire whether the premises and the conclusion of an argument are true. It is solely concerned with determining whether a given argument is valid, leaving the problem of determining its soundness to the various empirical sciences. To put this point differently, the task of Western logic is exclusively the investigation of logical relations between various thought-forms regardless of their content. For this reason, Western logic is often described as formal as distinct from material logic. This observation holds not only with respect to Aristotelian logic but also for modern logic.

In sharp contrast, Indian logic is at once formal and material. Indian logicians reject the verbalist view of logic —the view that logic is only concerned with thought-forms and symbols and not their content and referents. Another way of expressing this difference between Western and Indian logical traditions is, the former draws a sharp distinction between deductive (formal) and inductive (empirical) inquiries, whereas the latter regards deduction and induction as two inseparable aspects of one and the same process of reasoning to reach the truth. Nyāya defends this latter view as follows: Consider the syllogism, All men are mortal and Robert is a man, therefore Robert is mortal. Nyāya argues that although the conclusion is reached by deductive reasoning, it could not have been were it not for the universal proposition, namely, "All men are mortal," which is an inductive generalization. In other words, the validity of this categorical syllogism essentially depends upon a universal proposition, which is always an inductive generalization. According to the Indian logical tradition, inference is essentially the process of going from one particular to another through the universal; it is neither the passage from the particular to the universal nor that from the universal to the particular. We do not have to decide here which of the two views of logic, Western or Indian, is the correct one. Suffice it to point out that, whereas the Indian view is based on the conviction that logic is an instrument for the discovery and understanding of reality, and not a mere formal discipline wholly unrelated to the world, the Western view is not absurd but is quite intelligible in that logic can be done as a purely formal, structural inquiry without any regard to the world around us.[26] Nevertheless, it should be emphasized that the Western tradition, having sharply separated the formal from the empirical, is faced with the serious problem of accounting for the fact of the application of logic in the study of the world. Further, Western logicians are seriously divided on the issue of the status of the so-called laws of logic—whether they are purely linguistic, syntactical conventions or are grounded in reality. Indian philosophers would say that these problems are a direct consequence of the unwarranted initial separation between logical and empirical inquiries.

We should point out that our treatment of the Nyāya theory of inference is sketchy and by no means complete. We have only presented here the essential ideas underlying Nyāya inference and have not even touched upon the large number of topics treated by the Nyāya logicians: the conditions of validity of an inference, the various fallacies in argumentation, and a number of canons of inquiry known in Western philosophy as "Mill's methods" in the context of induction and scientific method.

We conclude our discussion of inference by pointing out

that Nyāya, like other Indian schools of philosophy, distinguishes between inference for oneself (*svārtha*) and inference for others (*parārtha*). In inference for oneself, there is no need for a formal statement of the inference. It is only when one has to demonstrate some truth to others that one has to offer a fully formal statement of the inference. The fully formal statement of the inference takes the form of a chain of steps which begins with *pratijñā,* goes through the intermediate steps of *hetu, udāharaṇa,* and *upanaya,* and terminates in *nigamana.*

Comparison (*Upamāna*). Comparison is the third source of valid knowledge. Nyāya defines "comparison" as the knowledge (or source of knowledge) of the relation between a word and its denotation (what the word refers to). The basis of comparison is resemblance or similarity—not, however, as commonly understood, between a word and another word or between a thing and another thing, but between a word and the thing it denotes. Suppose that a boy who has only heard the word "zebra" but never seen a zebra wants to know what a zebra is. We tell him that a zebra is like a donkey with stripes on its body. Then one day he comes across an animal and says that the animal is a zebra. According to Nyāya, the boy is able to correctly identify the animal by perceiving the similarity between the description of the animal and the animal.[27] It goes without saying that for comparison to serve as a source of knowledge one should already have a knowledge of the denotations of the terms constituting the description of the object. Thus, in the above example, the boy would not have been able to identify the animal as a zebra unless he already knew the denotations of "donkey," "body," and "stripes." [28] It may be noted in passing that Buddhists, Sāṁkhya, and Vaiśeṣika do not regard comparison as an independent source of knowledge. Buddhists reduce comparison to perception and testimony,[29] and Sāṁkhya and Vaiśeṣika reduce it to inference.[30]

Testimony (*Śabda*). Testimony is the fourth and last of the sources of knowledge recognized by Nyāya. "Testimony" is defined by Nyāya as valid verbal knowledge. Accordingly, testimony consists of the statements of a trustworthy person and our understanding them by understanding the meanings of their constituent terms. We may thus describe testimony as one's understanding of what a trustworthy and reliable person says.

Nyāya divides testimony into two kinds: (1) that which pertains to perceivable objects (*dṛṣṭārtha*) and (2) that which pertains to imperceivable objects (*adṛṣṭārtha*).[31] The former includes the statements of any reliable source whatever, human or divine, insofar as the statements are about perceivable objects. Thus the source of a given testimony may be that of an ordinary person, a scientist, a saint, or a scripture. The latter kind of testimony consists of all the assertions of any trustworthy source whatever, human or divine, insofar as the statements are about imperceivable objects—for example, the testimony of an ordinary person in everyday matters, that of the scientist about electrons, microbes, genes, that of the saint and the prophet about virtue and vice, and that of the scriptures concerning God, freedom, immortality, the afterlife, etc. It is to be noted that the difference between the first and the second kind of testimony does not lie in the nature of the source of testimony but in the kind of objects the testimony is about: if the objects are perceivable it is of the first kind, and if imperceivable it is of the second kind. It is of course necessary that the sources of both kinds of testimony be intelligible and trustworthy.

There is another Nyāya classification of testimony into two kinds: human (*laukika*) and divine (*vaidika*).[32] The former consists of statements of trustworthy human beings, irrespective of the perceivability of the objects the statements are about. The latter consists of scriptural (Vedic) statements, whose ultimate source is God. The point here is that human testimony is fallible, no matter how trustworthy the person may be, simply because human beings are not omniscient. In contrast, divine testimony is infallible, owing to the omniscience of God. It should be obvious that, whereas the earlier classification is based on the criterion of the perceivability of the objects of testimony, the second classification is based on the criterion of fallibility. Nevertheless, it is important to note that in both classifications testimony, irrespective of the nature of its source and the nature of its objects, must be reliable if it is to be a source of valid knowledge.

Metaphysics

Whereas Nyāya epistemology is an inquiry into the methods and criteria (*pramāṇas*) of valid knowledge, Nyāya metaphysics is concerned with delineating the various kinds of objects of knowledge (*prameyas,* knowables) constituting reality. According to Nyāya, the knowables are: (1) the self, (2) the body, (3) the senses, (4) the objects of the senses, (5) the mind (*manas*), (6) knowledge, (7) activity, (8) mental imperfections such as attachment and aversion, (9) rebirth, (10) pleasure and pain, (11) suffering, (12) absolute freedom from suffering, (13) substance, (14) quality, (15) motion, (16) universals (*sāmānya*), (17) particularity (*vaiśeṣa*), (18) inherence (*samavāya*), and (19) nonexistence (*abhāva*).[33] This list is not intended to be exhaustive; but it is comprehensive in that it includes all those objects the knowledge of which is essential to the attainment of freedom and liberation from all forms of bondage and suffering.

A moment's reflection shows that not all knowables in the above list are physical; some are physical, and others nonphysical. For example, the self and knowledge are not physical. It is worth emphasizing here that Nyāya accepts the Vaiśeṣika account of the knowable which we treated in detail in the chapter on Vaiśeṣika. As such, we shall give here just one example of a knowable. Nyāya, like the Vaiśeṣika, recognizes five different physical substances, namely, earth, water, fire, air, and ether. The ultimate constituents of the first four substances are the eternal, unchanging, infinitesimal atoms of earth, water, fire, and air respectively. On the other hand, ether is an infinite and nonatomic substance.

Self and Liberation

Like the Vaiśeṣika, Nyāya holds that the self is an individual substance, eternal and all-pervading. Cognition, feeling, willing, knowledge, etc., belong to the self as the unique subject.[34] It would be a mistake, according to Nyāya, to attribute such nonphysical properties as knowing, feeling, and willing to a physical substance, since a physical substance is, by definition, one which can only have physical properties. Thus, it would be absurd to say that a stone is not only heavy, grey, and rectangular but also happy and joyful. The Nyāya point here is that just as physical properties can only be attributed to physical substances, so also nonphysical properties can only be attributed to nonphysical substances. The self is not to be identified with either the body, the senses, or the objects of the senses, for none of these can account for imagination, feeling, ideation, etc. Nor can the self be identified with mind (*manas*), because mind is atomic and imperceivable and hence can only have imperceivable properties, but not such perceivable qualities as pleasure and pain. According to Nyāya, the self cannot be identified with pure consciousness either, for pure consciousness, understood as consciousness belonging to no subject, is a fiction; all consciousness is necessarily consciousness of some self or other. The self, then, is the substance to which belongs consciousness. That is, consciousness is not the self but only an attribute of the self, which is the "I," the knower, and the enjoyer.[35]

It should, however, be pointed out that, according to Nyāya, although consciousness is an attribute of the self, it is not an essential but only an accidental attribute. The self in its original state has no consciousness and hence no cognition and knowledge. It is through its association with the sense organs that the self comes to have consciousness. This is simply to say that consciousness arises as a property of the self owing to the latter's entanglement with the body. For this reason, Nyāya regards consciousness as a purely adventitious attribute of the self.[36] To the question how one knows that the self exists, Nyāya answers by saying that the self is known through direct internal perception.[37] Some Nyāya philosophers, however, maintain that the self as such can never be an object of perception, whether external or internal, but can only be inferred from cognition, feeling, and willing. In other words, on the basis of the various modes of consciousness one infers the existence of the self. It is of interest to note here that this Nyāya argument for the existence of the self is strikingly similar to that of Descartes: "I think, therefore I am." [38] There is, however, a difference: whereas Descartes asserts the existence of self on the basis of thinking, Nyāya affirms the existence of self on the basis of the very fact of consciousness. According to Nyāya, each person can only perceive his own self and not those of others. The existence of other selves is inferred by analogy.

The aim and goal of Nyāya, like that of all the other Indian schools of philosophy, is the salvation of the self. What is salvation? Salvation is the state of total liberation from all forms of suffering and bondage arising out of the self's association with the body. Because of its association with the body, the self acquires consciousness and therewith cognition, knowledge, and attachment to the non-self. Attachment is the source of pain and suffering.[39] As long as the self is attached, it goes through the cycles of birth and death. Needless to say, Nyāya, like all other Indian schools, subscribes to the universal law of *karma,* which determines the lot of the self in accordance with its past *karma.* In this manner, the self gets enmeshed in the karmic chain and its suffering is perpetuated through the rounds of birth and death. The goal of Nyāya is the liberation of the self from suffering—the cessation of the karmic chain. In its state of liberation, the self is wholly disentangled from the body and is consequently free from pain as well as pleasure, sorrow as well as joy.[40] According to Gautama, the founder of the Nyāya school, such a state is the state of absolute freedom—freedom from birth and death and hence freedom from pain and pleasure for all time. However, some later Nyāya philosophers teach that release is the state of eternal bliss.[41]

But how is one to attain liberation and freedom? The Nyāya answer to this question is in conformity with that of the Indian tradition in general. One attains liberation upon the cessation of all activity as a result of the knowledge that the self is distinct from all other things such as the body, the mind, the senses, and their objects.[42] Such knowledge is the result of a discipline comprised of three phases: (1) reading and listening to (*śravaṇa*) the scriptural (Vedic) intimations of the existence and nature of the self; (2) intellectual comprehension of the truth of these intimations through analysis in the light of reason and experience (*manana*); and (3) existential realization (*nididhyāsana*) through Yogic meditation of the intellectually apprehended truth. According to Nyāya, the first two phases alone are inadequate for liberation, for genuine liberation cannot come from secondhand knowledge, no matter how authoritative its sources and how impeccable the process of reasoning behind it. True liberation is the result of knowledge certified by one's own experience. However, it is important to note that according to Nyāya liberating knowledge, while in the last analysis personal and direct, should be consonant with reason and experience. It is clear, then, that liberation is not something one can look forward to after death. On the contrary, it is to be attained during one's lifetime, here and now. He who thus attains liberation is known as *jīvanmukta* (one who is free while still in bodily existence). On death, such a person attains *mokṣa,* total freedom from all fetters of existence. By bringing the karmic chain to an end he has overcome both birth and death and consequently is beyond pain and pleasure.

God

In his *Nyāya-sūtras,* Gautama, the founder of the Nyāya system, recognizes God, but he does not deal with the problem of the existence of God in any detail. Later Nyāya philosophers constructed a number of proofs for the existence of God and theorized as to his nature and relation to man and the world. We might mention here that while the Vaiśeṣika system in the original formulation of Kaṇāda is atheistic, subsequent Vaiśeṣika philosophers are avowed ly theistic and consequently incorporated God into their system. Further, since Nyāya accepts the Vaiśeṣika metaphysics, there emerged in course of time an amalgamation of the two schools, known as the Nyāya-Vaiśeṣika. The proofs for the existence of God are mostly the work of the Nyāya-Vaiśeṣika school—in particular, of Udayana in his *Nyāya-kusumāñjali*.[43]

1. *Cosmo-teleological Argument.* The cosmo-teleological argument combines the concept of cause with that of purpose. Every composite object of the world, being by definition made up of parts, is an effect of some cause or other. For example, a mountain is a composite object and is constituted of the ultimate atoms of earth. But, according to Nyāya, atoms are infinitesimal, eternal substances. In other words, atoms are the material cause of the objects of our experience of the physical world. Thus it would appear that material causes alone bring about the various objects of the world. Nyāya rejects this conclusion by saying that without the guidance of some intelligence material substances, no matter how many and how subtle, cannot produce unique objects.[44] A tree is different from a mountain, and copper is different from gold. The Nyāya point here is that atoms are only the ultimate material causes of finite objects and as such lack anything in themselves which can direct and coordinate their combinations so as to result in the production of unique objects. That is, the material causes are to be guided by a final cause endowed with knowledge, purpose, and power: knowledge of the material causes, the purpose for which the material causes are to be directed, and the power to realize that purpose. The final cause is also omniscient because it cannot guide the material causes unless it has a direct and unerring knowledge of the imperceivable, infinitesimal atoms. According to Nyāya, such a final cause is none other than God.

2. *Argument from the Unseen Power* (*Adṛṣṭa*). We said earlier that Nyāya recognizes the universal law of *karma,*

according to which every event, be it thought, word, or action, is causally efficacious in bringing about other events, which in turn act as causes for yet other events, and so on. The law of *karma* is the Unseen Power (*adṛṣṭa*) bringing about the happiness or unhappiness of human beings according to their past actions. Now, according to Nyāya, the law of *karma,* though by itself it can be considered the sum total of the moral merit and demerit of a man, lacks any consciousness and hence cannot itself apportion joy or sorrow to man. It therefore requires for its operation the guidance of a supremely intelligent and moral being.[45] Such a being is indeed God.

3. *Argument from Atomism.* According to Nyāya, the ultimate atoms constituting the physical world originally lack motion and cannot begin to form the finite objects unless set into motion by an agency. Such an agency is God, the prime mover. We may note in passing that we have presented here only a few of the Nyāya arguments for the existence of God;[46] and since we have already discussed in detail the various objections to arguments for the existence of God (in the chapters on Sāṁkhya and Vaiśeṣika), there is no need to repeat them here.

In conclusion, we may briefly present the Nyāya conception of the relation of God to man and the world. God is not creator in the sense that he creates the world out of nothing. Like God, all ultimate substances, both physical and nonphysical, are eternal and hence can neither be created nor be destroyed. God is thus merely the designer of the universe. He is said to create the world only in the sense that he imparts motion to atoms and guides their interactions by his intelligence, purpose, and power. He is said to destroy the world only in the sense that he dissolves the world of finite objects into their constituent atoms which are ultimate and eternal. God is the sustainer of the world in that he guides the law of *karma,* the Unseen Power, in the just and proper dispensation of happiness and unhappiness to men in accordance with their deeds.[47] It is clear that the God of Nyāya, being limited by the law of *karma* as well as the many eternal substances, cannot be omnipotent. According to some Nyāya philosophers, the individual self cannot attain liberation without the grace of God; that is, the individual self cannot acquire the liberating knowledge without the grace of God.[48] Accordingly, these philosophers exhort men seeking liberation to cultivate in themselves, through prayer and worship, genuine humility and piety, thereby making themselves worthy of the grace of God.

Chapter IX

Vedānta

Introduction

The literal meaning of the term *Vedānta* is "the end of the *Vedas,* the concluding parts of the *Vedas,* the culmination of the *Vedic* teachings and wisdom." [1] Thus the term originally referred to the Upaniṣads, the last literary products of the Vedic period. However, *Vedānta* has subsequently come to include the various elaborations and interpretations of the Upaniṣads. In course of time, there emerged three principal schools of Vedānta: (1) *Advaita* (nondualism) of Śaṁkara, (2) *Viśiṣṭādvaita* (qualified nondualism) of Rāmānuja, and (3) *Dvaita* (dualism) of Madhva. It is worth noting here that from a historical standpoint one speaks of the *Pūrva Mīmāṁsā* (the earlier schools) and the *Uttara Mīmāṁsā* (the later schools), subsequently referred to simply as *Mīmāṁsā* and *Vedānta,* respectively.[2] *Mīmāṁsā* is generally understood as being concerned with the ritualistic side (*karmakāṇḍa*) of the Vedic teachings, and Vedānta with the philosophical, speculative (*jñānakāṇḍa*) aspects. In the light of this distinction, the three schools of Vedānta listed above come under Uttara Mīmāṁsā. However, it would be a serious mistake to think, as many do, that the Mīmāṁsā schools, in their prime concern with ritualism, wholly avoid speculative-philosophical matters. Quite the contrary, the term *mīmāṁsā* means "solution of problems by reflection and critical examination." Accordingly, the Mīmāṁsā looked upon its task as twofold: (1) to provide a method by which the complex and seemingly conflicting ritualistic injunctions of the Vedas may be harmoniously interpreted and practiced; and (2) to provide a philosophical justification of Vedic ritualism. The realization of this twofold objective necessarily involved the Mīmāṁsā in serious philosophical questions, both methodological and substantive. The philosophical investigations of the Mīmāṁsā schools are considerable, and their results important. Particularly noteworthy is their treatment of knowledge, truth, and error.[3] The Vedānta schools are indebted to the Mīmāṁsā schools in that they not only recognize the *pramāṇas* (criteria of valid knowledge) as formulated by the Mīmāṁsā but incorporate and employ them in their own systems.

We shall first present the Vedic background and the fundamental insights of the Upaniṣads (the foundation of all Vedāntic schools) and then discuss the three chief schools of Vedānta. We shall not deal with the Mīmāṁsā schools, but shall present under Advaita Vedānta their account of the *pramāṇas.* As and when appropriate, we shall discuss other important ideas of the Mīmāṁsā.

A. THE VEDIC BACKGROUND

The Vedas are probably the oldest (1500–800 B.C.) scriptures in the recorded history of man. They are the source of the sacred knowledge and wisdom of orthodox Hinduism in its various forms. *Veda* is etymologically related to "wit," meaning knowledge. The Vedas are regarded by Hindus as divine in origin and not the work of human authors; accordingly, they are looked upon as timeless and eternal. This is not to deny that at a certain time in human history the Vedas acquired a specific verbal form, oral or written; it only means that the truths proclaimed by the Vedas are regarded as eternal truths and in no way dependent upon the manner, time, and place of their recording. The Vedas are four in number: the *Ṛg,* the *Sāma,* the *Yajur,* and the *Atharva.* Each of these may be regarded as consisting of four parts, the first three pertaining to rituals and sanctions, and the last to knowledge, philosophic and transcendental. The four parts of each Veda are as follows: (1) the *Saṁhitās,* (2) the *Brāhmaṇas,* (3) the *Āraṇyakas,* and (4) the *Upaniṣads.* We may note here that the literal meaning of *upaniṣad* is "sitting close to the teacher and listening to his teachings" as well as "that which destroys ignorance and illusion and brings man knowledge of ultimate reality." [4]

The Saṁhitās are hymns and chants in praise of various gods, such as air (Vāyu), fire (Agni), rain (Parjanya), thunder (Indra), sun (Mitra).[5] The hymns are sung in order that man may please the gods and thereby receive from them the blessings of worldly goods such as health, wealth, power, and fame. The Brāhmaṇas are manuals for performing various kinds of rituals and ceremonies as well as guides for the conduct of everyday life. They describe in detail procedures for performing different rituals for pleasing different gods, as well as the kinds of sacrifices to be offered to them; they also lay down the rules of conduct and duties of men toward each other.[6] It is worth pointing out that the undue emphasis of the Brāhmaṇas on the performance of rites, ceremonies, and duties has in course of time resulted in the degradation of religious consciousness: the mere chanting of certain words, the performance of certain rites, and acting in certain ways have totally replaced genuine religious consciousness. Thus empty utterances and mechanical gestures have themselves come to be regarded as constituting the core of religious life. From such degeneration it is but a short step to the emergence of an all-powerful priest class and therewith the rigid institutionalization of religion. However, these remarks are not to be construed as implying that the Brāhmaṇas are wholly devoid of anything valuable. Indeed, they emphasize self-control and exhort men to cultivate love, kindness, and charity toward all living beings, including animals. Further, the Brāhmaṇas forbid murder, theft, greed, and jealousy. The Brāhmaṇas therefore surely deserve to be commended for their lofty ethical teachings.[7] Nevertheless, their excessive emphasis on rituals and ceremonies did result in the gradual eclipse of genuine and sublime religious consciousness.

Like the Brāhmaṇas, the Āraṇyakas (literally "forest treatises") deal with rites and ceremonies. But, unlike the Brāhmaṇas, they go beyond rites and ceremonies to remind man that true and liberating wisdom does not consist in the mere performance of rites and ceremonies but in spiritual insight into ultimate reality. The *Āraṇyakas* call upon men to inquire into and grasp the spiritual significance behind the Vedic sanctions, rituals, and ceremonies. In other words, the Āraṇyakas are the transition from the outward symbols to the inner reality. In this manner, the Āraṇyakas pave the path to the Upaniṣads, the flower of the Vedic wisdom.

Before proceeding to a discussion of the central insights of the Upaniṣads, let us briefly present the evolution of the concepts of nature, man, and God in the Saṁhitās, the Brāhmaṇas, and the Āraṇyakas. The idea permeating the *Ṛgveda* is that nature in all its diversity and multiplicity is not a chaos but is governed by a basic cosmic law (*Ṛta*).[8] To this law are subject not only all natural phenomena, such as the movement of the planets and the generation, decay, and death of organisms, but also truth and justice. At this stage of the Vedic thought, many gods are said to exist; that is, the Vedas seem to subscribe to polytheism. Hymns are sung in praise of each god in order to receive his favors; but on closer examination it turns out that each god is praised in the respective hymns as the highest and supreme lord and creator of the universe.[9] How does one make sense of this paradoxical and contradictory belief and attitude? Max Müller, the great Indologist of the nineteenth century, distinguished this kind of belief and attitude from polytheism and referred to it as "henotheism."[10] Thus, while belief in many gods is common to both polytheism and henotheism, only the latter holds that each god is the highest and supreme. One might argue that the elevation of each god to the highest status is either romantic hyperbole or an act of opportunistic exaggeration and sycophancy motivated by selfish ends and, consequently, that the henotheism of the Vedas is really no different from polytheism. Such a view is not tenable, however; for we have good reason to believe that the Vedic exaltation of each god to the supreme status is governed by the belief that the different gods are manifestations of one single underlying reality: "To what is one, sages give many a title: they call it Agni, Yama, Mātariśvan." [11] In light of this utterance, it is neither absurd nor paradoxical to think of each god as the most high and supreme. This interpretation can be further substantiated by the explicit declaration of the unity of all existence. Thus, according to the celebrated hymn known as the *Puruṣasūkta:*

> Thousand-headed was the Puruṣa (person or man personified), thousand-eyed, thousand-footed. He embraced the earth on all sides, and stood beyond the breadth of ten fingers.
>
> The Puruṣa is this all, that which was and which shall be. He is Lord of immortality, which he grows beyond through (sacrificial) food.
>
> Such is his greatness, and still greater than that is the Puruṣa. One fourth of him is all beings. The three fourths of him is the immortal in Heaven.
>
> Three fourths on high rose the Puruṣa. One fourth of him arose here (on the earth). Thence in all directions he spread abroad, as that which eats and that which eats not.[12]

It is clear that the theme of this hymn is the unity of all existence, inorganic and organic. Such unity is expressed by the Vedic seers, in their grand visual imagery, in the form of what they call "the Puruṣa." According to this hymn, "the Puruṣa" is not to be equated with the universe, for not only does he pervade the universe but he is also beyond it. In philosophical terms, the supreme reality is both immanent and transcendent—immanent, because it pervades all existence, thereby rendering it a unity; transcendent, because it is not exhausted by existence but goes beyond it. In theological terms, God, while pervading the universe, is also more than the universe. In other words, the Vedic conception of God is not pantheistic but panentheistic (pantheism is the view that God and the universe are identical, whereas panentheism is the view that God is not exhausted by the universe but is greater than it and hence transcends it). It is in this manner, then, that the Vedic vision of the unity of existence leads to panentheism, which may be alternatively expressed by saying that the totality of existence is *in* God but *not equal to* God.

We have seen that the *Ṛgveda* refers to the supreme reality underlying and unifying all existence by the term "the Puruṣa" (person or man personified). The question now arises, Is this conception of ultimate reality anthropomorphic? The Vedic answer to this question is a clear "no," for the famous hymn of creation, also known as the *Nāsadīyasūkta,* unequivocally declares that ultimate reality (the Puruṣa) is not only impersonal but beyond all names and forms, and hence is inexpressible and indescribable:

> Non-being then existed not nor being:
> There was no air, nor sky that is beyond it.
> What was concealed? Wherein? In whose protection?
> And was there deep unfathomable water?
>
> Who knows for certain? Who shall here declare it?
> Whence was it born, and whence came this creation?
> The gods were born after this world's creation:
> Then who can know from whence it has arisen?
>
> None knoweth whence creation has arisen;
> And whether he has or has not produced it:
> He who surveys it in the highest heaven,
> He only knows, or haply he may know not.[13]

It is clear that according to this hymn all existence is the manifestation of a single ultimate reality, which, being beyond thoughts and words, is indescribable, indeterminate, and absolute. To be sure, this grand conception of ultimate reality is not grounded in discursive, philosophical speculation but in the loftiest of poetic, mystical, intuitive insights. It is also worth noting that this vision of reality also goes beyond all gods to the primordial ground of all existence. It goes beyond polytheism and monotheism to pure monism. Such a vision is the inspiration of all the Upaniṣads as well as all the subsequent philosophical speculations of the Vedantic schools. To sum up, then, even the extra-Upaniṣadic Vedic literature contains in itself the highest monistic vision of reality. In the light of this, it would be a grave mistake to think, as many do, that the religious consciousness informing the Vedic hymns is at best polytheism and at worst animism and nature worship. Through their sublime and lofty vision of reality the Vedic hymns reveal a profound religious consciousness.

B. THE UPANIṢADS

The *Upaniṣads* are the concluding parts of the Vedas and are the culmination of the Vedic knowledge and wisdom. How many Upaniṣads existed originally we do not know. One hundred and eight Upaniṣads have survived. Some of them are composed in prose, others in verse, and still others partly in one and partly in the other. The style of the Upaniṣads is direct, forceful, often didactic and dialogic. We are wholly in the dark as to who wrote them and when they were written. It is of interest to note that it was a common custom in ancient India for authors to remain anonymous. The reason for this was their strong conviction that what mattered was the truths proclaimed and not the identity or history of the authors, who looked upon themselves as merely the vehicles for communicating impersonal and eternal truths. Thus the names of the great sages whose extraordinary insights are the Upaniṣads forever remain a mystery.

Of the hundred and eight extant Upaniṣads, ten have come to be regarded as the cream of the Upaniṣadic teachings. They are as follows: *Īśa, Kena, Kaṭha, Praśna, Muṇḍaka, Māṇḍūkya, Chāndogya, Bṛhadāraṇyaka, Aitareya,* and *Taittirīya.* These Upaniṣads are the subject of innumerable commentaries, ancient, modern, and contemporary. The commentaries of Śaṁkara, the founder of Advaita Vedānta, are by far the most important and influential.

It is important to bear in mind that the Upaniṣads are not philosophical treatises. The authors of the Upaniṣads did not look upon themselves as builders of philosophical systems, but as men conveying their own experiences of and insights into reality. Consequently, it would be fruitless to look in the Upaniṣads for a systematic, coherent, logical development of ideas. One should be prepared to encounter apparent inconsistencies, undue emphasis on one idea here and another there, and sometimes even wholly unconnected digressions in the articulation of a given idea or theme. Further, the Upaniṣads are sometimes repetitious. The same idea may be dealt with in several places in more or less the same fashion. How do we account for this peculiar character of the style and texture of the Upaniṣads? One answer is that they are not the work of a single author, but the accumulation of the insights of different men over a long period of time. Another explanation for the nonsystematic character of the Upaniṣads is that their authors were concerned not so much with minutiae as with providing a comprehensive picture of their vision and insights. In short, their attention was not upon parts but on the whole. Thus the Upaniṣads abound in terse and aphoristic statements replete with inspiring meanings. Scintillating significance and dynamic intuition are packed into such short and powerful utterances. Precisely for these reasons the Upaniṣads give rise to diverse interpretations. This is not to say that there is no unity in the Upaniṣads. Quite the contrary, there are some fundamental concepts and meanings which run through all the Upaniṣads, thereby bestowing a unity on their content. As such, the various commentaries, no matter what their differences, share these fundamental concepts, which we shall now present.

Brahman. When the ancient sages turned their gaze on the external world, they found it to be one of ceaseless change. The birth, growth, and death of the stupendous variety of life-forms, the waxing and waning of the moon, the coming and going of seasons, all suggested to them that change and transience permeate the entire external world. Nothing seems to remain the same. Awed by the panorama of perennial change and impermanence around them, the Upaniṣadic inquirers asked: Is this all that there is to the world? Is there nothing but change, impermanence, birth, growth, and death? Or is there something amidst and behind the changing world that remains the same and endures eternally? They answered these questions affirmatively by saying that there is indeed something that is unchanging and eternal behind the fleeting world. That something they called *Brahman*.[14] It is of the utmost importance to note that the existence of the world of change itself is what has suggested to the seers the notion of the unchanging Brahman. For in the absence of any change, how could one be led to the idea of the unchanging? But soon they are confronted with the pressing questions: What is the relation between the unchanging Brahman and the changing world? Are Brahman and the world two different realities? Or are they one and the same? The answers to these questions are at the same time a clarification of the concepts "Brahman" and "world."

According to the Upaniṣads, Brahman is the imperishable and unchanging reality underlying every sector and facet of the world of change. Thus,

> In the heart of all things, of whatever there is in the universe, dwells the Lord.[15]
>
> This is the truth of *Brahman* in relation to nature: whether in the flash of lightning, or in the wink of the eyes, the power that is shown is the power of *Brahman*.[16]
>
> This is the truth of *Brahman* in relation to men: in the motions of the mind, the power that is shown is the power of *Brahman*.[17]
>
> The Imperishable is the Real. As sparks innumerable fly upward from a blazing fire, so from the depths of the Imperishable arise all things. To the depths of the Imperishable they again descend.[18]

> Self-luminous is that Being, and formless. He dwells within all and without all. He is unborn, pure, greater than the greatest, without breath, without mind.[19]

It is clear from these passages that Brahman is the selfsame power, the unchanging reality behind the world of ceaseless change. At this stage, the Upaniṣadic conception of reality seems to be dualistic—the changing world on the one hand and the unchanging Brahman on the other. But such a view is mistaken, for the Upaniṣads untiringly declare that Brahman is the sole reality. Just as different objects made of clay are different from each other only in name and form, so also the world of change is a world of names and forms only, while its substance alone is the reality, the eternal and imperishable Brahman: "In words or speech alone the modification [change] originates and exists. In reality there is no such thing as modification. It is merely a name, and the clay alone is real." [20] These sayings make it unmistakably clear that the Upaniṣadic conception of reality, far from being one of dualism constituted of the changing world and the unchanging Brahman, is thoroughly monistic: Brahman is the sole reality.

Brahman, unlike the world of our senses and intellect, is beyond names and forms. Consequently, nothing can be positively affirmed of Brahman; one can only say what Brahman is not. All description is relation, and since there can be nothing besides Brahman, Brahman cannot be described. Yet Brahman is the power that pervades all existence. This point is poignantly expressed by the Upaniṣads as follows:

> *Brahman* is he whom speech cannot express, and from whom the mind, unable to reach him, comes away baffled.[21]

> That which cannot be expressed in words but by which the tongue speaks—know that to be *Brahman*. *Brahman* is not the being who is worshipped of men.[22]

> That which is not comprehended by the mind but by which the mind comprehends—know that to be *Brahman*. *Brahman* is not the being who is worshipped of men.[23]

> That which is not seen by the eye but by which the eye sees—know that to be *Brahman. Brahman* is not the being who is worshipped of men.[24]

> That which is not drawn by the breath but by which the breath is drawn—know that to be *Brahman. Brahman* is not the being who is worshipped of men.[25]

Thus Brahman is the inexpressible, invisible, inaudible, and unthinkable ground of all existence. Brahman is neither a he nor a she but is the It. Brahman is not to be identified with any God or gods men worship. Brahman can never be captured by the senses or intellect, but can only be experienced in a flash of the highest mystical intuition.

To sum up, there are no two realities, the world of change and the unchanging Brahman. Rather, there is one and only one reality, the inexpressible Brahman. The world of our senses and intellect is merely a world of names and forms having no reality apart from Brahman. It is indeed Brahman itself appearing to us through the multiplicity of names and forms. Clay is one reality, one substance, although it may manifest itself through different names and forms.

Ātman. When the Upaniṣadic *ṛṣis* turned their attention inward, they found there a vast world, which, like the outer world, was one of incessant change. The inner world was a phantasmagoria of sensations, perceptions, thoughts, emotions, images, memories, and feelings. There seemed to be nothing there that was permanent and enduring. They then asked: Is the inner world just a passing phenomena of shifting and fleeting things? Or is there something in it that is permanent and imperishable? They answered again that there is indeed something amidst and behind the inner world of tumult and turmoil that remains permanent and unchanging. That something they called *Ātman,*[26] the silent, imperishable witness of all change. Ātman is the inmost Self of man and is not to be confused with the empirical ego, which, far from being the unchanging silent witness, is subject to unceasing change. It is the empirical ego that we are ordinarily aware of and call "self" and study in psychological laboratories. That the empirical ego is not to be identified with the Ātman is clear from the following passage:

> As a lump of salt when thrown into water melts away and the lump cannot be taken out, but wherever we taste the water it tastes salty, even so, O, Maitreyi, the individual self, dissolved, is the Eternal—pure consciousness, infinite and transcendent. Individuality arises by identification of the Self, through ignorance, with the elements; and with the disappearance of consciousness of the many, in divine illumination, it disappears. Where there is consciousness of the Self, individuality is no more.[27]

Ātman is pure spirit, unborn, uncreated, and eternal: "Ah, Maitreyi, my beloved, the Intelligence which reveals all—by that shall it be revealed? By whom shall the Knower be known? The Self is described as *not this, not that.* It is incomprehensible, for it cannot be comprehended; undecaying, for it never decays; unattached, for it never attaches itself; unbound, for it is never bound." [28] Ātman exists not just in man but in all beings—seas and stars, trees and thunder, birds and beasts. In the heart of all things, of whatever there is in the universe, dwells the Self: "The Self is the lord of all beings. As the spokes are held together in the hub and in the felly of a wheel, just so all beings, all creatures, all gods, all worlds, all lives, are held together in the Self." [29] The phenomenal world is a hierarchy of beings, with the inanimate at one end and man at the other. But—this is the important point—Ātman is present in all beings, irrespective of their place in the hierarchy. To put it differently, every existent is at the core spiritual.

From what has been said thus far, it should be clear to the reader that according to the Upaniṣads there is the Ātman on the one hand and the Brahman on the other. Brahman is the substance of all existence—the unchanging reality, of which the world of change is a mere manifestation through names and forms. Ātman is the eternal, silent witness in all beings; it is the pure spirit, all pervading. Further, both Ātman and Brahman, being beyond names and forms, are inexpressible and are to be experienced only in intuition. Both are unborn, uncreated, immutable, and eternal. There arise now two questions: Are Ātman and Brahman two different realities, the former underlying the inner world, and the latter the outer? What is the relation between Ātman and Brahman?

The Upaniṣadic answers to these questions constitute the greatest insight of the sages. Brahman, the unchanging reality amidst and behind the external world, although infinite and eternal, lacks spirituality. On the other hand, Ātman, the unchanging reality amidst and behind the internal world, although spiritual, lacks infinitude. That is, there is no self-contradiction in thinking that the infinite Brahman is a purely material reality; nor is it self-contradictory to think that Ātman is a finite spiritual reality. But now the *ṛṣis* noticed that by identifying Brahman and Ātman, they could in one stroke render Ātman spirit *infinite* and Brahman infinite *spirit*. Thus the sages declared that *Ātman* and *Brahman* do not refer to two different realities, but are two different labels for one and the same unchanging reality underlying the changing world of phenomena, external as well as internal. Here is reached the pinnacle of the Upaniṣadic wisdom: *Tat Tvam Asi* (That thou art), *Aham Brahma asmi* (I am Brahman);[30] *Ayam Ātmā Brahma* (This Self is Brahman);[31] *Prajñānam-Brahma* (Pure Consciousness is Brahman).[32]

> What is within us is also without. What is without is also within. He who sees difference between what is within and what is without goes evermore from death to death.[33]
>
> The Self who understands all, who knows all, and whose glory is manifested in the universe, lives within the shrine of the heart, the city of Brahman.[34]
>
> That which is the subtle essence—in that have all beings their existence. That is the truth. That is the Self. And that, O Svetaketu, That art Thou.[35]
>
> Formless is he, though inhabiting form. In the midst of the fleeting he abides forever. All-pervading and supreme is the Self. The wise man, knowing him in his true nature, transcends all grief.[36]

Knowledge and Freedom (Mokṣa). The Upaniṣads distinguish between two kinds of knowledge: the lower knowledge (*aparāvidyā*) and the higher knowledge (*parāvidyā*). The former is the product of the senses and intellect and is accordingly limited to the finite, objective world of change and impermanence. On the other hand, the higher knowledge is that by which the infinite and imperishable Brahman is attained:

> There are two kinds of knowledge, the higher and the lower. The lower is knowledge of the *Vedas* (the *Rik,* the *Sāma,* the *Yajur,* and the *Atharva*), and also of phonetics, ceremonials, grammar, etymology, meter, and astronomy. The higher knowledge is of that by which one knows the changeless Reality. By this is fully revealed to the wise that which transcends the senses, which is uncaused, which is undefinable, which has neither eyes nor ears, neither hands nor feet, which is all-pervading, subtler than the subtlest—the everlasting, the source of all.[37]

The higher knowledge, unlike the lower, is nonperceptual, nonconceptual, and intuitive. It is immediate and direct and is attained only by those who have stilled their senses and intellect. Further, the higher knowledge is neither objective nor subjective, for it transcends all three categories of empirical experience, namely, the knower, the known, and the act of knowing. Neither the performance of rituals and sacrifices nor the singing of the hymns nor the chanting of the mantras can bring one the higher knowledge: "The Self is not known through the study of scriptures, nor through subtlety of the intellect, nor through much learning. But by him who longs for him is he known. Verily unto him does the Self reveal his true being." [38]

Mokṣa, freedom from ignorance and bondage, is to be attained here and now, in this life. He who attains the knowledge of Brahman while still in bodily existence is the *jīvanmukta,* the living free. He has conquered ignorance and delusion once and for all. Gone is he beyond birth and death. He has attained immortality. At his death, the jīvanmukta attains *kaivalya,* complete freedom, the state beyond birth and death: "Having fully ascertained and realized the truth of Vedānta, having established themselves in purity of conduct by following the yoga of renunciation, these great ones attain to immortality in this very life." [39] It should be emphasized that in the context of the Upaniṣads immortality is not to be understood as endless existence in some unknown, distant corner of the cosmos, but as the state of consciousness in which one gains insight into the ground of all existence. To attain such consciousness is to attain immortality. Immortality is *saccidānanda* (*sat* = pure being, *cit* = pure consciousness, *ānanda* = pure bliss).

As the path to the realization of Brahman, the Upaniṣads recommend the fourfold discipline: (1) cultivation of moral purity as well as the disposition and will to seek the liberating knowledge, namely, the knowledge of Brahman, of Ātman; (2) listening attentively to a teacher (*guru,* the liberated man) as he expounds the Upaniṣadic truths; (3) reflecting upon the truths thus heard; and (4) meditation:

> To many it is not given to hear of the Self. Many though they hear of it, do not understand it. Wonderful is he who speaks of it; intelligent is he who learns of it. Blessed is he who, taught by a good teacher, is able to understand it.[40]

> The truth of the Self cannot be fully understood when taught by an ignorant man, for opinions regarding it, not founded on knowledge, vary one from another. Subtler than the subtlest is this Self, and beyond all logic. Taught by a teacher who knows the Self and *Brahman* as one, a man leaves vain theory behind and attains to truth.[41]

> Words cannot reveal him. Mind is unable to reach him. The eyes do not see him. How then can he be comprehended save when taught by those seers who indeed have known him?[42]

> Affix to the *Upaniṣad,* the bow incomparable, the sharp arrow of devotional worship; then, with mind absorbed and heart melted in love, draw the arrow and hit the mark, the Imperishable *Brahman. Om* is the bow, the arrow is the individual being, and *Brahman* is the target. With a tranquil heart, take aim. Lose thyself in him, even as the arrow is lost in the target. In him are woven heaven, earth, and sky, together with the mind and all the senses. Know him, the Self alone. Give up vain talk. He is the bridge of immortality.

> Within the lotus of the heart he dwells, where, like the spokes of a wheel, the nerves meet. Meditate on him as *Om*. Easily mayest thou cross the sea of darkness.[43]

Such, then, is the sublime nondualism of the Upaniṣadic teaching of the identity of Ātman and Brahman. Man's state of bondage and unfreedom is due to his ignorance of his real being and true nature. By destroying this primordial ignorance, man knows himself as the eternal and infinite Brahman.

Nothing could be a more fitting conclusion to our admittedly brief discussion of the Upaniṣadic teachings than the following delightful fable, told by the great seer Śrī Rāmakrishṇa:

> A lioness in search of prey came upon a flock of sheep, and as she jumped at one of them, she gave birth to a cub and died on the spot. The young lion was brought up in the flock, ate grass and bleated like a sheep, and it never knew that it was a lion. One day a lion came across this flock and was astonished to see in it a huge lion eating grass and bleating like a sheep. At his sight the flock fled and the lion-sheep with them. But the lion watched his opportunity and found the lion-sheep asleep. He woke him up and said, "You are a lion." The other said, "No," and began to bleat like a sheep. But the stranger lion took him to a lake and asked him to look in the water at his own image and see if it did not resemble him, the stranger lion. He looked and acknowledged that it did. Then the stranger lion began to roar and asked him to do the same. The lion-sheep tried his voice and was soon roaring as grandly as the other. And he was a sheep no longer.[44]

In truth, every one of us is Brahman, but in our ignorance we think that we are finite, perishable beings. The Upaniṣads exhort us to cut through the cloud of ignorance and discover ourselves to be Brahman, infinite, eternal, and immortal.

C. SCHOOLS OF VEDĀNTA

Introduction

The Upaniṣads are not systematic philosophical treatises, but are primarily the record of the utterances of various sages concerning their intuitive insights into and direct experience of ultimate reality. For this reason, one encounters in the Upaniṣads apparently inconsistent statements, different degrees of emphasis on the same idea at different times, and sometimes seemingly irrelevant digressions. Further, the terse and aphoristic style of the Upaniṣads and the esoteric nature of the subject of their teachings make it difficult to grasp the ideas. It is therefore not surprising that in course of time different people understood the Upaniṣads in different ways and accordingly a need for systematizing the fundamental ideas of the Upaniṣads was keenly felt. The earliest attempt to present the Upaniṣadic thought systematically was the celebrated *Brahma-sūtras* (also known as *Vedānta-sūtras* and *Śārīraka-sūtras*) of Bādarāyaṇa, which may justly be called the cornerstone of all Vedāntic thought. The *Brahma-sūtras* has been the source of inspiration for all Vedāntic thinkers, great and small alike. It should be pointed out, however, that the *Brahma-sūtras* itself is couched in brief and epigrammatic statements, which lend themselves to a variety of meanings and interpretations. Consequently, subsequent Vedāntic thinkers wrote elaborate commentaries, each interpreting the *Brahma-sūtras* and the Upaniṣads in his own way. In this manner there arose various schools of Vedānta, of which the most important are Śaṁkara's Advaita Vedānta, Rāmānuja's Viśiṣṭādvaita Vedānta, and Madhva's Dvaita Vedānta.

1. ADVAITA VEDĀNTA: NONDUALISM

Introduction

The life and times of Śaṁkara are shrouded in legend. On the basis of references to him in the writings of others, it is generally believed that Śaṁkara flourished sometime during the eighth or ninth century A.D. He was born of Brāhmin parentage in Kālādi, a village in the present Kerala state. He was a disciple of Govindapāda, who in turn was a disciple of the great Gauḍapāda. Attaining liberating knowledge at a very early age, Saṁkara traveled widely across the subscontinent, teaching Advaita Vedānta and debating with his opponents. According to tradition, he died at the early age of thirty-two. Given the brief span of his life, Saṁkara's achievements were truly extraordinary. He was an intellectual and religious genius, poet, philosopher, mystic, and saint. Among his most important works are *Brahma-sūtra-bhāṣya* (commentary on Bādarāyaṇa's *Brahma-sūtras*) and commentaries on the Upaniṣads and the Bhagavad-gītā.

Pramanas

Advaita Vedānta recognizes the six *pramāṇas* (sources and criteria of valid knowledge) as formulated by the Mīmāṁsā school of Kumārila Bhaṭṭa. They are as follows: (1) perception (*pratyakṣa*), (2) inference (*anumāna*), (3) testimony (*śabda*), (4) comparison (*upamāna*), (5) postulation (*arthāpatti*), and (6) noncognition (*anupalabdhi*).[45] The Advaita Vedānta treatment of perception, inference, and testimony is essentially the same as that of the Nyāya school. But as regards the other three *pramāṇas* its views are somewhat different from those held by the Nyāya thinkers. We shall therefore deal with these now.

Comparison (Upamāna). Comparison is an independent source of valid knowledge. It is a nonperceptual source in that it is not reducible to perception; nor can it be reduced to any of the other nonperceptual means, such as inference. Knowledge arrived at through comparison is expressed in the form of the judgment "A is like B," where B is an object being perceived at the time of the judgment, and A an object perceived sometime in the past, that is now remembered and asserted to be similar to B. Let us clarify this point by an example. Suppose a man has some time ago seen a cow in a barn and later comes across a wild cow in a forest and claims, "The cow I saw in the barn is like the wild cow I now perceive in the forest." According to the Advaitin, this claim cannot be one of perception, for of the two objects involved in the judgment only one is now being perceived; nor can the claim be regarded as memory-based, for what was perceived in the past and is now remembered is the cow in the barn and not its similarity to the wild cow now being perceived in the forest. Consequently, the similarity cannot be said to be the object of memory. Nor can it be said that knowledge by comparison is knowledge by inference; the reason for this is that inference always requires a universal premise stating an invariable relation (*vyāpti*) between two terms. But no such premise is employed here. To put the point explicitly, in order to infer from the proposition that the wild cow in the forest is like the cow in the barn the proposition that the cow in the barn is similar to the wild cow in the forest, one needs the universal premise, given any two objects, say X and Y, if X is similar to Y then Y is similar to X. But, evidently, in knowledge by comparison no such premise is employed. A man who has seen a cow in the barn and then sees a wild cow in the forest judges without any inference that the former is similar to the latter. Another way of putting this same point is that the similarity of X to Y is numerically distinct from the similarity of Y to X.

Postulation (Arthāpatti). Postulation is an independent source of valid knowledge. One employs postulation in order to account for an observed fact which cannot otherwise be explained. Suppose, for example, that a man says that he is fasting day and night, but he is nevertheless observed to be gaining weight. Now suppose further that we can observe him only during the day and find him to be fasting. Under these circumstances, the only way to account for the fact that he is gaining weight is to postulate that he eats during the night.[46] It is to be noted that postulation is neither perception nor inference: it is not perception, because we have not perceived him eating in the night; nor is it inference, because there is no invariable connection between growing fat and eating in the night. Postulation is like hypothesis in Western logic. There is, however, a difference between the two. Whereas hypothesis is tentative and may be rejected later on, postulation is held to be the only possible explanation of an observed state of affairs. It may further be noted that, whereas postulation is concerned with explaining observed facts, inference is concerned with drawing conclusions from observed facts. Briefly, postulation is the search for grounds, and inference is the search for the consequences of grounds.[47]

Anupalabdhi (noncognition).[48] As a source of knowledge, noncognition is a kind of cognition; it is our immediate cognition of the nonexistence of an object. It is concerned with negative facts and therefore with the nonexistence of objects and states of affairs. For example, the nonexistence of an elephant in my study is known through the absence of my cognition of an elephant in the study. Such noncognition is known as *anupalabdhi*. According to Advaita Vedānta, noncognition cannot be reduced to any of the other five *pramāṇas*. It would be a mistake to think that the nonexistence of an object is *inferred* from its noncognition; for inference requires a universal proposition asserting an invariable relation (*vyāpti*) between two terms, and there is no such proposition employed in my perception of the absence of an elephant in my study. It is important to note that to say that noncognition is a species of inference is to beg the issue, namely, establishing that when something is not perceived it does not exist. It is obvious that noncognition cannot be a case of perception, comparison, testimony, or postulation, either. For these reasons, the Advaitin regards noncognition as an independent source of valid knowledge.

It is worth emphasizing that not all cases of noncognition are necessarily cases of nonexistence. Thus, we do not perceive a table in a dark room. But this does not mean that there is no table in the room. To put the point differently, it is only when an object is not perceived under circumstances in which it should have been perceived that its nonperception means its nonexistence. If we do not perceive the table in a room which is fully lighted, then we are entitled to claim the nonexistence of the table in the room. Only cases of such nonperception are to be counted as the source of knowledge of nonexistence.

To conclude, Advaita Vedānta recognizes six *pramāṇas*, all of which are taken over from the Mīmāṁsā school of Kumārila Bhaṭṭa.

Śaṁkara's Theory of Reality

The Criterion of Sublation and Levels of Being. Central to Śaṁkara's theory of reality is the concept of sublation.[49] Sublation is essentially the mental process of correcting and rectifying errors of judgment.[50] Thus one is said to sublate a previously held judgment when, in the light of a new experience which contradicts it, one either regards the judgment as false or disvalues it in some significant sense. It is obvious that sublation of a given judgment necessarily results in its being replaced by a new one. Not only judgments but also concepts, objects, relations, and in general any content of consciousness, can be sublated. For Śaṁkara sublatability is the criterion of the ontological status of any content of consciousness; anything that is in principle sublatable is of a lesser degree of reality and value than that which replaces it as a result of sublation.[51] It is through the concept of sublation that Śaṁkara arrives at his ontological hierarchy.

On the criterion of sublatability, Śaṁkara distinguishes reality, appearance, and unreality. Reality is that which in principle cannot be sublated by any other experience. Appearance is that which in principle can be sublated by other experiences. Unreality is that which in principle neither can nor cannot be sublated.

Reality, Appearance, and Unreality. Let us first note that the act of sublation presupposes an essential dualism between the experiencer and the experienced, the subject and the object, consciousness and the contents of consciousness. It also presupposes a plurality of objects, concepts, judgments—contents of consciousness in general. The distinction between subject and object is necessary for sublation because it is the subject who sublates the object. Plurality of objects is necessary for sublation because sublation analytically implies juxtaposing one object or experience against another incompatible object or experience and judging that the first has a lesser degree of reality (or is of lesser value) than the second. In the light of these remarks, to say that the experience of reality is unsublatable is to say that no other experience can conceivably contradict the experience of reality. The reason for this is that reality is devoid of all distinctions—not only the distinction between one object and another but also that between the subject and the object, the self and the non-self. Thus the experience of reality transcends all distinctions and is therefore the experience of pure identity between the subject and the object, the self and the non-self. It is clear that the experience of reality is unsublatable, since there can be nothing besides the unitary experience which may conceivably controvert the experience. Reality is unsublatable because it is wholly bereft of any distinctions, oppositions, qualifications, or relations. It is the experience of reality that sublates all else, itself being unsublatable by any other experience whatsoever.

Appearance ("phenomenon," in the terminology of Plato and Kant) is that which in principle can be sublated. In contrast with reality as Pure Being, appearance may be construed as the realm of existents.[52] Śaṁkara divides existents into three kinds: real existents, existents, and illusory existents. Real existents are those which can only be sublated by reality. Unlike reality, real existents are experienced in the matrix of subject-object distinctions. It follows, then, that the only experience which can sublate the experience of a real existent is that which transcends the subject-object dichotomy—in short, the experience of the real. Let us illustrate this point by two examples. In the religious context, man experiences himself as creature and God as the creator, toward whom he has an attitude of dependency, devotion, and obedience. According to Śaṁkara, this experience of the dualism between creator and creature cannot be sublated by any experience within the realm of variety and plurality. It is only the experience of reality as transcending names and forms, and hence all distinctions, that can sublate the experience of the distinction between creator and creature.[53] To take another example: one accepts the law of noncontradiction as the touchstone of propositional truth; that is, one takes "p" as true insofar as "not-p" is false, and vice versa. And as long as men organize their experience of the world in accordance with the law of noncontradiction, no proposition, and hence no truth which they formulate, can conceivably violate or sublate the principle of noncontradiction. Only the experience of reality wholly transcending logic and language can sublate the principle of noncontradiction. This observation has far-reaching consequences for the enterprise of scientific, rational knowledge. The mind can grasp neither itself nor reality. It can only function by drawing distinctions, and for it to grasp itself it should function without drawing distinctions—a self-contradiction. In a word, the mind cannot catch itself, just as a knife which cuts everything else cannot cut itself. The mind can't grasp reality, because reality wholly transcends the realm of the mind—the realm of distinctions.

The second category under appearance is existent. Whereas a real existent can only be sublated by reality, an existent can be sublated by a real existent as well as by reality. The domain of existents can simply be characterized as that of conventional knowledge, knowledge based on rules and canons agreed upon by conventions, which may be commonsensical, logical, scientific, social, etc. For example, from the point of view of commonsense I assert that my desk is a solid body. But this commonsensical view is sublated by the scientific claim that the desk is a colony of electrical charges in constant motion with empty space between them. That is, the commonsensical notion of solid body is replaced by the scientific notion of moving electrical charges. But the notion of moving electrical charges is sublated by the experience of reality as being above and beyond all distinctions. This is what is meant by saying that an existent may be sublated by another existent or by reality. But since all real existents are sublatable by reality, it follows that "sublation" is a transitive relation with respect to existents, real existents, and reality. Thus let X be an existent, Y a real existent, and Z reality; then "Z sublates Y and Y sublates X" implies "Z sublates X."

The third category of appearances is illusory existent, which can be sublated by all other kinds of experience. Under illusory existents come illusions, hallucinations, dreams, and all erroneous perceptions. An illusory existent is distinguished by the fact that it fails to fulfill the criteria for empirical, everyday, conventional truth. Thus, a thirsty man traveling in a desert rushes to a certain spot to quench his thirst. But on reaching the spot he finds that there is no water and realizes that his perception of water is an illusory perception, a mirage, which fails to meet the criteria for water as existent. Consequently, the Advaitin says that the experience of the mirage is sublated by another experience.

We come now to the concept of unreality. According to Śaṁkara, unreality neither can nor cannot be sublated by other experiences. Anything which cannot become an object of our experience, actual or possible, is unreal. The reason why an unreal object cannot be experienced is that the concept of the unreal object is self-contradictory. Square circles, children of barren woman, married bachelors are examples of unreal objects. For anything to be sublatable, it must in principle be an object of our experience; and since unreal objects can never enter into our experience, it would be misleading to say that they are sublatable or not sublatable. For this reason, Śaṁkara says that unreal objects are neither sublatable nor not sublatable. It is worth pointing out that an illusory existent is one which *as a matter of fact* does not have an objective counterpart in our experience, whereas an unreal object is one which *in principle cannot* have an objective counterpart. In short, the unreal is nonbeing.

We shall presently see that according to Śaṁkara's criterion of sublatability only Brahman (Ātman) is reality,

Pure Being; the empirical world (world of our senses and intellect) is appearance; and nonbeing is unreality. But before examining Śaṁkara's arguments for this position, it is necessary to understand his theory of causation.

Śaṁkara subscribes to the *satkāryavāda* view of causation.[54] *Satkāryavāda* is the doctrine that the material effect is identical with (or preexists in) the material cause. Up to this point, Śaṁkara agrees with Sāṁkhya. We pointed out in the chapter on Sāṁkhya that there are two different versions of *satkāryavāda: pariṇāmavāda* and *vivartavāda.* According to the former, although the effect preexists in the cause, the cause undergoes a *real* transformation in bringing about the effect; according to the latter, the transformation is not real but only *apparent.* Śaṁkara emphatically rejects the *pariṇāmavāda* and upholds the *vivartavāda.*[55] His arguments against *pariṇāmavāda* are as follows: If *pariṇāmavāda* is true, then it contradicts *satkāryavāda;* for if the change undergone by a cause in bringing about an effect is a real change, then it would be absurd to say that the effect is identical with (or preexisted in) the cause. Śaṁkara readily grants that the efficient cause serves to change the material cause from one form into another. Thus the goldsmith makes rings and necklaces from a lump of gold. But these objects differ only in form and not in substance. Does this mean then that as efficient cause the goldsmith brings into existence forms which did not exist before? Śaṁkara answers this question negatively by saying that all that the efficient cause—in our example the activity of the goldsmith—does is to make manifest forms concealed in the material cause. According to Śaṁkara, it cannot be said that the forms do not preexist in the original material substance; for if they do not preexist, one should be able to produce oil from stone, and milk from metal.[56] But this is clearly impossible and absurd. Śaṁkara therefore concludes that the *pariṇāmavāda* interpretation of *satkāryavāda* is self-contradictory and hence false. When a cause produces an effect, it undergoes no *real* changes either in its substance or in its form. The changes of form that we observe are only *apparent* changes. This view that all changes which a cause is thought of as undergoing in bringing about effects are merely apparent changes is known as *vivartavāda*.

It should be pointed out that Śaṁkara's *vivartavāda* rests on his fundamental claim that forms do not and cannot have any reality of their own; their reality is inseparable from and dependent upon substance. According to Śaṁkara, we cannot even conceive of what it is for a form to exist apart from substance. As such, to regard changes in form as real is to regard substance as undergoing real changes. But substance is that which remains the same through all forms and changes in forms: the gold in the ring and the gold in the necklace are one and the same substance. Śaṁkara therefore concludes that all changes in form are only apparent changes. In brief, changes in form are not changes in reality but only in appearance. It may be noted that this argument for the apparent nature of changes in form can easily be extended to qualities. Qualities are inseparable from substance. If substance and quality are two distinct and independent realities, we need a third reality to relate substance and quality. But then we need a fourth reality to relate the third to the first two, and so on ad infinitum. According to Śaṁkara, the only way out of this threat of infinite regress (*anavasthā*) [57] is to regard qualities, not as independent reality, but as inseparable from and dependent upon substance, the only reality. Only changes in substance can be said to be real changes. But substance is that which remains unchanged through all changes in qualities. It now follows that changes in qualities are merely apparent changes.

We shall now discuss how the criterion of sublation and the *vivartavāda,* conjoined with the concepts of *māyā, avidyā,* and *adhyāsa,* lead to Śaṁkara's metaphysics, according to which Brahman is the sole reality and the world of our senses and intellect is merely an appearance.

Māyā. The term *māyā* is often translated as "illusion." However, such a translation is extremely misleading and is the source of serious misunderstandings of Śaṁkara's

Advaita Vedānta. The concept of *māyā* is best clarified by setting forth its psychological, epistemological, and ontological meanings. Needless to point out, there are analytical connections between the three kinds of meaning. Psychologically speaking, *māyā* is our persistent *tendency* to regard appearances as reality and vice versa. In terms of the criterion of sublatability, *māyā* is our constant *propensity* to regard the sublatable as the unsublatable and vice versa. From an epistemological point of view, *māyā* is our *ignorance* (*avidyā*) as to the difference between appearance and reality. Reality is that which cannot in principle be sublated by any other experience, whereas appearance is that which in principle can be sublated by other experiences. Sublation is possible only where distinctions exist. And since reality transcends all distinctions, the experience of reality cannot be sublated. On the other hand, the realm of appearances is necessarily one of distinctions and is therefore sublatable. Consequently, one appearance can be sublated by another, and all appearances can be sublated by reality. It is only by being unaware of this distinction between the sublatable and the unsublatable that men mistakenly believe that appearances are reality. In other words, ignorance as to the nature of reality is the foundation of *māyā*.[58] It is clear then that only the unsublatable, undifferentiated Pure Being is reality. The changing world of our senses, emotions, and intellect is merely an appearance. According to Śaṁkara, *māyā* is beginningless and endless, unthinkable and inexpressible.[59] *Māyā* is unthinkable because all thinking has its origin in it, and inexpressible because language has its basis in it.[60] *Māyā* is thus the warp and woof of the world of appearances—the world of senses, intellect, and emotion.

From an ontological point of view, *māyā* is the creative power of reality (Brahman) by virtue of which the world of variety and multiplicity comes into existence.[61] Sometimes *māyā* as the creative power of reality is referred to as "the sheer cosmic playfulness ('*līlā*') of reality." [62]

It is to be emphasized that when Śaṁkara talks about the phenomenal world as *māyā* in the sense of illusion, he is not saying that the phenomenal world is unreality, but that it is an appearance, which has its foundation in reality.[63] Appearance, unlike unreality, is sublatable. For this reason, there can be no such thing as pure illusion. Every illusion is grounded in reality. Thus one cannot experience a mirage in one's closet but only under certain objective, empirical circumstances. In other words, illusions and appearances, unlike unreality, are not pure nothing and nonbeing. The very fact that illusions are sublatable shows that they are genuine components of our experience. It is clear then that when Śaṁkara says that the phenomenal world is an illusion, he is not saying that it is nonexistent and unreal. Quite the contrary, he is affirming that the phenomenal world, like illusions, is not an independent reality but is grounded through and through in the sole reality of Pure Being.

Avidyā. The term *avidyā* means ignorance, which may be characterized as not knowing the real and also thinking that appearances are real. Often Śaṁkara and other Advaita Vedāntins speak of *māyā* and ignorance interchangeably. This is understandable in view of the fact that *māyā* in one of its senses means our persistent tendency to regard appearances as real and vice versa.[64] Like *māyā,* ignorance is also beginningless and endless. From a logical point of view *māyā* and ignorance are coeval, in that there cannot be the one without the other. However, from an epistemological point of view, ignorance may be regarded as prior to *māyā,* in that the latter presupposes the former. That is, ignorance is the necessary condition for *māyā.* This also means that *māyā* vanishes as soon as ignorance is overcome by knowledge of the real.[65] The magician's trick best illustrates this point. Suppose a magician makes one thing appear as another or apparently produces something out of nothing. Śaṁkara's point here is that it is we, being ignorant of the magician's trick, who mistake appearance for reality. For the magician himself, as the master of the trick, there can be no illusion.[66] But once we discover the trick by which the magician makes things appear, disappear, and reappear, we no longer fall victim to illusion but recognize the magician's performance for what it is. Just as the magician by his power of manipulation creates in us illusions, so also reality (Brahman) by its creative power, namely, *māyā,* produces in us the illusion of the phenomenal world of variety, multiplicity, and diversity. Once ignorance is overcome by knowledge of the real, one is no longer held captive by *māyā.* One might now ask: How is ignorance produced? To answer this question, we turn to a consideration of Śaṁkara's concept of *adhyāsa.*

Adhyāsa (Superimposition). The literal meaning of *adhyāsa is* "superimposition," which Śaṁkara defines as "the apparent presentation in the form of remembrance, to consciousness of something previously observed in some other thing." [67] As an act, superimposition is our thinking mistakenly that an object has certain attributes which in fact it does not have.[68] In general, we may say that superimposition consists in attributing qualities not immediately presented to consciousness to a thing that is immediately given to consciousness.[69] The classic illustration of superimposition is the rope-snake example. A man steps on a rope in the dark and thinks it is a snake. Here the rope is what is immediately present to consciousness, the snake is an object of past experience, and superimposition is the person's mistakenly attributing the remembered qualities of the snake to the rope. The present experience of the rope and the past experience of a snake are necessary conditions for one to be able mistakenly to claim that what is now experienced is a snake. In other words, the snakelike experience cannot be had in the absence of the rope. But when one brings a lamp and discovers that what one has stepped on is only a rope, one's snakelike experience is recognized as being illusory. In a similar manner, the empirical world arises as a result of our superimposing qualities on the undifferentiated, unsublatable reality. Just as under superimposition the rope is experienced as a snake, so also under the superimposition of names and forms reality, which is beyond names and forms, is experienced as the world of appearances. On attaining knowledge of reality, ignorance, *māyā,* and the world of appearances vanish away simultaneously. It is clear by now that superimposition is the source of ignorance.[70] One can talk about *adhyāsa* in two senses: (1) with respect to particular experiences in the world of appearances and (2) with respect to the world of appearances in general. In the former case *adhyāsa* is the attribution of qualities remembered to a thing now being experienced. In the latter case, *adhyāsa* is the superimposition of names and forms on the undifferentiated, unitary reality. We might mention here that Śaṁkara also distinguishes between two kinds of ignorance: primordial (universal ignorance) and individual (temporary ignorance). The former has neither beginning nor end, whereas the latter can be ended by the individual's attaining knowledge of the real. Moreover, universal ignorance serves to account for the common empirical world of appearances.

Having explicated the central epistemological concepts of Śaṁkara's Advaita Vedānta, we are now in a position to present his account of Brahman, Ātman, and the empirical world.

Brahman. According to the criterion of sublatability, Brahman is the sole reality—that which cannot be sublated by any other experience. That is to say, Brahman transcends all distinctions, such as subject and object and self and non-self. Consequently, Brahman is unthinkable, imperceivable, and inexpressible. Brahman can only be experienced in nonperceptual, nonconceptual, direct, intuitive insight. We note that this is precisely the Upaniṣadic account of Brahman.

World. The world of phenomena is the realm of *māyā,* the product of ignorance, which in turn is generated by our superimposing names and forms on the unitary unsublatable, nameless, formless reality (Brahman). The empirical world is thus the world of appearances. This is not to say, however, that the world of appearances is unreal. On the contrary, since the world of appearances is sublatable by reality, namely, Brahman, it is not nonbeing and unreality.[71] Just as a man stepping on a rope in the dark thinks in his ignorance that it is a snake that he has stepped on, so also man in his ignorance of Brahman, the unchanging reality, thinks that the changing world of appearances is the reality, What then, one might ask, is the ontological status of the snake the man thinks he has stepped on? Or, on a cosmic scale, what is the ontological status of the world of appearances? According to Śaṁkara, the snake is neither real nor unreal. It is not real, because it can be sublated; it is not unreal, because if it were it neither could nor could not be sublated. Similarly, the world of appearances is neither real nor unreal. Hence Śaṁkara's ontological hierarchy: the unreal, the neither real nor unreal, and the real. Further, just as no snakelike experience is possible without the empirical reality of the rope, so also there can be no experience of the world of appearances without the underlying reality of Brahman. Most importantly, just as there are no two numerically distinct realities called "the rope" and "the snake" but only one reality, the rope appearing as snake under certain conditions of superimposition, so also there are no two numerically distinct realities called "the empirical world" and "Brahman," but only one reality, Brahman, which appears to us as the empirical world under the superimposition of names and forms. When men free themselves from ignorance and *māyā,* the world of appearances itself will be seen as Brahman.[72] We note again that this is exactly the Upaniṣadic teaching that Brahman is the sole reality underlying the world of appearances.

Ātman. According to Śaṁkara, Ātman, the inmost Self of man, is pure, undifferentiated consciousness.[73] Like Brahman, Ātman is nameless and formless and hence spaceless, timeless, imperceivable, unthinkable, and inexpressible.[74] It is the unchanging, silent witness of the world of change and appearance.[75] Like Brahman, Ātman transcends all distinctions. Consequently, it is reality, unsublatable by any other experience.[76] Men in their ignorance mistakenly identify the Ātman with one or other of the appearances (names and forms), such as the body, the brain, the mind, etc. Ātman as reality is none of these things. Just as is the case for Brahman, Ātman cannot be an object in the world of appearances alongside other objects. On the contrary, it is the light which illumines all objects (that which the eye cannot see but by which the eye sees, etc.).[77] How does Śaṁkara establish the existence of Ātman? His argument is somewhat similar to Descartes' "*Cogito ergo sum*" ("I think, therefore I am"). According to Śaṁkara, one cannot doubt Ātman without falling into self-contradiction, for the very act of doubting presupposes the doubter.[78] We may point out that this argument is defective, because what it establishes is the existence of the empirical self (*jīva*), the changing ego, and not that of Ātman, the unchanging Self. This is not surprising, for Ātman, being beyond names and forms, eludes all thought and argument. *Jīva,* the empirical self, is the appearance of Ātman under superimposition. We may introduce here Śaṁkara's concept of *upādhi,* meaning limitation, limiting adjunct.[79] Ātman, which is infinite and eternal, appears to us as finite, time-bound *jīva* owing to limiting conditions, both mental and physical, belonging in the realm of appearances. Thus, space, which is formless, one, and indivisible, assumes the form of the container, such as a pot or a room. Similarly, Ātman which is nameless, formless, eternal, and infinite, appears as finite *jīva* owing to limitations such as the body and mind. When one overcomes ignorance arising out of superimposition and limitation, one knows the Ātman as the sole unsublatable reality.

Śaṁkara now establishes the central insight of the Upaniṣhads—the identity of Ātman and Brahman.[80] Ātman and Brahman are not two distinct realities but two different labels for one and the same reality.[81] Knowledge of Brahman coincides with knowledge of Ātman. One experiences Brahman as the sole unsublatable reality when one transcends all distinctions, in particular that between the subject and the object; the subject and the object coalesce into each other; the subject is also the object and vice versa. In such an experience, Brahman, the unchanging reality underlying the changing world of external appearances, is also Ātman, the unchanging reality underlying the changing world of internal appearances.[82] In other words, where all distinctions between the external and the internal vanish, the distinction between the Self and the non-Self vanishes and one experiences Pure Being as Pure Consciousness (Pure Intelligence).[83] Such an experience is also one of Pure Bliss.[84] For this reason Advaita Vedānta refers to the experience of reality (Brahman, Ātman) as saccidānanda (*sat* = Pure Being, *cit* = Pure Consciousness, *ānanda* = Pure Bliss).[85] We may note here that Śaṁkara's thesis of the identity of Ātman and Brahma is none other than the Upaniṣadic teaching that what is within is also what is without, and what is without is also what is within, and whosoever sees any difference between what is within and what is without goes evermore from death to death.[86] It is because of its emphatic rejection of any distinction between Ātman and Brahman, Self and non-Self that Śaṁkara's school of Vedānta is known as Advaita Vedānta. A word of clarification concerning *Advaita* is in order. *Advaita* means nondualistic and is not to be translated as monistic. The reason for this is that no positive attributes can be predicated of reality; one can only say what it is not. Thus to say that reality is nondual is not the same as saying that it is one. However, as long as one keeps this point in mind, no harm is done in referring to Śaṁkara teaching as monistic Vedānta.

Two Kinds of Knowledge[87]

Consistent with the Upaniṣads, Śaṁkara distinguishes two kinds of knowledge and truth: the lower, conventional, practical, relative knowledge and truth (*vyavahārika-satya*) and the higher, absolute knowledge and truth (*paramārthika-satya*).[88] The lower knowledge is the product of the senses and intellect—that is, knowledge obtained through superimposition. Consequently, it is of the changing, finite, objective world of our empirical experience. It is necessarily governed by the subject-object distinction.[89] With respect to lower knowledge one can always ask, "Who is the knower? What is the known? What is the act of knowing? All lower knowledge is propositional, constructed through names and forms. In brief, lower knowledge is knowledge of the world of appearances, the realm of *māyā*.[90] On the other hand, the higher knowledge is nonperceptual, nonconceptual, and hence nonpropositional. It is the knowledge of the real, of Braham (Ātman). It is to be attained through intuitive,[91] mystical insight of the *nirbījasamādhi* of Yogic discipline. The higher knowledge is neither subjective nor objective and therefore transcends all three categories of lower knowledge, namely, the knower, the known, and the act of knowing.[92]

At this point, it is appropriate to dispel some misunderstandings concerning Śaṁkara's teaching that the lower knowledge is only knowledge of appearances. Some of Śaṁkara's opponents, both ancient and modern, interpret him as having claimed that the world of appearance is an illusion and consequently that the knowledge of such a world is false and useless. Such an interpretation is wholly groundless. For Śaṁkara clearly maintains that the lower knowledge is valid and pragmatically efficacious in the realm of phenomena, the world of appearances.[93] Much like Nāgārjuna, Śaṁkara emphasizes that to say that a given truth is a lower truth is not to say that it is falsehood, but only that it is a truth conditioned by other truths and hence cannot be claimed to be absolute truth (truth about Brahman, the unsublatable reality). Śaṁkara readily grants that lower truths are useful in dealing with the objective world of appearances. Common sense, logic, science, and philosophy are all to be pursued for their fruitfulness for understanding particular domains of the empirical world. Further, to say that the world of appearances is an illusion is not to say it is nothing and nonexistent. More importantly, he who has not experienced reality has no business declaring that the phenomenal world is an illusion or a mere appearance. The phenomenal world is an illusion and appearance only in the light of the experience of reality. Just as the unreality of the imaginary standpoint (*prātibhāsika*) can only be certified by attaining the empirical standpoint (*vyavahārika*), so also the neither-real-nor-unreal status of the empirical standpoint can only be realized by attaining the absolute standpoint (*paramārthika*).[94] It is to be emphasized that even on attaining the absolute standpoint, the empirical world does not become unreality, but is only realized to be an illusion, which, we may recall, is not nonbeing. Thus, contrary to his opponents' charges, Śaṁkara teaches neither the unreality of the empirical world nor the falsity of empirical truths.

God

Consistent with his distinction between appearance and reality, Śaṁkara distinguishes two conceptions of God: God with qualities and God without qualities, respectively known as *Saguṇa-Brahman* (also called Īśvara) and *Nirguṇa-Brahman.*[95] It is obvious that the former conception belongs to the lower, conventional, relative, practical standpoint, and the latter to the higher, absolute standpoint. Saguṇa-Brahman is God thought of as the cause, creator, sustainer, and destroyer of the universe.[96] It is Saguṇa-Brahman that men worship in different names and forms, such as Rama, Kṛṣṇa, Śiva, Jesus. It is God as Saguṇa-Brahman that is endowed with such qualities as love, kindness, mercy. Saguṇa-Brahman is God who stands in relation to man and the world. In short, Saguṇa-Brahman is personal God.[97] But since qualities and relations can only belong in the realm of appearances, Saguṇa-Brahman is God as appearance and not as reality. On the other hand, Nirguṇa-Brahman, being reality beyond names and forms, is neither the cause nor the creator nor the sustainer nor the destroyer of the universe. God as Nirguṇa-Brahman can be neither worshiped nor prayed to. God as Nirguṇa-Brahman is Pure Being, Pure Consciousness, and Pure Bliss.

It may be pointed out here that there is a parallel between the individual self (*jīva*) and Saguṇa-Brahman on the one hand and between the Ātman and Nirguṇa-Brahman on the other. Both the individual ego and Saguṇa-Brahman are products of *māyā,* whereas both Ātman and Nirguna-Brahman are beyond māyā. Just as the Ātman appears as the individual ego under the limitations of body and mind, so also Nirguṇa-Brahman appears as Saguṇa-Brahman owing to cosmic ignorance, *māyā.*

It is obvious that it is only with respect to God as Saguṇa-Brahman that one can talk about omnipotence, omnipresence, omniscience, and omnibenevolence and accordingly hold him responsible for the good and evil in the world of appearances. On the other hand, God as Nirguṇa-Brahman, being the sole reality, is beyond good and evil. Śaṁkara recognizes the need for the concept of Saguṇa-Brahman as engendering genuine religious consciousness in as yet unenlightened men. It is conducive to the cultivation of moral virtues and piety necessary for the realization of Nirguṇa-Brahman.[98] Saguṇa-Brahman therefore serves as the stepping-stone in one's striving for knowledge of reality. However, Śaṁkara emphatically maintains that knowledge of reality cannot be attained unless one transcends the Saguṇa-Brahman. Only knowledge of Nirguṇa-Brahman is knowledge of reality—liberating knowledge.

Bondage and Freedom (Mokṣa)

True to the spirit of the Indian tradition, Śaṁkara holds that man's state of bondage and suffering is due not to any original sin on his part but to original ignorance (*avidyā*).[99] It is by conquering this ignorance by the knowledge of reality—the identity of Ātman and Brahman—that man attains *mokṣa,* the state of absolute freedom from ignorance, *māyā,* bondage, and suffering.[100] For this reason, knowledge of reality is called "liberating knowledge." It is also called "soteriological knowledge" in that it radically transforms man. The man who has attained *mokṣa* is freed once and for all from ignorance, illusion, delusion, fear, and attachment. By overcoming ignorance by the knowledge of the real, he has brought the karmic chain to an end and thereby has broken out of the circle of births and deaths.[101] He has thus gone beyond birth and death and attained immortality. It should be pointed out that in the context of Advaita Vedānta, as in that of the Upaniṣads, "immortality" is not to be understood in the sense of endless existence in some distant and unknown world. Rather, it means that man has discovered that birth and death are products of *māyā* and ignorance confined to the world of appearances and that in his true being he is infinite and eternal, untouched by birth and death. *Mokṣa,* absolute freedom, is not a state to be looked forward to after death. On the contrary, *mokṣa* is the attainment of the highest state of consciousness (of the identity of Ātman and Brahman) to be attained here and now while one is still in one's bodily existence.[102] He who attains such consciousness is *jīvanmukta,* the living free.[103] At death, he attains *videhamukti,* the final and absolute freedom from all fetters of *māyā*. To attain *mokṣa* is to attain knowledge into oneself as the ultimate reality that permeates all existence. The mokṣic man is thus one who has overcome all the distinctions and oppositions that plague men in igorance and bondage. In particular, he has overcome that nightmare of ignorant philosophies—the opposition between freedom and necessity and good and evil.[104] Having attained the knowledge of the real, one has overcome all forms of alienation—alienation from the world, from other men, and from oneself. *Mokṣa,* then, is the state of self-knowledge, peace, freedom, and wisdom. In a word, the mokṣic man is *saccidānanda,* Pure Being, Pure Consciousness, and Pure Bliss.

According to Advaita Vedānta, *mokṣa* is attained through *jñāna-yoga,* which may be characterized as intellectual-spiritual discipline (or simply the path of knowledge).[105] Advaita Vedānta recommends the fourfold discipline (*sādhana-catuṣṭaya*) as a practical aid to the aspirant to *mokṣa*. The discipline consists of: *samanyasa, śravaṇa, manana,* and *dhyāna.* We shall now briefly discuss these in turn.

Samanyasa consists in cultivating in oneself the following qualities: (*a*) the ability to discriminate between the real on the one hand and appearances and the unreal on the other; the capacity to discern between the timeless and the time-bound, the eternal and the transient, the infinite and the finite; (*b*) total indifference to both pleasure and pain under all circumstances, either here or elsewhere; renunciation of all worldly desires and attachments; (*c*) tranquillity, self-control, dispassion, fortitude, power of mental concentration, and faith; (*d*) single-minded desire for true freedom.

Śravaṇa is listening to the sages as they expound the great truths of the Upaniṣads and Advaita Vedānta as well as studying the Vedāntic texts. Through *śravaṇa* one learns the sole reality of Brahman and the identity of Ātman and Brahman (That thou art). In *śravaṇa,* the role of the *guru* (master) as a living example of the liberated man cannot be overemphasized.

Manana is the stage of reflection, in which the disciple subjects to systematic analysis and investigation what he has learned from his *guru* and the works of the sages. He examines the teachings and weighs them in the light of reason—arguments, counterarguments, analogy from everyday experience, etc.—and becomes intellectually convinced of their truth. But intellectual understanding and conviction, no matter how clear, firm, and convincing, can only provide mediate knowledge. Moreover, intellectual understanding and conviction are subject to change, especially under the burden of old habits of thought, resulting in the doubting and rejecting of what has hitherto been held as infallible truth. What is needed is to transform the intellectually grasped mediate knowledge into one's own immediate experience. The aspirant therefore now undertakes *dhyāna* (Yogic meditation) on the central Advaitic truth "That thou art." Through prolonged and intense meditation he comes to see in a flash of intuition that he is indeed Brahman, the sole reality.

2. VIŚIṢṬĀDVAITA VEDĀNTA: QUALIFIED NONDUALISM

Introduction

As opposed to the absolute and unqualified nondualism of Śaṁkara's Vedānta, Viśiṣṭādvaita Vedānta is qualified nondualism. According to tradition, Rāmānuja was the founder of Viśiṣṭādvaita Vedānta. Born in A.D. 1017 of Brāhmin parentage, at Śrīperumbudur in South India, Rāmānuja studied under such great *ācāryas* (teachers) and *ālvārs* (poet-saints) as Yādava Prakāśa, Yāmuna, Peria Nambi, and Gosṭhipūrna, all of whom held a theistic-personalistic interpretation of Vedānta. Regarding Śaṁkara's Absolute as an arid and bloodless abstraction, not only unwarranted by the scriptures but also incapable of fulfilling man's genuine religious aspiration, Rāmānuja set himself the task of providing an interpretation of Vedānta that would at once preserve the identity of and difference between Ātman and Brahman—between man and God. To this end, Rāmānuja composed several works, the most important of which are *Śrībhaṣya* and *Gitābhasya,* commentaries on the *Brahma-sūtras* and the Bhagavad-gītā, respectively. As a theistic Vedāntin, Rāmānuja worshiped God as Viṣṇu, established many temples of Viṣṇu and converted many to Vaiṣṇavism. He died in 1137.

We shall not treat Viśiṣṭādvaita in any great detail, but will confine ourselves to a discussion of its main tenets—especially as objections to and criticisms of Śaṁkara's Advaita Vedānta.

Brahman and Selves

Rāmānuja agrees with Śaṁkara that Brahman is the sole reality. But whereas for Śaṁkara Brahman, as reality devoid of any and all distinctions, is pure identity-without-difference, for Rāmānuja Brahman is the unity of the differences constituting the world of our empirical experience[106]—in brief, Rāmānuja's Brahman is identity-in-difference (*bhedābheda*).[107] Much like Hegel, Rāmānuja holds that pure identity such as Śaṁkara's is an abstraction, a pure nothing. One can talk about identity only when there is also difference. Identity-without-difference, just as difference-without-identity, is an empty concept and hence cannot point to any reality. Rāmānuja finds justification for his doctrine that Brahman is identity-in-difference in some rare Upaniṣadic passages. For example, the *Śvetāśvatara Upaniṣad* declares that there are three ultimate existences constituting the Absolute: the eternal, omniscient, omnipotent God, the eternal but powerless soul, and the eternal matter.[108] Thus, for Rāmānuja, Brahman is the unity of the different selves and material objects of the phenomenal world. Brahman as the identity of these different constituents is the underlying substratum. It should be pointed out that, correctly speaking, Rāmānuja's concept of unity is not unity but union; for from a logical point of view it is only union and not unity that can be thought of as being constituted of ultimately distinct and separate parts. That this is indeed the case is clear from Rāmānuja's own threefold categorial distinctions: *ādhāra* (the support) -*ādheya* (the supported) ; *niyāmaka* (the controller) -*niyamya* (the controlled), and *śeṣin* (the Lord) -*śeṣa* (the servant).[109] The first member of each of these refers to Brahman, and the second to the world. That is to say, for Rāmānuja the distinction between Brahman and the world is ultimate and indissoluble. That this is so is further supported by the fact of Rāmānuja's claim that Brahman is related to the cosmos as the soul to the body.[110] Just as the soul of man, although distinct from his body, controls and guides the body, so also Brahman, although different from the cosmos, controls and guides it. Brahman is thus the ruler and controller of the world. In other words, reality is like a person: [111] the various selves and material objects are its body, and Brahman its soul. Further, since there can be no genuine relation of any kind whatever between two entities of which one is real and the other unreal, it follows that the world of variety and multiplicity, in that it is related to Brahman, is real, although not independently real. This is the same as saying that individual selves and objects are real qualities and modes of Brahman.[112] Individual selves and material objects are related to Brahman as parts to a whole.[113] Each part is separate and yet not different in substance from the whole. Just as qualities are real but cannot exist independently of substance, so also the selves and objects are real as parts of ultimate reality but cannot exist independently of it. It is for this reason that Rāmānuja's Absolute, unlike Śaṁkara's, is not unqualified identity but identity-in-difference.[114] Hence Rāmānuja's Vedānta is known as Viśiṣṭādvaita (qualified nondualism). It is obvious that Rāmānuja's teaching that the world of phenomena is as real as Brahman is diametrically opposed to Śaṁkara's view that the phenomenal world is appearance and is therefore neither real nor unreal. It should be pointed out in defense of Śaṁkara that Rāmānuja's view is based on the shaky ontological argument from the concept of person as well as an inadequate analysis of how we experience and produce knowledge of the phenomenal world.

The second important difference between Śaṁkara and Rāmānuja concerns knowledge. Śaṁkara recognizes two kinds of knowledge (consciousness): the lower, governed by the distinctions between the knower, the known, and the act of knowing; and the higher, which transcends these distinctions. According to Śaṁkara, knowledge of the empirical world is subject to the above distinctions, whereas knowledge of Brahman (reality transcending the subject-object distinction) is itself Pure Being, Pure Consciousness, and Pure Bliss (*saccidānanda*). In short, Śaṁkara identifies Ātman (the Self) with the higher knowledge. Rāmānuja, on the other hand, holds that knowledge analytically implies the knower and the known and hence cannot be identified with the knower or the known; where there is no knower, there can be nothing to be known either.[115] Consequently, argues Rāmānuja, experience of reality is not an experience in which the self–non-self distinction is obliterated, but one in which the self becomes conscious of the unity of reality. In the terminology of Yoga, Śaṁkara admits *nirbījasamādhi,* and Rāmānuja rejects it. Once again in defense of Śaṁkara it should be pointed out that Rāmānuja's claim that the self remains distinct even in the experience of ultimate reality is based on a confusion between the empirical ego and the Ātman.[116] True, in our experience of the empirical world, the disinction between the knower and the known holds through and through; the knower here is not the Ātman but the empirical ego. But, and this is the important point, the Advaitin would say that it is absurd to argue thereby that the self remains distinct even in the experience of reality transcending all distinctions, because in such experience there can be nothing from which the self can be distinguished. It is precisely for this reason that Śaṁkara, in the true spirit of the recurrent theme of the Upaniṣads "That thou art," [117] sharply distinguishes between the empirical ego and the Ātman (Brahman, reality). That is, the "That" in "That thou art" does not refer to the empirical ego but to the Ātman, which is not consciousness of this or that object but Pure Consciousness, the awareness beyond the collapse of the intentional structure of empirical consciousness. The Advaitin draws attention to the fact that the quintessential teaching of the Upaniṣads reads "That thou art" without qualification, not "Thou in this or that respect or as this or that part art that."

Māyā

For the purposes of our discussion of Rāmānuja's criticism of Śaṁkara's concept of *māyā*,[118] we shall take *māyā* in two of its senses, namely, ignorance as well as the power of Brahman by which the empirical world is manifested. Rāmānuja's first objection is: If ignorance is what produces the world, where does ignorance exist? Surely, it cannot be said to exist in the *jīva* (individual), for individuality itself is produced by ignorance, and it is absurd to say effect produces cause. Nor can it be said that ignorance exists in Brahman, for in that case Brahman could not be omniscient. The Advaitin replies by saying that this objection is misguided, for *māyā* as ignorance is not an existent alongside other existents. Only of existents does it make sense to ask where they exist and what produces them; it simply does not make sense to ask where ignorance itself exists. Ignorance and individuality are two aspects of the same existent, the *jīva.* The *jīva* is individual in that it is produced by the power of Brahman; the *jīva* is ignorance in that it mistakenly thinks that in its true being it is finite and limited. *Māyā,* the power of Brahman to manifest the empirical world, no more affects the omniscience of Brahman than the power of the magician to produce illusions in us affects his knowledge. Thus Rāmānuja's objection is simply powerless against Śaṁkara.

The second objection is as follows: If, as Śaṁkara claims, ignorance is the veil that concels Brahman, then, contrary to the Advaitin's claim, Brahman cannot be said to be self-revealing. The Advaitin's reply is that to say that ignorance conceals Brahman is merely to say that it prevents the *jīva* from realizing its true being as Brahman; it is not to say that ignorance either diminishes the reality of Brahman or destroys Brahman's self-revealing power; in brief, ignorance cannot limit Brahman in any manner whatever. To illustrate this point, let us take an example. The sun is self-luminous and self-revealing. But on a cloudy day we cannot see the sun because the clouds obstruct our vision of it. But this is not to say that the clouds have diminished the reality of the sun or destroyed the self-luminous nature of the sun. In a similar manner, the *jīva's* inability to realize Brahman no more diminishes the reality and self-manifesting nature of Brahman than a group of blind men can render the sun unreal and non-self-lumious.

The third objection of Rāmānuja is: Śaṁkara teaches that ignorance is inexpressible and is neither real nor unreal. But the phrase "neither real nor unreal" is a strange and absurd locution, for it violates the principle of noncontradiction, according to which anything is either real or unreal. In reply, the Advaitin points out that Rāmānuja fails to understand Śaṁkara's criterion of sublation. Anything is sublatable if and only if it can in principle be a datum of our experience. *Māyā* is a datum of our experience; therefore it is sublatable and hence is not reality. On the other hand, since unreality cannot in principle be a datum of our experience, *māyā* is not unreality. It follows that *māyā* is neither real nor unreal. Further, to say that something is inexpressible is not to say that it violates the principle of noncontradiction. It is merely to say that it defies all our modes of thought, necessarily governed by the principle of noncontradiction. It is clear that Rāmānuja's objection is untenable.[119]

God

Rāmānuja's Brahman, unlike that of Śaṁkara, is unity-in-difference and therefore contains within itself ultimate and indissoluble distinctions. The individual selves and material objects of the world are related to Brahman as parts to a whole. In other words, Brahman, according to Rāmānuja, is not qualityless, undifferentiated Pure Being but has real qualities. The three essential attributes of Brahman are *satyam* (reality), *jñānam* (consciousness), and *anantam* (infinitude).[120] In contrast, Śaṁkara maintains that Brahman is beyond all attributes, positive as well as negative. However, Śaṁkara does admit that Saguṇa-Brahman, which is an appearance, does have qualities. It is obvious now that Rāmānuja's ultimate reality is none other than Śaṁkara's Saguṇa-Brahman.[121] Accordingly, Rāmānuja, unlike Śaṁkara, holds that God is the creator, sustainer, and destroyer of the world. God creates the world out of his will. But creation does not mean creation from nothing. Since selves and matter are coexistent with God, creation means God's bringing about the world of variety and multiplicity which is potentially present in him. God wills himself to be many and divides himself into the manifold of the animate and inanimate. Further, creation is not an event in time in the sense of having an absolute beginning in time. The world goes through cycles of evolution (*sṛṣṭi*) and dissolution (*pralaya*)[122] as willed by God, who is the Lord of *karma*. At the time of dissolution, God withdraws the world into himself. According to Rāmānuja, even in the state of dissolution there remain distinct in Brahman selves and undifferentiated matter. The reason for this is that like Brahman matter and selves are eternal. According to Rāmānuja, selves are subtle (*sūkṣma*) and infinitesimal (*aṇu* = atomic) but eternal.[123] It is worth noting that this view is contrary to the Upaniṣadic teaching (which is also Śaṁkara's) that selves are not only eternal but also infinite (all-pervading). It is clear from this that the Self of Rāmānuja's Vedānta is not the Ātman but the empirical "I," the ego. At the time of creation, God by his act of will manifests himself as selves and material objects. The kind of body a self receives depends upon its *karma*.[124] God gives every self freedom of will and is therefore not responsible for its good or evil deeds and *karma*. Each self, acting freely out of the will God has graciously bestowed upon it, is wholly responsible for its state of existence. Consequently, Rāmānuja maintains that evil in the world cannot be traced to God, who is the embodiment of all (and only) the positive virtues in highest perfection.[125] God is Perfect Personality.[126] Needless to say, Rāmānuja's theodicy is beset with all the standard difficulties associated with philosophies which uphold the conception of God as omiscient, omnibenevolent, and omnipotent.[127]

From these considerations, it is easy to see that Rāmānuja, unlike Śaṁkara, rejects complete identity of man and God.[128] For Rāmānuja, man is identical with God only in the sense that God pervades and controls the whole universe. Accordingly, Rāmānuja's interpretation of the Upaniṣadic declaration "That thou art" is radically different from that of Śaṁkara. For Rāmānuja, the "that" here refers to God, the omniscient, omnibenevolent, omnipotent, infinite creator of the world; the "thou" refers to God as existing in the form of man, the embodied Self. Consequently, says Rāmānuja, the identity between God and man is really the identity between God with certain qualifications and God with certain other qualifications. In brief, God and man are of one substance but possess different qualities. Hence the name *Viśiṣṭādvaita* ("qualified identity") for Rāmānuja's Vedānta. It should, however, be pointed out that Rāmānuja's interpretation of "That thou art" is not only far-fetched and arbitrary, but wholly incompatible with the spirit of absolute and unqualified identity of man and God that so unmistakably permeates the Upaniṣads.

Bondage and Salvation

According to Rāmānuja, the self's bondage to the body is due to its *karma,* which is generated and sustained by the self's ignorance as to its true being.[129] In its ignorance, the self identifies itself with the body or some part thereof and thereby develops desires and attachments to bodily existence. The general tendency of the self to identify itself with the non-self is known as *ahaṁkāra* (egoism).

Salvation, freedom from ignorance, *karma,* and bondage, is to be attained through work, knowledge, and devotion. Man should perform the rites and ceremonies commensurate with his caste and station in life as enjoined upon him by the Vedas. For this reason, the study of Mīmāṁsā, whose central concern is the right performance of rites and duties, is essential to the Viśiṣṭādvaitin. Man should study the Vedāntic texts in order to intellectually comprehend the true nature of himself, the world, and God. As a result of study and reflection, man comes to know that in reality he is not identical with his body or any other material entity but is part of God himself, the creator, sustainer, and destroyer of the universe; man also comes to realize that salvation cannot be attained either by the performance of duties and rites or by intellectual understanding alone, but only by the free, loving grace of God.[130] Consequently, man should devote himself completely to the service of God. Accordingly, Rāmānuja regards *bhakti-yoga*[131] (the path of devotion) as opposed to Śaṁkara's *jñāna-yoga* (the path of knowledge), as the sole means to salvation. *Bhakti-yoga* consists in constant meditation (*dhyāna*), *upāsanā* (prayer), and devotion (*bhakti*). Man should be in constant remembrance of God as his Lord and Savior; he should pray for God's grace and mercy; and he should love God with all his heart and soul and surrender himself completely to him. Such complete self-surrender is known as *prapatti.* It is through *prapatti* that man makes himself worthy of divine grace, which, by destroying ignorance, egoism, and *karma,* liberates man. In sharp contrast with Śaṁkara, Rāmānuja holds that liberation does not result in the effacement of the self or its uniqueness but in eternal union with God; the liberated self, instead of losing itself in God, retains its individuality and consciousness and eternally enjoys the highest bliss in the infinite glory of God.[132] Salvation, according to Rāmānuja, is thus not unity with God but eternal communion with him.

3. DVAITA VEDĀNTA: DUALISM

Introduction

Dvaita Vedānta, as its very name indicates, rejects Śaṁkara's nondualism as well as Rāmānuja's qualified nondualism and upholds thoroughgoing dualism between the world and Brahman. The school of Dvaita Vedānta was founded by Madhva. Born of Brāhmin parentage in A.D. 1199, at Biligram in southwestern India, Madhva began his philosophic studies under Achyutaprekṣa. But, dissatisfied with his teacher's nondualistic interpretation of Vedānta, Madhva left Achyutaprekṣa. After several years of independent study and reflection, he produced his own interpretation of Vedānta which developed into the school of Dvaita Vedānta. He was the author of thirty-seven works, among which the most important are *Madhvabhāṣya* and *Gītābhaṣya,* commentaries on the *Brahma-sūtras* and the Bhagavad-gītā, respectively. Consistent with his unremitting dualism, Madhva's religion is personalistic theism. He worshiped Brahman in the form of Viṣṇu and founded the sect of Sad-Vaiṣṇavism, also known as Brāhma-Vaiṣṇavism. Madhva traveled widely teaching his philosophy and religion and debating with his opponents. Among his converts was his former teacher. Madhva died in 1278.

Theory of Reality

The philosophic foundation of Madhva's dualism is his theory of perception and knowledge. According to Madhva, to perceive is to become aware of something as being unique and different from other things as well as from the perceiving self.[133] Genuine knowledge is the articulation of perceived differences between things as well as between things and the perceiving self. Consequently, to deny perception is to deny the very possibility of knowledge; those who affirm identity but deny difference, argues Madhva, are in the absurd position of claiming knowledge by rejecting its very foundation. The gist of this argument is that perception necessarily implies the perceiver and the perceived as distinct existents; and knowledge, too, in that it is based on perception, analytically implies the knower and the known as distinct existents. In other words, all knowledge is relative—relative to some knower and some known. As such, no claim to knowledge can conceivably reject this distinction without rendering itself absurd. Accordingly, Madhva rejects as untenable the nondual, absolute knowledge (transcendental consciousness) of the *nirbījasamādhi* of Yoga.

It should be obvious from the foregoing that Madhva is both an epistemological and an ontological realist: not only do we perceive the world as constituted of different selves and material objects, but in reality it is so. In short, the empirical world is real and pluralistic. Further, according to Madhva, Brahman, the creator and Lord of the world, is distinct from the world.

Madhva's philosophy is thus through and through a philosophy of difference—distinctionism. He recognizes five fundamental and absolute distinctions. These are (1) between Brahman and individual selves, (2) between Brahman and matter, (3) between matter and individual selves, (4) between one individual self and another, and (5) between one material object and another. Madhva divides the universe into independent (*swatantra*) and dependent (*aswatantra*) beings. Brahman is the sole independent being; selves and material objects depend upon Brahman for their existence.[134] Brahman is omniscient, omnipresent, and omnipotent.[135] To the question how Brahman as a distinct being can be omnipresent without being limited by the equally real selves and material objects, Madhva replies that the latter, being dependent upon Brahman, lack the power to resist and limit Brahman.

God

For Madhva, reality, then, consists of three eternal, absolutely real, and irreducibly distinct entities, namely, Brahman, selves, and matter, although the last two are absolutely dependent on the first. True to the spirit of distinctionism, Madhva regards Śaṁkara's Nirguṇa (unqualified) -Brahman not as reality but as an empty and absurd concept, and takes Śaṁkara's Saguṇa (qualified)-Brahman as ultimate reality. That is, Madhva's Brahman is Śaṁkara's Saguṇa-Brahman.[136] Madhva teaches that Brahman is God, the creator, sustainer, and destroyer of the world (selves and material objects) and is the Lord of *karma*. God creates the world only in the sense that by his will he brings into existence the world of variety and multiplicity.[137] At the time of dissolution of the world, God transforms all material objects into homogeneous primordial matter, and selves into disembodied intelligences. It is important, however, to note that even in the state of dissolution, there remain the distinctions between selves, matter, and God. God, according to Madhva, is a person, whose essence is reality, consciousness, and bliss. He possesses all positive qualities in infinite perfection. He is both transcendent and immanent.

Bondage and Salvation

Selves are eternal and atomic; consciousness and bliss are intrinsic to them.[138] But owing to their past *karma*,[139] selves become entangled with bodies and suffer pain and misery. God endows selves with free will; consequently, each self is wholly responsible for its state of existence. Evil in the world is thus not traceable to God, who possesses all and only positive perfections. Madhva divides souls into three kinds: eternally free (*nityamukta*), freed (*mukta*), and bound (*baddha*). Like Rāmānuja, Madhva recognizes total devotion and self-surrender to God as the only means of salvation.[140] Accordingly, *bhakti-yoga* is the sole path to liberation. We may note here that in the entire Indian philosophical-religious tradition Madhva is alone in teaching the doctrine of eternal damnation.[141]

We need not go into a detailed criticism of Dvaita Vedānta. Suffice it to point out that it is vulnerable to all the standard objections that can be raised against any philosophy of radical and absolute dualism—for example, that of Descartes. In the light of the Mādhyamika analysis of the concept of relation, we can formulate the most devastating objection to Dvaita Vedānta as follows: If Brahman, selves, and matter are all absolutely and irreducibly distinct entities, how can any relation obtain between them?

Concluding Remarks

We bring to a close our discussion of the three principal schools of Vedānta by summarizing their important similarities and differences. (1) Śaṁkara's Vedānta is absolute and unqualified nondualism, according to which reality (Brahman, Ātman) is pure identity (identity-without-difference). Rāmānuja's Vedānta is qualified nondualism, according to which reality (Brahman) is qualified identity (identity-in-difference). Madhva's Vedānta is unqualified dualism, according to which Brahman and the world are equally and irreducibly distinct. (2) For Śaṁkara, the empirical world is appearance, which is neither real nor unreal; consequently, there are no two numerically distinct realities—Brahman and the world—but only Brahman appearing as the world under the superimposition of names and forms. For Rāmānuja, too, Brahman alone is independently real, but Brahman is not without qualities; selves and material objects constituting the empirical world are real qualities and modes of Brahman; therefore, selves and material objects are real as differentiations *within* and *not from* Brahman; just as qualities are inseparable from substance and parts from whole, selves and material objects have no being apart from Brahman. For Madhva, Brahman, selves, and material objects are all equally real and absolutely different from each other. Thus, whereas for Rāmānuja selves and material objects are distinctions *within* Brahman, for Madhva they are differentiations *from* Brahman. (3) Śaṁkara upholds the doctrine of *māyā* in all three senses of the term: power of Brahman to manifest itself as the empirical world, illusory nature (from the standpoint of higher knowledge) of the empirical world, and ignorance. Rāmānuja teaches that as part of Brahman the empirical world is real, and accordingly rejects Śaṁkara's *māyā* in the second of the above three senses but accepts it in the other two. Madhva categorically rejects *māyā*. (4) Whereas Śaṁkara subscribes to the *vivartavāda* (doctrine of apparent change) version of *satkāryavāda,* Rāmānuja upholds the *pariṇāmavāda* (doctrine of real change) version. Madhva rejects *satkāryavāda* in both versions and maintains *asatkāryavāda.* (5) According to Śaṁkara, the God of ordinary religious consciousness is Saguṇa (qualified) -Brahman, an appearance and not reality; only Nirguṇa (unqualified) -Brahman is reality. Rāmānuja and Madhva reject Śaṁkara's Nirguṇa-Brahman (identity-without-difference) as being not reality at all but an empty concept, and accordingly regard Śaṁkara's Saguṇa-Brahman itself as reality. Consequently, for them Brahman as God has real qualities and modes. He is the creator, sustainer, and destroyer of the world. (6) In the true spirit of nondualism, Śaṁkara's God is Brahman, the impersonal Absolute. For Rāmānuja and Madhva God is Perfect Personality. (7) According to Śaṁkara, salvation is to be attained through knowledge of Brahman—knowledge of the identity of Ātman and Brahman. Accordingly, *jñāna-yoga* (path of knowledge) is the means of liberation. In contrast, Rāmānuja and Madhva, consistent with qualified nondualism and dualism, respectively, reject Śaṁkara's teaching of the unqualified identity of God and man, and maintain that man cannot attain salvation by his own efforts but only through the free, loving grace of God. Accordingly, they regard *bhakti-yoga* (path of devotion)—complete surrender to God—as the sole means to liberation. (8) For Śaṁkara, salvation consists in the loss of personal self and individuality in the impersonal Absolute. For Rāmānuja and Madhva, salvation does not result in the loss of self or its individuality. On the contrary, the liberated self retains its individuality and consciousness and enjoys eternal bliss in the infinite glory of God. (9) Whereas according to Rāmānuja the self on liberation becomes similar to but not identical with God, according to Madhva the liberated self is only partially similar to God. (10) Madhva is alone in the entire Indian tradition in his teaching that God condemns some selves to eternal damnation. It is generally believed that Madhva may have been influenced by Christian missionaries in his radical dualism, realism, and doctrine of eternal damnation.

Chapter X

Time and History in the Indian Tradition

Introduction

We have thus far studied the various Indian philosophical systems, both orthodox and unorthodox. There are, however, two important topics which we have not discussed, namely, time and history.[1] How a given culture understands and interprets time and history depends upon its fundamental philosophical concepts and presuppositions—especially those pertaining to ontology. In the present chapter, we shall uncover the views on time and history implicit in the Indian philosophical tradition. We may, without doing violence to the specific doctrines of the various Indian schools of philosophy, regard Śaṁkara's Advaita Vedānta as representing the Indian tradition in both thought and spirit. The reason for this is twofold: (1) Śaṁkara's Advaita Vedānta is the most systematic articulation of the Upaniṣadic insights and vision of man and world; as such, it is the flower of Hindu wisdom, which subsumes under itself the best in all the other orthodox systems. (2) It is the most dominant and influential of all the living currents in Indian philosophy and is thus the Weltanschauung of the majority of Hindus. In short, Śaṁkara's Advaita Vedānta is the flesh and blood of the Hindu culture. We shall also consider Buddhism and show that, although

Buddhism and Advaita Vedānta are generally regarded as rival systems, they both give rise to identical conceptions of time and history. For this very reason, we may regard these conceptions as characteristic of the Indian tradition as a whole.

Basic Concepts of Advaita Vedanta

The central concepts of Advaita Vedānta are Brahman, Ātman, ignorance *(avidyā)*, *māyā, karma, mokṣa,* and knowledge. For clarity and ready reference, we shall now provide summary explications of these concepts. (1) Brahman is the unchanging reality underlying the variety and multiplicity of phenomena. Brahman is eternal, unborn, uncreated, and immutable. (2) Ātman is the inmost Self of man. It is eternal, unborn, uncreated, and immutable. It is not to be confused with the empirical ego, whose distinguishing feature is constant change. Further, and most importantly, Brahman and Ātman are identical; that is, they are two different labels for one and the same ultimate reality. Brahman is beyond names and forms. Brahman is not to be thought of as creator or God. Brahman is neither a he nor a she but is the It. (3) Ignorance *(avidyā)* consists in our thinking on the one hand that the empirical ego is an ultimate reality, and on the other that our knowledge of the world obtained through senses and reason is the knowledge of ultimate reality. Ignorance, although beginningless *(anādi),* can be put an end to. The end of ignorance is the realization of the identity of Ātman and Brahman and therewith of the nonultimacy of individuality characteristic of phenomena, including the empirical ego. (4) *Māyā* is the power of Brahman by which it manifests itself as the phenomenal world. It is beginningless and endless, being coexistent with Brahman itself. It would be a serious mistake to construe this statement as implying that there are two ultimate realities, namely, Brahman and *māyā,* for *māyā* has no existence apart from Brahman. Very often the phenomenal world is referred to as *māyā* and *māyā* is translated and interpreted as illusion and unreality, thereby presenting the Advaita Vedāntin as claiming that the phenomenal world is illusory and unreal. Such an interpretation of the Advaita Vedāntin's conception of *māyā* is unwarranted, for the Advaita Vedāntin does not deny the phenomenal world or its reality. What he does deny is its ultimacy. Correctly speaking, then, for the Advaita Vedāntin reality is that which exists without depending for its existence on anything other than itself. In this sense, only Brahman is the reality, while the phenomenal world, being dependent on Brahman, is not ultimate. Such nonultimate existence the Advaita Vedāntin describes as "neither real nor unreal nor both," meaning thereby that it is neither ultimately real nor wholly unreal, illusory, and nonexistent. We may keep in mind here the celebrated rope-snake illustration of the Advaita Vedāntin, as well as his observation that there can be no such thing as a pure illusion—every illusion is grounded in reality. (5) *Karma* is the state of bondage arising out of man's ignorance and is generated by man's own thoughts, words, and deeds; and through rebirth *karma* acquires a peculiar psychomoral continuity. *Karma* (i.e., bondage) can be exhausted and brought to an end by attaining the knowledge of ultimate reality through the realization of the identity of Ātman and Brahman. *Mokṣa* (also known as *kaivalya*) is freedom from *karma* and bondage (which in turn is freedom from ignorance) and is to be attained through the knowledge of ultimate reality. *Mokṣa* is not something looked forward to after death but is to be attained here and now. He who attains it is known as *jīvanmukta,* one who is absolutely free even while existing as part of the phenomenal world. (7) Knowledge and truth are of two kinds: the lower and phenomenal (*vyavahāra*) and the higher and supraphenomenal (*paramārtha*). The first kind of knowledge and truth is the product of senses and intellect; name and form are the warp and woof of such knowledge and truth. Consequently, opposition, relativity, limited validity, and sublatability are of the essence of the lower knowledge and truth. On the other hand, the higher knowledge and truth are absolute and unsublatable. They are not the product of senses and intellect but of primordial intuitive insight into the nature of existence. Unity, nonrelativity, absolute certainty, and unsublatability are their distinguishing features. Such knowledge and truth surpass all distinctions and oppositions. More importantly, unlike the lower knowledge and truth, the higher knowledge and truth are soteriological, in that they bring about a total transformation of him who attains them. In a word, they bring one wisdom, peace, and freedom.

Basic Concepts of Buddhism

The following are the basic metaphysical concepts of Buddhism: existence, suffering *(duḥkha),* ignorance, *karma,* Nirvāṇa, and knowledge. (1) For the Buddhist, existence is pure flux, there being no eternal and unchanging entities either within man or without. It is craving *(taṅhā)* which produces and sustains the illusion of such entities. For the Buddhist existence is impermanence. (2) Being impermanence, existence is painful and is the source of suffering of all kinds, physical, moral, psychological, etc. The term *duḥkha* is to be understood, then, not in the sense of this or that suffering but as the very impermanence of all existence. (3) Ignorance is not only the absence of knowledge of reality but also the holding of wrong views concerning it. It is this ignorance which is the source of man's state of suffering, bondage, and unfreedom. (4) The law of *karma* is the principle of universal causality, according to which every event, be it thought, word, or deed, produces effects which in turn serve as causes bringing about further effects, and so on. *Karma* is generated by ignorance, lack of knowledge of the nature of existence. *Karma* acquires a kind of psycho-moral continuity through rebirth. (5) Nirvāṇa, freedom from ignorance and suffering, is attainable by man here and now by gaining insight into reality. (6) Knowledge is of two kinds: the lower and mundane, and the higher and supramundane, respectively known as *saṁvṛti-satya paramārtha-satya.* The former, which is the product of the senses and the intellect, is relative, governed by the opposition of identity and difference, and of limited validity. The latter is nonconceptual, nonrelative, and intuitive, but is not opposed to the relative. Unlike *saṁvṛti-satya, paramārtha-satya* is soteriological in that it effects a profound transformation of man, leading to blissful calm, wisdom, and freedom.

Implications to History

What views of time and history are implied by the above metaphysical concepts of Advaita Vedānta and Buddhism? It is clear that both Advaita Vedānta and Buddhism consider the world of phenomena to be marked by impermanence manifesting itself as plurality, division, distinction, opposition, conflict, tension, pain, and suffering. The impermanent and fleeting nature of phenomenal existence is keenly felt by man in the inevitability of his own death. Death is the constant and climactic reminder of the inexorably painful and suffering-ridden existence of man as a phenomenal being. The king and the beggar, the mighty and the lowly, the plebeian and the patrician, are all powerless in the face of death and submit themselves equally to this unique and ineluctable existential indignity. Neither power nor glory, neither wealth nor learning, has any sway over fear of death and death itself. With death constantly hovering over him ready to strike him down any moment, man becomes profoundly disturbed about whether his own existence as well as that of his species has any meaning and significance at all. In search of an answer, he turns from one thing to another. But what he finds is not an answer to this disquietude, but only something which makes him temporarily forget the unalterable predicament by immersing himself in some kind of activity or other, only to be soon confronted with redoubled intensity by the ever-present fear of vanishing away. The Advaita Vedāntin and the Buddhist tell us that efforts to conquer suffering and death by means which are themselves an integral part of phenomenal existence are doomed to failure, for such efforts betray a profound lack of understanding of the nature of phenomenal existence. What then is its nature? Phenomenal existence, according to Advaita Vedānta and Buddhism, is existence in the grip of the all-consuming temporality (*kāla*). In other words, everything that exists in time is, by the very nature of such existence, subject to change, decay, and death. As such, all attempts to overcome pain and death by means and methods which are themselves time-bound are destined to failure. It is only through knowledge which transcends everything that is characteristic of existence in time and which provides the insight into the ground of time-bound existence that man can conquer suffering, fear of death, and death itself, and thereby attain immortality. That is, it is knowledge of the eternal ground and basis of phenomenal, temporal existence that emancipates man from the fetters and shackles of time. To put it differently, man overcomes the pain and suffering of time-bound existence by the knowledge of the eternal and timeless. Brahman is the timeless and eternal ground of all existence; accordingly, it is the knowledge of Brahman which liberates man from the grip of time. But how does one know Brahman? Since, according to the Advaita Vedāntin, Brahman and Ātman are identical, one knows Brahman by knowing the Ātman, the inmost Self of man. Similar considerations hold with respect to Buddhism, except that the liberating knowledge here is neither of Brahman nor of Ātman but of the fundamental emptiness (Śūnyatā) underlying all existence. Such knowledge is what constitutes Nirvāṇa, the release from the pain and suffering of phenomenal existence. It is worth pointing out here that, although the Brahman of Advaita Vedānta and the Śūnyatā of Buddhism differ in many respects, there are striking similarities between them. Both defy logic and language and are hence beyond all names and forms and can only be described in negative terms; and the knowledge of both is thus nonconceptual and intuitive. Further, both Brahman and Śūnyatā, themselves nonrelative, absolute, and timeless, are the ground of all time-bound existence. More importantly, according to the Advaita Vedāntin, Brahman and the world of phenomena are *not* two numerically different ontological realms. Quite the contrary, they are one and the same reality seen from two different standpoints, the higher and the lower. The phenomenal world, seen by penetrating through the veil of names and forms is Brahman; conversely, Brahman concealed by names and forms is the phenomenal world. In a similar manner, in Buddhism Saṁsāra (the phenomenal world) and Nirvāṇa (Śūnyatā) are one and the same reality, seen from the lower and the higher standpoints, respectively. It is clear, then, that in both Advaita Vedānta and Buddhism time is of the essence of the phenomenal world. And since the phenomenal world has no independent reality, time too is not an independent reality. Time and the phenomenal world are the products of *māyā,* working through our senses, concepts, and imaginative constructions. Much like Kant, Advaita Vedānta and Buddhism regard time as an *a priori* form of our sensible intuition, which is a presupposition of the possibility of our experience of the phenomenal world. From the higher standpoint, time has no reality *of its own;* and since time is of the essence of the phenomenal world, the latter too, viewed from the higher standpoint, has no reality *of its own.* In other words, in both Advaita Vedānta and Buddhism, time is a secondary, dependent reality with no ultimate ontological status.

History is part and parcel of the phenomenal world, that is, of time-bound existence. We may include under the term "history" all varieties of history, celestial, geological, biological, and the specifically human. It is a truism that all history takes place in time (where else can it take place?). Thus time is the matrix in which history is embedded. But if time is devoid of any ultimate ontological status, then it follows that history cannot have any ultimate ontological status either. Like every other facet of the phenomenal world, history is only a secondary reality. Consequently, the Advaita Vedāntin and the Buddhist warn us against the temptation of trying to gain liberating knowledge (knowledge of the ultimate, timeless, eternal reality underlying all phenomenal existence) through history, which bleeds like a wounded animal under the gnawing blows of time—its vicissitudes, the rise and fall of civilizations, human greed and misery, wars, plague, pestilence, death, and the ominous possibility of the extinction of the overcerebrated ape himself by weapons into the forging of which went a great deal of his skill and knowledge acquired over thousands of years.

In the light of the above analysis, it should be clear that according to Advaita Vedānta and Buddhism what the study of history reveals to us is man in bondage, not man in his primordial reality; what history shows us is man in the state of ignorance, not the liberated man. Further, as long as he labors under the illusion of the ultimacy of historical reality and seeks freedom through history, man will remain in ignorance and bondage. It is for this reason that the Indian tradition attaches only a secondary significance to history and to its inner dynamic, namely, temporality.

It is time now to consider certain clichés which, though stale and well-worn, are still very much in vogue and are purported to be criticisms of the above-discussed Indian position on time and history. One often hears the charge that Indian thought teaches that the world of phenomena and hence time and history are unreal and illusory, and therefore that Indians utterly lack historical consciousness. It is unnecessary to document this charge, for one can find it by opening at random any Western work on Indian civilization.[2] Let it be first pointed out that such a criticism betrays a grave and deplorable ignorance of both Indian philosophical and religious traditions. Does such a charge have any basis either in Advaita Vedānta and Buddhism or in any other philosophico-religious tradition of India? Śaṁkara teaches that the phenomenal world is neither illusory nor nonexistent. On the contrary, it is practical reality. But it is not ultimate reality, for only the undifferentiated, unitary Brahman, on which depends the phenomenal world, is the ultimate reality. Just as the unreality of the imaginary standpoint (*prātibhāsika*) can only be judged from the standpoint of the empirical (*vyavahārika*), so also the neither real nor unreal status of the latter can only be judged from the standpoint of the ultimate *(paramārthika)*. He who has not attained the ultimate standpoint has no business declaring that the phenomenal world is unreal.[3] Thus the criticism that Indian philosophies and religions teach that the world of phenomena is unreal and illusory is both unwarranted and false with respect to Advaita Vedānta. Let us consider it now with respect to Buddhism. The Hīnayāna schools, far from holding that the world of phenomena is unreal and illusory, explicitly maintain that it is constituted of a certain number of *dharmas,* basic elements of existence. The Mahāyāna, even in its most radical form, the Mādhyamika school, does not claim that the empirical world is unreal and illusory. Quite the contrary, much like Advaita Vedānta, Mādhyamika distinguishes the lower and higher standpoints and teaches that the phenomenal world has relative reality and that our rational-scientific knowledge of the world provides us with truths which are certainly valid and efficacious within particular domains of empirical experience.[4] On the other hand, the higher truth is nonconceptual, nonrelative, intuitive insight into the Śūnyatā of all *dharmas.* Where, then, one wonders, is the basis in Indian thought for the hackneyed criticism that India regards the world of phenomena as unreal and illusory?

It is important in this connection to lay bare a basic confusion behind this empty and absurd criticism. It is quite correct to say that Indian thought denies the world of phenomena ultimate ontological status, regarding it as only a dependent and secondary reality, because the empirical world is one of constant change, relativity, conflict, opposition, and tension. Our knowledge of the empirical world, *saṁvṛti-satya* ("practical knowledge"), is based upon names and forms; as such, it is in principle possible for there to be a variety of systems of such knowledge. But liberating knowledge *(paramārtha-satya),* being different from but not opposed to practical knowledge, cannot be attained through a study of the empirical world, no matter how powerful and penetrating such a study may be. Liberating knowledge can only be attained by transcending the time-bound existence of the empirical world. That is, history and the empirical world, both being time-bound, cannot serve as means for liberation and freedom from bondage and ignorance. In other words, from the point of view of *mokṣa* and *Nirvāṇa,* history and the phenomenal world have only a secondary and pragmatic significance. But this is not to say that history and the empirical world are unreal and illusory. Professor Zimmer correctly grasps this point when he speaks in his *Philosophies of India*[5] of the philosophies of time and the philosophies of eternity. Under the former, Indian thought has a lot to say about pleasure, success, politics, economics, and other matters of temporal existence. Consistent with their ontological hierarchy, Indian thinkers also originated and expounded the philosophies of eternity—philosophies whose aim it is to enable man to transcend temporality and gain freedom through the knowledge of the eternal, thereby surpassing the human condition. We may now point out the source of the confusion behind the charge that the Indian tradition regards the world as unreal. The Western critics, having correctly observed that the Indians, while attaching ultimate ontological status and significance to the eternal, assign only a secondary ontological status and significance to the empirical world, went on to mistakenly proclaim that Indians therefore regard the empirical world as unreal and illusory. What is amazing here is not that men could be mistaken in their understanding of an alien philosophy and culture, but that such a misunderstanding could go unchecked for so long and acquire a permanent and celebrated place in the world of Western Indological scholarship. It should be obvious to anyone that men—Indians or Westerners—cannot help existing in history, whether they like it or not, and so cannot simply pretend that history, the phenomenal world, and time itself are unreal and illusory. To quote Professor Eliade:

> We ought, however, to point out *one misunderstanding which distorts the Western picture of India and of Indian spirituality.* It is not at all the case that the discovery of the cosmic illusion

and the metaphysical quest of Being express themselves, in India, by a total devaluation of Life or belief in a universal vacuity. We are now beginning to realise that, perhaps more than any other civilization, that of India loves and reverences Life, and enjoys it at every level. For *Māyā* is not an absurd and gratuitous cosmic illusion, it knows nothing of the absurdity that certain European philosophers ascribe to human existence as they conceive it, issuing out of Nothingness and proceeding to Nothingness. For Indian thought *Māyā* is a divine creation, a cosmic *play,* of which the end and aim is human experience, as well as deliverance from that experience. It follows that to become conscious of the cosmic illusion does not mean, in India, the discovery that all is Nothingness, but simply *that no experience in the world or of history has any ontological validity and, therefore, that our human condition ought not to be regarded as an end in itself.* But when he has come to consciousness of this, the Hindu does not withdraw from the world; if he did India would long ago have disappeared from History, for the conception of *Māyā* is accepted by the great majority of Indians.[6]

We shall conclude by making one observation concerning what may be called "the paradox of historicism." By "historicism," we mean that view or attitude according to which history is ultimate reality. A historicist civilization, therefore, is a civilization which holds such an attitude. Western civilization, by this definition, is the historicist civilization *par excellence.* The beliefs which make Western civilization historicist are as follows: History is the unfolding and realizing of God's will and purpose, for example, the Christian drama of the crucifixion of Jesus; God intrudes into history, thus involving himself in human affairs and conflicts.[7] History is thus sanctified and accorded the status of ultimate reality, and is therefore to be viewed with the utmost solemnity; for if history is ultimate reality, there can be nothing more worthy of man's attention, effort, and devotion. Consequently, the highest that man is capable of can only be realized through the historical process. But since man has not yet attained that highest perfection, he has to make progress toward that goal through history alone, for there can be no other realm as ultimate and real as history through which man may seek it. It is in this manner that the doctrines of progress, millenarianism, and utopianism have come to be the essential ingredients of historicism. By "paradox of historicism," we mean the strange fact that those civilizations which are uncomprisingly historicist have, in their quest for perfection through history, arrived at a point where history itself is in danger of being abolished by none other than themselves. How explain this paradox? Before answering this question, let us note that nonhistoricist civilizations such as the Indian and Chinese have not succumbed to this paradox, and that they have long histories, much longer than those of the historicist civilizations. It deserves to be emphasized that the paradox of historicism is not an accident. Quite the contrary, it is an analytic consequence of the historicist attitude itself. Thus, once one sees history as reality sanctified and made ultimate by the intrusion of God, one has no other way of understanding and evaluating history and temporal existence than by the categories of the historicist attitude itself. If history is the primordial and highest reality, what higher reality can one turn to by which to understand the nature and meaning of history? As an analogy to illuminate this point, think of the plight of thoroughgoing empiricism as the method of science. According to thoroughgoing empiricism, no term whose meaning cannot be exhaustively explicated through the observable should be allowed into science. If someone were to take this prescription seriously, he would not be able to do science, for scientific explanation of the observable cannot come from terms and concepts all of which can be exhaustively explicated observationally. In short, without theoretical terms there can be no science. Thus, for science to be possible, we should recognize at any stage of development of science a dimension of reality, not wholly translatable into the observable.[8] In a similar manner, assigning to history the status of exhaustive and ultimate reality cannot produce an understanding of history. Having no higher perspective from which to grasp the nature of historical existence, one becomes victim to delusion and rationalization. Whatever happens in history has somehow to be interpreted and understood as contributing to man's progress toward perfection. Small wonder then that Hegel, for whom history was the unfolding of the Absolute Idea, proclaimed as sublime truth that most absurd of philosophical slogans, "The real is the rational and the rational is the real." Like every other historicist, by gazing into the blazing face of the Absolute in history, Hegel became blind to the greed, misery, cruelty, and stupidity which are unmistakably the flesh, blood, and bones of history. According to Hegel, it is right and rational that millions of nameless masses should be trampled under the majestic feet of the Absolute Spirit when it marches in the form of, for example, a Napoleon, for one has no right to judge the Absolute Spirit by standards of morality that can only apply to faceless men. Their suffering and death, we are told, are necessary moments in the dialectic of the Idea, the dialectic which leads men to the pinnacle of freedom. Such are the monstrous delusions and shameless rationalizations of the warped vision of historicism. In our own day, historicist civilizations have reached the acme of historicist thinking through the production, use, and piling up of nuclear weapons as the *modus operandi* of the historicist's holy war against evil. The paradox is now complete, for the historicist civilizations now possess the power to abolish history itself by committing collective suicide, a power which they themselves enthusiastically produced in their vision of guiding man triumphantly along the path of progress toward perfection.

Nonhistoricists such as the Indians would say that if the historicist had had even a vague glimpse into the ultimate, eternal, timeless reality, in the light of which history and temporal existence could be seen as only relative and secondary, he would not have fallen victim to the worship of history and its mistress, the goddess of progress. It is significant, however, that even the most committed historicist and prophet of progress cannot escape the occasional tormenting doubt whether perfection through progress in history is anything more than an ever-receding mirage. He thus becomes a nihilist and a propounder and expounder of philosophies of the Absurd, Angst, and Nothingness. The nonhistoricist civilizations teach us that insight into a reality which is ultimate and more fundamental than history is what sustains life and history and prevents men from becoming nihilists and absurdists. It is the intuitive vision of the timeless reality that enables man to know himself and comprehend historical reality for what it is, thereby making it possible for him to be sane, tolerant, compassionate, wise, and free. It would not do for the theistic historicist to retort that he recognizes God as the ultimate reality behind and beyond history. For once one has sanctified history by making it the theater of God, one must admit that history is as real and ultimate as God himself. To this the contemporary historicist might reply that he no longer believes in a God. But then, for him, history *is* God, for there is now no other reality.[9] One can only reply at this point that he is surely wise who said: You shall not worship at the altar of the goddess of history, for she will seduce you into devouring yourself.

Chapter XI

A Glimpse at the Contemporary Scene

Introduction

In this final chapter, we shall provide a survey of the contemporary Indian philosophic scene. But before doing this, it would be well to describe briefly the historical forces which influenced Indian civilization leading up to its present state.

The Muslim invasions on the one hand and the European invasions on the other constitute the two most powerful alien influences on Indian civilization. The earliest Muslim invasion of India dates back to the eighth century A.D. and was followed by a series of others culminating in the Mughul Empire (A.D. 1550–1710). Many of the early Muslim invaders and conquerors were plunderers and looters and not in any significant sense rulers or founders of kingdoms. Not until the victory of the able Turk Muhammad Ghori over the Hindu king Prithvi Raj in A.D. 1192 did the Muslim civilization begin to exercise political control and dominance on India. From this time onward, the Muslim conquerors began to consolidate their victories and carve out kingdoms and dynasties eventually leading up to the founding of the great Mughul Empire. At the height of the Mughul Empire, most of India was under the rule of the dynasty, and the greatest interaction took place between Indian and Muslim civilizations on all fronts—social, political, economic, artistic, philosophic, and religious. Akbar the Great sought unity between Hinduism and Islam and went so far as to appoint a commission of scholars and religious leaders to formulate a universal faith, *Dīn-i-Ilāhi,* by integrating the two philosophic-religious traditions. And in spite of the zealotry and fanaticism so characteristic of Islam (as of its sister religions, Judaism and Christianity), it should be admitted that under enlightened Muslim rulers there developed genuine mutual understanding and appreciation between the Hindu and Islamic cultures. The Muslims acquired an insight into the profound and sublime teachings of the Upaniṣads, and in turn the Hindus, moved by the Muslims' simple devotion and self-surrender to Allah, revived the *bhakti-yoga* (the path of devotion) of their own tradition. The revival of Hindu devotionalism gave rise to a long line of illustrious poet-saints, such as Kabir, Tulasidas, Tukaram, Chaitanya, and to superb devotional literature.[1] Such in brief, are the effects of the Islamic conquests on India. It is worth noting that the conquests did not destroy Hindu religion or culture but served as a challenge to Hinduism to discover its extraordinary adaptability to alien, puzzling, and, sometimes, hostile influences.[2]

The coming of the Europeans to India was part of the great European wave of expansion which began in the late fifteenth century. The first Europeans to arrive in India were the Portuguese expedition of 1498 led by Vasco da Gama. Other expeditions—French, British, and Dutch—soon followed. Many of these adventurers were first interested in trade and business with India. They sought trade concessions from the Mughul emperors; and as a result of competition among themselves, they fought each other for possession of trade routes and monopolies. Thus for a good length of time the Europeans in India were primarily traders and merchants not interested in territorial conquests. But with the death of the Mughul emperor Auranga-zib in 1707 the central political authority broke down and chaos and turmoil became the order of the day. There soon ensued bitter struggles for power, and from the rubble of the Mughul Empire some Indian princes attempted to found kingdoms and dynasties. At this time, the French and the British were the chief European rivals vying for power and wealth. Not only did they fight each other, but most importantly, they took sides in the power-struggles among the Indian rulers. Before long the British vanquished the other European powers, emerging as victors and gaining political control over India. Still, there were here and there some pockets of Indian resistance which the British successfully defeated in 1818. In this manner began the historic British imperial hegemony over India which lasted until 1947.

The political, social, and economic effects of the British conquest on India were far more profound than those due to the Islamic conquests. Thus, although the culture and the life-style of both the Muslims and the British were different from those of the Indians, what made the Indian encounter with the British historic and unique was the fact that the latter represented Western modernity—modern political, social, and economic organizations, and the emerging scientific and technological culture. It was this modernity, wholly lacking in the non-Western world of the time, that was responsible for major changes in Indian culture under the British rule. It is neither appropriate nor possible for us to discuss here in any detail the long and interesting interaction between the Indian and Western cultures. We shall therefore merely indicate some of the highlights of the cultural encounter, and their significance for understanding contemporary India.

Upper-class Hindus, particularly the Brāhmins, were the first to come into close contact with Western thought patterns, organizations, and cultural forms. The reason for this was simply that, traditionally, upper-class Hindus formed the bulk of the educated, urban middle class. These people studied, absorbed, and used the Western social and political concepts to deal with the problems arising out of the contact between the ruling Western people and the subject natives. In this manner, the Indians found themselves in need of examining their own culture and heritage in the light of their new experience, not always pleasant, with alien people. In time, there arose among Indians social reformers, political leaders, religious innovators, and culture critics. Following Ainslie Embree, we can distinguish four different kinds of reaction on the part of Indians to the growing impact of the West on Indian culture. For the sake of completeness, we shall quote Embree at some length:

> One reaction was indifference, and this was not purely negative in its results, for it meant that religious and social movements that had their roots in the Hindu tradition continued to flourish, and the nineteenth century saw a remarkable proliferation of cults and sects of all kinds with Hinduism. But even though these movements seem completely indigenous in their inspiration, it is quite possible that they were reflecting a general malaise caused by the intrusion of the West. . . . Another, and very different response, was the rejection of the old tradition and the acceptance of everything Western, including Christianity. This attitude was not very common, but it contributed something to the general process of growth and change that characterized the time. More common, and of much greater significance, was the reaction to the West that was both critical and selective. Aware of the weaknesses within traditional Hindu society, many sought to reform it by using features of Western culture, particularly its political arrangements or its science or its technology. This classification covers a wide spectrum of opinion, including individuals of the most antithetical views, such as Rammohan Roy, K. C. Sen, the Tagore family, Vivekananda, Aurobindo Ghose, Gokhale, Ranade, and Gandhi. The fourth reaction was outright and hostile rejection of the values and ideas of the Western world . . . but here again the range of opinion, and degree of rejection, varied greatly.[3]

As a result of these different reactions there emerged in the nineteenth and twentieth centuries a great and unparalleled cultural exchange and integration between a Western and a non-Western tradition at all levels, intellectual, social, political, and religious. And although for a while the Hindus were puzzled and bewildered by the Western culture, in time Hinduism successfully responded to the cultural challenge by asserting its greatness. And this fact is a testimony to "the enduring richness and variety of the Hindu tradition." [4]

While the Indians were reacting to the Western culture, the British, having established themselves in secure political power, began to study the Indian tradition in its various aspects. For philologists there was the excitement of the discovery that Sanskrit is an ancient Indo-Āryan tongue, bearing a striking resemblance to Greek and Latin and modern European languages. In this excitement was born the discipline of Indology. Study of the Sanskrit language soon led the band of Western Indologists into the vast treasure-house of Indian philosophic literature, in particular the Upaniṣads and the Bhagavad-gītā. British, French, and German Indologists spent their lives translating, editing, and commenting upon various Indian works. The discovery of the Upaniṣads and Yoga was a particularly exhilarating experience to the West. Admirers of the Upaniṣads were to be found in Europe and even the New World.[5] In America the Upaniṣads and the Bhagavad-gītā profoundly influenced the Transcendentalists, such as Emerson, Thoreau, and Whitman. In course of time, European Indologists brought to light the great achievements of the Indian civilization in literature, logic, mathematics, metaphysics, theory of knowledge, painting, sculpture, architecture, and a number of minor arts and crafts. In this manner, knowledge of Indian culture began to spread far and wide, and although it was at first confined to some narrow and isolated circles of scholars, the study of Indian thought and culture became a serious academic pursuit in the major European and American centers of higher learning. In all this what struck the Western student of Indian civilization most was the extraordinary spirituality of the Indian mind and the sublime heights to which Indian philosophy and religion soared. With more detailed study of the hitherto inaccessible texts, Western academicians began to appreciate the subtle dialectical skills of Indian philosophers and their pattern of close argumentation in the treatment of philosophical problems. Today, as a result of the labors of countless Indologists—philosphers, logicians, philologists, historians, anthropologists, archaeologists, and students of civilization—we are in a better position than ever before to appreciate the full breadth and depth of Indian culture. With greater understanding of Indian thought, scholars began the exciting work of comparing Indian and Western thought patterns, and in this manner arose the discipline of comparative studies.

Just as the Western students of Indian thought were influenced by it, so also the Indians were influenced by Western intellectual tradition. Educated Indians were exposed to the classics of the Western world as well as Western science, technology, and social and political organizations. Soon it was not uncommon to find Indians who were as much at home with Plato and Aristotle as with Śaṁkara and Nāgārjuna. The impact of Western science and technology on Indians was equally noteworthy. There arose among Indians many creative scientists and technologists, for example, J. C. Bose and C. V. Raman. Equally noteworthy was the influence of Western social and political concepts on Indian society. Great Indian leaders such as Gandhi and Nehru, themselves educated in England, brought about a revolution in the Indian sociopolitical scene. It is important to remember, however, that Indian educators, social reformers, and political leaders were not blindly accepting everything Western. On the contrary, they were engaged in the task of synthesizing Indian and Western traditions in the most fruitful and significant manner. Thus it is correct to say that although the Indians drew freely upon Western knowledge and institutions, "in their personal style of living and in the intimacy of family life they maintained the traditional values and customs." [6] One of the main goals of Indian leaders in various fields today, as it was during the British rule, is to formulate a vision of man and the world which integrates the best in the Indian and Western traditions.

In the field of philosophy, the interaction between India and the West is both interesting and significant. While

Western students are enriching their understanding of Kant by comparing him with Śaṁkara, Indians are doing the reverse. And just as Western scholars write treatises on Indian philosophy, so also the Indian scholars write treatises on Western philosophy. The most significant result of such scholarly interaction is comparative philosophy, a discipline which promotes and enriches mutual understanding and appreciation.

We shall discuss briefly two of the best-known and most influential syntheses of Indian and Western philosophical traditions—one due to Sri Aurobindo and the other to Radhakrishnan.

Sri Aurobindo

Aurobindo Ghose (1872–1950) was born in a Bengali family of wealth and culture. Desiring his son to become a high-ranking civil servant in the British government, Aurobindo's father sent him as a young boy to England to receive a thoroughly Western education. On returning to India in 1893, however, Aurobindo became deeply involved in the Indian nationalist movement and emerged as a charismatic leader. His goal at this time was to forge a nationalist ideology and program free from all foreign influences and wholly Indian in character. Accordingly, he formulated an ideology in which the struggle for political freedom was interwoven with a mystical interpretation of India's past. The power of the ideology, combined with Aurobindo's extraordinary personality, was such that millions of Indians were drawn to it, and before long Aurobindo and his followers found themselves in active resistance of the British rule. Shortly thereafter, Aurobindo was accused by the British of fomenting violence and terror. At this time, he abruptly withdrew from all political activities and retired to the French colony of Pondicherry, near Madras, where he spent the rest of his life in study, meditation, and the practice of Yoga.

Aurobindo is the mystical philosopher *par excellence* of contemporary India. Through and through his aim as philosopher-mystic is to construct a vision of man and the world which does justice to all aspects of existence. Aurobindo's great merit lies in his synthesis of Western and Hindu thought in an original manner to formulate a philosophy of life that can serve as a guide for man in the modern world. *The Life Divine* is Aurobindo's masterpiece. His other works include *The Human Cycle, The Ideal Human Unity,* and *The Synthesis of Yoga.*

Aurobindo's philosophy may be referred to as "Spiritual Evolutionism." The central idea of it is that reality is essentially spiritual. Every existent, animate or inanimate, is spiritual at core, and the universe itself is a manifestation of the evolution of the spirit into various forms. Further, whereas the power of the spirit underlies the manifoldness of the universe, it is the spirit itself which provides the unity of the universe. According to Aurobindo, although it is undeniable that man suffers from ignorance and discord, it is equally undeniable that there is in him the spiritual urge to overcome ignorance by knowledge, and discord by harmony, and thereby attain the highest spiritual goal—unity, harmony, wisdom, peace, and joy. In order to attain this goal man needs philosophy. But what kind of philosophy must it be? According to Aurobindo:

> The problem of thought therefore is to find out the right idea and the right way of harmony; to restate the ancient and eternal spiritual truth of the Self, so that it shall re-embrace, permeate and dominate the mental and physical life; to develop the most profound and vital methods of psychological self-discipline and self-development so that the mental and psychical life of man may express the spiritual life through the utmost possible expansion of its own richness, power and complexity; and to seek for the means and motives by which his external life, his society and his institutions may remould themselves progressively in the truth of the spirit and develop towards the utmost possible harmony of individual freedom and social unity.[7]

Without going into any details of Aurobindo's complex system of philosophy, we shall simply point out that in full conformity with the teachings of the Upaniṣads Aurobindo holds that Brahman is pure existence and it is the very nature of the power of Brahman to manifest itself as the world of finite objects and selves. In short, the universe is nothing but the power of Brahman manifesting itself. Moreover, the evolution of the universe is neither haphazard nor capricious. Quite the contrary, in the process of evolution, all existents constantly return to Brahman, the very source of their being. This return to the primordial power of Being results in the evolution of the spirit into higher forms of consciousness. At this point, it is important to note a significant difference between Aurobindo's spiritual evolutionism and other evolutionary doctrines, including Darwinism. The former, unlike the latter, is not confronted with the problem of explaining how one kind of object, for example, inanimate, becomes another kind, animate. The reason is that for Aurobindo all existents are the evolutes of the spirit. As such, every existent has something in common with every other existent. The ordinary distinction between the lower, say a plant, and the higher, say an animal, is not an essential and ineradicable distinction but only one of degree. According to Aurobindo, the lower is constantly struggling to evolve into the higher, and the higher is always reflected in the lower. In brief, the universe is an unceasing evolutionary play between the lower and the higher, and the pinnacle of evolution is the attainment of *saccidānanda* (Pure Being, Pure Consciousness, and Pure Joy). The implications of this vision to man are clear. First, man is not a stranger in the world; on the contrary, he has a kinship to all existents, the core of the kinship being spiritual; second, man as he is now, is only a pale and insignificant measure of what he can be. At the present time, man, in his ignorance, having circumscribed himself as a mere empirical-rational being, is oblivious to his extraordinary potential to become pure spirit. The potential is realized by attaining consciousness that transcends his sensory-intellectual modes of being. Such consciousness Aurobindo calls "Supermind or Truth-Consciousness":

> In supermind being, consciousness of knowledge and consciousness of will are not divided as they seem to be in our mental operations; they are a trinity, one movement with three effective aspects. Each has its own effect. Being gives the effect of substance, consciousness the effect of knowledge, of the self-guiding and shaping idea, of comprehension and apprehension; will gives the effect of self-fulfilling force. But the idea is only the light of the reality illumining itself; it is not mental thought nor imagination, but effective self-awareness. It is real-idea.[8]

Clearly according to Aurobindo it is within the power of man to evolve into the highest spiritual being, thereby realizing the Upaniṣadic truth "I am Brahman, *Tat tvam asi*." What is more, men who have attained Truth-Consciousness (Supermind), being themselves free from ignorance, egoism, and discord, can guide others to attain that consciousness and thereby make possible the establishment of a world order in which peace, freedom, and justice prevail. Such a world order will enable everyone to realize the essential spirituality of existence.

But one might ask how one is to attain this spiritual insight. Aurobindo answers that it is to be attained through the practice of "Integral Yoga." Let it be first noted that Integral Yoga is not rejection of the world of toil and tears and withdrawing into the cave and the jungle and living in seclusion. The Integral Yoga of Aurobindo ignores no part of man's being, but takes into account all facets of it and harmoniously integrates them so that the lower is brought under the control and direction of the higher, thus enabling man to live in peace and joy according to the laws of the spirit within. Aurobindo is fully aware that most men crumble under economic and social hardships, and therefore he regards as absurd and senseless any philosophy which pays little or no attention to the material and social conditions of men but exhorts them to realize their spirituality. Accordingly, an essential component of the practice of Integral Yoga consists in working toward the creation of a social-political order which insures the material and social well-being of men, thereby making it possible for them to strive toward realizing the life divine.

By "social well-being" Aurobindo means justice and freedom. Thus he tells us that the aim and goal of every society must be

> first to provide the conditions of life and growth by which individual Man—not isolated men according to their capacity—and the race through the growth of its individuals, may travel towards its divine perfection. It must be secondly, as mankind generally more and more grows near to some figure of it—for the cycles are many and each cycle has its own figure of the Divine in man—to express in the general life of mankind, the light, the power, the beauty, the harmony, the joy of the Self that has been attained and that pours itself out in a freer and nobler humanity.[9]

It should be obvious now that Aurobindo's philosophy is an original synthesis of the Indian and Western traditions. He integrates in a unique fashion the great social, political, and scientific achievements of the modern West with the ancient and profound spiritual insights of Hinduism. The vision that powers the life divine of Aurobindo is none other than the Upaniṣadic vision of the unity of all existence:

> The gnosis [Supermind] is the effective principle of the spirit, a highest dynamis of the spiritual existence. The gnostic individual would be the consummation of the spiritual man; his whole way of being, thinking, living, acting would be governed by the power of a vast universal spirituality. . . . All his existence would be fused into oneness with the transcendent and universal Self and Spirit [*Ātman, Brahman*]; all his action would originate from and obey the supreme Self and Spirit's divine governance of Nature.[10]

The influence of the West on Aurobindo can easily be seen in, for example, his acceptance of the dominant Western view that Śaṁkara teaches through his *māyāvāda* that the world is unreal and illusory. This is quite puzzling, especially in view of the fact that Aurobindo himself was an astute student of Vedānta. We cannot discuss here Aurobindo's reason for understanding and interpreting Śaṁkara as he does. We can only point out that nowhere does Śaṁkara say that the world is unreal and illusory.

Quite the contrary, through the concept of sublation he teaches that the world is neither real nor unreal. That this is indeed his teaching is further borne out by his distinction between lower and higher truths. As such, Aurobindo's characterization of Śaṁkara's Vedānta as a world-negating philosophy[11] is unfounded. It is possible that in his enthusiasm to synthesize Hindu and Western modes of thought Aurobindo hastily and mistakenly identifies Śaṁkara's *māyāvāda* with the subjective idealism of Berkeley, which undoubtedly stands in sharp contrast to the realism of the Western philosophical tradition in general.

In conclusion, it is to be emphasized that such criticisms as the above do not diminish Aurobindo's stature as a great philosopher-mystic. The vision of man and the world emerging from Aurobindo's synthesis of the East and West will remain an inspiration for generations of men and women in their quest for wisdom, peace, harmony, and joy.

S. Radhakrishnan

Servapalli Radhakrishnan (1888–   ) is the most famous Indian philosopher of the twentieth century. Born in a Brāhmin family in South India, Radhakrishnan was educated in his native country. His education comprised a study of both Indian and Western philosophical traditions. He served with great academic distinction as professor of philosophy at Calcutta University, vice-chancellor of Andhra and Banaras universities, and as the Spalding Professor of Eastern Religions at Oxford. But his career was not confined to the field of education. In 1952 he was elected to the vice-presidency of the Indian Republic, and in 1962 to the presidency. It is as though Plato's dream of the philosopher-king had come true, for as educator-statesman Radhakrishnan has rendered illustrious service to his country and to the world. Radhakrishnan is a gifted teacher, and like all other gifted teachers he profoundly influenced his students. A master of English prose, Radhakrishnan is a superb lecturer and a brilliant writer. He has authored scores of articles and books. *Indian Philosophy,*

An Idealist View of Life, The Hindu View of Life, The Philosophy of the Upaniṣads, Eastern Religions and Western Thought are among his best-known works.

Radhakrishnan's philosophy is esssentially Śaṁkara's Advaita Vedānta interpreted in the light of the circumstances of the modern world. Like Śaṁkara, Radhakrishnan holds that ultimate reality is the absolute, undivided, unitary Brahman. Notwithstanding his elaborate denials and arguments to the contrary, Śaṁkara is often understood and interpreted in the West as having taught that the world is unreal and illusory. One of Radhakrishnan's main contributions to philosophy is the dispelling of this misunderstanding by a fresh and authoritative interpretation of Śaṁkara's doctrine of *māyā*.[12] In the true spirit of Śaṁkara's Vedānta, Radhakrishnan regards the world of our senses and intellect—the phenomenal world—as appearances of the one absolute Brahman, the ground of all existence. According to Radhakrishnan, the experience of ultimate reality—that is, the realization of the Upaniṣadic truth of the identity of Ātman and Brahman—is the goal of human life. Thus for Radhakrishnan the chief problem of philosophy is to construct a theory which on the one hand does justice to the phenomenal world of finite objects and selves and on the other explicates the relation of this world to its ground, namely, Brahman. Needless to say, such a theory should not only recognize the efficacy and validity of our senses and reason in dealing with the world of phenomena but also acknowledge the mystical, intuitive insight which transcends the senses and intellect. And it is no exaggeration to say that by a bold and rich interpretation of Vedānta Radhakrishnan succeeded in formulating a philosophy of religion which subsumes under itself in a consistent manner epistemology, metaphysics, science, axiology, social-political theory, and mysticism.

Radhakrishnan takes a dynamic view of Brahman. The phenomenal world of finite objects and selves is the dynamic manifestation of the power of Brahman. Brahman is eternally active, and selves and objects *are* its activity. It would be a mistake, Radhakrishnan emphasizes, to think that Brahman and the power by which Brahman manifests itself as the world are two distinct realities. Quite the contrary, the power *is Brahman* itself. That is, the existence and power of Brahman are one and the same. This view is somewhat similar to that of Thomas Aquinas, according to which in God, unlike finite beings of the phenomenal world, existence and essence are identical. The reader should, however, be cautious not to push this similarity between Aquinas and Radhakrishnan too far; for whereas the former is an avowed ontological dualist, the latter is a thoroughgoing monist. Consistent with his interpretation of the phenomenal world as the manifestation of the power of Brahman, Radhakrishnan maintains that the numerically different selves of the phenomenal world are neither identical with nor different from Brahman as the totality of existence. In other words, Brahman is not exhausted by any of its particular manifestations, but is the unity underlying the entire manifested world. This at once leads Radhakrishnan to the distinction between the lower and the higher self. The lower self is the self of man in his empirical-logical modes of experience, and as one among many manifestations it is only an aspect of Brahman. On the other hand, the higher self is the self which transcends all empirical-logical modes and hence can only be experienced in nonconceptual, nonperceptual, mystical intuition. The higher self, being free from all determinations and limitations, is pure spirit identical with Brahman itself. Religious quest, then, according to Radhakrishnan, is the struggle and the striving of man as lower self to realize the truth that in his inmost being as the higher self he is indeed the absolute spirit (Ātman-Brahman). Radhakrishnan emphasizes that, contrary to the widespread misunderstanding, such realization does not result in the annihilation of the self but in the transformation of man from mundane state to the supramundane state of *saccidānanda.*

We shall bring our brief discussion of Radhakrishnan's philosophy to a close by noting his characterization of the essence of religion and the nature of religious experience. According to Radhakrishnan, the essence of religion is not to be identified with theology, dogma, belief, sentiment, and such external trappings as ritual and ceremony; nor is it to be identified with morality or philosophy:

> Religion has been identified with feeling, emotion and sentiment, instinct, cult and ritual, perception, belief and faith, and these views are right in what they affirm, though wrong in what they deny. Schleiermacher is not wrong in saying that there is a predominant feeling element in the religious consciousness. Religious feeling, however, is quite distinct from any other kind of feeling. Nor is it to be identified with a sense of creaturely dependence. . . . If we assimilate religious experience to the moral consciousness, as Kant is inclined to do, we overlook the distinctive characters of the two activities. Religion is not mere consciousness of value. There is in it a mystical element, an apprehension of the real and an enjoyment of it for its own sake which is absent in the moral consciousness. Religion is not a form of knowledge as Hegel sometimes urged. While religion implies a metaphysical view of the universe, it is not to be confused with philosophy. . . . It [religion] is not an apologetic for the existing social order; nor is it a mere instrument for social salvation. It is an attempt to discover the ideal possibilities of human life, a quest for emancipation from the immediate compulsions of vain and petty moods. It is not true religion unless it ceases to be a traditional view and becomes personal experience. . . . It is the reaction of the whole man to the whole reality.[13]

Religious experience, according to Radhakrishnan, is a unique mode of consciousness of the unity of the knower, the known, and the activity of knowing. It is mystical experience *par excellence,* which transcends the senses and intellect and is what the Upaniṣadic sages call *saccidānanda:*

> It [religious experience] is a type of experience which is not clearly differentiated into a subject-object state, an integral, undivided consciousness in which not merely this or that side of man's nature but his whole being seems to find itself. It is a condition of consciousness in which feelings are fused, ideas melt into one another, boundaries broken and ordinary distinctions transcended. Past and present fade away in a sense of timeless being. Consciousness and being are not there different from each other. All being is consciousness and all

> consciousness being. Thought and reality coalesce and a creative merging of subject and object results. Life grows conscious of its incredible depths. In this fulness of felt life and freedom, the distinction of the knower and the known disappears. The privacy of the individual self is broken into and invaded by a universal self which the individual feels as his own.[14]

It is clear from the above that for Radhakrishnan religious experience is the realization of the apex of the Upaniṣadic wisdom expressed variously as *Aham Brahmāsmi* ("I am Brahman"), *Prajñānaṁ Brahma* ("Pure Consciousness is Brahman"), "*Ayam Ātmā Brahma* ("This Self is Brahman"), and *Tat Tvam asi* ("That thou art").

The power, persuasiveness, and exalted character of Radhakrishnan's philosophy lie in the inspiring vision of reality he provides by a masterly integration of the multifarious achievements and possibilities of the human spirit in all times and climes.

Nothing could be a more fitting conclusion to a book on Indian philosophy than the following observation of Professor Robert Hume:

> The *Upanishads* undoubtedly have great historical and comparative value, but they are also of great present-day importance. No one can thoroughly understand the workings and conclusions of the mind of an educated Hindu of today who does not know something of the fountain from which his ancestors for centuries past have drunk, and from which he too has been deriving his intellectual life. . . . Furthermore, although some elements [of the *Upanishads*] are of local interest and past value, it is evident that the monism of the *Upanishads* has exerted and will continue to exert an influence on the monism of the West, for it contains certain elements which penetrate deeply into the truths which every philosopher must reach in a thoroughly grounded explanation of experience.[15]

Notes

Chapter I. General Introduction

1. Frank Thilly, *A History of Philosophy,* revised and updated by Ledger Wood (New York: Henry Holt & Co., 1955), p. 7 (emphasis added).
2. *Ibid.,* p. 3 (emphasis added).
3. For a stimulating discussion of the parallels between Indian and European philosophies, see Th. Stcherbatsky, "Some European Parallels," in *Buddhist Logic* (New York: Dover Publications, 1962), Vol. I, 529-46. For a thorough and highly systematic treatment of the various problems, methods, and solutions in the Indian philosophical tradition, with appropriate comparison and contrast with the Western tradition, the reader is referred to Karl H. Potter, *Presuppositions of India's Philosophies* (Englewood Cliffs, N.J.: Prentice-Hall, 1963).
4. *Ibid.*
5. Heinrich Zimmer, *Philosophies of India* (Princeton: Princeton University Press, 1969), Ch. II (sections entitled "Philosophy as a Way of Life" and "Philosophy as Power"), pp. 48-50, 56-66.
6. "This Indian view of the identity of personality and conduct with teaching is well rendered in the apt comment of a Hindu friend of mine in criticism of a certain popular book on Oriental Philosophy. 'After all,' he said, 'real attainment is only what finds confirmation in one's own life.' The worth of a man's writing depends on the degree to which his life is itself an example of his teaching." *Ibid.,* p. 50.
7. Edward Conze, *Buddhist Thought In India* (Ann Arbor: University of Michigan Press, 1967), p. 214. Conze's references are to Koestler's *Arrow in the Blue* (New York: The Macmillan Co., 1970), p. 213, and *The Lotus and the Robot* (New York: Harper & Row, 1972), pp. 219, 225.

8. E. A. Burtt, "What Can Western Philosophy Learn from India?" *Philosophy East and West,* Vol. V, No. 3 (October 1955), pp. 206-7.
9. Puruṣārthas (the four aims, ends, attitudes of life) and social organization—division of men into the four castes (*brāhmin,* the priest-teacher; *kṣatriya,* the warrior-ruler; *vaiśya,* the trader; and *śūdra,* the servile class), the four stages of human life (*āśramas:* namely *brahmacarya,* the student; *gārhastya,* the householder; *vānaprastha,* the forest-dweller; and *sannyāsa,* the wandering ascetic) and the duties of each man toward himself and others—are widely discussed in Indian literature: the Bhagavad-gītā, the *Mahābhārata,* the *Laws of Manu,* and Kauṭilya's *Arthaśāstra.* See excerpts in *A Source Book in Indian Philosophy,* ed. by S. Radhakrishnan and Charles A. Moore (Princeton: Princeton University Press, 1967), pp. 101-223. See also Zimmer, *Philosophies of India,* pp. 34-42; and Potter, *Presuppositions of India's Philosophies,* pp. 5-10.

Chapter II. Cārvākism: Materialism

1. The following are some of the chief sources on materialism: (*a*) Jayarāśi Bhaṭṭa, *Tattvopaplava-siṁha,* Ch. VII, tr. by S. N. Shastri and S. K. Saksena, rev. by S. C. Chatterjee, from *Tattvopaplava-siṁha,* ed. by Pandit Sukhlaji Sanghavi and Rasiklal C. Parikh, Gaekwad's Oriental Series, LXXXVII (Baroda: Oriental Institute, 1940). (*b*) Kṛṣṇa Miśra, *Prabodha-candrodaya,* tr. by J. Taylor (Bombay, 1811), pp. 19-22. (*c*) Mādhava Ācārya, *Sarva-darśana-saṁgraha,* tr. by E. B. Cowell and A. E. Gough (London: Kegan Paul, Trench, Trubner, 1904), pp. 2-11. (*d*) Śaṁkara, *Sarva-siddhānta-saṁgraha,* tr. by Prem Sundar Bose (Calcutta, 1929), pp. 4-6. (All these materials are conveniently brought together in Radhakrishnan and Moore, *A Source Book in Indian Philosophy,* Ch. VII, pp. 227-49. In order to facilitate ready verification, all the notes in the text are referred to this work, hereafter cited as *Sourcebook.*)
2. *Sarva-darśana-saṁgraha* (*Sourcebook,* p. 229).
3. *Ibid.,* p. 231.
4. *Tattvopaplava-siṁha* (*Sourcebook,* pp. 236-46).
5. *Sarva-darśana-saṁgraha* (*Sourcebook,* pp. 231-33).
6. John Stuart Mill, *A System of Logic* (London, 1870). See the section "Of the function and logical value of the syllogism."
7. *Sarva-darśana-saṁgraha* (*Sourcebook,* p. 231).
8. *Ibid.,* pp. 233-34.
9. *Ibid.,* p. 230.
10. *Ibid.*
11. *Sarva-siddhānta-saṁgraha* (*Sourcebook,* p. 235).
12. *Ibid.*
13. *Ibid.*
14. *Sarva-darśana-saṁgraha* (*Sourcebook,* p. 229).
15. *Sarva-siddhānta-saṁgraha* (Sourcebook, p. 235).

NOTES

Chapter III. Jainism

For excerpts from some of the original Jaina works, see Radhakrishnan and Moore, *A Source Book in Indian Philosophy.*

1. Siddhasena Divākara, *Sanmati Tarka,* tr. by Pandit Sukhlalji Sanghavi and Pandit Bechardasji Doshi (Bombay: Shri Jain Shivetamber Education Board, 1939), 1. 14.
2. Umāsvāmī, *Tattvārthādhigama-sūtra* cited as *Tat. Sut.*), tr. by J. L. Jaini (Arrah: The Central Jaina Publishing House, 1920), 5. 38.
3. *Sanmati Tarka* 1. 12.
4. *Ibid.,* 1. 17.
5. Nemichandra, *Dravyasaṁgraha,* ed. and tr. by S. C. Ghoshal (Arrah: Central Jaina Publishing House, 1917), 24.
6. Haribhadra, *Ṣaḍ-darśana-samuccaya* (cited as *Ṣaḍ*), Commentary by Guṇaratna (Calcutta: Asiatic Society, 1905), 47. Also *Tat. Sut.* 2. 8.
7. *Tat. Sut.* 5. 16.
8. *Ibid.,* 10. 1, 2, 3.
9. *Ibid.,* 6. 3, 12, 13.
10. *Ibid.,* 6. 12-25.
11. *Ibid.,* 2. 22, 23.
12. *Ibid.,* 5. 25.
13. *Ibid.,* 5. 19.
14. *Ibid.,* 5. 24.
15. *Ibid.,* 2. 22. Also see *Ṣaḍ.* 49 for Guṇaratna's arguments for the existence of life in minerals and plants.
16. "The cosmic matter passed with them [the Milesians] for something in itself living: they thought of its as animated, just as are particular organisms, and for this reason their doctrine is usually characterized from the standpoint of the later separation in conceptions as *Hylozoism.*" Wilhelm Windelband, *A History of Philosophy* (New York: Harper & Brothers, 1958), p. 32 (see also pp. 44, 48, 179).
17. *Tat. Sut.* 5. 18.
18. *Ṣaḍ.* 49.
19. *Ibid.,* p. 172.
20. *Ibid.,* 49.
21. *Ibid.,* p. 163.
22. *Dravyasaṁgraha* 21.
23. H. Bergson, *Time and Free Will,* tr. F. L. Pogson (New York: Harper & Brothers, 1960), pp. 106-10.
24. *Tat. Sut.* 1. 9.
25. Siddhasena Divākara, Nyāyāvatāra, tr. with introduction by S. C. Vidyābhūṣaṇa (Calcutta: The Indian Research Society, 1909), p. 4.
26. *Ṣaḍ.* 55.
27. *Nyāyāvatāra* 29. Also *Tat. Sut.* 1. 33.
28. Mallisena, *Syādvāda-Mañjarī,* Commentary by Hemachandra, ed. by A. B. Dhruva, Sanskrit and Prakrit Series LXXXIII (Bombay: Bhandarkar Oriental Reserch Institute, 1933).
29. *Ibid.,* XXIII. Also *Tat. Sut.* 1. 33.
30. *Syādvāda-mañjarī* VI presents elaborate arguments in defense of atheism.

31. *Dravya-Saṁgraha* 49.
32. *Tat. Sut.* 7–10.

Chapter IV. Buddhism

Wherever possible, citations from original sources will be referred to the following readily accessible works:
Buddhist Texts Through the Ages, ed. by E. Conze and others (New York: Harper & Row, 1962) (cited as *Texts*).
A Source Book in Indian Philosophy, ed. S. Radhakrishnan and Charles A. Moore (cited as *Sourcebook*).
Buddhism in Translations, ed. by Henry Clark Warren (New York: Atheneum, 1963, originally published by Harvard University Press in the Harvard Oriental Series, 1896) (cited as *Translations*).
World of the Buddha: A Reader—from the Three Baskets to Modern Zen, ed. by Lucien Stryk (Garden City, N.Y.: Doubleday & Co., 1969), (cited as *World*).
The Buddhist Tradition in India, China and Japan, ed. by William Theodore De Bary (New York: Vintage Books, 1972) (cited as *Tradition*).

1. *Majjhima-Nikāya* 63 (*Translations,* p. 120).
2. "Questions which tend not to Edification," *ibid.,* pp. 117-28. A monk named Mālunkyaputta once asked the Buddha why he always refused to answer certain questions. These are: (1) Is the universe eternal? (2) Is it not eternal? (3) Is the universe finite? (4) Is it infinite? (5) Is the soul the same as the body? (6) Is it different from the body? (7) Does the *Tathāgata* (the thus-gone, one who has come to truth, one who has put an end to ignorance and suffering, one who is enlightened) exist after death? (8) Does he not exist after death? (9) Does he both (at the same time) exist and not exist after death? (10) Does he both (at the same time) not exist and not not-exist? These ten questions become sixteen when we state the four alternatives for each of the problems, as in the case of the last. These are known as "indeterminate questions" (*avyākatāni*). The Buddha answered Mālunkyaputta by saying that the reason why he refused to answer these questions was that inquiry into them is neither relevant nor profitable to knowledge of the cause of suffering and of the means to its cessation and therewith to attaining supreme wisdom and Nirvāṇa.
3. "First Sermon," *Saṁyutta-Nikāya,* v. 420, in Edward J. Thomas, *The Life of Buddha as Legend and History* (New York: Alfred A. Knopf, 1927), pp. 87-88.
4. For an excellent discussion of *duḥkha* as impermanence, see Walpola Rahula, *What the Buddha Taught* (New York: Grove Press, 1962), pp. 17-28.
5. *Mahā-Nidāna-Sutta* of the *Dīgha-Nikāya* (*Translations,* pp. 202-8).
6. *Saṁyutta-Nikāya* XXII. 90 (*Translations,* pp. 165-66); *ibid.,* XII.

35 (*Translations,* pp. 167-68); *Visuddhi-Magga,* Ch. XVII (*Translations,* pp. 168-82); *Milindapañha* 62 (*Translations,* pp. 182-83;); *Majjhima-Nikāya, sutta* 38 (*Translations,* pp. 183-84). For a detailed discussion of the links in the chain of causation, see excerpts from *Visuddhi-Magga,* Chs. XVII, XVIII (Chs. XXIV, XVII, XVIII, XX in *Translations,* pp. 168-82, 184-86, 187, 189-202); excerpts from *Saṁyutta-Nikāya* XXII, XII (*Translations,* pp. 165-68, 186); excerpts from *Milindapañha* 60, 62 (*Translations,* pp. 182-83, 186); excerpts from *Majjhima-Nikāya, sutta* 44 (*Translations,* p. 187).

7. *Mahā-Vagga,* opening sections (*Translations,* p. 84).
8. *Dīgha-Nikāya, sutta* 22 (*Translations,* pp. 372-74).
9. "The Arhat," in *The Dhammapada* (*The Path of Virtue*), Ch. VII (*Sourcebook,* pp. 299-300).
10. The concept of Nirvāṇa is immensely complex and has been the subject of a variety of conflicting interpretations. The main source of difficulty in explicating Nirvāṇa lies in the fact that since Nirvāṇa transcends the senses and intellect, no positive characterization of it is possible. This is what is meant by saying that Nirvāṇa is ineffable. This does not, however, mean that we are completely helpless and that the concept of Nirvāṇa is to be left as wholly unintelligible. Quite the contrary, the concept can be discussed and rendered intelligible to the extent possible within the limits of logic and language. But—this is the important point—no discourse on Nirvāṇa, however subtle and illuminating it may be, can be a substitute for actual experience. Everyone has to do his own thinking and analysis on the subject. Only thus can one command some understanding of the whole notion of Nirvāṇa. As aids to further study, we shall furnish here some original sources and secondary commentaries on the subject. "Nirvāṇa," *Texts,* sections 72, 76, 78, 84-89, 111, 121-22 (v. 12), 123, 154, 165, 178-79, 186, 188, (vv. 13, 27, 40, 41, 102, 103, 110), 189 I, 201; "Meditation and Nirvāṇa," *Translations,* ch. VI, pp. 280-391; *World,* pp. 109-24; *Tradition,* pp. 30-32, 75-76, 82, 87, 100, 121, 128, 162, 172; *Buddhist Wisdom Books: The Diamond Sūtra and the Heart Sūtra,* tr. by E. Conze (New York: Harper & Row, 1972), pp. 26, 47, 82-83, 97, 104-5. Secondary works: E. Conze, *Buddhism: Its Essence and Development* (New York: Harper & Brothers, 1959); Louis de La Vallée Poussin, *Nirvāṇa* Paris: G. Beauchesne, 1925); Th. Stcherbatsky, *The Conception of Buddhist Nirvāṇa* (The Hague: Mouton & Co., 1965); Nyanaponika Thera, *Anatta and Nibbāna* (Ceylon: The Wheel Publications, 1959); Edward J. Thomas, *The History of Buddhist Thought* (London: Routledge & Kegan Paul, 1933). For a variety of Western interpretations of Nirvāṇa, see Guy R. Welbon, *Buddhist Nirvāṇa and Its Western Interpreters* (Chicago: University of Chicago Press, 1968).
11. "I will pull the wick right down (into the oil)—the going out (nibbāna) of the lamp itself was deliverance of the mind." *Therīgātha* 116 (*Texts,* p. 92). "For those who in mid-stream stay, in great peril in the flood—for those adventuring on ageing and dying—do I proclaim the Isle. Where is nothing, where

naught is grasped, this is the Isle of No-beyond. Nirvāṇa do I call it—the utter extinction of ageing and dying." *Milindapañha* (*World,* pp. 112-13).

12. *Suttanipāta* 204 (*Texts,* p. 93).
13. "By passing quite beyond the plane of no-thingness, he enters into and abides in the plane of neither-perception-nor-non-perception. By passing quite beyond this plane, he enters into and abides in the stopping of feeling and perceiving." *Majjhima-Nikāya* I. 160 (*Texts,* p. 64). Also "Great King," a person possessed of magical power, possessed of mastery over mind, could estimate the quantity of water in the great ocean and the number of living beings dwelling there; but that person possessed of magical power, possessed of mastery over mind, would never be able to make clear the form or figure or age or dimensions of Nibbana, either by an illustration or by a reason or by a cause or by a method." *Milindapañha* (*World,* pp. 112-13).
14. H. Hackmann, *Buddhism as a Religion* (London: Probsthain & Co., 1910), pp. 289-99.
15. "*Ontology* . . . [is] a metaphysical theory as to the most general formal relations of reality." Windelband, *History of Philosophy,* p. 199. This is an authoritative work on the history of Western philosophy from the Greeks to Nietzsche. It provides a succinct account of the ontologies of different thinkers.
16. For a detailed discussion of the development of substance and process ontologies in India, see T. R. V. Murti, *The Central Philosophy of Buddhism* (London: George Allen & Unwin, 1960), Ch. III.
17. *Saṁyutta-Nikāya* III. 66 (*Sourcebook,* pp. 28-281); *Milindapañha* 25, 28 (*Translations,* pp. 128-33); *Visuddhi-Magga,* Ch. XVII (*Translations,* pp. 133-35); *Mahā-Nidāna-Sutta* of the *Dīgha-Nikāya* (*Translations,* pp. 135-37); *Saṁyutta-Nikāya* XXII. 85 (*Translations,* pp. 138-45); *Visuddhi-Magga,* Ch. XXI (*Translations,* pp. 145-46); *Saṁyutta-Nikāya* XII. 62 (*Translations,* pp. 150-52).
18. See excerpts under "Conditioned Genesis Collectively" and "Con ditioned Genesis Separately," *Texts,* pp. 65-82.
19. *Saṁyutta-Nikāya* II. 64-65 (*Texts,* p. 66).
20. "That things have being, O Kaccāna, constitutes one extreme of doctrine; that things have no being is the other extreme. These extremes, O Kaccāna, have been avoided by The Tathāgata, and it is a middle doctrine he teaches." *Saṁyutta-Nikāya* XXII. 90 (*Translations,* p. 166). Also see *Visuddhi-Magga,* Ch. XVII (*Translations,* pp. 194-201).
21. For detailed discussions of *karma,* see *Saṁyutta-Nikāya* III. 2. 10 (*Translations,* pp. 226-28). The Buddhist notion of rebirth is not to be confused with transmigration. On this see *Milindapañha* 32, 41, 71, 77 (*Translations,* pp. 232-38); and *Visuddhi-Magga,* Ch. XVIII (*Translations,* pp. 172-82).
22. *Vinaya-Piṭaka* I. 1 (under "Conditioned Genesis Collectively," *Texts,* p. 66).
23. *Saṁyutta-Nikāya* II. 64-65 (*Texts,* p. 66).
24. F. C. Copleston, *A History of Philosophy* (Garden City, N.Y.:

Doubleday & Co., 1966), Vols. I, IV, VI.

25. "The wise one [i.e., the Ātman, the Self] is not born, nor dies.
This one has not come from anywhere, has not become anyone.
Unborn, constant, eternal, primeval, this one
Is not slain when the body is slain."
—*Kaṭha Upaniṣad* II. 18. R. E. Hume, *The Thirteen Principal Upanishads* (New York: Oxford University Press, 1971) (*Sourcebook,* p. 45).
26. *Visuddhi-Magga,* Ch. XIV (*Translations,* pp. 154-57); *Milindapañha* 25 (*Translations,* pp. 129-35).
27. "For my part, when I enter most intimately into what I call 'myself,' I always stumble on some particular perception or other, of heat or cold, light or shade, love or hatred, pain or pleasure. I never catch 'myself' at any time without a perception, and never can observe anything but the perception." David Hume, *A Treatise of Human Nature,* ed. by L. A. Selby-Bigge (New York: Oxford University Press, 1951), p. 252. It should be emphasized, however, that the similarity of Hume's analysis of the self to that of the Buddha should not be allowed to obscure the fundamental differences between their philosophical orientations. This point is ably developed by N. P. Jacobson, *Buddhism: The Religion of Analysis* (New York: Humanities Press, 1966), Ch. VIII ("The Buddha and Hume"), pp. 162-77.
28. *Saṁyutta-Nikāya* III, 127-28 (*Texts,* p. 74). Also see the following sections in *Texts:* 14, 32.
29. *Aṅguttara-Nikāya* III, 399-401 (*Texts,* p. 73); *Majjhima-Nikāya* I. 8 (*Texts,* p. 74).
30. These are the very questions which King Milinda puts to the monk Nāgasena, and the latter answers them with copious illustrations. The whole discussion is concerned with the question of rebirth. Nāgasena repeatedly teaches that rebirth is not transmigration but takes place without anything transmigrating. See *Mlindapañha* 71 (*Translations,* pp. 234-38). Further, "it is only elements of being possessing a dependence that arrive at a new existence: none transmigrated from last existence, nor are they in the new existence without causes in the old." *Visuddhi-Magga,* Ch. XVII (*Translations,* p. 238).
31. "For twenty years past I have mistrusted 'consciousness' as an entity. . . . To deny plumply that 'consciousness' exists seems so absurd on the face of it—for undeniably 'thoughts' do exist—that I fear some readers will follow me no further. Let me then immediately explain that I mean only to deny that the word stands for an entity, but to insist most emphatically that it does stand for a function." William James, "Does Consciousness Exist?" *Essays in Radical Empiricism and A Pluralistic Universe* (London: Longmans, Green & Co., 1940), pp. 1-38. Compare this with

"Misery only doth exist, none miserable.
No doer is there; naught save the deed is found.
Nirvāṇa is, but not the man who seeks it.
The Path exists, but not the traveler on it."
—*Visuddhi-Magga,* Ch. XVI (*Translations,* p. 146).

32. During his long travels, the Buddha once visited a town called Kesaputta in the kingdom of Kosala. On hearing that the Buddha was in their town, its inhabitants, known as the Kālāmas, paid him a visit and told him thus: "Sir, there are some recluses and brāhmaṇas who visit Kesaputta. They explain and illuminate only their own doctrines, and despise, condemn and spurn others' doctrines. Then come other recluses and brāhmaṇas, and they, too, in their turn, explain and illumine only their own doctrines, and despise, condemn and spurn others' doctrines. But, for us, Sir, we have always doubt and perplexity as to who among these venerable recluses and brāhmaṇas spoke the truth and who spoke falsehood."

    To the confused Kālāmas, the Buddha gave the following advice: "Yes, Kālāmas, it is proper that you have doubt, that you have perplexity, for a doubt has arisen in a matter which is doubtful. Now, look you Kālāmas, do not be led by reports, or tradition, or hearsay. Be not led by the authority of religious texts, nor by mere logic or inference, nor by considering appearances, nor by the delight in speculative opinions, nor by seeming possibilities, nor by the idea: 'this is our teacher.' But, O Kālāmas, when you know for yourselves that certain things are unwholesome *(akusala),* and wrong, and bad, then give them up. . . . And when you know for yourselves that certain things are wholesome (*kusala*) and good, then accept them and follow them." *Aṅguttara-Nikāya,* ed. by Devamitta Thera, (Colombo, 1929), p. 115.

    What is more, the Buddha neither considered himself nor expected his followers to consider him to be an exception to the above advice and exhortation. For equally explicitly and emphatically he told his disciples that they should carefully examine the teaching of the *Tathāgata* (the Buddha) himself, in order that they may fully convince themselves of the true value of their teacher. *Vīmaṁsaka-sutta,* No. 47, in *Majjhima-Nikāya,* Pali Text Society of London edition.
33. For an authoritative treatment of the development of the various Buddhist schools, major and minor, see E. Conze, *Buddhist Thought in India* (Ann Arbor: University of Michigan Press, 1967). Also see the chart displaying Buddhist history in Conze, *Buddhism: Its Essence and Development,* immediately following p. 212.
34. For original Mahāyāna criticisms of Hīnayāna, see excerpts under "Criticisms of the Hīnayāna Position," *Texts,* pp. 119-35. An excellent discussion of *Arhat* is to be found in Conze, *Buddhism: Its Essence and Development,* pp. 93-95.
35. See sections "*Bodhisattva*" and "The Six Perfections," *Texts,* pp. 127-39. For a discussion of the Bodhisattva as the ideal of the *Mahāyāna,* see Conze, *Buddhism: Its Essence and Development,* pp. 125-30.
36. *Pañcaviṁśatisāhasrikā* 40-41 (*Texts,* p. 119); and *Aṣṭasāhasrikā* XXII, 402-4 (*Texts,* p. 128).
37. *Ratnagotravibhāga* I, v. 72 (*Texts,* p. 130).
38. *Ibid.,* 71.

39. Commenting on God (and gods) in the context of Buddhism, Herbert V. Guenther writes: "Buddhism, however, is a thoroughly atheistic doctrine. The host of gods which appears on the stage of life are ethically inferior to man, superior only in their power and duration of life. In many circumstances these gods are symbols which have significant functions and through which we are enabled to see 'meaning.' Atheism, to be sure, is in no way opposed to true religiosity. It is only dogmaticism with its artificial restrictions and its thoroughgoing disorientation that prevents any true religiosity to express itself and in this violation of a living process endangers mental health." *Philosophy and Psychology in the Abhidharma* (Lucknow: Buddha Vihara, 1957), pp. 173-74. For an illuminating discussion of the question: Is Buddhism atheistic? see Conze, *Buddhism: Its Essence and Development,* pp. 38-43; and Helmuth V. Glasenapp, *Buddhism: A Non-theistic Religion,* tr. by I. Schloegl (New York: George Braziller, 1966).
40. For a masterly discussion of this point as well as the general characteristics of Mahāyāna, as distinguished from those of Hīnayāna, see D. T. Suzuki, *Outlines of Mahāyāna Buddhism* (London: Luzac & Co., 1907). Also see excerpts under "The Buddhism of Faith," *Texts,* pp. 170-206.
41. For a discussion of the Buddha as the unconditioned and transcendent reality, see Conze, *Buddhist Thought in India,* pp. 225-34.
42. "Because the Buddha-cognition is contained in the mass of beings,
Because it is immaculate and non-dual by nature,
Because those who belong to the Buddha's lineage go towards it as their reward,
Therefore all animate beings have the germ of Buddhahood in them."

"As to its Suchness identical in common people, Saints and perfect Buddhas,
Thus has the *Jina's* Germ been shown to be in beings, by those who have seen the true Reality."
—*Ratnagotravibhāga* I, vv. 27, 45 (*Texts,* p. 181).
43. "*Saṁsāra* (i.e., the empirical life-death cycle) is nothing essentially different from *nirvāṇa. Nirvāṇa* is nothing essentially different from *Saṁsāra*"; "The limits (i.e., realm) of *nirvāṇa* are the limits of *Saṁsāra*. Between the two, also, there is not the slightest difference whatsoever." Nāgārjuna, *Mūlamadhyamakakārikā,* tr. by Kenneth K. Inada (Tokyo: The Hokuseido Press, 1970), Ch. XXV, 19, 20, p. 158.
44. "But the difference lies in that common people are perverted in their views,
Whereas those who have seen the Truths have undone this perversion;
The Tathagatas again are unperverted as to what truly is,
And without intellectual impediments."
—*Ratnagotravibhāga* (*Texts,* p. 181).
45. "The meaning of '*dharma*' is as follows: They bear their intrinsic

nature, or they are supported by conditions, or they are supported according to their intrinsic nature. However, all these factors or *dharmas* are so entirely dependent upon the innumerable conditions that in no way they can or will retain their individuality above all conditions, hence they are called 'having no individuality of their own.'" Guenther, *Philosophy and Psychology in the Abhidharma,* pp. 6-7. Guenther bases this statement on *Atthasālinī* II. 9, 10. An extremely analytical treatment of the concept of *dharma* in Buddhist philosophy is to be found in Conze, *Buddhist Thought in India,* Ch. 7: "the Buddhist science of salvation regards the world as composed of an unceasing flow of simple ultimates, called 'dharmas,' which can be defined as (1) multiple, (2) momentary, (3) impersonal, (4) mutually conditioned events" (p. 97).

46. "Not dependent on anything else, calm, unimpeded by discursive ideas,
Indiscriminate, undifferentiated, those are the marks of true reality."
—Candrakīrti, *Prasannapadā* XVIII (*Texts,* p. 169).
"Where there is eye and forms, ear and sounds, etc., to: where there is mind and dharmas, where there is enlightenment and the unenlightened, that is duality. Where there is no eye and forms, nor ear and sounds, etc., to: no mind and dharmas, no enlightenment and enlightened, that is non-duality."
—Śatasāharikā LIII, f. 279-83 (*Texts,* p. 175). Also see "The Synonyms of Emptiness," *Texts,* pp. 170-72.

47. No *dharmas,* not even the teaching of the Buddha, are to be grasped as ultimate reality. The teaching is the means for liberation from ignorance and suffering and is not something to be clung to: "The Lord: Bodhisattvas, great beings have no notion of a dharma, Subhuti, nor a notion of non-dharma. They have no notion or non-notion at all. For if these Bodhisattvas should have the notion of a dharma, then they would thereby seize on a self, on a being, on a soul, on a person. A Bodhisattva should therefore certainly not take up a dharma, nor a non-dharma. Therefore this saying has been taught by the Tathāgata in a hidden sense: "Those who know the discourse on dharma as a raft should forsake dharmas, and how much more so non-dharmas.'" *Vajracchedikā* 6 (*Texts,* p. 173).

48. For a detailed treatment of *Saguṇa-Brahman* and Nirguṇa Brahman, see under "Ádvaita Vedānta" in Ch. IX on Vedānta.

49. "The Dharma-body should be known as twofold:
The completely immaculate element of Dharma,
And its outpourings, the demonstration of the principle (of Dharma),
In its depth and in its variety."
—*Ratnagotravibhāga* I, v. 145 (*Texts,* p. 183).
Conze defines *dharmakāya* as "the absolute body of Buddhahood free of all definite qualities." *Texts,* p. 315.

50. The sect of Buddhism centered around the concept of Amitābha Buddha is known as "Pure Land Buddhism" and is popular in China, Japan, and Korea. The main tenet of this sect is salva-

tion through faith and devotion. Pure Land Buddhists worship the Buddha as God, offer him prayers, and seek love and mercy from him. Thus Honen exhorts a disciple to lay aside all pedantry and subtle scholarly preoccupations and repeat the name of Amitābha Buddha with a pure heart and simple faith: "The method of final salvation that I have propounded is neither a sort of meditation, such as has been practiced by many scholars in China and Japan, nor is it a repetition of the Buddha's name by those who have studied and understood the deep meaning of it. It is nothing but the mere repetition of the "Namu Amida Butsu,' without a doubt of His mercy, whereby one may be born into the Land of Perfect Bliss. . . . Those who believe this, though they clearly understand all the teachings of Shākya [the Buddha] taught throughout his whole life, should behave themselves like simple-minded folk, who know not a single letter, or like ignorant nuns and monks whose faith is implicitly simple. Thus without pedantic airs, they would fervently practice the repetition of the name of Amida, and that alone." H. H. Coates and R. Ishizuka, *Honen the Buddhist Saint, His Life and Teaching* (Tokyo: Kodokaku, 1930), pp. 728-9 (*Tradition,* p. 331).

51. There is some ambiguity concerning the meaning of the term *Abhidhamma.* It may mean further doctrine or supreme, higher doctrine. In any case, the term is usually rendered as higher doctrine, meant only for those who are intellectually highly developed. Thus Conze writes: "The *Abhidharma* books, however, were meant for the very core of the Buddhist elite, and it was assumed that the Wisdom acquired from their perusal would be sufficient reward and incentive of study." *Buddhism: Its Essence and Development,* p. 106. According to another scholar, "'*Abhidhamma*' means the Higher Doctrine because it enables one to achieve one's Deliverance, or because it exceeds the teachings of the *Sutta Piṭaka* and *Vinaya Piṭaka* (the other two parts of the *Tipiṭaka* (Three Baskets) of the *Pali Canon*)." *Manual of Abhidhamma,* tr. and ed. by Narada Thera (Colombo: Vajirarama Publications, 1956), p. 2. *The Abhidhamma Piṭaka* consists of seven treatises: "1. *Dhamma-Saṅgaṇi,* Enumeration of psychic and material properties, i.e., the elements and objects of consciousness; 2. *Vibhaṅga,* Eighteen treatises upon various themes of a philosophical, psychological and ethical character; 3. *Kathā-Vatthu,* Book of disputed questions, with regard to the (heretical) views of other Buddhist sects; 4. *Puggala-Paññati,* Book of qualities of character, or types of individuals; 5. *Dhātu-Kathā,* Expositions of the functions of the senses in their eighteen fundamental elements; the six organs, the six classes of objects corresponding to them, and the six classes of consciousness resulting from the mutual relationship of the two; 6. *Yamaka,* Book of the pairs of opposites; and 7. *Paṭṭhāna,* Book of the arising of psychic and material states: Causal connexions and mutual dependence." Lama Anagarika Govinda, *The Psychological Attitude of Early Buddhist Philosophy* (London: Rider & Co., 1969), p. 146. It might be noted that the exact date of composition of the *Abhidhamma* works is not known. Scholars generally assign

them to the first two centuries after the death of the Buddha. A list of *Abhidhamma* translations and commentaries is supplied in the Bibliography.

52. The term *vaibhāṣa* means extensive annotation or variety of views and opinions. The *Vaibhāṣa Śāstra* is a commentary on Katyāyaniputra's *Jñāna-prasthāna* (*Source of Knowledge*) of the Sarvāstivāda school, closely related to the orthodox Theravāda school. Sarvāstivada is the doctrine that all things exist. In all probability, the *Vaibhāṣa Śāstra* was composed in the second century A.D. "and this title indicates that many opinions of the time were gathered and criticized in detail and that some optional ones were selected and recorded. The chief object of the *Vaibhāṣa* commentary was to transmit the correct exposition of the *Abhidharma* School which has since then come to be called the *Vaibhāṣika* School." Junjiro Takakusu, *The Essentials of Buddhist Philosophy* (Honolulu: Office Applicance Co., 1956), p. 59. The *Abhidhamma-mahāvaibhāṣa* is Pārśva's great commentary on the *Jñāna-prasthāna.*
53. For a thorough treatment of the Vaibhāṣika school, see H. V. Guenther, *Buddhist Philosophy in Theory and Practice* (Baltimore: Penguin Books, 1972), Ch. 2.
54. "Buddhism assumes no substance, no abiding individual self, no soul, no Creator, no root principle of the universe. But this by no means implies that all beings and things do not exist. They do not exist with a substratum or a permanent essence in them, as people often think, but they do exist as causal relatives or combinations." Takakusu, *Essentials of Buddhist Philosophy,* p. 72.
55. "Existence, real existence, is nothing but efficiency. Consequently, what is non-efficient, or what is a non-cause, does not exist." Th. Stcherbatsky, *Buddhist Logic* (New York: Dover Publications, 1963), Vol. I, p. 124.
56. "They [the Vaibhāṣikas] claimed that we have an immediate apprehension of the nature of things as they are in themselves, but as they never lost sight of 'experience,' which may be described as the sum total of appearances and feelings together with ordering thought they at once were aware of the distinction between (a) data available for ordering and (b) thought as ordering activity. More precisely, they held that we are directly aware of external material objects and that therefore the senses give us trustworthy knowledge." Guenther, *Buddhist Philosophy in Theory and Practice,* p. 34.
57. "Since the past and future exist *substantialiter* in their own rights, the three divisions of time exist now as substances." *The Summary of Philosophical Systems* (*YID-BZHIN-MDZOD-KYI GRUB-MTHA' BSDUS-PA,* a Tibetan work), extract in *ibid.,* p. 63. This Vaibhāṣika view of the equireality of past, present, and future was criticized by other schools, e.g., the Sautrāntikas. See under the Sautrāntika school.
58. For a concise and up-to-date discussion of the problem of universals and the controversy between realists and nominalists, see H. Staniland, *Universals* (Garden City, N.Y.: Doubleday & Co., 1972).

59. "The *Vaibhāṣikas* recognized immediate apprehension and influence as the means providing us with valid knowledge." Guenther, *Buddhist Philosophy in Theory and Practice,* p. 41.
60. The Sautrāntika school is not represented by a single theory or set of doctrines. Rather, it is a movement with a variety of theories, all of which share certain characteristics. They all deny that *Abhidhamma* has scriptural authority and place exclusive emphasis on the *sutras;* they all criticize the Sarvāstivada and the Vaibhāṣika; and their inquiries are dominated by epistemological concerns. As a result of these common characteristics, certain doctrines are held by the Sautrāntika movement as a whole. It is these doctrines that we discuss here.
61. "According to the *Sautrāntika's* view, the objective constituents of perceptual situations are particular existents of a peculiar kind; they are not literally parts of the perceived object, although they resemble physical objects as ordinarily conceived." Guenther, *Buddhist Philosophy in Theory and Practice,* p. 73.
62. See Copleston, *History of Philosophy,* Vol. 5, Part I, p. 99.
63. See the section on the Yogācāra school.
64. "Not from one's own Self, not from another Self, not at haphazard are the things produced. In reality they are not produced at all, they arise in functional dependence upon their causes. There is no causation in the sense of one eternal stuff changing its forms in a process of evolution, because there is no such stuff at all, this stuff is a fiction." Stcherbatsky, *Buddhist Logic,* Vol. I, p. 122.
65. "Existence and non-existence are thus different names given to the same thing 'just as a donkey and an ass are different names given to the same animal.'" *Ibid.,* p. 95.
66. Asaṅga (A.D. 5) was the founder of the Yogācāra school. He authored the text *Yogācāra-bhumi.* Vasubandhu (A.D. 420-500), after his conversion to Mahāyāna by his older brother Asanga, systematized the philosophical doctrines of the Yogācāra school in *Vijñāpti-mātrata-triṁśikā.* Dignāga, Dharmapāla, Guṇamati, Sthiramati, Paramārtha, and Jayasena are among the illustrious figures of the Yogācāra school.
67. As to ontology, the Yogācāra school "adheres neither to the doctrine that all things exist, because it takes the view that nothing outside the mind (mental activity) exists, nor to the doctrine that nothing exists because it asserts that ideations do exist." Takakusu, *Essentials of Buddhist Philosophy,* p. 80.
68. For a summary of Yogācāra arguments against the reality of the external world, with citation of original sources, see Stcherbatsky, *Buddhist Logic,* Vol. I, pp. 513-29.
69. "It [the argument] starts with the declaration that the external object must be either an atom or an aggregate of atoms. If it can be proved that it is neither an atom nor an aggregate of atoms, it is nothing but an idea without a corresponding external reality." From Dignāga's *Ālambana-parikṣa,* cited in *ibid.,* p. 518.
70. "The object of cognition is the object internally cognized by introspection and appearing to us as though it were external. The ultimate reality is thus the 'idea' consciousness." *Ibid.,* pp. 519-20.
71. "The absolute existence of unthinking things without any rela-

tion to their being perceived seems perfectly unintelligible. Their *esse* is *percipi,* nor is it possible they should have any existence out of the minds of thinking things which perceive them." Copleston, *History of Philosophy,* Vol. 5, Part II, p. 26.

72. "Indeed it is not the eyeball that represents the organ, but a respective sensuous faculty. In assuming a subconscious store of consciousness instead of an extèrnal world and a Biotic Force [*karma*] instead of the physical sense-organs, we will be able to account for the process of cognition. There will be no contradiction." From Dignāga's *Ālambana-parikṣa,* cited in Stcherbatsky, *Buddhist Logic,* Vol. I, pp. 520-21.
73. "When all things are reflected on our mind, our discriminating or imaginative power is already at work. This is called our consciousness (*vijñāna*). Since the consciousness co-ordinating all reflected elements stores them, it is called the store-consciousness or ideation-store—I prefer to use the word ideation-store." Takakusu, *Essentials of Buddhist Philosophy,* p. 82.
74. "The *Ālaya*-consciousness itself is not an unchangeable fixed substance (*dravya*) but is itself ever changing instantaneously (*kṣaṇika*) and repeatedly." *Ibid.,* p. 90.
75. "As it [store-consciousness] grows up by self-culture, it gradually subjugates the false nature of the eighth consciousness [Ālaya-consciousness] and as the result of this subjugation the life of error becomes a refined one until the highest stage of enlightenment is attained." *Ibid.,* p. 91.
76. *Nāgārjuna: A Translation of His Mūlamadhyamakakārikā with an Introductory Essay,* by Kenneth K. Inada (Tokyo: The Hokuseido Press, 1970). The *Mūlamadhyamakakārikā* will hereafter be cited as *Kārikā,* and all references are to Inada's translation.
77. According to Heraclitus, "there is nothing abiding either in the world or its constitution taken as a whole. Not only individual things, but also the universe as a whole, are involved in perpetual, ceaseless revolution: all flows, and nothing abides. . . . That, then, which abides and deserves the name of deity, is not a thing, and not a substance or matter, but motion, the cosmic process, *Becoming* itself. . . . The number and variety of things presented in co-existence and succession by experience had given the Milesians occasion to ask for the common abiding ground of which all these things are metamorphoses. When, however, the conception of cosmic substance or world-stuff has culminated with Parmenides in the conception of Being, there seems so little possibility of uniting these individual things with it, that reality is denied them, and the one unitary Being remains also the *only* being." Windelband, *History of Philosophy,* pp. 36, 38.
78. For a thorough treatment of the development of the Ātman and Anātman traditions in India, see Murti, *Central Philosophy of Buddhism,* Ch. III.
79. "They [philosophical systems] seek to comprehend the entire universe in their scope and attempt to reach the unconditioned. In the absence of any objective criterion that might eliminate questionable and inadequate views, the formulation of innumer-

able systems of thought and their inevitable conflict are necessary consequences." *Ibid.,* p. 210.

80. K. Venkata Ramanan, *Nāgārjuna's Philosophy: As Presented in The Mahā-Prajñapāramita-Śāstra* (Banaras: Bharitiya Vidya Prakashan, 1971), p. 238.
81. *Critique of Pure Reason,* tr. by N. K. Smith (New York: St. Martin's Press, 1965), pp. 120-75.
82. For a detailed treatment of this point, see R. Puligandla, "The *Mādhyamika* and the Impossibility of Transcendental Deductions," *Proceedings of the Ohio Philosophical Association* (University of Akron), April 1972, pp. 112-22; and "How Does Nāgārjuna Establish the Relativity of all Views?" *The Maha Bodhi* (Calcutta), Vol. 81, Nos. 5-6 (May-June 1973), pp. 156-64.
83. "*Tṛṣṇā* (craving) as the origin of *kleśa* stands for thirst, passion, as the root of seizing and clinging. *Kleśa* is the painful state of emotional conflict which results from the failure to fulfill the thirst, from the disparity between the expected and the realized. Ignorance, functioning again through *tṛṣṇā,* gives rise to *dṛṣṭi,* which is to seize the specific concepts and the conceptual systems that embody them as themselves absolute and limitless. This is dogmatism, claiming absoluteness for the relative, completeness for the fragmentary." Ramanan, *Nāgārjuna's Philosophy,* p. 105.
84. "Philosophy, for the Mādhyamika, is not an explanation of things through conceptual patterns. That is the way of dogmatic speculation (*dṛṣṭi*); but this does not give us the truth. The Dialectic is intended as an effective antidote for this dogmatic procedure of reason; it is the criticism of theories (*śūnyatā-sarva-dṛṣṭīnām*). The Dialectic itself is philosophy. . . . Dialectic is the consciousness of this conflict in reason. . . . The essence of the Mādhyamika attitude, his philosophy (the *madhyamā pratipad*), consists in not allowing oneself to be entangled in views and theories, but just to observe the nature of things without standpoints (bhūta-pratyavekṣā)." Murti, *Central Philosophy of Buddhism,* p. 209.
85. "Freedom from pain is achieved by the elimination of kleśas—the unconscious primordial passions impelling man towards attachment and bondage. Prajñā is the negation of all vikalpa—conceptual constructions; it is the reaching of non-dual knowledge, a state beyond the discursive level of Reason." *Ibid.,* p. 221.
86. "It is usual to ask of a system of philosophy to give us its views about ultimate existences—God, soul and matter. Systems are labelled Monism, Dualism, Idealism, Realism, etc., according to the nature of the answers given. The Mādhyamika philosophy is not a system in this sense. Nowhere is there any attempt to raise such problems on its own initiative. The Dialectic is not a body of doctrines, but their criticisms. . . . The Dialectic itself is Philosophy." *Ibid.,* p. 209.
87. Candrakīrti, *Mādhyamika-vṛtti* (*Prasannapadā*) (cited as *Vṛtti*), commentary on Nāgārjuna's *Kārikā,* ed. by Louis de La Vallée Poussin, Bibliotheca Buddhica, No. IV (St. Petersburg, 1903-13), p. 24.
88. "*Prasanga* is not to be understood as an apogogic proof in which we *prove* an assertion *indirectly* by disproving the opposite.

Prasanga is disproof simply, without the least intention to prove any thesis. All the arguments which Kant adduces to prove the thesis and the antithesis in his *Antinomies of Reason* are well-known examples of the apogogic proof. . . . Such proofs, however plausible they may appear, fail to carry conviction. For, the disproof of the opponent, even if it is cogent, does not necessarily mean the establishment of one's own position as true. For, both the opponent's view, as well as one's own view may be false. The apogogic proof can have cogency and compulsion in spheres where by the nature of the subject matter, such as mathematics, we so completely possess the field *in concreto* that the alternatives are narrowed down to two, and by rejecting one we indirectly prove the other. It must fail with regard to the empirical facts and especially with regard to the supersensuous." Murti, *Central Philosophy of Buddhism*, p. 131.

89. *Mahā-prajñāpāramitā-śāstra* (cited as *Śāstra*), commentary by Nāgārjuna on the original *Pañcaviṁsati-sāhasrikā*, was translated into Chinese by Kumārajīva and reproduced in *Taisho-Shinshu-daizokyo*, ed. by Takakusu and Watanabe (Tokyo, 1922-33), Vol. 25, 641*c*, 644*a*, 658*c*, 662*a*, 686*a*, 706*b*, 707*c*; Āryadeva's *Catuḥśatakā*, restored into Sanskrit by V. Bhattacharya (Santiniketan: Visva-Bharati, 1931), XIV, 21; *Abhisamayālaṁkarāloka* of Haribhadra, Gaekwad's Oriental Series (Baroda), n.d., p. 61; and Ramanan, *Nāgārjuna's Philosophy*, p. 155.
90. *Kārikā* I. 1.
91. *Vṛtti*, pp. 14, 22.
92. *Ibid.*, p. 36.
93. *Kārikā* XIV. 5-8.
94. The Mādhyamika treatises do not subject the third alternative to any elaborate criticism. The reason for this is that the refutation of it follows from the conjunction of the refutations of the first two alternatives. It can easily be seen that the argument for the refutation of the third alternative is a special case of the argument for the mutual opposition of existence (*sat*) and non-existence (*asat*), in *Kārikā* XXV. 14.
95. *Ibid.*, I. 1.
96. "All elements, physical as well as mental, are *śūnya*, i.e., relative and non-substantial, conditioned and changing." Ramanan, *Nāgārjuna's Philosophy*, p. 210; "Pratītyasamutpāda (doctrine of dependent origination), the cardinal doctrine of Buddhism. means, according to the Mādhyamika, the dependence of things on each other, their having no nature or reality of their own (nissvabhāvatva or śūnya)." Murti, *Central Philosophy of Buddhism*, p. 122.
97. There is nothing absolutely fixed as the qualifier and the qualified. That which is the qualifier in one situation can itself be the qualified in another and vice versa. Again, it is only in relation to the qualified (substance) that there is the qualifier and it is only in relation to the qualifier that there is the qualified." *Śāstra*, p. 549*a* (translation in Ramanan, *Nāgārjuna's Philosophy*, p. 208).
98. See *Kārikā*, *Vṛtti*, and *Śāstra*; for a masterly exposition and sum-

maries of the arguments, see Murti, *Central Philosophy of Buddhism,* Ch. 7; Ramanan, *Nāgārjuna's Philosophy,* Chs. 7, 8.

99. Like Nirvāna, Śūnyatā is an extremely difficult and complicated concept and has consequently been the subject of great controversy. Nevertheless, one can grasp its meaning and significance by careful reading of the Mādhyamika treatises—in particular Kārikā XXIV, XXV.

100. "The 'no-doctrine' attitude of the Mādhyamika is construed by Vedānta and Vijñānavāda as a 'no-reality' doctrine; they accuse the Mādhyamika, unjustifiably, of denying the real altogether and as admitting a theory of appearance without any reality as its ground (niradhiṣṭhāna bhrama). In fact, the Mādhyamika does not deny the real; he inly denies *doctrines* about the real. For him, the real as transcendent to thought can be reached only by the denial of the determinations which systems of philosophy ascribe to it. When the entire conceptual activity of reason is dissolved by criticism, there is a Prajñā-Pāramitā. The *Aṣṭasāhasrikā* declares in the clearest terms that Prajñāpāramitā is not to be construed as a doctrine of Elements, of Groups, etc. These conceptual devices do not obtain in reality. The non-apprehension of things (yo'nupalambaḥ sarvadharmāṇām) is *Prajñāpāramitā.*" Murti, *Central Philosophy of Buddhism,* p. 218 (the reference to *Aṣṭasāhasrikā* is as follows: *Aṣṭasāhasrikā-prajñāpāramitā,* ed. by Rajendralal Mitra, Bibliotheca Indica [Calcutta, 1888], p. 177).

101. "The 'being dependent nature' of existing things; that is called 'emptiness.' That which has a nature of 'dependent'—of that there is a non-self-existent nature." Nāgārjuna, *Vigrahavyāvarttanī,* Part II, 22 (translation by Frederick J. Streng, *Emptiness: A Study in Religious Meaning* [Nashville: Abingdon Press, 1967], Appendix B, pp. 221-27).

102. "Rejection of all thought categories [concepts] and views [theories] is the rejection of the competence of reason to apprehend reality. the real [according to the Mādhyamika] is transcendent to thought; it is non-dual (śūnya), free from the duality of 'is' and 'not-is.'" Murti, *Central Philosophy of Buddhism,* p. 208.

103. "In order to prove actual relation between two things we refer to the concept of relation and say that had there been no relation the concept of relation would never have arisen. But the Mādhyamika would pay the realists back in their own coin, because, for them, if there had been no concept of relation, actual relation itself would never have been assumed. Therefore, we can say with justification that the concepts are responsible for the notion of actually existing things, but we cannot say the converse because except concepts we have no other means to ascertain the actual state of affairs. Thus, the notion of causality for the Mādhyamika is not rooted in actual co-ordination of factors. It means only dependence of one concept upon another (hetupratyāyapekṣa)." R. C. Pandeya, "The Mādhyamika Philosophy: A New Approach," *Philosophy East and West,* Vol. XIV, No. 1 (April 1964), p. 10; see *Vṛti,* pp. 78-85 and 250-58, and *Kārikā,* I. 8.

104. *Śāstra* 319*a*.
105. *Kārikā*, "Examination of Dogmatic Views," XXVII.
106. Nāgārjuna explicitly states that *Pratītyasamutpāda* (dependent origination), the Middle Way (*madhyamā-pratipad*), and *Śūnyatā* are all one and the same: "We declare that whatever is relational [dependent, conditioned] origination is *śūnyatā*. It is a provisional name (i.e., thought construction) for the mutuality (of being) and, indeed, it is the middle path." *Ibid.*, XXIV. 18.
107. "I pay homage to the Fully Awakened One,
the supreme teacher who has taught
the doctrine of relational origination,
the blissful cessation of all phenomenal thought constructions.
(Therein, every event is 'marked' by):
non-origination, non-extinction,
non-destruction, non-permanence,
non-identity, non-differentiation,
non-coming (into being), non-going (out of being)."
—*Ibid.*, I, dedicatory verse,
108. *Ibid.*, XXIV. 8, 9; Candrakīrti provides three definitions of *saṁvṛti*: (1) the categorizing activity of the mind which conceals the real nature of things—in short *avidyā* (ignorance); (2) phenomena as contrasted with nondual, ultimate reality; and (3) that which is of conventional nature—knowledge and truth which are based on linguistic and social conventions and underlie our everyday transactions (*Vṛtti*, p. 492).
109. *Kārikā* XXIV. 8, 9; *Vṛtti*, p. 473; *Prajñākaramati, Bodhicaryāvatārapañjikā* (commentary on Śāntideva's *Bodhicaryāvatāra*), ed. Bibliotheca Indica (Calcutta, 1901-5), pp. 354, 366, 367.
110. The translation of *prajñā* as "intuition" (intuitive insight) is the source of many misunderstandings. Thus one tends to uncritically identify the *prajñā* the Mādhyamika speaks of with the intuition of Henri Bergson (*An Introduction to Metaphysics*, tr. by T. E. Hume (New York: Bobbs-Merrill, 1955). One should guard oneself against such identification: "Anti-conceptualism notwithstanding, the intellectual intuition of the Mādhyamika must not be confounded with the Bergsonian view of intuition. For Bergson, Reason spatialises things, it freezes reality which is movement, *élan vital*—the life principle. The real can be apprehended, according to him, only by sympathetically identifying oneself with it. From the examples that Bergson suggests and his interpretations of the course of evolution, it is evident that intuition for him is *instinctual* in nature; its position is *infra-rational*. It would not be very wrong to say that Bergson wants us to sink down to the level of birds and insects. He does not prescribe any discipline for acquiring this faculty or for suppressing reason. The Prajñā of the Mādhyamika, on the other hand, is not instinct and cannot be identified with any biotic force. It is supra-rational." Murti, *Central Philosophy of Buddhism*, p. 219. As knowledge, *Prajñā* is nondual (*advayā*) and nonbifurcated (*advvaidhīkārā*), and as intuition it is contentless—that is, its content is not any particular object but the entire reality. Further, *prajñā* is unfathomable, immeasurable, and infinite. As such, it

is beyond the reach of language, logic, and the senses (*Aṣṭasāhasrikā,* p. 467).

111. *Śāstra* 138*c*. That Nāgārjuna fully acknowledges the validity of *saṁvṛti-satya* (relative truth) in mundane experience is unmistakably clear from the following: "Without relying on everyday common practices (i.e., relative truths), the absolute truth cannot be expressed. Without approaching the absolute truth, *nirvāṇa* cannot be attained." Further, "whatever is in correspondence [harmony] with *śūnyatā,* all is in correspondence (i.e., possible). Again whatever is not in correspondence with *śūnyatā,* all is not in correspondence." *Kārikā* XXIV. 10, 14. "The Mādhyamika is not only not opposed to system-building, but he would himself institute systems, not as ends in themselves, but as the means to widen one's understanding, deepen one's comprehension. Analysis, synthesis and criticism have all their respective places and functions in this comprehensive understanding. . . . It is the revelation of this all-comprehensive nature of true understanding that is the basic meaning of *śūnyatā* in regard to views; this is the underlying idea of the Mādhyamika's rejection of all views and not having any view of his own." Ramanan, *Nāgārjuna's Philosophy,* p. 318.
112. "*Saṁsāra* (i.e., the empirical life-death cycle) is nothing essentially different from *nirvāṇa. Nirvāṇa* is nothing essentially different from *saṁsāra.* The limits (i.e., realm) of *nirvāṇa* are the limits of *saṁsāra.* Between the two, also, there is not the slightest difference whatsoever." *Kārikā* XXV. 19, 20.
113. "The wise men (i.e., enlightened ones) have said that *śūnyatā* or the nature of thusness is the relinquishing of all false views. Yet it is said that those who adhere to the idea or concept of *śūnyatā* are incorrigible." *Ibid.,* XIII. 8.
114. *Ibid.,* XXV. 4-16.
115. "Existence is the grasping of permanency (i.e., permanent characteristics) and non-existence the perception of disruption. (As these functions are not strictly possible), the wise should not rely upon (the concepts of) existence and non-existence." Further, "those who delight in maintaining, 'Without the grasping, I will realize *nirvāṇa; Nirvāṇa* is in me;' are the very ones with the greatest grasping." *Ibid.,* XV. 10; XVI. 9.
116. This section is a slightly revised version of the following article: R. Puligandla, "The Buddhist Analysis of Identity and Its Psychological Implications," *The Maha Bodhi* (Calcutta), Vol. 79, Nos. 5 and 6 (May-June 1971), pp. 144-57.
117. Glasenapp, *Buddhism: A Non-theistic Religion,* pp. 50-51.
118. Chögyam Trungpa, *Meditation in Action* (Berkeley: Shambala Publications, 1970), p. 55 (emphasis added). For an honest and illuminating discussion of the gnawing doubt of the believer, see Father James Kavanaugh, *A Modern Priest Looks at His Outdated Church* (New York: Pocket Books, 1968), p. 24.
119. Trungpa, *Meditation in Action,* pp. 36-37.
120. I owe this illustration to my student, Miss Kaisa Puhakka, formerly of the Department of Philosophy, The University of Toledo, Toledo, Ohio, U.S.A.

121. For a comparison of the Buddhist and Marxist conceptions of revolution and freedom, see R. Puligandla and K. Puhakka, "Buddhism and Revolution," *Philosophy East and West,* Vol. 20, No. 4 (October 1970), pp. 345-54.
122. Jacobson, *Buddhism: The Religion of Analysis,* pp. 135-41.
123. *Ibid.,* p. 65.
124. Nyanatiloka, *Buddhist Dictionary* (Colombo: Frewin & Co., 1956), pp. 11-12.
125. Conze, *Buddhism: Its Essence and Development,* p. 23.
126. See E. Conze, *Buddhist Meditation* (New York: Harper & Row, 1970), and Nyanaponika Thera, *The Heart of Buddhist Meditation* (Colombo, 1956).
127. Charles Hartshorne, "Recollections of Famous Philosophers and Other Important Persons," *Southern Journal of Philosophy,* Vol. 8, No. 4 (1970), p. 72.

Chapter V. Sāṁkhya

(For excerpts from some of the original Sāṁkhya works, see Radhakrishnan and Moore, *A Source Book in Indian Philosophy.*)

1. References to the Sāṁkhya (and Yoga) doctrines are to be found in, among others, the Upaniṣads, the *Mahābhārata,* the Bhagavadgītā (or, simply Gītā). There are many excellent and authoritative translations of these, some of which are cited in the Bibliography: *Chāndogya Upaniṣad VI.* iv. 1; *Praśna Upaniṣad* VI. 2; *Kaṭha Upaniṣad* I. iii. 10-13; *Śvetāśvatara Upaniṣad* LV. 5, 10, 12; *Mahābhārata, Śāntiparva* 303-8; *Bhagavad-Gītā* II. 11-39; III. 42; V. 4-5.
2. "The ultimate ground of the unfolding universe is *prakriti,* a formless, limitless, undifferentiated, indestructible, ungrounded, uncontrolled, and eternal matter." Dale Riepe, *The Naturalistic Tradition in Indian Thought* (Delhi: Motilal Banarsidass, 1964), p. 193.
3. *The Sāṁkhya-kārikā of Īśvarakṛṣṇa* (cited as *SK*), tr. by T. H. Colebrooke (Bombay: Tookaram Tatya, 1887), 15.
4. *Vijñānabhikṣu's Sāṁkhya-pravacana-bhāṣya* (cited as *SPB*) ed. by R. G. Bhaṭṭa, Chowkhamba Sanskrit Series (Banaras), n.d., 1. 67-68, 76-77; 6. 36.
5. "As the unintelligent and unconscious principle, it [prakṛti] is called Jada." Chandradhar Sharma, *A Critical Survey of Indian Philosophy* (Delhi: Motilal Banarsidass, 1964), p. 153.
6. *SK* 16.
7. "The Guṇas are said to be everchanging. They cannot remain static even for a moment." Sharma, *Critical Survey of Indian Philosophy,* p. 155.
8. The *guṇas* are "interdependent moments in every real or substantive existence." B. N. Seal, *The Positive Sciences of the Ancient Hindus* (London: Longmans, Green & Co., 1915), p. 2.
9. "Effect subsists (antecedently to the operation of cause); for what exists not, can by no operation of cause be brought into existence. Materials, too, are selected which are fit for the purpose;

everything is not by every means possible: what is capable, does that to which it is competent; and like is produced from like." *SK* 9, in S. C. Banerji, *Sāṇkhya Philosophy with Gauḍapāda's Scholia and Nārāyaṇa's Gloss* (cited as *Sāṇkhya Philosophy*) (Calcutta: Hare and Co., 1898).

10. For the Sāṁkhya version of arguments for *satkāryavāda* and against *asatkāryavāda,* see *SK,* as well as *SPB* 1. 113-21.
11. "But even in the stage of dissolution, we must remember, Prakṛti does not cease to be dynamic, motion conceived as original to it." M. Hiriyanna, *The Essentials of Indian Philosophy* (London: George Allen & Unwin, 1967), p. 110.
12. According to Professor Joseph Kaplan, a well-known American physicist, the Sāṁkhya theory of objects as dynamic energy complexes is in full harmony with modern physics: "The transmutability of the elements has been shown in many ways. For example, it is possible, by bombarding certain elements with extremely rapidly-moving electrical particles, to change them into others, and to even produce elements which do not occur in nature because they are unstable (radioactive). We go even further. It is possible to produce matter, such as electrons, from radiation (light). Thus the Sāṁkhya theory is in absolute agreement with the latest results of physics. It is interesting here to make the following comment. The atomic theory is the product of the Western mind. In his naive way the Western scientist generalizes the experience that one can subdivide matter until one meets an ultimate particle into an atomic theory assuming many elements. The Hindu [Sāṁkhya] philosopher goes much further and reduces everything to one element." Commenting on the Sāṁkhya doctrine of the three *guṇas,* Professor Kaplan observes that the role of the three *guṇas* is "in entire accord with the point of view of the modern physicist. By this I mean that if a modern physicist were to discuss the *guṇas,* he would, in the light of his knowledge and experience, use the same arguments [as the Sāṁkhya's]. To put it differently, the thought processes of the Western philosopher are such that he is antagonistic to the physicist whereas the Hindu [Sāṁkhya] philosopher is sympathetic. Only in the relatively unimportant realm of classical [Newtonian] physics—unimportant as regards its fundamental character—does the Western philosopher have any sympathy." Quoted in Swami Prabhavananda and Frederick Manchester, *The Spiritual Heritage of India* (Garden City, N.Y.: Doubleday & Co., 1964), pp. 242-44. Observations such as these provide further justification for the widely accepted view that the Sāṁkhya system is naturalistic, in the sense that it is an attempt to explain the world without appealing to any supernatural entities and agencies such as God.
13. *The Vedānta Sūtras of Bādarāyaṇa with the Commentary by Śaṁkara* (also known as *Vedānta-sūtra-bhāṣya, Śārīraka-bhāṣya, Brhama-sūtra-bhāṣya*), tr. by George Thibaut. (New York: Dover Publications, 1970), I. 4; also see Eliot Deutsch, *Advaita Vedānta: A Philosophical Reconstruction* (Honolulu: East-West Center Press, 1969), p. 35.

14. *Vācaspati Miśra's Sāṁkhya-tattva-kaumudī* (cited as *STK*), ed. by B. Rama Sastri, Chowkhamba Sanskrit Series (Banaras, 1921), 21-41; *SPB* 1. 64-74; 2. 10-32.
15. *Sāṁkhya-pravacana-sūtra* (cited as *SPS*) with Aniruddha's *Vṛtti*, ed. by Kalivara Vedantavagisa (Calcutta), n.d., 1. 71.
16. *SK* 36-37; *SPS* 2. 40-43.
17. *SK* and *STK* 25.
18. *SK* and *STK* 17-20; *SPB* and *Vṛtti* 1. 66; 1. 138-64; 5. 61-68.
19. For a comparison of the Puruṣa-Prakṛti dualism of the Sāṁkhya with the mind-body dualism of Descartes, see Riepe, *The Naturalistic Tradition in Indian Thought,* pp. 202-3.
20. "It [Puruṣa] is the principle of sentience, a principle generally held by the Samkhya philosophers to be completely independent of *Prakriti.*" *Ibid.,* p. 199.
21. "*Purusha* supplies the element of awareness to the physical world of *prakriti.*" *Ibid.*
22. *SK* 17.
23. *Ibid.*
24. *Ibid.*
25. "Since birth, death, and the instruments of life are allotted severally . . . and since qualities affect variously; multitude of souls [selves] is demonstrated." *Ibid.,* 18.
26. See the section "Advaita Vedānta" in Ch. IX on Vedānta.
27. There is considerable dispute as to the correct interpretation of the Sāṁkhya view of the relation between Prakṛti and Puruṣa. Thus, while there are perfectly good grounds to say that in general Sāṁkhya philosophers hold that Prakṛti and Puruṣa are two independent, noninteracting realities, there are certain passages in the Sāṁkhya texts which suggest some interaction between the two. For example: "And from the contrast (before set forth) it follows, that soul is witness, solitary, bystander, spectator, and passive. Therefore, by reason of *union* with it insensible body seems sensible . . . and though the qualities be active the stranger (soul) *appears* as agent. . . . For the soul's contemplation of nature, and for its abstraction, the *union* takes place, as of the halt and blind. By that *union* a creation is framed." *SK* 19-21.
28. *Ibid.,* 21.
29. *SK* and *STK* 4-6; *SPB* 1. 87-89, 99-103; 5. 27, 37, 42-51.
30. The Sāṁkhya distinction between indeterminate and determinate perceptions is parallel to Bertrand Russell's distinction between knowledge by acquaintance and knowledge by description. See "Knowledge by Acquaintance and Knowledge by Description," in *The Basic Writings of Bertrand Russell,* ed. by Robert E. Egner and Lester E. Dennon (New York: Simon & Schuster, 1967), pp. 217-24.
31. The Sāṁkhya conception of inference may be expressed as follows: "*Linga-linga* [mark-marked] relation means the relation of sign and signification, or meaning and symbol. It is a connection of meaning or logical connection. Of this two varieties may be noticed. They are (1) the causal relation and (2) the relation of kind and instance of *sāmānya* and *viśeṣa.* Inference may thus be

defined as the systematic construction or explanation of the objective world of perception by the disimplication of the connection of meaning hidden from sense-perception. It is distinguishable but not separable from perception. Perception and inference are continuous." *SK* 5, in Banerji, *Sāṅkhya Philosophy*. It is interesting to note that in conformity with the general Indian conception of logic, Sāṁkhya holds that perception and inference are not separable but continuous. For a detailed discussion of this point, see Ch. VIII on Nyāya.

32. Broadly speaking, Sāṁkhya accepts with slight modification the Nyāya classification of inference. Accounts of the Sāṁkhya classification differ depending upon whether or not one ignores the modification. Thus our account differs from Banerji's, according to which Sāṁkhya classifies inference into (1) Śeṣavvat, reasoning from effect to cause. (2) Pūrvavat, reasoning from cause to effect, and (3) *Sāmānyatodṛṣṭa,* reasoning from analogy. An example of the first is reasoning from the rise of a river that it has rained; of the second, reasoning from a cloudy sky that it will rain; and of the third, reasoning from the general observation that actions require instruments to the proposition that seeing, an action, requires an instrument, namely, the eye (from Banerji, *Sāṅkhya Philosophy,* 34 f) . It is to be noted that Banerji's account ignores the Sāṁkhya modification of the Nyāya classification of inference. The root of these differences is to be found in the Sāṁkhya texts themselves; thus Vācaspati Miśra's treatment of inference is somewhat different from Īśvara Kṛṣṇa's, on which is based Banerji's exposition.

33. "Perception, Inference and Authoritative Statement [testimony, *āptavacana*] are the three kinds of approved proof, for they comprise every mode of demonstration. The complete determination of the demonstrable is verily by proof." *SK* 4.

34. It is extremely important to distinguish the Sāṁkhya conception of authoritative statement (*āptavacana*), also known as "true revelation," from those of other doctrines, in particular the Christian. A statement is "authoritative not because somebody has said it but because it has survived the test of reason." J. N. Mukerji, *Sāṁkhya or the Theory of Reality* (Calcutta, 1930), p. 24; further, "though there is nothing prescribed, yet what is unreasonable cannot be accepted, else we should sink to the level of children, lunatics and the like." *Sāṁkhya Sūtras* i. 26, in Banerji, *Sāṅkhya Philosophy,* p. 47. "What is called 'revelation' by writers on Sāṁkhya turns out to be considerably different from 'revelation' as understood by Tertullian [*ca.* A.D. 155–222] or St. Thomas Aquinas. . . . Tertullian['s] . . . famous sentence in *De Carne Christi,* 5, unqualifiedly places revelation above reason. It reads: 'It is believable, because it is absurd; it is certain, because it is impossible.' This was written at about the same time as the *Sāṁkhya Kārikā. . . . Sāṁkhya* revelation is authoritative statement. It is authoritative because it squares with the evidence of perception and inference. There is no split between what is known by faith and what is known by reason, or between faith without evidence as opposed to faith with evidence. It is not cor-

rect, then, to say that *Sāṁkhya's āptavacana* is superrational or dependent ultimately on external authority or authority of *śruti* [revelation]. . . . Even if the *Vedas* are not of personal authorship, yet they must be communicated by *āptas* to disciples. The truth of *āptas* is established by experience and by reason, which is to say that they must agree with what is accepted in other branches of knowledge such as treatises on medicine." Riepe, *Naturalistic Tradition in Indian Thought,* pp. 190-91.

35. *SK* 5, 11.
36. *SK* and *STK* 56-67, 61; *SPS* and *Vṛtti* 1. 92-95; 3. 56-67; 5. 2-12.
37. The existence of a supreme lord is unproved. "Since he could not be either free (from desires and anxieties) or bound by troubles of any kind, there can be no proof of his existence. Either way he could not be effective of any creation (That is, if he were free from anxieties he could have no wish to create; and if he were bound by desires of any kind, he would then be under bondage, and therefore deficient in power)." Kapila, *Aphorisms* 96, quoted in Monier-Williams, *Indian Wisdom* (London: George Allen & Unwin, 1875), p. 98.
38. A slightly different version of this argument is as follows: Theistic opponents of the Sāṁkhya maintain that God (Īśvara) and self (soul) are devoid of qualities. The Sāṁkhya argues that this view leads to contradictions; for "how can beings endowed with qualities proceed from *Īśwara,* who is devoid of qualities? or how from soul, equally devoid of qualities? Therefore (the causality) of nature is rendered probable. Thus, from white threads white cloth is fabricated; from black threads black cloth; and in the same manner, from nature, endowed with the three qualities [*guṇas*] [various kinds of objects arise]. . . . But it is claimed that *Īśwara* is without qualities." *Sāṁkhya-kārikā-bhāṣya of Gauḍapāda,* tr. by H. H. Wilson (Bombay: Tookaram Tatya, 1887). 61.
39. *Vṛtti* 1. 92-94.
40. "The attempt to give a theistic colour to the [*Sāṁkhya*] doctrine appears quite late in its history. Vijñānabhikṣu is anxious to find a place for God in the Sāṁkhya scheme, but the support for it even in the late *Sūtra* is slender." M. Hiriyanna, *Outlines of Indian Philosophy* (London: George Allen & Unwin, 1967), p. 282.
41. *SK* and *STK* 44-68; *SPB* and *Vṛtti* 3. 65-84.
42. *SK* and *STK* 44, 63; *SPB* and *Vṛtti* 3. 23-24.
43. *SK* and *STK* 64; *Vṛtti* 3. 66, 75.
44. *Vṛtti* 5. 74-83.
45. *SK* and *STK* 67-68; *Vṛtti* 3. 78-84.

Chapter VI. Yoga

For excerpts from some of the original Yoga works, see Radhakrishnan and Moore, *A Source Book in Indian Philosophy.*

1. Parts of this section are taken from R. Puligandla, "Phenomenological Reduction and Yogic Reduction," *Philosophy East and West,* Vol. 20, No. 1 (January 1970), pp. 19-33.

2. "The excavations undertaken in Punjab some thirty years ago by Sir John Marshall and his collaborators, and continued by E. Mackay, Vats, and Wheeler, have brought to light a civilization whose high point may be placed between 2500 and 2000 B.C. . . . But the most important fact for our investigation is the discovery, at Mohenjo-daro, of an iconographic type that may be considered the earliest plastic representation of a yogin. Here the great God himself, in whom the prototype of Śiva has been identified, is represented in the specifically yogic posture." Mircea Eliade, *Yoga: Immortality and Freedom* (Princeton: Princeton University Press, 1971), pp. 353-355. Stuart Piggott, an authority on prehistoric India, has this to say about the icon mentioned above: "There can be little doubt that we have here the prototype of the great god Shiva as Lord of the Beasts and Prince of Yogis." *Prehistoric India* (Baltimore: Penguin Books, 1950), p. 202; further, "as we have pointed out, the absence of the Yoga complex from other Indo-European groups confirms the supposition that this technique is a creation of the Asian continent, of the Indian soil." Eliade, *Yoga,* p. 361.
3. Patañjali's *Yoga-sūtras* (cited as *YS*) I. 23-28; II. 1, 32, 45. An excellent translation is by Rama Prasada, *Sacred Books of the Hindus, IV* (Allahabad: The Panini Office, 1924).
4. Copleston, *History of Philosophy,* Vol. 2, Part II, pp. 62-63.
5. "On account of his perfection, He serves as a pattern to man in regard to what he might achieve. In this respect, He resembles a *guru* [teacher] who ought, likewise, to be an embodiment of the ideal." Hiriyanna, *Essentials of Indian Philosophy,* p. 125.
6. *Patañjala-sūtra with Bhoja's Vṛtti* (Bhojarāja's commentary on the *Yoga-sūtras*), ed. by K. Vedantavagisa (Calcutta, 1930), i. 23.
7. "*Yoga* is the restraint of mental modifications." *YS* I. 2.
8. *Ibid.,* II. 29.
9. *Ibid.,* III. 1.
10. *Ibid.,* III. 2.
11. *Ibid.,* III. 3.
12. *Ibid.,* I. 41.
13. *Ibid.,* I. 49.
14. *Ibid.,* I. 49.
15. *Ibid.,* III. 49.
16. "Even if we could bring our intuition to the highest degree of clearness, we should not thereby come any nearer to the constitution of objects in themselves [noumena]. We should still know only our mode of intuition, that is, our sensibility." Immanuel Kant, *Critique of Pure Reason,* tr. by N. K. Smith (New York: St. Martin's Press, 1965), p. 83.

17 and 18. See chapters dealings with Vaiśeṣika, Nyāya, and Advaita Vedānta.

Chapter VII. Vaiśeṣika

For excerpts from some of the original Vaiśeṣika works, see Radhakrishnan and Moore, *A Source Book in Indian Philosophy* (cited as *Sourcebook*).

1. *Padārtha-dharma-saṁgraha of Praśastapāda, with the Nyāyakandalī of Śrīdhara* (cited as *PDS* and *NK*), tr. by Ganganatha Jha (Allahabad: E. J. Lazarus & Co., 1916), I. 1 (*Sourcebook*, pp. 397-98).
2. *The Vaiśeṣika-sūtras of Kaṇāda, with the Commentary of Śaṁkara Miśra, extracts from the Gloss of Jayanārāyaṇa, and the Bhāṣya of Candrakānta* (cited as *VSK*), tr. by Nanadalal Sinha, Vol. VI of *The Sacred Books of the Hindus* (Allahabad: The Panini Office, 1923), I. 1. 15 (*Sourcebook*, p. 388).
3. "The character of being dependent (upon something else) belongs to all things except the eternal [ultimate] substances." *PDS* III. 12 (*Sourcebook*, p. 399).
4. *VSK* II. 1. 1-5, 9 (*Sourcebook*, p. 389).
5. "The character of not being dependent and that of being eternal belong to all (substances) except those that are made up of certain constituent parts." *PDS* III. 21 (*Sourcebok*, p. 400).
6. "The arguments used to prove that indivisible atoms existed were as follows: (1) if they did not exist as the smallest things, this would lead to an infinite regress; and (2) if they did not exist, every material product would consist of an equally endless number of constituents which would exclude difference of dimension. The largest mountain might be equal to a sesame seed." Riepe, *Naturalistic Tradition in Indian Thought*, p. 240.
7. There are conflicting interpretations of the Vaiśeṣika notion of atoms. At the heart of the conflict is the question whether the Vaiśeṣika atoms have magnitudes. "According to Chatterji, the *paramāṇus* are not atoms in the Vaiśeṣika system; they should not be translated into English as 'atoms.' The reason he adduces for this rare viewpoint is that the *paramāṇus* have no magnitude, whereas 'Western atoms' do. D. H. H. Ingalls, on the other hand, has pointed out that the *paramāṇus* do have the qualities of visible substances. He says 'Necessarily, for otherwise there would be no *asamavāyi* cause of the qualities in the visible substances. The blue color of the atom is the *asamavāyi* cause of the blue color of the diad and this of the blue color of the visible triad." *Ibid.*, p. 240. Riepe is quoting from J. C. Chatterji, *The Hindus Realism* (Allahabad: The Indian Press, 1912), p. 19, and from Ingall's letter to Riepe (12 December 1956).
8. *PDS* IX. 157-58 (*Sourcebook*, pp. 422-23).
9. "According to Leucippus and Democritus there are an infinite number of indivisible units, which are called atoms. These are imperceptible, since they are too small to be perceived by the senses. The atoms differ in size and shape, but have no quality save that of solidity and impenetrability." Copleston, *History of Philosophy*, Vol. I, Part I, p. 90.
10. "Aristotle blames the Atomists for not explaining the source of motion but we ought not to conclude that Leucippus meant to ascribe the motion of atoms to change: to him the eternal motion and the continuation of motion required no explanation." *Ibid.*, p. 92.
11. "But in the atomic system that which perceives, the mind or soul, can consist only of atoms. To be more explicit, it consists,

according to Democritus, of the same atoms which constitute also the essence of fire: namely, the finest, smoothest, and most mobile." Windelband, *History of Philosophy,* p. 113. Also see Lancelot L. Whyte, *Essay on Atomism* (New York: Harper & Row, 1963).

12. Copleston, *History of Philosophy,* Vol I, Part II, pp. 56-57.
13. *VSK* II. 1. 27 (*Sourcebook,* p. 390); *PDS* III. 24 (*Sourcebook,* p. 400).
14. *PDS* III. 24 (*Sourcebook,* p. 400).
15. *Ibid.,* V. 43 (*Sourcebook,* p. 404).
16. *Ibid.,* V. 42 (*Sourcebook,* p. 404).
17. "Though from the uniformity of the distinguishing character of time, time is directly by itself, one only, yet, it is indirectly, or figuratively, spoken of as manifold, on account of the diversity among the conditions afforded by the production, persistence and cessation of all produced things." *Ibid.*
18. *Ibid.,* V. 44 (*Sourcebook,* p. 404).
19. "And thus the only thing to which consciousness could belong is the self, which thus is cognised by this consciousness." *Ibid.* (*Sourcebook,* p. 405).
20. *Ibid.,* (*Sourcebook,* p. 407).
21. *Ibid.,* (*Sourcebook.* p. 407).
22. *Ibid.,* V. 45 (*Sourcebook,* pp. 408-9).
23. "In consequence of non-existence of universal expansion, mind is atomic or infinitely small." *VSK* VII. 1. 23 (*Sourcebook,* p. 395).
24. *Ibid.,* III. 2. 3 (*Sourcebook,* p. 392).
25. "The absence of the all-pervading character in the mind is inferred from the nonsimultaneity of cognitions." *PDS* V. 45 (*Sourcebook,* p. 410).
26. "Inhering in substance, not possessing attribute, not an independent cause in conjunctions and disjunctions,—such is the mark of attribute [quality]." *VSK* I. 1. 16 (*Sourcebook,* p. 388).
27. Whereas "substance is not annihilated either by effect or by cause; attributes (are destroyed) in both ways." *Ibid.,* I. 1. 12, 13 (*Sourcebook,* p. 388).
28. *PDS* VI. 46-137 (*Sourcebook,* pp. 410-19).
29. "Residing in one substance only, not possessing attribute, an independent cause of conjunctions and disjunctions—such is the mark of action." *VSK* I. 1. 17 (*Sourcebook,* p. 388).
30. "Conjunctions and disjunctions also (are individually the products) of actions." *Ibid.,* I. 1. 30 (*Sourcebook,* p. 388).
31. *PDS* II. 6 (*Sourcebook,* p. 398).
32. "It [universal] pervades over all its objectives; has identically the same form (in all cases) inhering in many individuals; it brings about the idea of its own form in one, two or many things; and it is the cause or basis of the notion of inclusion, inhering as it does in all its substrates simultaneously." *Ibid.,* VII. 154 (*Sourcebook,* pp. 419-20).
33. For a concise but fine discussion of the problem of universals in Western philosophy, see Hilary Staniland, *Universals* (Garden City, N.Y.: Doubleday & Co., 1972).
34. "That these universals belong to a category distinct from sub-

stance, quality and action, is proved by the fact of their having a character totally different from these latter. For this same reason too they are eternal." *PDS* VII. 155 (*Sourcebook,* p. 421).

35. Vallabhācārya, *Nyāya-līlāvatī* (Bombay: Nirnaya Sagar Press, 1915), 80-81; *PDS* VII. 154 (*Sourcebook,* pp. 419-21).
36. "Individualities are the ultimate [i.e., final] specificatives or differentiatives of their substrates. They reside in such beginingless and indestructible eternal substrates, as the atoms, *ākāśa,* time, space, self, and mind,—inhering in their entirety in each of these, and serving as the basis of absolute differentiation or specification." *PDS* VIII. 146 (*Sourcebook,* p. 421).
37. *Ibid.*
38. "Inherence is the relationship between things that are inseparably connected, and which stand to each other in the relation of the container and the contained,—the relationship, namely, that serves as the ground of the notion that 'such and such a things subsists in this.'" *Ibid.,* IX. 157 (*Sourcebook,* p. 422).
39. "Inherence is not mere conjunction; (1) because the members of this relationship are inseparably connected; (2) because this relationship is not caused by the action of any of the members related; (3) because it is not found to end with the disjunction of the members; and (4) because it is found subsisting only between the container and the contained." *Ibid.,* IX. 158 (*Sourcebook,* p. 422).
40. "Even though the members related are transient, the inherence is not transient, like conjunction; because like being, it is not brought about by any cause. That is to say, in the case of being we have found that it is eternal, because we cannot cognise any cause for it, by any of the valid means of knowledge; and the same may be said to be the case with inherence also; as by none of the valid means of knowledge can we find any cause for it." *Ibid.,* IX. 161 (*Sourcebook,* p. 423).
41. "Nor is there a multiplicity of inherences, as there is of conjunctions; because like 'being,' inherence has the same distinguishing feature, and also because there are no reasons for making distinctions in regard to it; for these reasons, inherence, like 'being,' must be regarded as one only." And "in the case of 'being' with regard to substances, qualities and actions, we have seen that it has no connection with any other 'being'; and in the same manner, inherence, being inseparable (from its substrate) and of the very nature of a subsisting relation, could have no other relation; and hence it is regarded as self-sufficient. For this reason it has been regarded as imperceptible by the sense-organs; specially as it is not found to have an existence in the perceptible substances in the same manner that 'being' &c, have; and as it is not perceptible by itself, we conclude that it is only inferable from the notion that 'this is in that.'" *Ibid.,* IX. 159, 161 (*Sourcebook,* p. 423).
42. It is to be noted that Kaṇāda, the founder of Vaiśeṣika, does not list nonexistence as a separate category: "The Supreme Good [of the Predicables] (results) from the knowledge, produced by a particular *dharma,* of the essence of the predicables, substance,

attribute, action, genus, species, and combination [inherence], by means of their resemblances and differences." *VSK* I. 1. 4 (*Sourcebook,* p. 387). Nevertheless, in that elsewhere in the *VSK* (IX. 1. 1-10) he discusses nonexistence as a *padārtha* [possible object of knowledge] and later Vaiśeṣika commentators treat it as the seventh category, our own treatment of nonexistence as a separate category is not without justification: "A knowledge of the true nature of the six categories—substance, quality, action, generality, individuality and inherence—through their similarities and dissimilarities—is the means of accomplishing the highest bliss. . . . *Abhāva* [nonexistence], negation, is not mentioned separately, simply because it is dependent (for its conception) upon *bhāva* [existence] (the six categories enumerated), and *not because there is no such category." PDS* I. 1 (*Sourcebook,* pp. 397-98, emphasis added).

43. "'Non-existence' is of four kinds: (1) previous non-existence, (2) destruction, (3) mutual negation, and (4) absolute non-existence." *Ibid.,* VI. 110 (*Sourcebook,* p. 416).
44. "The appearance and non-appearance of knowledge, on contact of the self with the senses and the objects are the marks (of the existence) of the mind." *VSK* III. 2. 1 (*Sourcebook,* p. 391); *PDS* V. 45 (*Sourcebook,* pp. 408-9).
45. "The objects of the senses are universally known. The universal experience of the objects of the senses is the mark of (the existence of an) object different from the senses and their objects." *VSK* III. 1. 1, 2 (*Sourcebook,* p. 391).
46. *PDS* VI. 88 (*Sourcebook,* pp. 412-13).
47. *PDS,* pp. 19-23; *NK,* pp. 50-54.
48. *VSK* I. 1. 3; X. 2. 8 (*Sourcebook,* pp. 387, 397).
49. Udayana, *Nyāya-kusamāñjali,* Chowkhamba Sanskrit Series (Banaras, 1957).
50. *VSK* X. 2. 8 (*Sourcebook,* p. 397).
51. "The plurality of number appears in the atoms and the diads, according to the will of God." *PDS* VI. 86 (*Sourcebook,* p. 412).
52. "False knowledge (arises) from imperfection of the senses and from imperfection of impression. That (i.e., *avidyā*) is imperfect knowledge. (Cognition) free from imperfection, is (called) *vidyā* or scientific knowledge." *VSK* IX. 2. 10-12 (*Sourcebook,* p. 397).
53. *Ibid.,* X. 2. 8 (*Sourcebook,* p. 397); *PDS* VI. 136 (*Sourcebook,* p. 418).
54. *PDS* VI. 136 (*Sourcebook,* p. 418).
55. "*Mokṣa* [emancipation] consists in the non-existence of conjunction with the body, when there is at the same time no potential body existing, and consequently, re-birth cannot take place." *VSK V.* 2. 18 (*Sourcebook,* p. 394); "and thus there being a complete cessation [of action], the self becomes 'seedless' and the present body falling off, it takes no other bodies, and this cessation of equipment with bodies and organs, being like the extinguishing of fire on all its fuel being burnt up, constitutes what is called '*mokṣa*' ('final deliverance')." *PDS* VI. 136 (*Sourcebook,* p. 418).
56. "What is the true nature of the self, the resolution whereunto would constitute deliverance? Some people hold that the nature

of the self consists in bliss. But this theory is not correct; as it will not bear an examination of the possible alternatives. . . . And when the mind is such as has all seeds of good and evil rooted out of it, it can never function towards any purpose of the self. It might be urged that the mind favours the self by the force of *dharma* born of Yogic practices. But even such *dharma* being a product, should be transient; and when this would be destroyed [by knowledge], what would be there to help the mind?" *PDS* VI. 136 (*Sourcebook,* pp. 418-19).

Chapter VIII. Nyāya

For excerpts from some of the original Nyāya works, see Radhakrishnan and Moore, *A Source Book in Indian Philosophy.*

1. "Supreme felicity is attained by the knowledge about the true nature of the sixteen categories, viz., means of right knowledge, object of right knowledge, doubt, purpose, familiar instance, established tenet, members [of a syllogism] . . . futility, and occasion for rebuke. Pain, birth, activity, faults (defects) and misapprehension [wrong notion]—on the successive annihilation of these in the reverse order, there follows release." *The Nyāya Sūtras of Gotama* (cited as *NS*), tr. by S. C. Vidyābhūṣaṇa, Vol. VIII of *The Sacred Books of the Hindus* (Allahabad: The Panini Office, 1930), I. 1. 1.
2. For a clear exposition of the fundamental tenets of the Navya-nyāya school, see B. K. Matilal, *The Navya-Nyāya Doctrine of Negation* (Cambridge, Mass.: Harvard University Press, 1968) (Part I: "The Basic Concepts of Navya-nyāya Philosophy"), pp. 3-95.
3. *NS* I. 1. 1–I. 2. 20.
4. See the discussion of *padārtha* in Ch. VII on Vaiśeṣika.
5. *Uddyotakara's Nyāya-Vārttika* (cited as *NV*), ed. by Vindhyesvariprasada Dvivedin, Kashi Sanskrit Series (Banaras, 1915), II. 1. 22.
6. *NS* I. 2. 4.
7. For an excellent discussion of the correspondence as well as coherence and pragmatic theories of truth, see A. D. Woozley, *Theory of Knowledge* (New York: Barnes & Noble, 1971).
8. "Perception, inference, comparison and word (verbal testimony) —these are the means of right knowledge." *NS* I. 1. 3.
9. *Annaṁbhaṭṭa's Tarkasaṁgraha with Tarkadīpikā and Vivṛti* (cited as *TS*), ed. by Jivananda Vidyasagara (Calcutta, 1897), p. 84.
10. " 'Something is useful because it is true' and 'something is true because it is useful' mean exactly the same thing." William James, *Pragmatism* (London: Longmans, Green & Co., 1929), p. 200; "If a theory conforms to human needs, it is in so far a true theory. If the established laws of nature have been accepted and recognized because they have met human needs, then there is a probability that a new hypothesis which satisfies some need or aspiration will accord with those laws. We must, in short,

judge the truth of a theory by the pragmatic criterion of its value in practical life." W. P. Montague, *The Ways of Knowing* (London: George Allen & Unwin, 1958), p. 136.

11. "Perception is that knowledge which arises from the contact of a sense with its object, and which is determinate [well-defined], unnameable [not expressible in words], and non-erratic [unerring]." *NS* I. 1. 4.
12. *Ibid.*, I. 1. 12-14.
13. "The name is not (necessarily present and) operative at the time that the apprehension of the thing takes place; it becomes operative (and useful) only at the time of its being spoken of, or communicated to other persons." *Gautama's Nyāyasūtras with Vātsāyana's Bhāṣya* (cited as *NS* & *B*), tr. by Ganganatha Jha (Poona: Oriental Book Agency, 1939), commentary on I. 1. 4. It may be noted that Nyāya distinguishes recognition (*pratyabhijñā*) as a species of perception different from both indeterminate and determinate perceptions. To re-cognize something is to cognize it as that which was cognized earlier. In short, recognition is identification.
14. "Thoughts [concepts] without content [percepts] are empty, intuitions [percepts] without concepts are blind." Kant, *Critique of Pure Reason,* tr. by N. K. Smith, p. 93.
15. *Viśvanātha's Bhāṣāpariccheda with Siddhāntamuktāvalī, Dinakarī and Rāmarudrī* (cited as *BP* & *SM*), ed. by A. N. Jere (Bombay: Nirnaya Sagar Press, 1927), 52.
16. For a detailed discussion of the Nyāya theory of extraordinary perception, see S. C. Chatterjee, *The Nyāya Theory of Knowledge* (Calcutta: University of Calcutta Press, 1939), Ch. X.
17. *The Yoga-sūtras of Patañjali, with the Yoga-bhāṣya of Vyāsa and the Tattva-vaiśāradi of Vācaspati Miśra,* tr. by Rama Prasada, Vol. IV of *The Sacred Books of the Hindus* (Allahabad: The Panini Office, 1924), Ch. 3, 44-48.
18. For a detailed discussion of the Nyāya theory of inference, as formulated through the apparatus of symbolic logic, see S. S. Barlingay, *A Modern Introduction to Indian Logic* (Delhi: National Publishing House, 1965), pp. 107-59.
19. "Inference is knowledge which is preceded by perception, and is of three kinds, viz., *a priori, a posteriori* and 'commonly seen.'" *NS* I. 1. 5.
20. *Ibid.,* I. 1. 32-39; *BP* & *SM* 66-67; *Keśava Miśra's Tarkabhāṣā* cited as *TB*), original text and tr. by Ganganatha Jha (Poona: Oriental Book Agency, 1924), pp. 48-49.
21. The diagrammatic representation used here is due to Karl H. Potter, *Presuppositions of India's Philosophies,* pp. 61-62.
22. For a detailed discussion of the rules of validity of the Nyāya syllogism, see *ibid.,* pp. 64-74.
23. See I. M. Copi, *Introduction to Logic* (New York: The Macmillan Co., 1972), Ch. VI.
24. See W. and M. Kneale, *The Development of Logic* (London: Oxford University Press, 1962).
25. See S. C. Vidyābhūṣaṇa, *A History of Indian Logic* (Delhi: Motilal Banarsidass, 1971).

26. "In the West logic has been primarily concerned with propositions or sentences. Navya-nyāya, like the older Indian systems of logic, deals with what is called *jñāna,* by which it means something close to 'particular instances of cognition.' An instance of cognition, it is true, can be shown to be ultimately related to some verbal form, namely, to a statement or a sentence. In the case of a determinate or qualificative cognition (*savikalpa* or *viśiṣṭa jñāna*), with which Navya-nyāya is chiefly concerned, the relation is very close. But the *jñāna* itself is not a form of language, and scholars have differed in their English translations of the term; it has been rendered as 'knowledge,' 'cognition,' 'awareness,' 'apprehension,' and 'judgment.' . . . In the Indian tradition logic and epistemology were always intertwined. The Nyāya school, which is often described as simply a system of Indian logic, actually developed as a separate discipline with a particular system of epistemology and ontology." Matilal, *Navya-Nyāya Doctrine of Negation,* pp. 6, 21.
27. *TS,* pp. 62-63.
28. "Comparison [analogy] is the knowledge of a thing through its similarity to another thing previously well known." NS I. 1. 6.
29. *NV* I. 1. 6.
30. *TS,* p. 63.
31. *NS* I. 1. 8.
32. *TS,* p. 73; *TB,* p. 14.
33. *NS* I. 1. 9-22.
34. "Desire, aversion, volition, pleasure, pain, and intelligence are the marks of the soul." *Ibid.,* I. 1. 10.
35. *Ibid.,* III. 1. 4; *BP* & *SM* 48-50.
36. *NV* II. 1. 22.
37. *TB,* p. 6; *BP* & *SM* 47-50.
38. "*Cogito, ergo sum* (I think, therefore I am)." Descartes, *Discourse on Method,* Part IV. *Descartes: Selections,* ed. by R. M. Eaton (New York: Charles Scribner's Sons, 1955), p. 29.
39. "Pain has the characteristic of causing uneasiness. . . . Everything (i.e., the body, etc., and also pleasure and pain), being intermingled with i.e., invariably accompanied by, never existing apart from—pain, is inseparable from pain; and as such is regarded as pain itself. Finding everything to be intermingled with pain, when one wishes to get rid of pain, he finds that birth (or life) itself is nothing but pain; and thus becomes disgusted (with life); and being disgusted, he loses all attachment; and being free from attachment, he becomes released." *NS* I. 1. 21, and *NS* & *B,* commentary on *NS* I. 1. 21.
40. "Release [salvation] is the absolute deliverance from pain." *NS* I. 1. 22.
41. "When there is a relinquishing of the birth that has been taken and the non-resumption of another—this condition, which is without end (or limit) is known as 'final release.' . . . This condition of immortality, free from fear, imperishable (unchanging), consisting in the attainment of bliss, is called '*Brahman.*'" *NS* & *B,* commentary on *NS* I. 1. 22.
42. *NS* I. 1. 2.

43. *Udayana's Nyāya-kusumāñjali with the commentary of Hari Dasa Bhattacarya* (cited as *NK*), tr. by E. B. Cowell (Calcutta: Baptist Mission Press, 1864).
44. "If it [the atom] acts independently, it ceases to be brute matter; if there be no cause there is no effect; a particular effect has a particular cause. There cannot be an effect without a causer. If the atom were endued with volition it would follow that the atom was intelligent, since an unintelligent thing can produce an effect only when impelled by an intelligent being." *Ibid.,* V. 4; *TS,* pp. 21-22.
45. *NK* I.
46. For a detailed account of the various Nyāya arguments for the existence of God, see *NK.*
47. *Ibid.,* I.
48. *Ibid.,* II. "The later Vaisheṣikas and particularly the later Naiyāyikas [adherents of the Nyāya school] have given an elaborate account of God and the latter have made God's grace an essential thing for obtaining true knowledge of realities which alone leads to liberation." Sharma, *Critical Survey of Indian Philosophy,* p. 208.

Chapter IX. Vedānta

For excerpts from the Vedas, the Upaniṣads, the Bhagavad-gītā, and original works of the three principal schools of Vedānta, see Radhakrishnan, *A Source Book in Indian Philosophy* (cited as *Sourcebook*).

1. See Paul Deussen, *The System of the Vedānta,* tr. by Charles Johnston (New York: Dover Publications, 1973), pp. 3-4.
2. Jaimini's *Mīmāṁsā-sūtras* and Bādarāyana's *Vedānta-sūtras* (also known as *Brahma-sūtras* and *Śarīraka-sūtras*) are the foundations of the Mīmāṁsā and Vedānta schools respectively.
3. In course of time, the Mīmāṁsā developed into two major schools, known as the *Kumārila Bhaṭṭa* and *Prabhākara,* after their founders. A number of major and minor thinkers contributed original writings, expositions, and commentaries to the literatures of these schools. The following are the most important works of these schools dealing with logical, epistemological, and metaphysical problems: (*a*) Prabhākara (seventh-eighth cent. A.D.), *Bṛhati,* ed. by S. K. Ramanatha Sastri (Madras: University of Madras, 1934); (*b*) Kumārila Bhaṭṭa (eighth cent. A.D.), *Ślokavartika,* Chowkhamba Sanskrit Series (Banaras, 1898) (tr. by Ganganatha Jha [Calcutta: Asiatic Society, 1909]); (*c*) Pārthasārathi Miśra (eleventh cent. A.D.), *Nyāyaratnākara* (commentary on *Ślokavartika*), published together with the latter, ed. by Rama Shastri Tailanga, Chowkhamba Sanskrit Series (Banaras, 1898), English tr. by Ganganatha Jha, Bibliotheca Indica (Calcutta, 1900); (*d*) Pārthasārathi Miśra, Śāstra-Dīpikā, Chowkhamba Sanskrit Series (Banaras, 1903), Ganganatha Jha's *Prabhākara School of Pūrva Mīmāṁsā* (Banaras: Banaras Hindu University Press, 1918), A. B. Keith's *The Karma Mīmāṁsā* (London: Oxford University Press,

1921), and Paśupatināth Śāstrī's *Introduction to the Pūrva Mīmāṁsā* (Calcutta, 1923) are well-known works in English. For a concise and lucid treatment of Mīmāṁsā, see Hiriyanna, *Outlines of Indian Philosophy,* Ch. XII.

4. "The word 'Upaniṣad' is derived from *upa,* near, *ni,* down, and *sad* to sit. Groups of pupils sat near the teacher to learn from him the truth by which ignorance is destroyed." Radhakrishnan and Moore. *A Source Book in Indian Philosophy,* p. 37; some scholars are of the view that the term *Upaniṣad* means "secret meaning, secret instruction, a secret." On this and other meanings, see Paul Deussen, *The Philosophy of the Upanishads,* tr. by A. S. Geden (New York: Dover Publications, 1966), "On the meaning of the word Upanishad," pp. 10-15.
5. Selections from the Vedas in *Sourcebook,* pp. 5-16.
6. *Ibid.,* pp. 27-31.
7. *Ibid.,* pp. 29-30.
8. *Ibid.,* pp. 25-27.
9. *Ibid.,* pp. 16-25.
10. Max Müller, *Six Systems of Indian Philosophy* (Vol. XIX of *Collected Works*) (London, 1899), p. 40.
11. *Ṛgveda* I. 164. 46, from R. T. H. Griffiths, *The Hymns of the Rigveda* (Banaras: E. J. Lazarus & Co., 3rd ed., 1920-26), *Sourcebook,* p. 21).
12. *Ṛgveda* X. 90. 1-4, from Edward J. Thomas, *Vedic Hymns,* wisdom of the East (London: John Murray, 1923), (*Sourcebook,* p. 19).
13. *Ṛgveda* X. 129. 1, 6, 7, from A. A. Macdonell, *Hymns from the Rigveda* (London: Oxford University Press, 1922), (*Sourcebook,* pp. 23-24).
14. The term *Brahman* derives from the root *brh* meaning "to grow" and "to burst forth." It is easy to see how this root meaning underlies the philosophic conception of Brahman as the primordial reality spontaneously bursting forth into the world of variety and multiplicity.
15. *The Upanishads,* tr. by Swami Prabhavananda and Frederick Manchester (Hollywood: Vedānta Press, 1947), *Īśa* 1. There are innumerable translations of the Upaniṣads. The reason why we have chosen this particular one is that it conveys best "in clear and simple English the sense and spirit of the original" and is easily accessible. The following are among standard translations: *The Upanishads,* tr. by Max Müller, 2 vols. (New York: Dover Publications, n.d.), and *The Principal Upanishads,* tr. by S. Radhakrishnan (London: George Allen & Unwin, 1953).
16. *Ibid., Kena* IV. 4.
17. *Ibid., Kena* IV. 5.
18. *Ibid., Muṇḍaka* II. i. 1.
19. *Ibid., Muṇḍaka* II. i. 2.
20. *Ibid., Chāndogya* VI. i. 4.
21. *Ibid., Taittrīya* II. 4.
22. *Ibid., Kena* I. 5.
23. *Ibid., Kena* I. 6.
24. *Ibid., Kena* I. 7.

25. *Ibid., Kena* I. 9.
26. In all likelihood, the original meaning of *Ātman* is "breath"; and since breath is the essence of life, the term has been subsequently used to signify the essential part or quality of anything. Thus in its philosophic sense *ātman* means the inmost self of man as well as of the universe. It is of interest to note that the German word *atmen* means "to breathe."
27. *Ibid., Bṛhadāraṇyaka* II. iv. 12.
28. *Ibid., Bṛhadāraṇyaka* II. iv. 14.
29. *Ibid., Bṛhadāraṇyaka* II. v. 15.
30. *Ibid., Kena* I.
31. *Ibid., Bṛhadāraṇyaka* I. iv. 10.
32. *Ibid., Bṛhadāraṇyaka* II. 5.
33. *Ibid., Aitareya* III. i. 3.
34. *Ibid., Kaṭha* II. iv. 10.
35. *Ibid., Chāndogya* VI. x. 3.
36. *Ibid., Kaṭha* I. ii. 22.
37. *Ibid., Muṇḍaka* I. i. 4-6.
38. *Ibid., Kaṭha* I. ii. 23.
39. *Ibid., Muṇḍaka* III. ii. 6.
40. *Ibid., Kaṭha* I. ii. 7.
41. *Ibid., Kaṭha* I. ii. 8.
42. *Ibid., Kaṭha* II. vi. 12.
43. *Ibid., Muṇḍaka* II. 3-6.
44. *The Complete Works of Swami Vivekananda* (Mayavati: Advaita Āshrama, 1950), Vol. I, pp. 324-25.
45. It may be noted that while Śaṁkara refers only to the three *pramāṇas* (perception, inference, and testimony), later thinkers of the Advaita school accept all six. See *The Vedānta-sūtras of Bādarāyaṇa, with the commentary by Śaṅkara* (cited as *VS*), tr. by George Thibaut (New York: Dover Publications, 1970), I. 3. 28; III. 2. 24; IV. 4. 20.
46. "*Arthāpatti* consists in the postulation, by a cognition which has to be made intelligible, of what will make (that) intelligible. . . . e.g., since in the absence of eating at night, the fatness of one who does not eat by day is unintelligible, that kind of fatness is what is to be made intelligible; or else, since in the absence of eating by night there is unintelligibility . . . eating by night is what makes (that) intelligible." *Dharmarāja's Vedānta-paribhāṣā* (cited as *VP*), tr. by S. S. Suryanarayana Sastri (Madras: Adyar Library, 1942), V. 1-2. For a critical discussion of *arthāpatti,* see D. M. Datta, *The Six Ways of Knowing* (Calcutta: University of Calcutta Press, 1960), Bk. V.
47. In Western logic one draws a similar distinction between argument and explanation, although both can be formulated in the pattern Q because P. "If we are interested in establishing the truth of Q, and P is offered as evidence for it, then 'Q because P' formulates an argument. However, if we regard the truth of Q as being unproblematic, as being at least as well established as the truth of P, but are interested in explaining why Q is the case, then 'Q because P' is not an argument but an explanation." Copi, *Introduction to Logic,* p. 20.

48. See *VP* VI; Datta, *Six Ways of Knowing*, Bk. III.
49. Some scholars use "subration" instead of "sublation." See, for example, Eliot Deutsch, *Advaita Vedānta: A Philosophical Reconstruction* (Honolulu: East-West Center Press, 1969), p. 15.
50. Sublation is the mental process whereby one disvalues some previously appraised object or content of consciousness because of its being contradicted by a new experience." *Ibid.*
51. "But passages such as 'Thou art that,' 'I am *Brahman*,' leave nothing to be desired because the state of consciousness produced by them has for its object the unity of the universal Self. For as long as something else remains a desire is possible; but there is nothing else which could be desired in addition to the absolute unity of *Brahman*. . . . Nor, again, can such consciousness be objected on the ground either of uselessness or of erroneousness, because, firstly, it is seen to have for its result the cessation of ignorance, and because, secondly, *there is no other kind of knowledge by which it could be sublated.*" *VS* II. 1. 14 (emphasis added). Also, according to the Advaitin Sureśvara (ninth cent. A.D.), "Wheresoever there is doubt, there, the wise should know, the Self [the Real] is not. For no doubts can arise in relation to the Self, since its nature is pure immediate consciousness." *Naiṣkarmya-Siddhi*, tr. by A. J. Alston (London: Shanti Sadan, 1959), III. 37.
52. *VS* II. 1. 22.
53. *Ibid.*, IV. 3. 15.
54. *Ibid.*, II. 1. 4, 14-17.
55. For Saṁkara's critique of the Sāṁkhya doctrines, in particular the *pariṇāmavāda*, see *ibid.*, I. 4 and II. 1. 10.
56. *Ibid.*, II. 1. 18.
57. *Ibid.*
58. "The *śāstra's* purport is not to represent *Brahman* definitely as this or that object, its purpose is rather to show that *Brahman* as the eternal subject (*pratyagātman*, the inward Self) is never any object, and thereby to remove the distinction of objects known, knowers, acts of knowledge, &c., which is fictitiously created by Nescience [*Māyā* as Ignorance]." *Ibid.*, I. 1. 4.
59. *Ibid.*, Introduction, p. xxv.
60. *Ibid.*
61. *Ibid.*, II. 1. 27, 37.
62. "But (Brahman's creative activity) is mere sport, such as we see in ordinary life." *Ibid.*, II. 1. 33.
63. "By that element of plurality which is the fiction of Nescience [*Māyā* as Ignorance] which is characterized by name and form, which is evolved as well as non-evolved, which is not to be defined either as the Existing or the Non-existing, *Brahman* becomes the basis of this entire apparent world with its changes, and so on, while in its true and real nature it at the same time remains unchanged, lifted above the phenomenal universe." *Ibid.*, II. 1. 27.
64. *Ibid.*, II. 1. 22.
65. "Moreover, as soon as, in consequence of the declaration of non-difference contained in such passages as 'that art thou,' the con-

sciousness of non-difference arises in us, the transmigratory state of the individual soul and the creative quality of *Brahman* vanish at once, the whole phenomenon of plurality, which springs from wrong knowledge, being sublated by perfect knowledge, and what becomes then of the creation and the faults of not doing what is beneficial, and the like? For that this entire apparent world, in which good and evil actions are done, &c., is a mere illusion, owing to the non-discrimination of (the Self's) limiting adjuncts, viz. a body, and so on, which spring from name and form the presentations of Nescience, and does not in reality exist at all, we have explained more than once." *Ibid.*

66. "As the magician is not at any time affected by the magical illusion produced by himself, because it is unreal, so the highest Self is not affected by the world-illusion." *Ibid.,* II. 1. 9, 21.
67. *Ibid.,* I. 1.
68. *Ibid.*
69. *Ibid.*
70. "The superimposition thus defined, learned men consider to be Nescience (*avidyā*), and the ascertainment of the true nature of that which is (the Self) by means of discrimination of that (which is superimposed on the Self), they call knowledge (*vidyā*)." *Ibid.*
71. "The non-existence (of external things) cannot be maintained, on account of (our) consciousness (of them)." *Ibid.,* II. 2. 28.
72. "As the cause, i.e., *Brahman,* is in all time neither more nor less than that which is, so the effect also, viz. the world, is in all time only that which is. But that which is is one only; therefore the effect (the world) is non-different from the cause." *Ibid.,* II. 1. 16.
73. *Ibid.,* I. 3. 19.
74. *Ibid.,* I. 2. 18.
75. *Ibid.,* I. 1.
76. *Ibid.,* II. 3. 18.
77. "The soul does not then perceive, not because perception is wanting but because the objects are wanting; just as light does not become visible in space, as long as there are no objects to be illuminated." Deussen, *System of the Vedānta.* p. 296.
78. "Just because it is the Self, it is impossible for us to entertain the idea even of its being capable of refutation. For the (knowledge of the) Self is not, in any person's case, adventitious, not established through the so-called means of right knowledge: it rather is self-established." *VS* II. 3. 7. "No one can doubt the fact of his own existence. Were one to do so, who could the doubter be? Only a deluded man could entertain the idea that he does not exist." *Pañchadaśī: A Treatise on Advaita Metaphysics by Swami Vidyaranya,* tr. by Hari Prasad Shastri (London: Shanti Sadan, 1956), III. 23-24.
79. *VS,* Introduction, pp. xxvi, xxx; I. 1; I. 1. 11. "The extension of the world and the plurality of wandering souls, this hybrid which is neither Being [real] nor non-Being [unreal] (*tattvaanyatvābhyām anirvacanīyam*) and comparable to an hallucination or to a dream, is produced by Ignorance by virtue of the *Upādhis,*

the limitations, literally 'the ascription' (with the secondary idea of the unpermitted) by means of which we 'ascribe' to Brahman what does not naturally belong to him, and through which, as we shall show in detail, he becomes 1) a personal God (Īśvara), 2) the world, 3) the individual soul. All this depends on the *Upādhis,* and the *Upādhis* on *Avidyā* (Ignorance). *Avidyā* alone is the cause of the origin of the *Upādhis.*" Deussen, *System of the Vedānta,* p. 303.

80. *VS* I. 4. 19-22.
81. "The existence of *Brahman* is known on the ground of its being the Self of every one. For everyone is conscious of the existence of (his) Self, and never thinks 'I am not.' If the existence of the Self were not known, everyone would think 'I am not.' And *this Self (of whose existence all are conscious) is Brahman." Ibid.,* I. 1. 1 (emphasis added). "This great unborn Self undecaying, undying, immortal, fearless is indeed *Brahman." Ibid.,* III. 3. 17; also see *ibid.,* I. 1. 4; I. 4. 1, 14; III. 4. 2.
82. ". . . and wrong knowledge itself is removed by the knowledge of one's Self being one with the Self of *Brahman." Ibid.,* I. 1. 4.
83. "For as long as the individual soul does not free itself from Nescience [Ignorance] in the form of duality—which Nescience may be compared to the mistake of him who in the twilight mistakes a post for a man—and does not rise to the knowledge of the Self, whose nature is unchangeable, eternal Cognition—which expresses itself in the form 'I am *Brahman*'—so long it remains the individual soul. But when, discarding the aggregate of body, sense-organs and mind, it arrives, by means of Scripture, at the knowledge that it is not itself that aggregate, that it does not form part of transmigratory existence, *but is the True, the Real, the Self,* whose nature is pure intelligence [consciousness]; then knowing itself to be of the nature of unchangeable, eternal Cognition, it lifts itself above the vain conceit of being one with this body, and itself becomes the Self whose nature is unchanging, eternal Cognition." *Ibid.,* I. 3. 19 (emphasis added).
84. "The Self consisting of bliss is the highest *Brahman." Ibid.,* I. 1, 2; also see I. 1. 13-19.
85. "The later Vedānta names three [positive characteristics of esoteric Brahman], which form the famous name of *Brahman: Sac-cid-ānanda,* that is "Existence, Intelligence and Bliss." Deussen, *System of the Vedānta,* p. 212.
86. *Kaṭha Upaniṣad* II. iv. 10.
87. *VS* II. 1. 13-14; IV. 2. 12-16.
88. "Moreover, two kinds of knowledge are enjoined there (in the Upanishad), a lower and a higher one. Of the lower one it is said that it comprises the *Rig-veda* and so on, and then the text continues, 'The higher knowledge is that by which the Indestructible is apprehended.' Here the Indestructible is declared to be the subject of the higher knowledge. . . . The distinction of lower and higher knowledge is made on account of the diversity of their results, the former leading to merely worldly exaltation, the latter to absolute bliss." *Ibid.,* I. 2. 21.

89. "The mutual superimposition of the Self and the Non-Self, which is termed Nescience [Ignorance], is the presupposition on which there base all the practical distinctions—those made in ordinary life as well as those laid down by the Veda—between means of knowledge, objects of knowledge (and knowing persons), and all scriptural texts, whether they are concerned with injunctions and prohibitions (of meritorious and non-meritorious actions), or with final release." *Ibid.,* I. 1.
90. "The whole practical world exists only in the sphere of Nescience." *Ibid.,* I. 2. 26; also see *ibid.,* I. 4. 22.
91. *Ibid.,* II. 3. 21.
92. "And when parts that are due to nescience are dissolved through knowledge it is not possible that a remainder should be left. The parts therefore enter into absolute non-division from *Brahman.*" *Ibid.,* IV. 2. 16. According to Deussen: "The perception [it is unfortunate that the author uses this term here; 'experience' is the appropriate term] of unity is final, for, as it contains everything in itself, it does not leave anything beyond itself to be desired, as do the ritual precepts; it is attainable, as the Scripture shows by its examples and exhortations; it is not aimless, for its fruit is the cessation of Ignorance; and it is infallible, for there is no further knowledge which could remove it, for the *Brahman* unlike everything else, is not a mere transformation; He is the Highest, free from all change, and all qualities; only by the knowledge of *Brahman* [that is, by higher knowledge], not by that of his transformations [that is, by lower knowledge], can liberation be attained." Deussen, *System of the Vedānta,* p. 271.
93. "The declaration of the difference of the embodied Self and the internal ruler has its reason in the limiting adjunct [*upādhi*], consisting of the organs of action, presented by Nescience [names and forms], and is not absolutely true [to say that something is not absolutely true is not the same as saying that it is false; rather, it is to say that it is relatively true—true from the lower standpoint]. For the Self within is one only; two internal Selfs are not possible. But owing to its limiting adjunct the one Self is practically treated as if it were two; just as we make a distinction between the ether [space] of the jar and the universal ether. Hence there is room for those scriptural passages which set forth the distinction of knower and object of knowledge, for perception and the other means of proof, for the intuitive knowledge of the apparent world, and for that part of Scripture which contains injunctions and prohibitions." *VS* I. 2. 20. According to Deussen: "Only unity exists; plurality does not exist. This statement abolishes not only the empirical means of knowledge, perception, etc., but also the Vedic canons. . . . But does it not also abolish the canon of liberation? For this certainly presupposes the duality of pupil and teacher, and thus rests upon untruth; and how can the teaching of unity from a false standpoint be true? To this, it is to be replied that *all empirical action* [*and knowledge*], *until* [*higher*] *knowledge comes, is just as true as are all dream faces, until awakening comes.*" Deussen, *System of the Vedānta,* p. 270 (emphasis added).

94. "The entire complex of phenomenal existence is considered as true as long as the knowledge of *Brahman* being the Self of all has not arisen; just as the phantoms of a dream are considered to be true until the sleeper wakes. . . . Hence, *as long as true knowledge does not present itself, there is no reason why the ordinary course of secular and religious activity should not hold on undisturbed.*" VS II. 1. 14 (emphasis added).
95. *Ibid.,* III. 2. 11-21.
96. *Ibid.,* I. 1. 11, 20.
97. "The *Brahman* of Śaṅkara is in itself impersonal, a homogeneous mass of objectless thought, transcending all attributes; a personal God it becomes only through its association with the unreal principle of *Māyā* [names and forms], so that—strictly speaking—Śaṅkara's personal God, his *Īśvara,* is himself something unreal." *Ibid.,* Introduction, p. xxx.
98. "Where, again, for the purpose of pious meditation, the texts teach *Brahman* as qualified by some distinction depending on name, form, and so on, using such terms as 'He who consists of mind, whose body is *prāṇa,* whose shape is light.'" *Ibid.,* IV. 3. 14.
99. "You must therefore admit that the relation of cause of suffering and of sufferers is not real, but the effect of Nescience [Ignorance]." *Ibid.,* II. 2. 10.
100. "Even the most meritorious works necessarily lead to new forms of embodied existence. . . . The pious worshipper passes on his death into the world of the lower [*Saguṇa-*] *Brahman* only, where he continues to exist as a distinct individual soul—although in the enjoyment of great power and knowledge—until at last he reaches the highest knowledge, and, through it, final release [*mokṣa*].—That student of the Veda, on the other hand, whose soul has been enlightened by the texts embodying the higher knowledge of *Brahman,* whom passages such as the great saying, 'That art thou,' have taught that there is no difference between his true Self and the highest Self, obtains at the moment of death immediate final release, i.e., he withdraws altogether from the influence of *Māyā,* and asserts himself his true nature, which is nothing else but the absolute highest *Brahman.*" *Ibid.,* Introduction, p. xxvii.
101. "A previous stage of the world such as the one assumed by us must necessarily be admitted, since it is according to sense and reason. For without it the highest Lord could not be conceived as creator, as he could not become active if he were destitute of the potentiality of action. The existence of such a causal potentiality renders it moreover possible that *the released souls should not enter on new courses of existence, as it is destroyed by perfect knowledge.*" *Ibid., I.* 4. 3 (emphasis added).
102. "The Sanskrit word *mokṣa* (or *mukti*) connotes to the Advaitin 'freedom from *karma*' and also this other kind of spiritual freedom [the overcoming of all oppositions such as freedom-versus-necessity and good-versus-evil]. *Mokṣa,* in the positive sense, means the attaining to a state of 'at-one-ment' with the depth and quiescence of Reality and with the power of its creative becoming.

Spiritual freedom means the full realization of the potentialities of man as a spiritual being. It means the attaining of insight into oneself; it means self-knowledge and joy of being." Deutsch, *Advaita Vedānta,* p. 104.

103. *VS* III. 3. 27; IV. 1. 15.

104. "As it is established that good as well as evil works—which are both causes of bondage—do, owing to the strength of knowledge, on the one hand not cling and on the other hand undergo destruction, there necessarily results final release of him who knows as soon as death takes place." *Ibid.,* IV. 1. 15. Compare this with: "When the seer beholds the Effulgent One, the Lord, the Supreme Being, then, transcending both good and evil, and freed from impurities, he unites himself with him." *Muṇḍaka Upaniṣad* III. i. 3. The Advaitin (and Upaniṣadic) view that the mokṣic man is gone beyond good and evil is open to grave misunderstandings; thus, one might think that the mokṣic man is a callous human being who with impunity inflicts pain and suffering on others. Quite the contrary, we submit, "to be beyond good and evil is not of course to be able to do evil with impunity, but rather to be incapable of it." Prabhavananda and Manchester, *Spiritual Heritage of India,* p. 54.

105. *VS* I. 1. 1.

106. "Those who maintain the doctrine of a substance devoid of all difference have no right to assert that this or that is a proof of such a substance, for all means of right knowledge have for their object things affected with difference." *The Vedānta Sūtras of Bādarāyaṇa, with the Commentary of Rāmānuga* (also known as *Śrībhāṣya* and cited as *SB*), tr. by George Thibaut (Oxford: Clarendon Press, 1904), I. i. 1. (*Sourcebook,* p. 543).

107. *Bhedābheda* (*bheda,* difference; *abheda,* identity) is the phrase which is commonly employed to describe Rāmānuja's conception of Brahman as well as its relation to self. However, there are passages in his *SB* which are conflicting on this point. Thus some passages support identity alone, and others difference alone: "Rāmānuja's conception of the relation between the self and God cannot be easily brought under any well-known logical category (such as identity, difference and identity-in-difference). While refuting Śaṅkara's view that this relation is one of identity (*abheda*) he emphasizes so much the difference between the self and God that the reader would be quite justified to suppose that according to Rāmānuja the relation is one of difference (*bheda*). This supposition is further confirmed when one reads his commentary on Bādarāyaṇa's *sūtra* (2. 1. 22) which points out that *Brahman* is other than the embodied self. But the impression is reversed when one reads his commentary on the *sūtra* (2. 1. 15) teaching the non-difference (*ananyatva*) of the world (including the *Jīvas* [selves]) from its cause, *Brahman.* He thus seems to support two contradictory views. This conflict disappears, however, on reading his commentary on the *sūtra* (2. 3. 42) purporting that the individual self is a part of *Brahman.* . . . In short, as there are both difference and identity (*bhedābheda*) between the part and the whole, so also is there a similar relation be-

tween the self and God. It is reasonable to conclude then that according to Rāmānuja, in different respects, there are different kinds of relations between the self and God. . . . Sadananda [in his *Advaita-brahma-siddhi*] also describes him [Rāmānuja] as a *bhedābheda-vādin*. But unfortunately even this well-founded conclusion regarding Rāmānuja's view receives a rude shock from his rather surprising statements here and there in which he launches a wholesale attack on all the three kinds of philosophers who advocate respectively identity (*abheda*), difference (*bheda*) and identity-in-difference (*bhedābheda*) [see *SB*, I. 1. 1, 4]. The reader is thus swept away even from the last foothold and is left puzzled." S. C. Chatterjee and D. M. Datta, *An Introduction to Indian Philosophy* (Calcutta: University of Calcutta Press, 1968), pp. 421-22.

108. "There is one unborn [*prakriti*]—red, white, and black—which gives birth to many creatures like itself. An unborn [individual soul] becomes attached to it and enjoys it, while another unborn [individual soul] leaves it after his enjoyment is completed." "Know, then, that *prakriti* is *māyā* and that the Great God is the Lord of *māyā*. The whole universe is filled with objects which are parts of His being." *Śvetāśvatara Upanishad,* IV. 5, 10, from *The Upanishads,* tr. and ed. by Swami Nikhilananda (New York: Harper & Row, 1963); also see *SB* I. iv. 8.

109. *SB* II. i. 9.

110. "From all this it follows that the entire aggregate of things, intelligent and non-intelligent, has its Self in *Brahman* in so far as it constitutes *Brahman*'s body." *Ibid.,* I. i. 1. (*Sourcebook,* p. 552).

111. "The divine Supreme Person, all whose wishes are eternally fulfilled, who is all-knowing and the ruler of all, whose every purpose is immediately realised, having engaged in sport befitting his might and greatness and having settled that work is of a two-fold nature, such and such works being good and such and such being evil, and having bestowed on all individual selves bodies and sense-organs capacitating them for entering on such work and the power of ruling those bodies and organs, and having himself entered into those selves as their inner self, abides within them, controlling them as an animating and cheering principle." *Ibid.,* II. ii. 3 (*Sourcebook,* p. 553).

112. "The ruling element of the world, i.e., the Lord, finally, who has the sentient and non-sentient beings for his modes, undergoes a change in so far as he is, at alternating periods, embodied in all those beings in their alternating states." *Ibid.,* II. iii. 18. (*Sourcebook,* p. 554).

113. "Hence there is no contradiction between the individual and the highest Self—the former of which is a distinguishing attribute of the latter—standing to each other in the relation of part and whole, and their being at the same time of essentially different nature." *Ibid.,* II. iii. 45 (*Sourcebook,* p. 555).

114. Rāmānuja's *Vedārtha-saṁgraha,* Chowkhamba Sanskrit Series (Banaras), 1894, pp. 30-31. "Rāmānuja recognizes as ultimate and real three factors (*tattva-traya*) of matter (*acit*), soul, (*cit*) and

God (*Īśvara*). Though equally ultimate, the first two are absolutely dependent upon the last, the dependence being conceived as that of the body upon the soul." Hiriyanna, *Outlines of Indian Philosophy,* p. 398.

115. "Hence mere Being does not alone constitute reality. And as the distinction between consciousness and its objects—which rests just on this relation of object and that for which the object is—is proved by perception, the assertion that only consciousness has real existence is also disposed of. . . . The essential character of consciousness or knowledge is that by its very existence it renders things capable of becoming objects, to its own substrate, of thought and speech. This consciousness . . . is a particular attribute belonging to a conscious self and related to an object. . . . How, then, should consciousness and the conscious subject be one?" *SB* I. i. 1. (*Sourcebook,* p. 546).

116. That Rāmānuja bases his metaphysical claim of ultimate distinction between self and its objects on everyday experiences (experiences of the empirical ego) is clear from his appeals to "ordinary judgments such as 'I know the jar,' 'I understand this matter,' 'I am conscious of (the presence of) this piece of cloth.'" *Ibid.* (*Sourcebook,* p. 546).

117. It is to be expected that Rāmānuja interprets "That thou art" in the light of his own metaphysics: "In texts, again, such as 'Thou art that,' the co-ordination of the constituent parts is not meant to convey the idea of the absolute unity of a non-differenced substance; on the contrary, the words 'that' and 'thou' denote a *Brahman* distinguished by difference." *Ibid.* (*Sourcebook,* p. 551).

118. Rāmānuja lodges seven charges (*anupapatti*) against Śaṁkara's theory of *Māyā* as *Avidyā* (Ignorance). *Ibid.* (*Sourcebook,* pp. 549-51).

119. "All these charges of Rāmānuja against *Avidyā* or *Māyā* are based on this misunderstanding of the meaning of this term. It is called 'indescribable either as real or as unreal' due to the genuine difficulty of our finite intellect to reach Reality. It is a self-contradictory notion. Rāmānuja takes it in the sense of something 'real' and demands a seat and a *pramāṇa* for it. However, we may say that *Brahman* is the seat of *Avidyā*. *Avidyā* being not real, the monism of *Brahman* is not destroyed. . . . Real means [for the Advaitin] 'absolutely real' and unreal means 'absolutely unreal' and *Avidyā* is neither. These two terms are not contradictories and hence the Laws of Contradiction and Excluded Middle are not overthrown. The Law of Contradiction is fully maintained since all that which can be contradicted is said to be false. The Law of Excluded Middle is not overthrown since 'absolutely real' and 'absolutely unreal' are not exhaustive. Again, since *Avidyā* is not 'real' but only a superimposition, it vanishes when the ground-reality is known. The rope-snake vanishes when the rope is known. It is only the direct and intuitive knowledge of Reality which is the cause of liberation. Even Rāmānuja admits it though he calls it highest *bhakti* [devotion] which dawns by the grace of God." Sharma, *Critical*

Survey of Indian Philosophy, pp. 360-61. Even those who have a general sympathy for Rāmānuja's philosophy admit that his arguments against Śaṁkara's theory of *māyā* are unsuccessful: "Though Rāmāṇuja tries to refute the doctrine of *māyā* as expounded by Śaṁkara, he is obliged to admit in the final analysis the existence of *māyā,* or ignorance, in man: for the self, he believes, has forgotten its divine origin and its divine destiny, and tends to identify itself with matter, until it becomes subject to the evils of *saṁsāra,* or empirical existence." Prabhavananda and Manchester, *Spiritual Heritage of India,* p. 366; "The true nature of these selves is, however, obscured by ignorance, i.e., the influence of the beginningless chain of works; and by release then we have to understand that intuition of the highest Self, which is the natural state of the individual selves, and which follows on the destruction of ignorance." *SB* I. ii. 12 (*Sourcebook,* p. 552).

120. "You have further maintained the following view:—In the text, 'one only without a second,' the phrase 'without a second' denies all duality on *Brahman*'s part even in so far as qualities are concerned. . . . What the phrase 'without a second' really aims at intimating is that *Brahman* possesses manifold powers, and this it does by denying the existence of another ruling principle different from *Brahman*. . . . If it were meant absolutely to deny all duality, it would deny also the eternity and other attributes of *Brahman*. . . . The . . . passage 'He who knows the bliss of that *Brahman* from whence all speech, together with the mind, turns away unable to reach it,' hence must be taken as proclaiming with emphasis the infinite nature of *Brahman*'s auspicious qualities. . . . We thus conclude that all scriptural texts enjoin just the knowledge of *Brahman* for the sake of final release. This knowledge is, as we already know, of the nature of meditation, and what is to be meditated on is *Brahman* as possessing qualities." *SB* I. i. 1 (*Sourcebook,* p. 548).

121. "Rāmānuja denies the distinction of the two Brahmans [*saguṇa* and *nirguṇa*]." George Thibaut, in his Introduction to *The Vedānta Sūtras of Bādarāyaṇa, with the Commentary by Śaṅkara,* p. xci.

122. *SB* II. ii, 3 (*Sourcebook,* p. 553).

123. *Ibid.,* II. iii. 18 (*Sourcebook,* p. 554).

124. *Ibid.,* II. ii. 3; II. iii. 18 (*Sourcebook,* pp. 553-54).

125. *Ibid.,* I. ii. 12 (*Sourcebook,* p. 552).

126. *Ibid.,* II. ii. 3 (*Sourcebook,* p. 553).

127. The main objection against the conception of God as being at once omniscient, omnibenevolent, and omnipotent is as follows: It is an undeniable fact that there is evil in the world. It follows then that either God is omniscient and omnibenevolent but lacks power over evil (that is, he is not omnipotent); or he is both omniscient and omnipotent, but since he permits evil he is not omnibenevolent; or he is both omnipotent and omnibenevolent but has no knowledge of the existence of evil, in which case he is certainly not omniscient. In short, each of the three properties usually attributed to God is incompatible with the other two.

128. "The individual self is a part of the highest Self; as the light issuing from a luminous thing such as fire or the sun is a part of that body. . . . The highest Self is not of the same nature as the individual self. For as the luminous body is of a nature different from that of its light, thus the highest Self differs from the individual self which is a part of it. It is this difference of character—due to the individual self being the distinguishing element and the highest Self being the substance distinguished thereby—to which all those texts refer which declare difference." *SB* II. iii. 45 (*Sourcebook,* p. 555).
129. "Bondage . . . consists in the experience of pleasure and pain caused by the connexion of selves with bodies of various kind, a connexion springing from good or evil actions." *Ibid.,* I. i. 1 (*Sourcebook,* p. 552).
130. "The cessation of such bondage is to be obtained only through the grace of the highest Self pleased by the devout meditation of the worshipper." *Ibid.,* I. i. 1 (*Sourcebook,* p. 552).
131. There are four principal forms of Yoga: *rāja-yoga* (the path of psychological exploration leading to self-knowledge and mastery); *jñāna-yoga* (the path of knowledge); *karma-yoga* (the path of action without attachment to the fruits); and *bhakti-yoga* (the path of devotion and utter surrender to the Lord); there are also other Yogic disciplines such as *Hatha Yoga* and *Mantra Yoga.* See Patañjali's *Yoga-sūtras* and the Bhagavad-gītā. For an excellent treatment of the theoretical and practical aspects of the various types of Yoga, see Eliade, *Yoga, Immortality, and Freedom.* A brief but extremely lucid work on Yoga is *Seven Schools of Yoga,* by Ernest Wood (Wheaton, Ill.: The Theosophical Publishing House, 1973).
132. *SB* I. i. 1.
133. "The non-existence (of external things, i.e., of the world) cannot be maintained, on account of our being conscious of them." "And on account of the difference of characteristics (the world is not non-existent), as those of dreams, etc., are." "The world is not *vijñāna* (consciousness or thought), for it is not so perceived." "And because of its (of consciousness) momentary duration." *Vedānta-sutras with the Commentary of Madhwāchārya* also known as *Madhwabhāṣya* and cited as *MB*), tr. by S. Subba Rao (Tirupati: Sri Vyasa Press, 1936), II. ii. 28-31.
134. "The glorious Lord, who is superior to and different from the persons of the world, and not limited by the three qualities, shows himself as many, and again the Lord untouchable by any defect, the first cause, becomes one again and goes to rest." *Ibid.,* I. i. 9.
135. "There is no equality in experience between the Lord and the self; for the Lord is all-knowing, all-powerful, and absolute; while the self is of little understanding, of little power and absolutely dependent, and so on." *Ibid.,* I. ii. 8.
136. "If it (that which is spoken of) is said to be the *saguṇa* (qualified) *Brahman,* we deny that, on account of the word *Ātman* (used in the text to denote the cause of the world). It is not proper to hold that it is the qualified *Brahman* that is spoken

of as capable of being seen and described, and not the *nirguṇa* (unqualified); for the word *Ātman* (Self) used to denote the Lord (precludes this view)." *Ibid.*, I. i. 6.

137. "And (*prakṛti* is *Brahman* only) on account of His (divine) will being called (*prakṛti* or of His being spoken of as Will, i.e., *prakṛti*)." *Ibid.*, I. iv. 25.
138. "Since the essence (i.e., the very nature) of the self consists only of wisdom, bliss and other qualities similar (in some degree) to those of *Brahman*, there proceeds the statement that the self is one with (like) *Brahman*." *Ibid.*, II. iii. 29.
139. "The Lord impels the self to action, only according to (the tendency of) his previous actions and his effort (or aptitude), so that the injunctions and prohibitions are not purportless, etc." *Ibid.*, II. iii. 42.
140. "*Brahman* and others are called selves, as *Ātman* is but one who is *Janārdana* (the saviour). In the case of others, the word *Ātman* is used only in a secondary sense. By means of the direct realisation of that *Ātman*, it is said, release is obtained. The others (selves) are bound up with qualities, it is said, and their knowledge does not lead to release. For the highest and perfect Lord is *Viṣṇu*. Hence the sages say that release comes through His grace." "As the Supreme Being of His own accord shows Himself in consideration of the self's devotion and bestows upon him final beatitude, devotion becomes the foremost of all means, and consequently it is spoken of as the only means." *Ibid.*, I. i. 7; III. iii. 54.
141. "This belief of Madhwa, that only a few attain salvation while the rest cannot, and some even suffer [eternal] damnation, is contrary to the teachings of all other Indian religious schools. Madhwa may possibly have been influenced by certain Christian missionaries who during his time may have penetrated into India." Prabhavananda and Manchester, *Spiritual Heritage of India*, p. 377.

Chapter X. Time and History in the Indian Tradition

1. Parts of this chapter are taken from R. Puligandla, "Time and History in the Indian Tradition," *Philosophy East and West*, Vol. 24, No. 2 (April 1974), pp. 164-70.
2. To be sure, there are exceptions to this observation. Nevertheless, it is still a widespread belief in the West, both within and without academia, that Indian civilization, past and present, suffers from a profound lack of historical consciousness and that such a lack can only be traced to its philosophies and religions. The fountainhead of this absurd fantasy is Hegel, the towering figure in nineteenth-century Western philosophy. At the time of Hegel, the West was just beginning to study Indian civilization, and source-materials were meager and fragmentary, although there was much by way of travelogues of British missionaries and employees of the East India Company (and subsequently of the Indian Civil Service). But Hegel was too mighty a spirit to

be daunted by lack of source-materials and systematic studies. Armed with his allegedly formidable philosophic weapon, the triadic dialectic forged with the blessings of the Absolute Spirit itself, he lays bare the very essence of Indian culture: "The Hindoos on the contrary are *by birth* given over to an unyielding destiny, while at the same time their Spirit is exalted to Ideality; so that their minds exhibit the contradictory processes of a dissolution of fixed rational and definite conceptions in their Ideality, and on the other side, a degradation of this ideality to a multiformity of sensuous objects. This makes them *incapable of writing History.* All that happens is dissipated in their minds into confused dreams. *What we call historical truth and veracity —intelligent, thoughtful comprehension of events, and fidelity in representing them—nothing of this sort can be looked for among the Hindoos.* We may explain this deficiency partly from *the excitement and debility of the nerves,* which prevent them from retaining an object in their minds, and firmly comprehending it, for in their mode of apprehension, a sensitive and imaginative temperament changes it into a feverish dream;—partly from the fact, that *veracity is the direct contrary to their nature. They even lie knowingly and designedly where misapprehension is out of the question.* As the Hindoo Spirit is a state of dreaming and mental transiency—a self-oblivious dissolution—objects also dissolve for it into unreal images and indefinitude. This feature is *absolutely characteristic; and this alone would furnish us with a clear idea of the Spirit of the Hindoos, from which all that has been said might be deduced.* . . . Among the Hindoos, on the contrary—instead of this Unity—*Diversity is the fundamental* characteristic. . . . With this is bound up a *monstrous, irrational imagination,* which attaches the moral value and character of men to an infinity of outward actions as empty in point of intellect as of feeling; sets aside all respect for the welfare of man, and even makes a duty of the cruellest and severest contravention of it. . . . Annihilation—the abandonment of all reason, morality and subjectivity—can only come to a positive feeling and consciousness of itself, by extravagating in a boundless wild imagination; in which, like a desolate spirit, it finds no rest, no settled composure, though it can content itself in no other way; *as a man who is quite reduced in body and spirit finds his existence altogether stupid and intolerable, and is even driven to the creation of a dream-world and delirious bliss in opium.*" Hegel, *The Philosophy of History,* tr. with a new introduction by C. J. Friedrich (New York: Dover Publications, 1956), pp. 162-67 (emphasis added). Lest the reader think that I have deliberately presented Hegel in an unfavorable light, I shall quote two evaluations of Hegel as a philosopher, one by Arthur Schopenhauer, a contemporary of Hegel and a close student of Hinduism and Buddhism, and another by Karl Popper, a well-known twentieth-century philosopher: "Hegel, installed from above, by the powers that be, as the Certified Philosopher, was a flat-headed, insipid, nauseating, illiterate charlatan, who reached the pinnacle of audacity in scribbling together and dishing up the craziest mystifying nonsense. This nonsense has been proclaimed as immortal wisdom, by mercenary followers and readily accepted as such by all fools, who thus joined into as perfect a chorus as had ever been heard before. The extensive field of spiritual influence with which Hegel was furnished by those in power has enabled him to achieve the intellectual corruption of a whole generation." *Schopenhauer's Works* (2nd ed., 1888), Vol. V, 103 f. "But as far as Hegel is concerned, I do not even think he was talented. He is an indigestible writer. As even his most ardent apologist must admit, his style is 'unquestionably scandalous.' And as far as the content of his writing is concerned, he is supreme only in his outstanding lack of originality. There is nothing in Hegel's writing that has not been said better before him. There is nothing in his apologetic method that is not borrowed from his apologetic forerunners. But he devoted these borrowed thoughts and methods with singleness of purpose, though without a trace of brilliancy to one aim: to fight against the open society, and thus to serve his employer, Frederick William of Prussia. Hegel's confusion and debasement of reason is partly necessary as a means to this end, partly a more accidental but very natural expression of his state of mind. And the whole story of Hegel would indeed not be worth relating, were it not for its more sinister consequences, which show how easily a clown may be a 'maker of history.'" Karl Popper. *The Open Society and Its Enemies* (New York: Harper & Row, 1962), Vol. II, p. 32. Although Hegelianism has been held in disrepute for quite some time now, there are still a considerable number of apologists and enthusiastic followers untiringly spreading the wisdom of the master—a fact which is largely responsible for keeping alive the Hegelian judgment on Indian civilization: "*The Philosophy of History* remains the heart and center of Hegel's philosophy. What is more, it is the work that has exerted the most profound influence over the years." C. J. Friedrich's introduction to the Dover edition of *The Philosophy of History*, 1956.

3. *The Vedānta Sūtras of Bādarāyaṇa, with the Commentary Śaṅkara*, tr. by George Thibaut, II. 1. 14.
4. *Nāgārjuna's Mūlamadhyamakakārikā*, tr. by Kenneth K. Inada, XXIV. 8, 9, 18; also see *Nāgārjuna's Vigraha-vyāvarttanī*, ed. by K. P. Jayaswal and R. Sankrityayana, as an appendix to the *Journal of Bihar and Orissa Research Society* (Patna), Vol. XXIII, 1937, Part III.
5. Heinrich Zimmer, *Philosophies of India*, ed. by Joseph Campbell (Princeton: Princeton University Press, 1951).
6. Mircea Eliade, *Myths, Dreams, and Mysteries* (New York: Harper & Brothers, 1960), p. 241 (emphasis added).
7. One might object to this by saying that modern Western historicists do not believe in God and therefore our characterization of historicism does not apply to them. We reply that our characterization takes into account the roots of Western historicism; further, it applies equally to theistic and atheistic historicists,

since both hold that history is ultimate reality. For the former, history is ultimate because it is the theater of God; for the latter, it is ultimate because there is, *ex hypothesi,* no other reality.

8. For a thorough treatment of this point, see C. G. Hempel, *Aspects of Scientific Explanation* (Glencoe, Ill.: The Free Press, 1965), pp. 173-221.
9. This argument is not to be construed as a nonhistoricist plea for belief in God, for belief in God is not an essential component of the nonhistoricist attitude, as witness the Indian and Chinese traditions.

Chapter XI. A Glimpse at the Contemporary Scene

For excerpts from the writings of Radhakrishnan and Aurobindo, see Radhakrishnan and Moore, *A Source Book in Indian Philosophy.*

1. It would be a grave error to think that devotionalism was unknown to Hinduism until its contact with Islam. Quite the contrary, devotion *(bhakti)* as a means to salvation is to be found in the Vedas and the Upaniṣads and, above all, in the Bhagavadgītā, where *bhatki-yoga* (the path of devotion)) is explicitly and elaborately discussed. Thus "the movement for expressing religious truth in the language of the people began in the South by at least the seventh century A.D. The time and place are both significant, for they make clear that the impetus towards devotional religion came from within the tradition itself, not, as has sometimes been suggested, from contact with Islam in the twelfth century." Ainslie T. Embree, *The Hindu Tradition: Readings in Oriental Thought* (New York: Vintage Books, 1972), p. 229.
2. "The effects of Islamic conquest on India were great—the most striking evidence of this is the existence of at least one hundred and thirty million Muslims in the area at the present time—but the long centuries of alien domination had not destroyed either Hindu religion or culture. In all history, no other civilization has ever been subjected to such a strain and managed to endure so unchanged in fundamentals as did the Hindu. There are many reasons for this, such as the vast Hindu population in comparison with the small number of invaders, the strength of the Hindu class system, and the attitudes of the Muslim rulers themselves, but much credit must be given to the poet-saints who made the immemorial tradition a living reality for the people of India. The songs of Hinduism were the products of a passionate faith that enabled men to live by old standards and old values by giving them relevance in a world that must have seemed hostile and menacing." *Ibid.,* p. 231.
3. *Ibid.,* pp. 275-76.
4. *Ibid.,* p. 277.
5. According to Arthur Schopenhauer, the great German philosopher of the nineteenth century, "It [Anquetil du Perron's Latin translation of a Persian rendering of the Upaniṣads] is the most re-

warding and the most elevating reading which (with the exception of the original text) there can possibly be in the world. It has been the solace of my life and will be of my death." *Parerga,* 2, § 185 (*Werke,* 6. 427). The American Transcendentalist Ralph Waldo Emerson has this to say about the Bhagavad-gītā: "I owed—my friend and I owed—a magnificient day to the Bhagavad-Gita—It was the first of books; it was as if an empire spake to us, nothing small or unworthy, but large, serene, consistent, the voice of an old intelligence which in another age and climate had pondered and thus disposed of the same questions which exercise us." *Journals of Ralph Waldo Emerson* (Cambridge, Mass.: Houghton, 1912), VII, pp. 510-11. According to Thoreau, "In the morning I bathe my intellect in the stupendous and cosmogonal philosophy of the Bhagavad Geeta, since whose composition years of the gods have elapsed, and in comparison with which modern world and its literature seems puny and trivial." *The Writings of Henry David Thoreau* (Cambridge, Mass.: Houghton, 1949), II, p. 306.

6. Embree, *Hindu Tradition,* p. 275.
7. Aurobindo, *Arya* (Calcutta, 15 July 1918), pp. 764-65 (reprinted in *Sourcebook,* p. 577).
8. Aurobindo, *The Life Divine* (Calcutta: Arya Publishing House, 1947), p. 121 (*Sourcebook,* p. 599).
9. Aurobindo, *The Human Cycle* (Pondicherry: Sri Aurobindo Ashram, 1950), pp. 83-84.
10. Aurobindo, *The Life Divine,* p. 863 (*Sourcebook,* p. 605).
11. *Ibid.,* pp. 373-78 (*Sourcebook,* pp. 589-93).
12. S. Radhakrishnan, *Indian Philosophy* (London: George Allen & Unwin, 1931), Vol. II, Ch. VIII.
13. S. Radhakrishnan, *An Idealist View of Life* (London: George Allen & Unwin, 1929), Ch. III (*Sourcebook,* pp. 614-15).
14. *Ibid.* (*Sourcebook,* pp. 617-18).
15. *The Thirteen Principal Upanishads,* tr. with introduction by Robert E. Hume (New York: Oxford University Press, 1971), pp. 4-5.

Glossary

A. Pronunciation and Accent

A number of Sanskrit terms are used in this book. The reader not familiar with Sanskrit can learn to pronounce the terms reasonably correctly by adhering to the general rule that consonants are given their English value and vowels and diphthongs their German or Italian value. Exceptions to this general rule are as follows:

a: as *u* in but and gut
c: as *ch* in check but not so strongly aspirated
ḥ: occurs only at the end of syllables and is pronounced as a light *h* sound
ṁ or ṃ: nasalizes the preceding vowel
ph: as *ph* in uphill but not as in phenomena and phobia
ṛ: originally and properly pronounced as *ur* in the Scottish pronunciation of hurt and spurt; today it is acceptable to pronounce as *ri*
ś (or ç): as in *sh* in shun and shut
th: as *th* in penthouse but not as in thick and thin

The accenting of a Sanskrit word depends upon whether or not it contains a heavy syllable. A heavy syllable is one which contains a long vowel or diphthong (a, e, i, o, u, ai, au) or a short vowel followed by two or more consonants (bh, gh, kh, ph, th are each to be counted as a single consonant). If a word contains heavy syllables, the accent is usually on the last heavy syllable; and if a word contains no heavy syllable, the accent is on the third syllable from the end. Here are some examples: Lankavat*a*ra, Mahabh*a*rata, Mādhav*a*carya, Viśiṣṭādv*a*ita, Rām*a*nuja, Gaṇapatig*u*pta, g*a*rima, p*a*rama.

a: as *u* in but and gut
ā: as *a* in calm and father

ai: as *ai* in aisle
au: as *ou* in house and mouse
b: as *b* in bear
bh: ase *bh* in abhor
c: as *ch* in check (but not so strongly aspirated)
ç or ś (palatal) : as *sh* in shun and shut
ch: as *chh* in church hill
d: as *d* in dice and dime
ḍ: as *d* in drug and drum
dh: as *dh* in adhere
ḍh: as *dh* in mudhouse
e: as *e* in gray and prey
g: as *g* in go
gh: as *gh* in doghouse
h: as *h* in him and hit
ḥ: occurs only at the end of syllables and is a lightly aspirated *h* sound
i: as *i* in pin and pit
ī: as *i* in police
j: as *j* in jump and jungle
jh: as *dgeh* in hedgehog
k: as *k* in kind and kite
kh: as *kh* in inkhorn and sinkhole
l: as *l* in lull
ṁ: as *m* in mad and man
ṃ, m, or n: semi-nasal sound
ṅ: as *n* in not
ñ: as *n* in singe
ṇ: as *n* in nice and nine
ṅ or ñ: as *n* in sing
o: as *o* in go
p: as *p* in push and put
ph: as *ph* in uphill
r: as *r* in red
ṛ: as *ri* in ring, rip, and Rita
s: as *s* in sick and sin
ś or ç (palatal) : as *sh* in shun and shut
ṣ (sibilant) : as *sh* in shun and shut but with the tip of the tongue turned backward
t: as *t* in crater and water
ṭ: as *t* in tile and time
th: as *th* in nuthook
ṭh: as *th* in boathouse
u: as *u* in push and pull
ū: as *u* in prude and rude
v: as *v* in very (as *w* after consonant)
y: as *y* in yes

B. Alphabetical List of Sanskrit Terms

The following is the alphabetical list of Sanskrit terms. (Some Pali terms are also used in the text and they are included in the list in parentheses following the corresponding Sanskrit terms.)

abhāva: nonexistence, negation, absence

Abhidharma (Abhidhamma): higher (superior) *dharma,* collection of advanced (Buddhist) treatises on dharma (see *Abhidharma-Piṭaka*)

Abhidharma-Piṭaka (Abhidhamma-Piṭaka): the last of the *Three Baskets* (the Pali Canon, the *Tipiṭaka*)

ācāra: conduct, discipline, observance

acarya: great teacher, master

ādhāra: support

adharma: moral demerit, an extended substance (in Jaina metaphysics) which makes rest possible

ādheya: the supported

adhyāsa: superimposition

adṛṣṭa: Unseen Power (*karma*)

adṛṣṭārtha: imperceivable objects

Advaita: nondual (istic), a school of Vedānta

Agni: the Vedic god of fire

ahaṁkāra: egoism, ego-sense, sense of "I," "me," and "mine"

ajīva: non-soul, the inanimate

ākāśa: space, ether (substratum of sound in Nyāya-Vaiśeṣika metaphysics)

alaukika: extraordinary

Ālaya-vijñāna: storehouse consciousness

ālvār: one who through utter self-surrender and pure devotion has attained union with God; the term usually refers to the Vaiṣṇava poet-saints of South India

anādi: beginningless

ānanda: bliss

anantaṁ: infinite

Anātman (anattā): no permanent, eternal self

anavasthā: infinite regress

anekāntavāda: Jaina doctrine of the many-faceted character of reality

aṅga: organ, part

anitya: impermanent

antaḥ-karaṇa: internal organ constituted of mind

(*manas*), ego-sense (*antaḥ-karaṇa*), and intellect (*buddhi, mahat*)

antarindriya: internal sense (mind)

aṇu: atom (the indivisible)

anumāna: inference

anupalabdhi: noncognition (one of the six *pramāṇas* of Advaita Vedānta)

aparāvidyā: empirical, lower, mundane, relative knowledge (see *parāvidyā*)

aparokṣa: immediate, direct, without the mediation of the senses

apohavāda: the doctrine according to which to say that two things, e.g., two cows, are similar and therefore belong to the same class is not to say that they share certain positive characteristics, but merely that they share the negative character of not being non-cows

Āraṇyakas: Forest-treatises (that part of the Vedas primarily concerned with rites and ceremonies)

Arhat (Arhant): the worthy one, the perfected saint, the person who has attained the Buddhist enlightenment

artha: means of life, wealth (one of the four *puruṣārthas*), the nonperceptual, nonconceptual, intuitive knowledge of reality which the Yogic aspirant seeks

arthapatti: postulation (one of the six *pramāṇas* of Advaita Vedānta)

āsana: discipline of the body consisting of steady and comfortable postures necessary for attaining one-pointedness and stillness of the mind (a limb of *aṣṭāṅga-yoga*)

asatkāryavāda: the theory that effect is not identical with (does not preexist in) cause (as opposed to *satkāryavāda*)

aṣṭāṅga-yoga: Eight-limbed *yoga* (Yoga as systematized by Patañjali in his *Yoga-sūtras*)

aṣṭāngika-mārga: the Fourth Noble Truth (the Eightfold Path taught by the Buddha as the means for the cessation of suffering)

aswatantra: the unfree

Atharva: one of the four Vedas

Ātman: soul, the inmost Self which is eternal, nameless, and formless (not to be confused with the empirical ego)

avayava: organ, member (of the Nyāya syllogism)

avidyā: ignorance, nescience

avīta: negative inference (inference based on a universal negative proposition)

aviveka: lack of discrimination (between the real and the unreal, and the true and the false)

baddha: the unfree, the bound

bāhya: external (as distinct from internal)

bhakti: devotion (to God)

bhakti-yoga: the *yoga* (path) of devotion

bhava: existence, becoming

bhāva: being, nature, reality, true condition

Bhava-cakra: the wheel of existence (becoming) (another name for *Pratītyasamutpāda*)

bhedābheda: identity-in-difference

bhoktṛ: enjoyer

Bodhisattva (Bodhisatta): one who is a Buddha-to-be, one who aspires to *bodhi* (enlightenment) (the Mahāyāna ideal as contrasted with the Hīnayāna ideal of *Arhat*)

Brahman: the eternal, nameless, formless ultimate reality of which the world of phenomena is manifestation

Brāhmaṇas: that part of the Vedas primarily concerned with rites, ceremonies, duties, and conduct

buddhi: intellect (*mahat*)

carv: to chew, to eat (root from which derives Cārvāka)

Cārvāka: school of materialism, an adherent of the school of materialism

chala: an unfair reply by which one attempts to contradict or refute one's opponent's statement by taking it in a sense other than the one intended

citta: mind

darśana: vision (view) of truth and reality

dhāraṇā: concentration (a limb of *aṣṭānga-yoga*)

dharma:	what holds together, the basis of all order, one of the four *puruṣārthas,* law, moral merit, an extended substance (in Jaina metaphysics) which makes motion possible
Dharma-cakra:	wheel of law, wheel of existence, wheel of becoming (another name for *Pratītyasamutpāda*)
Dharma-kāya:	*dharma*-body (truth-body), one of the three aspects of the Buddha-nature
dhṛ:	bearing, upholding, supporting, that which forms the foundation (root from which derives *dharma*)
dhyāna:	meditation, contemplation (a limb of *aṣṭānga-yoga*)
Digambara:	sky-clad (nude), refers to the sect of Jainism the highest monks of which go about naked
dik:	space, direction
dravya:	substance
dravyatva:	substantiality, state of being a substance
dṛṣṭānta:	example, instance, an undisputed fact which illustrates a general rule, the third and last member of the Nyāya syllogism
dṛṣṭārtha:	perceivable objects
duḥkha:	suffering
Dvādaśa-nidāna:	the twelve sources (links) constituting the chain of causation (another name for *Pratītyasamutpāda*)
Dvaita:	dual(istic), a school of Vedānta
guṇa:	constituent, quality, product, cosmic constituent (in Sāṁkhya metaphysics)
hetu:	reason for something, second member of the Nyāya syllogism, the middle term of the Nyāya syllogism
hetvābhāsa:	something which only appears to be but is not in fact a valid reason, fallacy of inference
Hīnayāna:	one of the two major divisions of Buddhism (also known as *Theravāda Buddhism*)
Indra:	Vedic god of the heavens

Īśvara: God, creator, sustainer, and destroyer of the universe (see *Saguṇa-Brahman*)

Jaḍa: Prakṛti as unintelligent and unconscious

jalpa: a mere wrangling in which each party is concerned only with winning an argument rather than establishing truth

Janma-maraṇa-cakra: wheel of birth, old age, and death (another name for *Pratītyasamutpāda*)

jarā-maraṇa: old age and death (a link in the Buddhist twelvefold chain of dependent origination)

jāti: birth, class as determined by birth, universal (as distinct from particular), an unfair reply based on false analogy

Jina: spiritual conqueror, title by which Vardhamāna, the founder of Jainism, is known

jīva: animate substance, individual soul

jīvanmukta: he who is free while still alive

jñāna: knowledge

jñānakāṇḍa: the part of the Vedas which deals with knowledge of ultimate reality (refers to the Upaniṣads)

jñānalakṣaṇa: a certain kind of extraordinary perception (recognized by the Nyāya school), in which sensations and perceptions of different senses are so intimately associated that one feels that they are integral parts of a single perception—e.g., "I see the fragrance of the flower."

jñānam: knowledge, consciousness

kaivalya: perfect independence, absolute freedom, *mokṣa*

kāla: time

kāma: desire, pleasure, passion (one of the four *puruṣārthas*)

karma: action, effect of action

karmakāṇda: the part of the Vedas concerned with conduct, practice, and action—rituals and sacrifices (refers to the Saṁhitās, Brāhmaṇas, and Āraṇyakas)

kartṛ:	agent, doer
kevala-jñāna:	all-comprehensive (perfect) knowledge
khaṇḍana:	refutation
kṣaṇika-vāda:	Buddhist doctrine of momentariness, according to which things last not even for one indivisible moment (also known as theory of instantaneous existence)
laukika:	ordinary, secular (as distinct from scriptural)
līlā:	sport, cosmic playfulness of Brahman
Lokāyata-mata:	the world of common experience, the view of common folk (often derogatorily applied to the Cārvāka school)
Mādhyamika:	farer of the Middle Way
mahākaruṇa:	boundless compassion (an attribute of the Bodhisattva)
Mahāsāṁghikas:	the Great Assembly-ites (group of Buddhist monks who broke off from the rest of the order, fourth-third century B.C.)
mahat:	intellect (*buddhi,* the first evolute of Prakṛti)
Mahāvīra:	the great hero (Jina)
Mahāyāna:	one of the two major divisions of Buddhism
manana:	reflection
manas:	mind
mānasa:	mental, internal
māyā:	cosmic illusion, cosmic ignorance, the power of Brahman by which Brahman manifests itself as the phenomenal world
māyāvāda:	Śaṁkara's doctrine of *māyā,* according to which the phenomenal world is neither real nor unreal but an appearance
Mīmāṁsā:	revered thought, solution of problems by reflection and critical examination, a school of Vedānta
mokṣa:	absolute freedom (*kaivalya*) (one of the four *puruṣārthas*)
muk:	to release, to free (the root from which derives *mokṣa*)
mukta:	he who has attained *mokṣa*

Naiyāyika: an adherent of the Nyāya school

nāma: name

nāma-rūpa: names and forms, concepts and percepts

Nāsadīyasūkta: the famous Ṛgvedic hymn of negation declaring that ultimate reality is indefinable, indescribable, imperceivable, etc.

Navya-nyāya: modern school of Nyāya (as distinct from *Pracīna-nyāya*)

naya: partial knowledge (judgment), in Jaina theory of knowledge

nididhyāsana: constant meditation which results in direct experience of truth and reality

nigamana: proposition which stands for conclusion in the Nyāya syllogism

nigrahasthāna: the basis on which an argument is conceded to have been lost

Nikāyas: the five collections of *sūtras* (*suttas*) constituting the *Sūtra-Piṭaka* (*Sutta-Piṭaka*) of the Pali Canon

nirbījasamādhi: the state of *samādhi* which is free from all seeds of bondage, actual or potential

Nirguṇa-Brahman: Brahman as ultimate reality transcending all perceptions and conceptions (names and forms)

nirṇaya: reliable and certain knowledge (about anything) obtained by any of the legitimate methods of knowledge (*pramāṇas*)

Nirvāṇa: the state of Buddhist enlightenment and hence of absolute freedom from ignorance and delusion (consequently of suffering)

nirvikalpa: indeterminate

nirvitarkasamādhi: that stage of Yogic meditation in which the mind loses its essential subjectivity and consequently knows the object as it really is

nityamukta: one who is eternally free

niyamya: self-culture which includes external and internal purification and moral virtues (a limb of *aṣṭānga-yoga*), the controlled

niyāmaka: controller

Nyāya: logic, an orthodox school of philosophy

padārtha:	category, object of experience, knowable
pakṣa:	side, part, minor term of the Nyāya syllogism
Pali:	language of the canonical texts of Theravāda Buddhism
Paramāṇu:	the infinitesimal Vaiśeṣika atoms
paramārtha-satya:	higher, ultimate truth, absolute standpoint
parārtha:	for others (as distinct from for oneself), Nyāya division of inference
parāvidyā:	higher knowledge (as distinct from lower knowledge), knowledge of Ātman, of Brahman
pariṇāmavāda:	the theory that when an effect is produced there is a real transformation of the cause into the effect (as distinct from *vaivartavāda*)
Parjanya:	Vedic god of the rain-cloud
parokṣa:	mediate
paryāya:	mode, accidental quality of a substance
Prācīna-nyāya:	Ancient (original) school of Nyāya
pradhāna:	first cause, eternal fundamental substance, Nature, Prakṛti
prajñā:	nonperceptual, nonconceptual, direct, intuitive insight into ultimate reality
prajñā-pāramitā:	perfect wisdom (perfection of wisdom)
Prakṛti:	primal matter
pralaya:	dissolution of the world into the primal, undifferentiated Prakṛti
pramā:	valid presentative knowledge
pramāṇa:	criterion (source, standard) of valid knowledge, way of knowing anything truly and objectively
prameya:	knowable, object of true knowledge, reality
prāṇāyāma:	control and regulation of breath (a limb of *aṣṭānga-yoga*)
prapatti:	complete self-surrender to God
prasanga:	Mādhyamika dialectical technique of *reductio ad absurdum*
prātibhāsika:	imaginary standpoint
pratijñā:	hypothesis (the first member of the Nyāya syllogism)
Pratītyasamutpāda (Paṭiccasamuppāda):	Doctrine of Dependent Origination of which *Bhava-cakra, Dharma-cakra,*

	Dvādaśa-nidāna, Janma-maraṇa-cakra are different names
pratyāhāra:	the withdrawal of the senses from their objects (a limb of *aṣṭāṅga-yoga*)
pratyakṣa:	direct, immediate (as distinct from *parokṣa,* mediate)
pratyaya:	the totality of object (s) concentrated upon at any given time
prayojana:	the object to attain or avoid which one acts
pudgala:	matter, substratum of personality
Puruṣa:	self (not to be confused with the empirical ego), spiritual substance
puruṣārthas:	the goals (ends) of human life, four in number: *dharma, artha, kāma, mokṣa*
Puruṣasūkta:	the celebrated Ṛgvedic hymn declaring the organic unity of the universe (the oneness of all existence)
Pūrva:	prior, early
Pūrva Mīmāṁsā:	a school of Vedānta primarily concerned with providing philosophical justification for the Vedic ritualism
pūrvapakṣa:	statement of the opponent's position before proceeding to refute it
rajas:	the active principle of existence, one of the three *guṇas* of Prakṛti
ṛṣi:	man of transcendent wisdom, sage
Ṛta:	cosmic law (order), principle of righteousness, sacrificial correctness
rūpa:	form
śabda:	sound, testimony
saccidānanda:	Pure Being, Pure Consciousness, Pure Bliss
ṣaḍāyatana:	the six organs of knowledge
sādhana-catuṣṭaya:	the fourfold discipline of Vedānta for the realization of ultimate reality
sādhya:	the major term of the Nyāya syllogism
Saguṇa-Brahman:	Brahman conceived as having name and form (*Īśvara*) (as distinct from *Nirguṇa-Brahman*)
sākṣin:	Ātman, the witness self
Śākyamuni:	the sage who hailed from the Śākya clan (the Buddha)

Sāma:	one of the four Vedas
samādhi:	mind's absorption in the object of contemplation (the last and eighth limb of *aṣṭānga-yoga*)
sāmānya:	generality, universal
sāmānyalakṣaṇa:	perception of universals (recognized by the Nyāya school as one of three types of extraordinary perception)
samanyasa:	cultivation of internal and external purity necessary for direct experience of ultimate reality (the first part of the *sādhana-catuṣṭaya*)
sāmānyatodṛṣṭa:	a type of Nyāya inference based on noncausal uniformity
samavāya:	the *Nyāya-Vaiśeṣika* category of inference
saṁgha:	community of Buddhist monks
Saṁhitās:	the parts of the Vedas dealing with mantras and hymns
Sāṁkhya:	an orthodox school of philosophy
Saṁsāra:	mundane existence, empirical reality, recurrent round of birth and death
Saṁsāra-cakra:	the wheel of existence (becoming), another name for *Pratītyasamutpāda*
saṁśaya:	doubt, state of uncertainty
saṁskāra:	karmic impressions
saṁvṛti:	lower, empirical standpoint
saṁvṛti-satya:	lower, empirical truth
samyagājīva (sammā-ājīva)	right conduct
samyagdṛṣṭi (sammādiṭṭhi):	right views
samyakkarmānta (sammākammanta):	right conduct
samyaksamādhi (sammāsamādhi):	right concentration
samyasaṅkalpa (sammāsaṅkappa):	right resolve
samyaksmṛti (sammāsati):	right mindfulness
samyagvāk (sammāvācā):	right speech
samyagvyāyāma (sammāvāyāma):	right effort
saṁyama:	*dhārana, dhyāna,* and *samādhi* taken together
saṁyoga:	Nyāya Vaiśeṣika category of conjunction

sapakṣa:	the fourth term of the Nyāya syllogism (represents the positive example)
saptabhangīnaya:	the sevenfold judgment schema of Jainism
sarvāstivāda:	a school of Buddhism according to which all things, physical as well as mental, exist
sat:	being, good
satkāryavāda:	the theory that effect is identical with (preexists in) cause (as opposed to *asatkāryavāda*)
sattva:	one of the three *guṇas* of Prakṛti (signifies everything pure, fine, and calm)
satya, satyaṁ:	reality, truth
Sautrāntika:	a Buddhist school of critical realism
savikalpa:	determinate
savitarkā-samādhi:	the stage of Yogic *samādhi* in which the three kinds of knowledge (*śabda, artha, jñāna*) exist in a mixed state
śeṣa:	servant (devotee)
śeṣin:	Lord (God)
siddha:	one who has attained extraordinary powers as a result of Yogic practice
siddhānta:	theory, view, doctrine, conclusion
skandhas:	components of human personality
sparśa:	contact, touch
śravaṇa:	attentive listening
sṛṣṭi:	creation
Sthaviras:	Elders
sūkṣma:	subtle, infinitesimal
Śūnyatā:	Emptiness, Void
sūtra (sutta):	aphorism
Sūtra-Piṭaka (Sutta-Piṭaka):	the second of the *Three Baskets* (*Tripiṭaka*)
svabhāva-śūnya:	no-self (own) -nature
svārtha:	for oneself
svarūpa:	essential form, internal form
Śvetāmbara:	the white-clad sect of Jainism
swatantra:	the free, the independent
syād:	somehow, relative to some standpoint
syādvāda:	the Jaina theory of the relativity of all judgments
tadvacana:	his (their) word
tamas:	one of the three *guṇas* of Prakṛti (sig-

nifies stupor, laziness, stupidity, and inaction in general)

taṅhā: craving

tanmātra: a simple or subtle element (as distinct from gross matter)

tarka: hypothetical argument by which one provides an indirect justification for a proposition by showing that its contradictory leads to absurdity (*reductio ad absurdum*)

tarkaśāstra: science of logic

Tathāgata: the thus-gone, the awakened one, the Buddha

tattva: truth, reality

Theravāda: doctrine of the Elders

Tīrthaṁkara: liberated man, saint (Jainism)

Tripiṭaka (Tipiṭaka): the *Three Baskets* (the Buddhist Pali Canon)

tṛṣṇā: thirst, craving

udāharaṇa: example, the third member of the Nyāya syllogism which gives, together with an example, the invariable connection between *pratijñā* and *hetu.*

upādāna: clinging

upādhi: limitation, limiting adjunct

upamāna: comparison (one of the six *pramāṇas* of Advaita Vedānta)

upanaya: application of a universal proposition to the present case (fourth member of the Nyāya syllogism)

Upaniṣad: secret teaching, sitting close to a teacher and receiving from him liberating knowledge, the concluding parts of the Vedas (concerned with knowledge of ultimate reality)

upāsanā: prayer, observance

uttara: posterior, later

Uttara Mīmāṁsā: that branch of Vedānta whose chief concern is knowledge of ultimate reality (as distinct from *Pūrva Mīmāṁsā*)

uttarapakṣa: the statement of a philosopher's own position after refuting those of his opponents *vāda:* theory, doctrine, view, any discussion in which all arguments are explicitly and fully stated in the format of the Nyāya syllogism and every relevant pramāṇa and principle of logic cited

Vaibhāṣika: a Buddhist school of realism

vaidika: pertaining to the Vedas, testimony of the Vedas

vaiśeṣa: the category of particularity (central to the Vaiśeṣika school)

Vāyu: the Vedic god of air

vedanā: sense experience

Vedānta: concluding parts of the Vedas, the culmination of the Vedic wisdom, name of a group of philosophical schools with their foundations in the Vedas

Vedas: the most sacred scriptures of the Hindus

videhamukti: freedom from all bodies (gross as well as subtle), absolute freedom from all fetters of existence

vijñāna: consciousness

Vijñāna-vāda: idealistic school of Buddhism (see *Yogācāra*)

vikalpa: subjective forms (imaginative constructions) which have no empirical grounding and are therefore *a priori*

vinaya: discipline, Discipline of the Buddhist Order

Vinaya-Piṭaka: the first of the *Three Baskets,* with matters of conduct and discipline of the order

vipakṣa: the fifth term of the Nyāya syllogism (represents the negative example)

Viśiṣṭādvaita: qualified nondualism

vīta: affirmative inference (inference based on a universal affirmative proposition), as contrasted with *avīta*

vitaṇḍā: any debate in which one attempts to refute the position of one's opponent rather than establishing one's own position

vivartavāda: doctrine of apparent change—when an effect is produced, there is only apparent but no real transformation of the cause into the effect (as opposed to *pariṇāmavāda*)

vivekajñāna: discriminative knowledge

vyāpti: the relation (in the Nyāya syllogism) of the invariable connection between *hetu* (the middle term) and sādhya (the major term) and therefore the logical ground of inference

vyavahārika: empirical (lower, mundane) standpoint

Yajur: one of the four Vedas

yama: Vedic god of death, and the first limb of *aṣṭānga-yoga,* consists of the cultivation of such qualities as nonviolence, truthfulness, contentment

Yogācāra: idealistic school of Buddhism (see *Vijñāna-vāda*)

yogaja: a type of extraordinary perception recognized by the Nyāya school (the intuitive perception of all objects, past, future, hidden, and infinitesimal, resulting from the practice of Yoga)

Bibliography

General

Akhilananda, Swami. *Spiritual Practices* (with an introduction by Walter G. Muelder). Boston: Branden Press, 1971.

Barborka, Geoffrey A. *The Pearl of the Orient: The Message of the Bhagvad-Gītā for the Western World.* Wheaton, Ill.: The Theosophical Publishing House, 1972.

Brown, Norman. *Man in the Universe: Some Cultural Continuities in India.* Berkeley: University of California Press, 1970.

Chatterjee, S. C., and Datta, D. M. *An Introduction to Indian Philosophy.* Calcutta: University of Calcutta Press, 1960.

Chettimattam, J. B. *Consciousness and Reality: An Indian Approach to Metaphysics.* Bangalore: Dharmaram College Press, 1967.

Dasgupta, Surendranath. *A History of Indian Philosophy.* 5 vols. London: Cambridge University Press, 1922-55.

________. *Indian Idealism.* London: Cambridge University Press, 1933.

Deutsch, Eliot, tr. *The Bhagavad Gītā.* With critical essays. New York: Holt, Rinehart and Winston, 1968.

Edgerton, Franklin, tr. *The Bhagavad Gītā.* With commentary. New York: Harper & Row, 1964.

Eliade, Mircea. *Myths, Dreams and Mysteries.* Tr. Philip Mairet. New York: Harper & Row, 1967.

Guenther, H. V. *Buddhist Philosophy in Theory and Practice.* Baltimore: Penguin Books, 1972.

________. *Tibetan Buddhism Without Mystification.* Leiden: E. J. Brill, 1966.

Heiman, Betty. *Indian and Western Philosophy: A Study in*

Contrasts. London: George Allen & Unwin, 1937.

Hiriyanna, M. *The Essentials of Indian Philosophy*. London: George Allen & Unwin, 1932.

________. *Outlines of Indian Philosophy*. London: George Allen & Unwin, 1932.

Humphreys, Christmas, ed. *The Wisdom of Buddhism*. New York: Harper & Row, 1972.

Johnson, Clive, ed. *Vedānta, An Anthology of Hindu Scriptures, Commentary and Poetry*. New York: Harper & Row, 1971.

Joshi, Lal Mani. *Brahmanism, Buddhism and Hinduism*. Kandy: Buddhist Publication Society, 1970.

Joshi, N. V. *The Three Fountainheads of Indian Philosophy*. Bombay: Somaiya Publications, 1972.

Kalghatji, T. G. *Karma and Rebirth*. Ahmedabad: L. D. Institute of Indology, 1972.

Kaveeshwar, G. W. *The Ethics of the Gītā*. Delhi: Motilal Banarsidass, 1971.

Kim, Yong C. *Oriental Thought: An Introduction to the Philosophical and Religious Thought of Asia*. Springfield, Ill.: Charles C. Thomas, 1973.

Koller, John M. *Oriental Philosophies*. New York: Charles Scribner's Sons, 1970.

Lal, R. B. *The Gītā in the Light of Modern Science*. Bombay: Somaiya Publications, 1971.

Ling, Trevor. *Buddha, Marx and God*. New York: St. Martin's Press, 1966.

Maitra, S. K. *The Spirit of Indian Philosophy*. Banaras, 1947.

Mehta, J. L., ed. *Vedānta and Buddhism*. Banaras: Banaras Hindu University Press, 1968.

Mitra, G. *Analytical Studies in Indian Philosophy*. Bhubaneshwar: Utkal University Press, 1971.

Moore, Charles A., ed. *The Indian Mind*. Honolulu: University of Hawaii Press, 1967.

________, ed. *The Status of the Inidvidual in East and West*. Honolulu: University of Hawaii Press, 1968.

Motwani, K. *Manu: The Origins of Social Thought*. Bombay: Bharatiya Vidya Bhavan, 1970.

Müller, F. Max. *The Six Systems of Indian Philosophy*. London: Longmans, Green & Co., 1928.

Munshi, K. M., Diwakar, R. R., eds. *Contemporary Indian Philosophy*. Bombay: Bharatiya Vidya Bhavan, 1970.

Northrop, F. S. C. *The Meeting of East and West: An Inquiry Concerning World Understanding*. New York: The Macmillan Co., 1946.

Organ, Troy W. *The Hindu Quest for the Perfection of Man*. Athens, Ohio: Ohio University Press, 1970.

Pardue, Peter A. *Buddhism: A Historical Introduction to Buddhist Values and the Social and Political Form They Have Assumed.* New York: The Macmillan Co., 1968.

Parrinder, Geoffrey. *Upanishads, Gītā and Bible: A Comparative Study of Hindu and Christian Scriptures.* New York: Harper & Row, 1972.

Potter, Karl H. *Presuppositions of India's Philosophies.* Englewood Cliffs. N.J.: Prentice-Hall, 1963.

________. comp. *The Encyclopedia of Indian Philosophies.* Vol. I. Delhi: Motilal Banarsidass, 1972.

Prabhavananda, Swami, and Manchester, Frederick. *The Spiritual Heritage of India.* Garden City, N.Y.: Doubleday & Co., 1964.

Radhakrishnan, S. *Indian Philosophy.* 2 vols. London: George Allen & Unwin. 1923, 1927.

Radhakrishnan, S., and Moore, Charles A., eds. *A Source Book in Indian Philosophy.* Prenceton: Princeton University Press, 1967.

Radhakrishnan, S., and Muirhead, J. H. eds. *Contemporary Indian Philosophy.* New York: The Macmillan Co., 1952.

Radakrishnan, S., *et al.*, eds. *History of Philosophy Eastern and Western.* London: George Allen & Unwin, 1953.

Raja, C. Kunhan. *Some Fundamental Problems in Indian Philosophy.* Delhi: Motilal Banarsidass, 1960.

Raja, Kunjunni. *Indian Theories of Meaning.* Wheaton, Ill.: The Theosophical Publishing House, 1971.

Raju, P. T. *Idealistic Thought of India.* Cambridge, Mass.: Harvard University Press, 1953.

________. *Introduction to Comparative Philosophy.* Carbondale, Ill.: Southern Illinois University Press, 1962.

________. *Lectures on Comparative Philosophy.* Poona: University of Poona Press, 1970.

________. *The Philosophical Traditions of India.* London: George Allen & Unwin, 1971.

Rao, P. Nagaraja. *Contemporary Indian Philosophy.* Bombay: Bharatiya Vidya Bhavan, 1970.

Riepe, Dale. *The Naturalistic Tradition in Indian Thought.* Delhi: Motilal Banarsidass, 1964.

________. *The Philosophy of India and Its Impact on American Thought.* Springfield, Ill.: Charles C. Thomas, 1970.

Saksena, S. K. *Essays on Indian Philosophy.* Honolulu: University of Hawaii Press, 1972.

Sangharakshita, Bhikshu. *The Three Jewels: An Introduction to Modern Buddhism.* Garden City, N. Y.: Doubleday & Co., 1970.

Sarkar, A. K. *Changing Phases of Buddhist Thought: A Study in the Background of East-West Philosophy.* Patna: Bharati Bhavan, 1968.

Sharma, Chandradhar. *A Critical Survey of Indian Philosophy*. Delhi: Motilal Banarsidass, 1964.

________. *Dialectic in Buddhism and Vedānta*. Banaras: Nand Kishore Brothers, 1952.

Sharma, I. C. *Ethical Philosophies of India*. New York: Harper & Row, 1970.

Sinari, Ramakant. *The Structure of Indian Thought*. Springfield, Ill.: Charles C. Thomas, 1969.

Singer, Milton. *When a Great Tradition Modernizes: An Anthropological Approach to Indian Civilization*. New York: Praeger Publishers, 1972.

Singh, Balbir. *Foundations of Indian Philosophy*. New Delhi, Orient Longman, 1972.

Singh, R. J., ed. *World Perspectives in Philosophy, Religion and Culture (Essays Prestented to Professor D. M. Datta)*. Bombay: Bharatiya Vidya Bhavan, 1968.

Sinha, Jadunath. *Indian Realism*. London: Kegan Paul. 1938.

________. *Introduction to Indian Philosophy*. Agra: Lakshmi Narain Agarwal, 1949.

Smart, Ninian. *Doctrine and Argument in Indian Philosophy*. London: George Allen & Unwin, 1968.

Suzuki, D. T. *Mysticism: Christian and Buddhist*. New York: Harper & Row, 1971.

Swearer, Donald K., ed. *Secrets of the Lotus: Studies in Buddhist Meditation*. New York: The Macmillan Co., 1971.

Tähtinen, Unto. *Indian Philosophy of Value*. Turku, Finland: Turun Yliopisto, 1968.

Upadhyaya, K. N. *Early Buddhism and the Bhagavadgītā*. Delhi: Motilal Banarsidass, 1971.

Walker, Benjamin. *The Hindu World: An Encyclopedic Survey of Hinduism*. Vol. I and II. New York: Praeger Publishers, 1968.

Warder, A. K. *Outlines of Indian Philosophy*. Delhi: Motilal Banarsidass, 1971.

West, M. L. *Early Greek Philosophy and the Orient*. London: Oxford University Press, 1971.

Zimmer, Heinrich. *Philosophies of India*. Ed. by Joseph Campbell. Princeton: Princeton University Press, 1969.

Cārvāka

Bose, Prem Sunder, tr. *Śaṁkara's Sarvasiddhāntasaṁgraha*. Calcutta, 1929.

Cowell, E. B., and Gough, A. E., trs. *Mādhavācarya's Sarvadarśana-saṁgraha*. London: Kegan Paul, Trench, Trubner & Co., 1904.

Haribhadra. *Ṣaḍ-darśana-samuccaya.* Calcutta: Asiatic Society, 1905.

Parikh, Rasiklal C., and Sanghavi, Pandit Sukhlalji, eds. *Jayarāśi Bhaṭṭa's Tattvopaplavasiṁha.* Gaekwad's Oriental Series, LXXXVII. Baroda: Oriental Institute, 1940.

Shastri, Dakshinaranjan. *A Short History of Indian Materialism.* Calcutta: Book Company, 1930.

Jainism

Desai, M. D., tr. *The Naya-karnika (by Sri Vinaya Vijaya Maharaj)*. Arrah: Central Jaina Publishing House, 1915.

Dhruva, A. B., ed. *Malliṣeṇa's Syādvādamañjarī with Anyayoga-vyavaccheda-dvātriṁśikā of Hemacandra.* Sanskrit and Prakrit Series, LXXXIII. Bombay: Bhandarkar Oriental Research Institute, 1933.

Ghoshal, S. C., ed. and tr. *Nemichandra's Dravya Saṁgraha,* Arrah: Central Jaina Publishing House, 1917.

Jacobi, Hermann, tr. *The Jaina Sūtras.* Sacred Books of the East. London: Oxford University Press, 1884.

Jaini, J. L. *Outlines of Jainism.* London: Cambridge University Press, 1916.

————, tr. *Umāswāmi's Tattvārtha-dhigama-sūtra.* Arrah: Central Jaina Publishing House, 1928.

Kalghatji, T. G. *Jaina View of Life.* Sholapur: Lalchand Harichand Doshi, 1969.

Mehta, Mohan Lal. *Outlines of Jaina Philosophy.* Bangalore: Jain Mission Society, 1954.

Mookerji, Satkari. *The Jaina Philosophy of Non-Absolutism: A Critical Study of Anekāntavāda.* Calcutta: Bharati Mahavidyalaya, 1944.

Sanghavi, Pandit Sukhlalji, and Becherdasji, Pandit, trs. *Siddhasena Divākara's Sanmati Tarka.* Bombay: Shri Jain Shivetamber Education Board, 1939.

Stevenson, S. *The Heart of Jainism.* London: Oxford University Press, 1915.

Tatia, Nathmal. *Studies in Jaina Philosophy.* Banaras: Jain Cultural Research Society, 1951.

Thomas, F. W., ed. *Syādvāda-mañjarī.* Delhi: Motilal Banarsidass, 1968.

Vidyabhusana, S. C., tr. *Siddhasena Divākara's Nyāyāvatāra,* Calcutta: Indian Research Society, 1909.

Buddhism

Chatterjee, Ashok Kumar. *The Yogācāra Idealism.* Banaras: Banaras Hindu University Press, 1962.

Conze, E. *Buddhism: Its Essence and Development*. New York: Harper & Brothers, 1959.

________. *Buddhist Thought in India*. Ann Arbor: University of Michigan Press, 1967.

________. *Thirty Years of Buddhist Studies: Selected Essays by E. Conze*. Columbia: University of South Carolina Press, 1968.

________, tr. *Aṣṭasāhasrikā Prajñāpāramitā*. Calcutta: The Asiatic Society, 1970.

________, tr. *Buddhist Wisdom Books: The Diamond Sūtra and The Heart Sūtra*. New York: Harper & Row, 1972.

Dahlke, Paul. *Buddhism and Its Place in the Mental Life of Mankind*. London: Macmillan & Co., 1927.

Davids, C. A. F. Rhys. *Buddhist Psychology*. London: Luzac & Co., 1924.

Davids, T. W. Rhys, tr. *Buddhist Sūtras*. New York: Dover Publications, 1965.

Dayal, Har. *The Bodhisattva Doctrine in Buddhist Sanskrit Literature*. London: Routledge & Kegan Paul, 1932.

De Bary, William Theodore, ed. *The Buddhist Tradition in India, China and Japan*. New York: Vintage Books, 1972.

Gard, Richard A. *Mādhyamika Buddhism: Introductory Lectures on Its History and Doctrines*. Bangkok: Mahamukuta University Press, 1956.

Goddard, Dwight, ed. *A Buddhist Bible*. With introduction by Huston Smith. Boston: Beacon Press. 1970.

Govinda, Lama Anagarika. *The Psychological Attitude of Early Buddhist Philosophy*. London: Rider & Co., 1969.

Guenther, H. V. *Buddhist Philosophy in Theory and Practice*. Baltimore: Penguin Books. 1972.

________. *Philosophy and Psychology in the Abhidharma*. Lucknow: Buddha Vihara, 1957.

Hakeda, Yoshito, tr. *The Awakening of Faith Attributed to Aśvaghoṣa*. New York: Columbia University Press, 1967.

Hattori, Masaaki, ed. *Dignāga on Perception (The Pratykṣaparicheda of Dignāga's Pramāṇasamuccaya from the Sanskrit and the Tibetan Version)*. Cambridge, Mass.: Harvard University Press, 1967.

Horner, I. B. *The Living Thoughts of Gautama the Buddha*. London: Cassell, 1948.

Inada, Kenneth K., tr. *Nāgārjuna: A Translation of His Mūlamadhyamakakārikā, with an Introductory Essay*. Tokyo: The Hokuseido Press, 1970.

Jacobson, N. P. *Buddhism: The Religion of Analysis*. Carbondale: Southern Illinois University Press, 1970.

Jayatilleke, K. N. *Early Buddhist Theory of Knowledge*. London: George Allen & Unwin, 1963.

Johansson, Rune E. A. *The Psychology of Nirvāṇa.* Garden City, N.Y.: Doubleday & Co., 1970.

Keith, A. B. *Buddhist Philosophy in India and Ceylon.* Banaras: Chowkhamba, 1963.

Mahathera, Nyanatiloka. *Guide Through the Abhidhamma-Piṭaka. Being a Synopsis of the Philosophical Collection Belonging to the Buddhist Pali Canon. Followed by an Essay on the Paṭicca-Samuppāda.* Kandy: Buddhist Publication Society, 1971.

Matics, Martin L., tr. *Entering the Path of Enlightenment: The Bodhicaryāvatāra of the Buddhist Poet Śāntideva.* New York, The Macmillan Co., 1970.

Murti, T. R. V. *The Central Philosophy of Buddhism.* London: George Allen & Unwin 1955.

Nanananda, Bhikku. *Concept and Reality in Early Buddhist Thought.* Kandy: Buddhist Publication Society, 1971.

Obeyesekere, Gananath, *et al. Essays on the Theravāda Tradition in India and Ceylon.* Chambersburg, Pa.: American Academy of Religion, 1972.

Poussin, Louis de La Vallée. *The Way to Nirvāṇa.* London: Cambridge University Press, 1917.

Radhakrishnan, S. *The Dhammapada, with Introductory Essays, Pali Text, English Translation and Notes.* London: Oxford University Press, 1954.

Rahula, Walpola. *What the Buddha Taught.* New York: Grove Press, 1962.

Ramanan, K. Venkata. *Nāgārjuna's Philosophy: As Presented in the Mahā-prajñāpāramitā-śāstra.* Banaras: Bharatiya Vidya Prakashan, 1971.

Robinson, Richard H. *The Buddhist Religion.* Belmont, Calif.: Dickenson Publishing Co., 1970.

________. *Early Mādhyamika in India and China.* Madison: University of Wisconsin Press, 1967.

Stcherbatsky, Th. *Buddhist Logic.* 2 vols. New York: Dover Publications, 1963.

________. *The Central Conception of Buddhism.* Calcutta: Sushil Gupta, 1956.

________. *The Conception of Buddhist Nirvāṇa.* The Hague: Mouton & Co., 1965.

Streng, Frederick J. *Emptiness: A Study in Religious Meaning.* Nashville: Abingdon Press, 1967.

Stryk, Lucien, ed. *World of the Buddha: A Reader from the Three Baskets to Modern Zen.* Garden City, N.Y.: Doubleday & Co., 1969.

Suzuki, D. T. *On Indian Mahāyāna Buddhism.* Ed. with an introduction by E. Conze. New York: Harper & Row, 1968.

________. *Outlines of Mahāyāna Buddhism*. With an introduction by Alan Watts. New York: Schocken Books, 1967.

________. *Philosophy of the Yogācāra*. Bibliothèque du Muséon. Louvain: Bureau du Muséon, 1904.

________. *Studies in Laṅkāvatāra Sūtra*. London: Kegan Paul, 1930.

________, tr. *The Laṅkāvatāra Sūtra*. London: Kegan Paul, 1930.

Takakusu, Junjiro. *The Essentials of Buddhist Philosophy*. Ed. by Wing-tsit Chan and Charles A. Moore. Honolulu: University of Hawaii Press, 1947.

Thera, Narada. *A Manual of Abhidhamma: Abhidhammattha Saṅgaha*. Vol. I, Chs. I-V, Pali text, translation and explanatory notes. Colombo: Vajirarama, 1956.

________. *The Buddha and His Teachings*. Colombo, n.d.

Thera, Soma. *The Way of Mindfulness: The Sati-patthana-sutta and Commentary*. Kandy: Buddhist Publication Society, 1967.

Thomas, E. J. *The History of Buddhist Thought*. London: Kegan Paul, 1933.

________. *The Life of the Buddha as Legend and History*. London: Kegan Paul, 1927.

Upadhyaya, K. N. *Early Buddhism and the Bhagavadgita*. Delhi: Motilal Banarsidass, 1971.

Warder, A. K. *Indian Buddhism*. Delhi: Motilal Banarsidass, 1970.

Warren, H. C., tr. *Buddhism in Translations*. New York: Atheneum, 1963.

Sāṁkhya

Banerjee, S. C., tr. *The Sāṅkhya Philosophy: Sāṅkhya-kārikā with Gauḍapāda's Scholia and Nārāyaṇa's Gloss*. Calcutta: University of Calcutta Press, 1909.

Bhatta, R. G., ed. *Sāṁkhya-pravacana-bhāṣya*. Banaras: Chowkhamba, n.d.

Colebrooke, H. T. and Wilson, H. H., trs. *The Sāṁkhya-kārikā, with the Bhāṣya or Commentary of Guaḍapāda*. Bombay: Tookaram Tatya, 1887.

Ghosh, Jagneswar. *Sāṁkhya and Modern Thought*. Calcutta: Book Company, 1930.

Gupta, Anima Sen. *Classical Sāṁkhya: A Critical Study*. Lucknow: Gour Ashram, 1969.

________. *Sāṁkhya and Advaita Vedānta: A Comparative Study*. Patna: Patna University Press, 1972.

Jha, Ganganatha, tr. *The Tattva-kaumudī (Vācaspati Miśra's Commentary on the Sāṁkhya-kārikā)*. Poona: The Oriental Book Agency, 1934.

Johnston, Edward H. *Early Sāṁkhya: An Essay on its Historical Development According to the Texts.* London: Royal Asiatic Society, 1937.

Keith, A. B. *The Sāṁkhya System.* Oxford: Clarendon Press. 1918.

Larsen, Gerald J. *Classical Sāṁkhya.* Delhi: Motilal Banarsidass, 1969.

Majumdar, A. K. *The Sāṁkhya Conception of Personality, or, a New Interpretation of the Sāṁkhya Philosophy.* Calcutta: University of Calcutta Press, 1930.

Mukerji, J. N. *Sāṁkhya or the Theory of Reality: A Critical and Constructive Study of Īśvarakṛṣṇa's Sāṁkhya-kārikā.* Calcutta, 1931.

Rao, K. B. Ramakrishna. *Theism of Pre-classical Sāṁkhya.* Mysore: University of Mysore Press, 1966.

Seal, B. N. *The Positive Sciences of the Ancient Hindus.* London: Longmans, Green & Co., 1915.

Sastri, S. S. Suryanarayana, tr. *The Sāṁkhya-kārikā of Īśvara Kṛṣṇa.* Madras: University of Madras Press, 1933.

Sinha, Nandalal, tr. *The Sāṁkhya Philosophy, Containing Sāṁkhya-pravacana-sūtra, with the Vṛtti of Aniruddha, the Bhāṣya of Vijñāna Bhikṣu, Extracts from the Vṛtti-sāra of Mahādeva Vedāntin, Tattva-samāsa, Sāṁkhya-kārikā, pañcaśikha Sūtra.* The Sacred Books of The Hindus, XI. Allahabad: The Panini Office, 1915.

Yoga

Behanan, Kovoor T. *Yoga, a Scientific Evaluation.* New York: The Macmillan Co., 1937.

Brahmachari, Dhirendra. *Yogāsana Vijñāna: The Science of Yoga.* New York: Asia Publishing House, 1970.

Brena, Stephen F. *Yoga and Medicine: The Merging of Yogic Concepts with Modern Medical Knowledge.* Baltimore: Penguin Books, 1973.

Coster, Geraldine. *Yoga and Western Psychology: A Comparison.* London: Oxford University Press, 1935.

Dasgupta, Surendra Nath. *The Study of Patañjali.* Calcutta: University of Calcutta Press, 1920.

________. *Yoga as Philosophy and Religion.* New York: E. P. Dutton & Co., 1924.

________. *Yoga Philosophy in Relation to Other Systems of Indian Thought.* Calcutta: University of Calcutta Press, 1930.

Eliade, Mircea. *Patañjali and Yoga,* tr. by Charles L. Markmann. New York: Funk & Wagnalls, 1969.

________. *Yoga, Immortality and Freedom.* Princeton: Princeton University Press, 1971.

Feuerstein, G., and Miller, J. *Yoga and Beyond.* New York: Schocken Books, 1972.

Jha, Ganganatha, tr. *The Yoga-darśana. The Sūtras of Patañjali with the Bhāṣya of Vyāsa.* Bombay: R. T. Tatya, 1907.

________, tr. *The Yogasārasangraha of Vijñāna Bhikṣu.* Bombay: Tattvavivechaka Press, 1894.

Johnston, Charles, tr. *The Yoga-Sūtras of Patañjali.* London: Stuart & Watkins, 1970.

Koelman, Gaspar M. *Patañjala Yoga: From Related Ego to Absolute Self.* Poona: Papal Athenaeum, 1970.

Prabhavananda, Swamy, and Isherwood, Christopher. *How to Know God: The Yoga Aphorisms of Pantañjali (tr. with new commentary).* New York: Harper & Row, 1953.

Prasada, Rama, tr. *The Yoga-Sūtras of Patañjali, with the Yoga-bhāṣya of Vyāsa and the Tattva-vaiśāradī of Vācaspati Miśra.* The Sacred Books of the Hindus, IV. Allahabad: The Panini Office, 1924.

Taimni, I. K. *The Science of Yoga: A Commentary on the Yoga-sutras of Patanjali in the Light of Modern Thought.* Wheaton, Ill.: The Theosophical Publishing House, 1967.

Wood, Ernest. *Great Systems of Yoga.* New York: Philosophical Library, 1954.

________. *Seven Schools of Yoga, An Introduction.* Wheaton, Ill.: The Theosophical Publishing House, 1973.

Vaisesika

Cowell, E. B. and Gough, A. E., tr. *Mādhavācārya's Sarva-darśana-saṁgraha.* London: Kegan Paul, Trench, Trubner & Co., 1904.

Gough, A. E., tr. *The Vaiśeṣika Sūtras of Kaṇāda, with Comments from the Upaskāra of Sankara-miśra and the Vivṛitti of Jayanārāyaṇa-tarkaparichānana.* Banaras. E. J. Lazarus & Co., 1873.

Jha, Ganganatha, tr. *The Padārthadharmasaṁgraha of Praśastapāda, with the Nyāyakandalī of Srīdhara.* Allahabad: E. J. Lazarus & Co., 1916.

Keith, A. B. *Indian Logic and Atomism: An Exposition of the Nyāya and Vaiśeṣika Systems.* Oxford: Clarendon Press, 1921.

Sinha, J. N. *Indian Realism.* London: Kegan Paul, 1938.

Sinha, Nandalal, tr. *The Vaiśeṣika Sūtras of Kaṇāda, with the Commentary of Saṁkara Miśra, Extracts from the Gloss of Jayanārāyana, and the Bhāṣya of Candrakānta.* The Sacred Books of the Hindus, VI. Allahabad: The Panini Office, 1923.

Vallabhācārya. *Nyāya-līlāvatī.* Bombay: Nirnaya Sagar Press, 1914.

Nyaya

Atreya, B. L. *The Elements of Indian Logic, with the Text and Hindi and English Translations of Tarkasangraha (Buddhikaṇḍa)*. Banaras: The Indian Bookshop. 1934.

Barlingay, S. S. *A Modern Introduction to Indian Logic.* Delhi: National Publishing House, 1965.

Bhaduri, Sadananda. *Studies in Nyāya-Vaiśeṣika Metaphysics.* Poona: Bhandarkar Oriental Research Institute, 1947.

Chatterjee, S. C. *The Nyāya Theory of Knowledge.* Calcutta: University of Calcutta Press, 1950.

Cowell, E. B., tr. *Udayana's Kusumāñjali, with the Commentary of Hari Dasa Bhattacarya.* Calcutta: Baptist Mission Press, 1864.

Ingalls, D. H. H. *Materials for the Study of Navya-Nyāya Logic.* Cambridge, Mass.: Harvard University Press, 1951.

Jha, Ganganatha. *The Nyāya Philosophy of Gautama.* Allahabad: Allahabad University Press, n.d.

________, tr. *Gautama's Nyāyasūtras, with Vātsāyana's Bhāṣya.* Poona: The Oriental Book Agency, 1939.

________, tr. *The Tarkabhāṣā (by Keśava Miśra), or Exposition of Reasoning.* Poona: The Oriental Book Agency, 1924.

Keith, A. B. *Indian Logic and Atomism* (full citation under Vaiśeṣika).

Madhavananda, Swami, tr. *Viśvanātha Nyāyapañcānana, Bhāṣāpariccheda with Siddhāntamuktāvalī.* Calcutta: Advaita Ashrama, 1940.

Mathuranatha. *Mathuri* or *Tattvacintāmaṇirahasya, A Commentary on Gaṅgeśa's Tattvacintāmaṇi.* Ed. by Pandit Kamakhyanātha Tarkavāgīsha. Bibliotheca Indica, 98, 4 parts. Calcutta: Asiatic Society of Bengal, 1884-1901.

Matilal, B. K. *The Navya-Nyāya Doctrine of Negation.* Cambridge, Mass.: Harvard University Press, 1968.

Misra, Umesh. *Conception of Matter According to Nyāya-Vaiśeṣika.* Allahabad: M. N. Pandey, 1936.

Randle, Herbert N. *Indian Logic in the Early Schools.* London: Oxford University Press, 1930.

Sastri, Kuppuswamy. *A Primer of Indian Logic According to Annambhaṭṭa's Tarkasaṁgraha.* Madras: P. Varadachary & Co., 1932.

Vidyabhusana, S. C. *A History of Indian Logic.* Delhi: Motilal Banarsidass, 1971.

———, tr. *The Nyāya Sutras of Gotama*. The Sacred Books of the Hindus, VIII. Allahabad: The Panini Office, 1930.

Vidyasagara, Jivananda, ed. *Nyāya-darśana, with Vātsāyana's Bhāṣya and Viśvanātha's Vṛtti*. Calcutta, 1919.

Vedānta

A. Vedic Hymns

Griffth, R. T. H., tr. *The Hymns of the Rigveda*. 2 vols. Banaras: E. J. Lazarus & Co., 1920-26.

Macdonell, A. A., tr. *Hymns from the Rigveda*. London: Oxford University Press, 1922.

Smith, H. Daniel, ed. *Selections from Vedic Hymns*. Berkeley: McCutchan Publishing Corporation, 1968.

Thomas, Edward J., tr. *Vedic Hymns*. London: John Murray, 1923.

B. The Upaniṣads

Deussen, Paul. *The Philosophy of the Upanishads*. Tr. by A. S. Geden. New York: Dover Publications, Inc., 1966.

Hume, R. E., tr. *The Thirteen Principal Upanishads*. New York: Oxford University Press, 1971.

Mahadevan, T. M. P., tr. *The Upaniṣads: Selections from the 108 Upaniṣads*. Madras: G. A. Natesan & Co., n.d.

Müller, F. Max, tr. *The Upaniṣads*. 2 vols. New York: Dover Publications, 1970.

Nikhilananda, Swami, tr. *The Upanishads*. 2 vols. New York: Harper & Brothers, 1951.

Prabhavananda, Swami, and Manchester, Frederick, trs. *The Upanishads*. Hollywood: Vedanta Press, 1947.

Radhakrishnan, S. *The Philosophy of the Upaniṣads*. London: George Allen & Unwin, 1935.

———, tr. *The Principal Upaniṣads*. London: George Allen & Unwin, 1953.

C. Advaita

Alston, A. J., tr. *The Naiṣkarmyasiddhi of Sri Sureśvara*. London: Shanti Sadan, 1959.

——— tr. *That Thou Art (From the Thousand Teachings of Sri Śaṁkara)*. London: Shanti Sadan, 1967.

Apte, V. M., tr. *Brahma-sūtra-Shaṅkara-Bhāṣya*. Bombay, Popular Book Depot, 1960.

Bhattacharyya, Kokileswar. *An Introduction to Advaita Philosophy*. Calcutta: University of Calcutta Press, 1924.

Bhattacharyya, Vidhushekhara, ed. and tr. The *Āgamaśāstra of Gauḍapāda*. Calcutta: University of Calcutta Press, 1943.

Date, Vinayak H., tr. *Vedānta Explained, Śaṁkara's Commentary on the Brahma-sūtras*. 2 vols. Bombay: Bookseller's Publishing Co., 1954.

Datta, D. M. *The Six Ways of Knowing: A Critical Study of the Vedānta Theory of Knowledge*. Calcutta: University of Calcutta Press, 1960.

Deussen, Paul. *The System of the Vedānta, According to Bādarāyaṇa's Brahmasūtras and Śaṅkara's Commentary*. Tr. by Charles Johnston. New York: Dover Publications, 1973.

Deutsch, Eliot. *Advaita Vedānta: A Philosophical Reconstruction*. Honolulu. East-West Center Press, 1969.

Deutsch, Eliot and Van Buitenen, J. A. B., eds. *A Sourcebook of Advaita Vedānta*. Honolulu: University of Hawaii Press, 1972.

Devanji, Prahlad Chandrashekha, tr. *Siddhāntabindu by Madhusūdanasarasvati: A Commentary on the Daśaśloki of Śaṁkarācārya,* Gaekwad's Oriental Series, LXIV. Baroda: Oriental Institute, 1933.

Devaraja, N. K. *An Introduction to Śaṅkara's Theory of Knowledge*. Delhi: Motilal Banarsidass, 1961.

Gupta, Anima Sen. *Sāṁkhya and Advaita Vedānta: A Comparative Study*. Patna: Patna University Press, 1972.

Hasurkar, S. S. *Vācaspati Miśra on Advaita Vedānta*. Darbhanga: Mithila Institute, 1958.

Iyer, K. A. Krishnaswami. *Vedānta, or the Science of Reality*. Madras: Ganesh & Co., 1930.

Jagadānanda, Swami, tr. *Upadesasāhasrī of Srī Śaṅkarācārya (A Thousand Teachings)*. Madras: Sri Ramakrishna, 1961.

Johnston, Charles, tr. *The Great Jewel of Wisdom (Śaṁkara's Vivekachūdāmaṇi)*. New York: Quarterly Book Department, 1925.

Joshi, Shanti. *The Message of Śaṁkara*. Ahmedabad: Lokbharati Publications, 1968.

Levy, John. *The Nature of Man According to Vedānta*. London: Routledge & Kegan Paul, 1956.

Mahadevan, T. M. P. *Gauḍapāda: A Study in Early Advaita*. Madras: University of Madras Press, 1954.

________. *The Philosophy of Advaita, with Special Reference to Bhāratītīrtha Vidyāraṇya*. London: Luzac & Co., 1938.

________, tr. *The Saṁbandha-Vārtika of Sureśvarācārya*. Madras: University of Madras Press, 1958.

Malkani, G. R. *Vedāntic Epistemology*. Amalner: The Indian Institute of Philosophy, 1953.

Mayeda, Sengaku, ed. *Śaṁkara's Upadesasāhasrikā*. Tokyo: The Hokuseido Press, 1973.

Mukharji, Nalini Mohan Sastri. *A Study of Śaṁkara.* Calcutta: University of Calcutta Press, 1942.

Murty, K. Satchidananda. *Revelation and Reason in Advaita.* New York: Columbia University Press, 1961.

Rao, K. Ramakrishna. *Advavita as Philosophy and Religion.* Mysore: University of Mysore Press, 1969.

Roy, S. S. *The Heritage of Śaṅkara.* Allahabad: Udayana Publications, 1965.

Sastri, Kokileswar. *An Introduction to Advaita Philosophy.* Calcutta: University of Calcutta Press, 1926.

________. *A Realistic Interpretation of Śaṅkara-Vedānta.* Calcutta: University of Calcutta Press, 1931.

Sastri, S. S. Suryanarayana, ed. and tr. *Vedāntaparibhāṣā by Dharmarāja Ahdvarin.* Madras: The Adyar Library, 1942.

Sastry, A. Mahadeva, tr. *The Bhagavad-Gītā, with the Commentary of Śrī Śaṅkarāchārya.* Madras: Ramaswamy Sastrulu & Sons, 1961.

Satprakāshānanda, Swami. *Methods of Knowledge (According to Advaita Vedānta).* St. Louis: The Vedanta Society of St. Louis, 1972.

Sharma, B. N. K. *The Brahmasūtras and Their Principal Commentaries: A Critical Exposition.* Vol. 1. Bombay: Bharatiya Vidya Bhavan, 1971.

Shastri, Hari Prasad, tr. *Panchadasi: A Treatise on Advaita Metaphysics by Swami Vidyāraṇya.* London: Shanti Sadan, 1956.

Shastri, Prabhu Datt. *The Doctrine of Māyā in the Philosophy of the Vedānta.* London: Luzac & Co., 1911.

Shrivastava, S. N. L. *Śaṁkara and Bradley.* Delhi: Motilal Banarsidass, 1968.

Sircar, Mahendranath. *Comparative Studies in Vedāntism.* Bombay: Humphrey Milford, 1927.

Staal, J. F. *Advaita and Neo-Platonism: A Critical Study in Comparative Philosophy.* Madras: University of Madras Press, 1961.

Sundaram, P. K. *Advaita Epistemology with Special Reference to Iṣṭasiddhi.* Madras: University of Madras Press, 1968.

Thibaut, George, tr. *The Vedānta Sūtras of Bādarāyaṇa, with the Commentary by Saṁkara.* 2 vols. New York: Dover Publications, 1970.

Urquhart, W. S. *The Vedānta and Modern Thought.* London: Oxford University Press, 1928.

Wood, Ernest. *The Pinnacle of Indian Thought: Verse-by-Verse Translation and Commentary in the Vivekachūdāmani of Shri Shaṅkarācārya.* Wheaton, Ill.: The Theosophical Publishing House, 1971.

D. Viśiṣṭādvaita

Govindācārya, A., tr. *Śrī Bhagavad Gītā with Sri Rāmānujāchārya's Viśiṣṭādvaita Commentary*. Madras: Vaijayanti Press, 1898.

Gupta, Anima Sen. *A Critical Study of Rāmānuja*. Banaras: Chowkhamba, 1967.

Johnston, J., tr. *The Vedāntatattvasāra Ascribed to Rāmānujācārya*. Banaras: E. J. Lazarus & Co., 1898.

Krishnamachary, Pandit V., and Narasimha Iyengar, M. B. *A Concise Viśiṣṭādvaita Commentary on the Brahma-sūtras of Bādarāyaṇa*. Wheaton, Ill.: The Theosophical Publishing House, 1953.

Krishnamacharya, V., ed. *Vedānta-sāra of Rāmānuja*. Wheaton, Ill.: The Theosophical Publishing House, 1971.

Raghavachar, S. S. *Srī Rāmānuja on the Gītā*. Mangalore:Sri Ramakrishna Ashrama, 1969.

Rangacharya, Malur Rao, and Aiyangar, Varadaraja, trs. *The Vedānta-sūtras with the Srī-Bhāshya of Rāmānujāchārya*. Madras: The Brahmavadin Press, 1919.

Sampatkumar, M. R., tr. *The Gītābhāshya (of Rāmānuja)*. Madras: Rangacharya Memorial Trust, 1969.

Srinivasachari, P. N. *The Philosophy of Bhedābheda*. Madras: The Adyar Library, 1950.

________. *The Philosophy of Viśiṣṭādvaita*. Madras: The Adyar Library, 1943.

________. *Rāmānuja's Idea of the Finite Self*. Calcutta: Longmans, Green & Co., 1928.

Thibaut, George, tr. *The Vedānta Sūtras with the Commentary of Rāmānuga*. Oxford: Clarendon Press, 1904.

Van Buitenen, J. A. B. *Rāmānuja on the Bhagavadgītā*. Delhi: Motilal Banarsidass, 1968.

Varadachari, K. C. *Srī Rāmānuja's Theory of Knowledge*. Tirupati: Tirumalai-Tirupati Devasthanams Press, 1943.

E. Dvaita

Maitra, Sushil Kumar. *Madhva Logic*. Calcutta: University of Calcutta Press, 1936.

Raghavendrachar, H. N. *Dvaita Philosophy and Its Place in the Vedānta*. Mysore: University of Mysore Press, 1941.

Rao, B. A. Krishnaswamy. *Outlines of the Philosophy of Sri Madhwāchārya*. Tumkur, 1951.

Rao, P. Nagaraja. *Epistemology of Dvaita Vedānta*. Wheaton, Ill.: The Theosophical Publishing House, 1972.

Rao, S. Subba. *The Bhagavad-Gītā (Translation and Commentary in English According to Srī Madhvāchārya's Bhāshya)*. Madras: The Minerva Press, 1906.

———, tr. *Vedānta-sūtras with the Commentary of Sri Madhvācharya*. Tirupati: Sri Vyasa Press, 1936.

Sarma, Nagaraja. *The Rein of Realism in Indian Philosophy: Exposition of Ten Works by Madhva*. Madras: The National Press, 1937.

Sri Aurobindo

Aurobindo, Sri. *Essays on the Gītā*. Sri Aurobindo Library. Calcutta: Arya Publishing House, 1926-44, 1950.

———. *The Human Cycle*. Pondicherry: Sri Aurobindo Ashram, 1949.

———. *The Ideal of Human Unity*. Pondicherry: Sri Aurobindo Ashram, 1950.

———. *The Life Divine*. 2 vols. Calcutta: Arya Publishing House, 1947.

———. *The Mind of Light*. Introduction by Robert A. McDermott. New York: E. P. Dutton & Co., 1971.

———. *More Lights on Yoga*. Pondicherry: Aurobindo Ashram, 1948.

———. *The Problem of Rebirth*. Pondicherry: Aurobindo Ashram, 1948.

———. *The Renaissance in India*. Calcutta: Arya Publishing House, 1946.

———. *The Riddle of the World*. Calcutta: Arya Publishing House, 1946.

———. *The Synthesis of Yoga*. Madras: Sri Aurobindo Library, 1952.

Bhattacharya, A. C. *Sri Aurobindo and Bergson: A Synthetic Study*. Gyanpur: Jagabandhu Prakashan, 1972.

Brutean, Beatrice. *Worthy Is the World: The Hindu Philosophy of Sri Aurobindo*. Rutherford, N.J.: Fairleigh Dickinson University Press, 1972.

Chaudhuri, Haridas. *Integral Yoga: The Concept of Harmonious and Creative Living*. San Francisco: California Institute of Asian Studies, 1970.

———. *The Philosophy of Integralism, or, the Metaphysical Synthesis Inherent in the Teachings of Sri Aurobindo*. Calcutta: Sri Aurobindo Pathamandir, 1954.

———. *Sri Aurobindo: The Prophet of Life Divine*. Calcutta: Sri Aurobindo Pathamandir, 1951.

Maitra, S. K. *An Introduction to the Philosophy of Sri Aurobindo*. Banaras: Banaras Hindu University Press, 1945.

———. *The Meeting of East and West in Sri Aurobindo's Philosophy*. Pondicherry: Sri Auribindo Ashram, 1956.

________. *Studies in Sri Aurobindo's Philosophy*. Banaras: Banaras Hindu University Press, 1945.

Singh, S. P. *Sri Aurobindo and Whitehead on the Nature of God*. Aligarh: Vigyan Prakashan, 1972.

Zaehner, R. C. *Evolution and Religion: A Study in Sri Aurobindo and Pierre Teilhard de Chardin*. New York: Oxford University Press, 1971.

S. Radhakrishnan

Radhakrishnan, S. *East and West in Religion*. London: George Allen & Unwin, 1949.

________. *Eastern Religions and Western Thought*. London: Oxford University Press, 1940.

________. *The Ethics of Vedānta and Its Metaphysical Presuppositions*. Madras: The Guardian Press, 1908.

________. *The Hindu View of Life*. London: George Allen & Unwin, 1927.

________. *Indian Philosophy*. London: George Allen & Unwin, 1931.

________. *The Philosophy of Rabindranath Tagore*. London: Macmillan & Co., 1918.

________. *The Philosophy of the Upaniṣads*. London: George Allen & Unwin, 1935.

________. *The Principal Upaniṣads*. London: George Allen & Unwin, 1953.

________. *The Reign of Religion in Contemporary Philosophy*. London: Macmillan & Co., 1920.

Joad, C. E. M. *Counter Attack from the East, the Philosophy of Radhakrishnan*. London: George Allen & Unwin, 1933.

McDermott, Robert A., ed. *Radhakrishnan: Selected Writings on Philosophy and Culture*. New York: E. P. Dutton & Co., 1970.

Schilpp, Paul Arthur, ed. *The Philosophy of Sarvepalli Radhakrishnan*. New York: Tudor Publishing Co., 1952.

Standard References

Encyclopaedia of Buddhism. Published by the Government of Ceylon.

Hastings Encyclopaedia of Religion and Ethics. New York: Charles Scribner's Sons.

The Pali Text Society Translation Series. London: Oxford University Press.

The Sacred Books of the Buddhists Translation Series. London: Oxford University Press.

The Sacred Books of the East Translation Series. Oxford: Clarendon Press.

The Sacred Books of the Hindus Translation Series. Allahabad: The Panini Office.

The following books provide extensive bibliographies on Indian philosophical literature:

Inada, Kenneth K. *Nāgārjuna: A Translation of his Mūlamadhyamakakārikā, with an Introductory Essay.* Tokyo: The Hokuseido Press, 1970.

Jayatilleke, K. N. *Early Buddhist Theory of Knowledge.* London: George Allen & Unwin, 1963.

Potter, Karl H. *Presuppositions of India's Philosophies.* Englewood Cliffs, N.J.: Prentice-Hall, 1963.

Radhakrishnan, S., and Moore, Charles A., ed. *A Source Book in Indian Philosophy.* Princeton: Princeton University Press, 1967.

Ramanan, K. Venkata. *Nāgārjuna's Philosophy: As Presented in the Mahā-prajñāpāramitā-śāstra.* Banaras: Bharatiya Vidya Prakashan, 1971.

Robinson, Richard H. *The Buddhist Religion.* Belmont, Calif.: Dickenson Publishing Co., 1970.

Periodicals

Indian Philosophy and Culture. Vrindaban, India.

Journal of Indian Philosophy. Dordrecht, the Netherlands.

Journal of the Oriental Institute. Baroda, India.

Monumenta Nipponica. Tokyo, Japan.

Philosophy East and West. Honolulu, Hawaii, U.S.A.

Prabuddha Bharata. Calcutta, India.

The Aryan Path. Bombay, India.

The Eastern Buddhist. Tokyo, Japan.

The Indo-Asian Culture. New Delhi, India.

The Maha Bodhi. Calcutta, India.

The Middle Way. London, U.K.

The Pakistani Philosophical Quarterly. Lahore, Pakistan.

The Vedanta Kesari. Madras, India.

Vivekananda Kendra Patrika. Madras, India.

Wiener Zeitschrift für die Kunde Südasiens. Vienna, Austria.

Index